AF477668

Zimbabwe

ZIMBABWE

Picking Up the Pieces

Edited by

Hany Besada

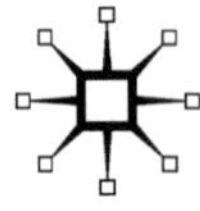

ZIMBABWE

Copyright © Hany Besada, 2011.

First published in 2011 by
PALGRAVE MACMILLAN®
in the United States—a division of St. Martin's Press LLC,
175 Fifth Avenue, New York, NY 10010.

Where this book is distributed in the UK, Europe and the rest of the world,
this is by Palgrave Macmillan, a division of Macmillan Publishers Limited,
registered in England, company number 785998, of Houndmills,
Basingstoke, Hampshire RG21 6XS.

Palgrave Macmillan is the global academic imprint of the above companies
and has companies and representatives throughout the world.

Palgrave® and Macmillan® are registered trademarks in the United States,
the United Kingdom, Europe and other countries.

ISBN: 978–0–230–11019–9

Library of Congress Cataloging-in-Publication Data

Zimbabwe : picking up the pieces / edited by Hany Besada.
     p. cm.
   ISBN 978–0–230–11019–9 (hardback)
     1. Zimbabwe—Politics and government—1980– 2. Zimbabwe—
   Economic conditions—1980– I. Besada, Hany.

JQ2925.Z545 2011
330.96891—dc22   2010025622

A catalogue record of the book is available from the British Library.

Design by Newgen Imaging Systems (P) Ltd., Chennai, India.

First edition: January 2011

10 9 8 7 6 5 4 3 2 1

Printed and bound in Great Britain by

CPI Antony Rowe, Chippenham and Eastbourne

Contents

Figures

Tables

Foreword: Reflections on the Prerequisites for a Sustainable Reconstruction in Zimbabwe

Adam Habib

It is very rare to witness a conversation about the current problems of Zimbabwe, and the solutions thereof, without it degenerating into emotional rhetoric laden with insults. Zimbabwe raises difficult questions about identities, the nature of public discourse, and the manipulation of a rights discourse by political elites both within and outside the country. Implicit in this debate are assumptions about race and how this speaks to national and continental identities. Also, the public debate on Zimbabwe is severely polarized, with opposition parties and critics accusing the Zimbabwe African National Union-Patriotic Front (ZANU-PF) of violating the rights of citizens and even murder, while the state's supporters openly argue that the Movement for Democratic Change (MDC) and human rights activists are pawns of imperialist powers intent on regime change. As if this is not enough, political elites in Zimbabwe, the Southern African Development Community (SADC), and in Western countries manipulate the rights discourse by highlighting issues that support their argument and downplaying other elements that contradict it—further polarizing the discourse on Zimbabwe and bringing to the fore the highest aspirations and deepest fears about the country's future.

Given this, the hosting of a workshop with such diversified participation—without it degenerating into emotional squabble—should be viewed as a victory in its own right. The production of a book recording the views of the participants, and the debates among them, is testimony to the commitment of the authors and, it is hoped, to a maturing of the debate on Zimbabwe. With the ideologically diverse nature of the participants, it would be impossible to have produced a unanimously endorsed, coherent set of recommendations. The pages that follow instead reflect a more heterogeneous and diverse set of recommendations advocated by the participants of the workshop. Their value lies in the provocative thinking about Zimbabwe and its future. Nevertheless, in the debate and the reflections that are likely to follow the publication of this book, five essential lessons should be borne in mind.

First, as does seem to be recognized by the vast majority of the authors, Zimbabwe's path to reconstruction has to begin from a political settlement that has at its core what Garth le Pere describes in the *Afterword* as "the normative imperatives of transitional justice, national healing and reconciliation." This solution, also described by the African scholar Mahmood Mamdani as "survivor's justice" in his *Saviours and Survivors,* is increasingly presented as a considered historical lesson from the South African transition from apartheid, and is, therefore, an African response to the historical dilemma bequeathed to the continent by colonialism and the nature of postindependence political conflict. Yet, while the necessity of such a conceptual framework for political negotiations in Zimbabwe cannot be disputed, it must be underscored that justice should only be tempered with if peace and progress are to be its beneficiaries. This is the principal lesson of the South African experience. South Africa can only truly be invoked if progress toward peace is recorded. Without peace and progress, there is no legitimacy to the tempering of justice.

It is also worth bearing in mind that the lessons from the South African experience do not preclude the notion of consequences for past injustices. Transitional justice in South Africa ensured that there were no legal prosecutions, but apartheid's political elites did pay penalties for their past actions. While they may not have been legally charged, they were cast into the political wilderness in the democratic era with even their previous supporters disassociating themselves from their political actions. Most of apartheid's political elites were ostracized through mainstream political opinion, and many died as lonely, dejected individuals. There were consequences, even if they were not legal, and this is necessary if autocrats of the future are to be measured in their subjugation of citizen's rights.

Second, it is worth bearing in mind that the reason that Zimbabwe is in its current predicament is because pragmatism prevailed over principle with the sacrifice of socioeconomic justice at the dawn of its independence. The land question was sacrificed in the Lancaster House negotiations, where its resolution was postponed until a future date so as not to rock the political boat. In the desire to effect political compromise, political and economic elites, national and foreign, were willing to sacrifice equitable development. This has also been the advice of mainstream, American political science, which has over the last three decades produced a body of empirical case studies on democratization that emphasize the importance of procedural rather than substantive democracy. From O'Donnell's, Schmitter's and Whitehead's classic 1986 four volume *Transitions to Democracy* to Samuel Huntington's 1991 *The Third Wave,* the advice to would-be democratizers has been simple: stay away from issues of economic justice for they will merely complicate the agenda of the transition. Such issues, they advised, weakened support for democratization from reformers within the regime, foreign governments, and other transnational actors. The choice they offered was one between formal democracy and authoritarian rule. Their advice was to take formal democracy rather than have nothing at all. The net effect of this choice in Zimbabwe is, two decades after the dawn of independence, an inequitable settlement manipulated by political elites, and Robert Mugabe in particular, to remain in power. The lack of substantive equality in the political settlement was reflected in the inequitable ownership of land in the country and compromised the sustainability of procedural democracy.

This is a lesson that must be remembered in the path toward reconstruction in Zimbabwe. Essentially, it underscores the need not to review the land redistribution program, but rather to recognize and revitalize it so that land inequality is comprehensively addressed. Similar lessons need to be applied in other sectors. Ownership of the nation's mineral resources should be similarly diversified and not overly concentrated in foreign hands, whether Western or Asian, lest this become a source of conflict in the future. Domestic dominance in the ownership of a nation's resources, which need not entail state ownership or control, has implicitly been the principle of all national development experiences, including those in Asia, Latin America, western Europe, and the United States. It should be recognized as a valid element of Zimbabwe's, and more broadly Africa's, developmental agenda. Obviously, Zimbabwe's need for foreign resources, investment, and a skilled workforce may require that this principle be applied pragmatically. But these requirements need not entail complete reliance on the free market and the abandonment of the goal of nationally ensconced but diversified ownership of the nation's resources. If this were to happen, then the seeds of future political conflict and instability will be sown as was the case in the Lancaster House settlement that gave birth to contemporary Zimbabwe.

Third, the recommendations contained in the pages that follow suggest a tension between advocates of market and state-oriented policy solutions. This is not surprising given the ideological diversity of Zimbabweans, and Africans more generally. It should be remembered that given the current lack of capacity in state institutions in Zimbabwe, and the ideological predispositions of international political elites and multilateral institutions whose resources are necessary for any reconstructive endeavor, state-oriented solutions alone are unlikely to be feasible. But unfettered market solutions have a tendency to reproduce historical inequities. In order to fashion a comprehensive solution to Zimbabwe's dilemma, both market forces and their conditioning by the state are going to be needed in a successful reconstruction effort. Obviously, this requires an accountable and responsive government in Zimbabwe. But if this were achieved, and in a world where markets are conditioned by states in almost all of the industrialized economies, it is necessary that progressives of all political hues be counted in ensuring that a similar practice is enabled and defended in Zimbabwe's reconstruction effort.

Fourth, there has emerged in certain circles, particularly in the business community, a belief that aid is no longer required for development. All that is required, according to these advocates, is free trade. Simply put, aid is perceived to create dependency and corrupt governments, whereas trade is seen to facilitate entrepreneurial activity and development. The comparative history of development, however, suggests the opposite lesson. Both aid and trade are necessary if development is to be realized.

The great success stories of development in the post–World War II period are seen as Europe, Japan, Korea, and Taiwan. In each of these cases, a mix of trade and aid created the enabling conditions that facilitated this end. Aid was absolutely necessary. The development of western Europe would have been unimaginable without the role of the Marshall Plan. Similarly, the abovementioned Asian countries were a major beneficiary of U.S. aid. The 2007 *Economic Development in Africa* report released by the *United Nations Conference on Trade and Development* (UNCTAD) estimates that US$500 million per year was given to Japan by the United States between 1950 and 1970.[1] Korea received economic and military investment that amounted to US$13 billion between 1946 and 1978, while Taiwan received US$5.6 billion.[2] But trade was as crucial as aid. The United States provided preferential access to its markets for both western Europe and its Asian allies. Moreover, it did not demand reciprocal access enabling these societies to develop their competitive capacities before they integrated into the global economy. This restructuring of international trade by the United States in favor of its allies was crucial for the development of western Europe and southeast Asia in the post–World War II period. The lesson for Zimbabwe is that a mix of aid and trade is going to be required if the country is to succeed in emerging from its current economic malaise.

Finally, if reconstruction is to become a reality, then it is important to note that equitable development in the current global context is always a condition of democratic accountability. In this sense, Nobel Laureate Amartya Sen is correct to argue that political freedom (read democracy) is necessary for economic growth and development. But the statement requires qualification: his insistence on the positive value of democracy to economic growth and development is founded on it enabling citizens to articulate their needs and creating a culture of debate and discussion that would facilitate effective public policy. This presupposes that these democracies always achieve their primary purpose, to diffuse power in society, and as a result, enhance the leverage of citizens and thereby promote the accountability of state elites to their citizenry. But what if such diffusion of power does not take place and such accountability is not realized? After all, this is the essential conclusion of much of the later literature on the third wave of democratization, lamenting the rise of the phenomenon of illiberal and delegative democracies in which representative political structures are weakened sufficiently to enable power to be centralized in leadership.

Elite contestation can therefore not be assumed, but must rather be actively promoted in both new and established democracies. This is because such contestation is necessary, as is social mobilization, for enhancing the leverage of citizens vis-à-vis their political elites, and thereby promoting the democratic accountability that is necessary for development to serve the interest of citizens. Development requires good political leaders, but they are merely instruments toward desired ends. If democratic accountability does not prevail—which is itself a product of citizen mobilization and elite political contestation—policies and solutions will merely produce inequitable outcomes. Only when political leaders fear for their future, and can institutionally do something about it, are they prompted to fashion policy solutions that are beneficial to the citizenry. In this sense, citizen empowerment is integral to Zimbabwe's reconstruction agenda.

All of these issues are touched upon in the pages that follow. A careful reading, however, will reveal that an implicit divide continues to plague progressive nationalists and liberal human rights activists. The former inevitably bring to the fore in their analysis the historical source of contemporary conflict and recommend that the historically produced systemic inequality—including among others the inequitable ownership of land and national mineral wealth—needs to be addressed if sustainable solutions are to be found. The latter speak of the failures of postindependence political elites, their abrogation of the rights of citizens, and the necessity to protect these very citizens from arbitrary political violence. The former fear that international political elites will turn the tide of national independence and use the abrogation of citizen rights to subvert Zimbabwe's independence. The latter fear that nonintervention leaves citizens to the mercies of avaricious domestic political elites.

Both perspectives speak to a partial reality. They each trade off one essential element of the development and human rights agenda for another. Progressive nationalists, in their desire for a comprehensive solution and in their fear of external intervention, implicitly trade off the rights and protection of their citizens for systemic reform and equitable solutions. Liberal activists, on the other hand, by either remaining silent or not emphasizing the historical nature of the conflict, implicitly trade off equitable development for the immediate protection of citizens from state repression. Yet both sets of tradeoffs are unacceptable for they essentially compromise reconstruction and the advancement of human rights. Systemic reform and citizen empowerment are essential ingredients of both socioeconomic reconstruction and human rights, and must therefore be undertaken simultaneously. Leadership for this agenda must obviously be provided domestically. Foreign human rights activists do have a role, but it is to engage in solidarity work and support progressive and democratic activists on the ground. Only if this is undertaken, and the divide bridged between progressive nationalists and liberal human rights activists can the social force emerge, both within the country and abroad, for the realization of sustainable reconstruction in Zimbabwe.

This divide has of course has been bridged in the past. The antiapartheid movement, both in South Africa and abroad, was essentially premised on such an alliance between progressive nationalists and human rights activists. If there is a lesson to be learned from South Africa's experience, then this is the one; for such an alliance is increasingly necessary not only for the realization of sustainable reconstruction in Zimbabwe, but also for addressing some of the other protracted conflicts that afflict our world.

Notes

1. United Nations Conference on Trade and Development (UNCTAD), *Economic Development in Africa*, New York and Geneva, 2007, 80.
2. Ibid., 81.

Acknowledgments

Zimbabwe: Picking Up the Pieces paints a picture of Zimbabwe's descent into economic and political turmoil, and lays out the way forward to resuscitate the nation. This volume brings together a variety of perspectives from some of southern Africa's leading academics and practitioners, looking at issues of peace building and good governance, economic recovery and development, and foreign direct investment and reconstruction.

The completion of this volume has hinged upon the support of numerous individuals, whose time and dedication made the compilation process a success. In particular, Nicky Moyo, the executive director of Development Enterprise Africa Trust (Zimbabwe), has been instrumental in providing intellectual and moral support, as well as guidance, throughout the book-writing process.

The timely assembly of the volume was made possible by Jason LaChappelle, a Balsillie Fellow with the Centre for International Governance Innovation (CIGI), (and Karolina Werner, project manager, Africa Portal with CIGI), who both assisted with the editing and formatting process. The fine-touching and compilation of the various chapters was expedited with the help of Ibi Brown, an exchange program coordinator with CIGI's the African Initiative; Ariane Goetz and Leah McMillan, PhD candidates at the Balsillie School of International Affairs. Timothy Shaw, professor and director at the Institute of International Relations at The University of the West Indies, St Augustine Campus, in Trinidad & Tobago, has provided invaluable advice and lent support that made publication possible. I thank each of them for their commitment and support.

Finally, many thanks go out to Boitumelo Helen Moatshe, project manager at the Development Bank of Southern Africa (DBSA), who co-organized a successful international conference in October of 2008 in Midrand, South Africa, which initiated the work behind this volume. Her work made the publication of this book possible, and special thanks go to Ravi Naidoo and Dr Paul Kibuuka, the executive managers at the DBSA, for their support.

The project's institutional partners have also been integral players in the creation of this volume. Specifically, the cooperation of CIGI, the Development Enterprise Africa Trust of Zimbabwe, and the Development Bank of Southern Africa facilitated the production process and without their support the project may have never gotten off the ground.

I am especially grateful to John English, Daniel Schwanen, Andy Cooper, and Max Brem, whose unwavering support remained integral in furthering my efforts. Without their leadership and mentorship this project could not have been completed.

HANY BESADA
Senior Researcher: Development Cooperation
North-South Institute

Contributor Biographies

Hany Besada is senior researcher, Development Cooperation at the North-South Institute (NSI), in Ottawa, Canada. He holds a BA and an MA in international relations from Alliant International University in San Diego, United States, where he specialized in peace and security studies. Previously, he was senior researcher and program leader, Health and Social Governance at the Centre for International Governance Innovation (CIGI) in Waterloo, Canada. Prio to that, he was the Business in Africa researcher at the South African Institute of International Affairs (SAIIA) in Johannesburg, South Africa, and research manager at Africa Business Direct, a trade and investment consulting firm in Johannesburg. Mr. Besada has worked for Amnesty International, United Nations associations, the Joan Kroc Institute of Peace and Justice, and the Office of U.S. senator Dianne Feinstein. Mr. Besada has widely published in international news media and academic journals. He is the editor of *Crafting an African Security Architecture: Addressing Regional Peace and Conflict in the 21st Century* (Ashgate, 2010); *From Civil Strife to Peace Building: Examining Private Sector Involvement in West African Reconstruction* (WLU Press, 2009); and *Unlocking Africa's Potential: The Role of Corporate South Africa in Strengthening Africa's Private Sector* (SAIIA, 2008).

Knox Chitiyo is a Zimbabwean researcher and head of the Royal United Services Institute's Africa Programme, an initiative generously supported by The Brenthurst Foundation and the Nelson Mandela Foundation. Dr. Chitiyo was a senior lecturer in war studies in the History Department at the University of Zimbabwe for ten years. He was also the deputy director and cofounder of the Centre for Defence Studies during the same period, and edited the *Journal of African Security and Conflict.* Currently based in the United Kingdom, Dr. Chitiyo has since published in journals that examine Zimbabwean, southern African, and broader African defense and security/developmental issues. He is also a regular contributor to the *Guardian* newspaper and is an African affairs commentator on the BBC, Al Jazeera, and other international news agencies.

Dianna Games has extensive experience working in and writing about Africa. She has twenty-two years' experience in the media, primarily in South Africa, but also writes articles for a variety of African and international publications. She has worked for leading South African newspapers including South Africa's top daily newspaper, *Business Day,* and was the editor of pan-African business magazine *Business in Africa* for more than three years before joining Africa @ Work, a company that aims to facilitate and improve business in Africa through the provision of research, information, and networking opportunities. Dianna travels extensively around the continent writing features and country reports. Among other things, Dianna currently writes a regular column on African issues for Business Day, compiles research reports on business in Africa for various clients, analyses African issues for business and the media, and gives occasional guest lectures on doing business in Africa. She is an Africa writer for the World Economic Forum and honorary chief executive of the South Africa-Nigeria Chamber of Commerce.

Steven Gruzd is head of the Governance and African Peer Review Mechanism (APRM) Program at the South African Institute of International Affairs (SAIIA). He joined SAIIA's NEPAD and Governance Project in April 2003, serving as research manager, and he was subsequently appointed to deputy head of the Governance and APRM Program in 2006, and head in 2008. Previously he worked as a researcher and then research coordinator at the Centre for Development and Enterprise (CDE). Steven's research interests include the African Peer Review Mechanism, South Africa's international relations, African affairs, the Middle East, conflict and peace studies, sport and politics, and urban studies. He holds an MSc in international relations from the London School of Economics and Political Science (LSE) and an honors and BA degree from the University of Witwatersrand.

Adam Habib is deputy vice chancellor Research, Innovation and Advancement at the University of Johannesburg. He has held distinguished academic appointments at a number of universities, including the University of KwaZulu-Natal, where he was a research professor in the School of Development Studies and founding director of the Centre for Civil Society. Dr. Habib also served as executive director of the Democracy and Governance Programme of the Human Sciences Research Council. In the past, he has held coeditor positions with academic journals such as *Transformation,* and has served on a number of boards and councils, including those of the University of Durban-Westville, International Society for Third Sector Research, and the Centre for Public Participation. In addition to presenting papers at a number of international conferences, Dr. Habib has published many books and articles on topics such as democratic consolidation in South Africa, contemporary social movements, poverty alleviation, and institutional reform.

Holger Bernt Hansen is a professor emeritus at the University of Copenhagen in the Centre of African Studies. He has been involved with the University of Copenhagen since 1967, serving as a research professor in African Studies and director of the Centre of African Studies. In the past, he was chairperson for the Danish Social Science Research Council and for the Council for Development Research. For twenty years he has been a board member of the Danish International Development Agency (DANIDA), serving as its chairperson 1996–2007. His major field of research focuses on Uganda, conducted in collaboration with Makerere University. He has published and edited several books on Uganda, dealing with topics such as religion and politics, the political development during the Museveni era, and donor attitudes toward Uganda. Since 1992, he has taken part in a major project on *Research and Education for Democracy in Tanzania* at the University of Dar es Salaam. He is attached to the Institute of Commonwealth Studies, University of

London, and he is a member of the Council for the International African Institute, London.

Prosper Kambarami is an MSc in political science candidate with the University of Zimbabwe. He is currently working with Zimbabwe's Department of Immigration. Prosper's research interests are mainly in the area of political economy and the distribution of resources within Zimbabwe.

George Katito has been a researcher on the Governance and African Peer Review Mechanism (APRM) Programme with the South African Institute of International Affairs since 2007. He has worked as a business analyst on African markets and political risk for Emerging Market Focus (EMF) and was previously a junior faculty member of the Department of Political Science of the University of Pretoria. He holds an honors degree in international relations from the University of Pretoria and is currently a masters of public affairs candidate at Sciences Po, Paris. His most recent publications are "Towards a More Responsive African Union: Lessons Learnt from Zimbabwe," *Southern African Yearbook of International Affairs* (2008/9) and an upcoming German Development Institute (DIE) publication on the role of development partners in the implementation of the APRM. George's research expertise covers the implementation of the APRM, civil society advocacy, and South Africa-Zimbabwe relations.

Jason LaChappelle is a Balsille Fellow at the Balsille School of International Affairs. He holds a master of arts degree in Global Governance at the University of Waterloo. He obtained a bachelor of arts degree from the University of Alberta, majoring in Middle Eastern and African Studies. Jason worked as a research fellow at the Centre for International Governance Innovation. His major research interest focuses on environmental governance in developing countries, particularly the climate change negotiations and the global forest regime, and the role that market-based solutions, international organizations, and nonstate actors play in bridging environmental protection and sustainable development. Jason has also extensively studied poverty alleviation in sub-Saharan Africa, with special emphasis on food security, HIV/AIDS, and Canadian development assistance policy. He was a long-term volunteer and board member with St. Albert Special Olympics in Alberta, Canada, and currently serves on the board of directors for Siyawela, an NGO engaged in development work in rural South Africa.

Albert Makochekanwa is a PhD (economics) finalist graduating September 2010 with University of Pretoria in South Africa. He is currently working as a trade policy analyst with the Commonwealth Secretariat's Hub & Spokes project, deployed to the Government of Ethiopia's Ministry of Trade and Industry. He has more than ten years of research experience in economic and social science fields, with his special interests including poverty analysis, monetary and political economy, and trade and regional integration in southern Africa. Albert has written a number of papers on the dynamics of hyperinflation and state fragility in the Zimbabwean economy. His recent research works include an analysis of Botswana's sectoral exports potential, and the impacts of SADC Trade Protocol implementation on the region's intra-agricultural trade. Among the reputable organizations for which he has conducted research are the World Bank Institute (WBI), the African Economic Research Consortium (AERC), and Trade and Industrial Policy Strategies (TIPS) in South Africa.

Helen Moatshe is project manager in the Project Management Unit at the Development Bank of Southern Africa (DBSA). She has served as project manager for the Eradication of Mud Structures Program in the Eastern Cape Department of Education, Infrastructure and Planning Unit, and codeveloped the policy development framework and processes for the DBSA. She played a vital role as project manager for the Knowledge Management Africa initiative (KMA), as well as with the NEPAD/SADC project management system interface, sponsored by the United Nations Development Programme (UNDP). She is a cofounder of the Tsogo Education Centre in De-Wildt and has been involved with a variety of initiatives: the Oukasie Community Computer Training and Development Centre; the Brits Civil Association (BCA), which is a community organizing committee that fought forced removals; Mopake Ka Ditiro, an NGO for youth and women's development; and the Young Christian Workers (YCW).

David Moore is a professor of development studies at the University of Johannesburg. His PhD, on the political and ideological formation of Zimbabwe's ruling class up to 1980, was granted by York University in Toronto. He then taught at Athabasca University in Alberta, Flinders University in Adelaide, and the University of KwaZulu-Natal in Durban. His latest edited book is *The World Bank: Development, Poverty, Hegemony* (University of KwaZulu-Natal Press, 2007). Recent work includes "Coercion, Consent, Context: *Operation Murambatsvina* and ZANU-PF's Illusory Quest for Hegemony," in *Zimbabwe: The Hidden Dimensions of Operation Murambatsvina in Zimbabwe,* ed. Maurice Vambe (Harare: Weaver Press, 2008); with Showers Mawowa, "*Mbimbos, Zvipamuzis* and Primitive Accumulation in Zimbabwe's Violent Mineral Economy: Crisis, Chaos, and the State," *The Political Economy of Africa*, ed. Vishnu Padayachee (Routledge, 2010); and "A Decade of Disquieting Diplomacy: South Africa, Zimbabwe and the Ideology of the National Democratic Revolution, 1999–2009," *History Compass*, 8, 8 (August 2010).

Sam Moyo is Executive Director of the African Institute for Agrarian Studies (AIAS) in Harare, Zimbabwe, and is the current President of Council for the Development of Social Research in Africa (CODESRIA). He served as Vice President of CODESRIA (1998–2002) and a member of the Executive Council (1995–1998). He received his PhD in environmental and rural development issues, with a focus on land reform and agrarian change. His works explore the political economy and dynamics of rural transformations, including the nature of social movements which advocate reforms. His major publications include: African Land Questions, Agrarian Transitions and the State: Contradictions of Neoliberal Land Reforms, (2008); Land Reform Under Structural Adjustment in Zimbabwe: Land Use in the Mashonaland Provinces (2000); The Land Question in Zimbabwe (1995), [co-edited with Paris Yeros]: Reclaiming the Land: The Resurgence of Rural Movements in Africa, Asia and Latin America<http://www.amazon.com/Reclaiming-Land-Resurgence-Movements-America/dp/1842774255/ref=sr_1_2?

ie=UTF8&s=books&qid=1202056028&sr=1-2> (2005); [co-edited with Kojo Sebastian Amanor<http://www.amazon.com/exec/obidos/search-handle-url/103-3233725-3277437?%5Fencoding=UTF8&search-type=ss&index=books&field-author=Kojo%20Sebastian%20Amanor>]: Land and Sustainable Development in Africa<http://www.amazon.com/Sustainable-Development-Africa-Sebastian-Amanor/dp/1842779133/ref=sr_1_1?ie=UTF8&s=books&qid=1202055834&sr=1-1> (2008).

Sanusha Naidu is research director of the Emerging Powers in Africa project with Fahamu, a social justice network with offices across Africa. She was recently part of the United Nations Conference on Trade and Development (UNCTAD) consultant team for the 2008 World Investment Report on the development impact of Chinese, Indian, and South African TNC activity in Africa. Sanusha has been a research fellow at the Centre for Chinese Studies based at Stellenbosch University and a research specialist with the democracy and governance research program at the Human Sciences Research Council. She also served as the coordinator of the trade and poverty program of the Southern African Regional Poverty Network (SAPRN) for a number of years. Previously, Ms. Naidu was the senior Africa researcher at the South African Institute of International Affairs. Her research specialties include the implications of Africa's engagment with the Emerging Actors for governance and sustainable development.

Simon Pazvakavambwa worked for the government of Zimbabwe for twenty-eight years, serving in various capacities and retiring in 2008. He attained many senior positions, including permanent secretary for the Ministries of Rural Resources and Water Development; permanent secretary for the Ministry of Lands, Land Reform and Rural Resettlement; permanent secretary for the Ministry of Rural Housing and Social Amenities; and finally permanent secretary for the Ministry of Agriculture. He was also the technical coordinator for the Water Resources Management Strategy Project, which drew up the Water Resources Management Strategy for Zimbabwe. He has contributed to a number of publications throughout his career, including a number of World Bank Publications. More recently, Simon has been involved in consultancy work related to agricultural policy, and he is currently a full-time farmer. Simon is a graduate of Fourah Bay College at the University of Sierra Leone and The National College of Agricultural Engineering in the United Kingdom.

John Robertson is a writer and commentator on the Zimbabwean economy. After many years in the radio and television industries, he received his economics degree from the University College of Rhodesia and Nyasaland. After completing the degree, he became a financial journalist for *The Rhodesia Herald*. He was promoted to financial editor a few years later and spent nine years with the paper. In 1978, he joined First Merchant Bank as its chief economist, where he spent the next sixteen years. In 1994 he formed his own economic consultancy, Robertson Economic Information Services. John is a leading and well-respected economist in Zimbabwe who continues to write frequently on the country's financial situation.

Elizabeth Sidiropoulos is national director and programme head of the EU-Africa Project with the South African Institute of International Affairs (SAIIA). Previously she was director of studies at SAIIA, and she has also held positions as research director at the South African Institute of Race Relations and as editor of the *South African Survey*. She served for a time as the editor-in-chief of the *South African Journal of International Affairs* and the *South African Yearbook of International Affairs*. Her many publications include: "India and Africa: India Calling," *The World Today* 64, no. 4 (2008); "South Africa's Regional Engagement for Peace and Security," *FRIDE Comment,* October 2007; and *Apartheid Past, Renaissance Future: South Africa's Foreign Policy 1994–2004* (Johannesburg: SAIIA, 2004). Her research focuses on South African foreign policy and global governance, as well as EU-Africa relations.

Karolina Werner is project manager of the African Initiative at the Centre for International Governance Innovation (CIGI) in Waterloo, Canada, a position she has held since 2007. Before returning to Canada, she lived in Austria where she worked at the United Nations Industrial Development Organization and the International Institute for Applied Systems Analysis. She has lived in a variety of countries, including South Africa, through which she has developed a special interest in African issues. Ms. Werner has an MA in conflict resolution from the University of North Carolina, and a BSc honors degree in peace and conflict studies and psychology from the University of Toronto. Ms. Werner's research interests include security and international conflict, as well as grassroots and indigenous approaches to conflict transformation.

Siphamandla Zondi is executive director at the Institute for Global Dialogue (IGD). Trained in African studies at the former University of Durban-Westville (UDW), South Africa, and University of Cambridge, United Kingdom, Dr. Zondi went on to teach part-time in social development studies at UDW. He then worked for the Africa Institute of South Africa before joining the Institute for Global Dialogue (IGD) as head of the Africa Programme. In January 2010, he was promoted to his current post of director. His work spans areas such as SA's foreign policy, contintental governance, social policy, and regional governance.

Chapter 1

Zimbabwe's Recovery Path

A Conceptual Framework

Hany Besada and Jason LaChapelle

Once one of sub-Saharan Africa's most prosperous and promising states, Zimbabwe has endured a traumatic decade, socially and economically, under a government led by President Robert Mugabe since its independence from the United Kingdom in 1980. As Zimbabwe emerges from a decade marked by economic mismanagement, political violence, and international isolation, the national government faces enormous challenges ahead. Formerly the envy of its neighbors for its abundant mineral deposits, thriving agricultural sector, and one of the continent's most skilled and educated workforces, Zimbabwe has since become politically unstable and an economic disappointment of unprecedented proportions.

The current socioeconomic situation is dire: Zimbabwe has an unemployment rate hovering around 94 percent[1]; its poverty rate exceeds 78 percent,[2] with more than half of the population relying on remittances from Zimbabweans living abroad; its life expectancy is thirty-seven years for men and thirty-four for women,[3] down from fifty-nine in 1990; its health system is in a sorry state of rehabilitation, with scores of Zimbabweans dying from HIV/AIDS and cholera daily; and approximately two million Zimbabweans out of a population of thirteen million desperately need food.[4]

With the signing of the power-sharing agreement in September 2008, and the formation of a Government of National Unity (GNU) in February 2009 between the ruling Zimbabwe African National Union-Patriotic Front (ZANU-PF) party, led by longtime president Robert Mugabe, and the main opposition party, the Movement for Democratic Change (MDC), led by Prime Minister Morgan Tsvangirai, plus an MDC splinter group led by Arthur Mutambara, Zimbabwe has taken an important first step toward rebuilding its fractured political system and shattered economy.

There are signs that things are slowly improving. Back in 2008, Zimbabwe's inflation had rocketed to an astronomical 231 percent. A loaf of bread would have cost between Z$7,000 and Z$10,000, when it could be found. Officially, US$1 used to trade for Z$180 back in October 2008, but on the black market, it would have fetched Z$8,000. For bank transfers, the rate was Z$1.5 million to 1. With the Zimbabwean dollar being abandoned and replaced with the U.S. dollar and South African rand as the currency for financial transactions, hyperinflation has effectively disappeared. Wages are slowly rising, particularly in the private sector. Some schools are gradually reopening, while goods are flooding back into supermarkets, stocking their empty shelves. In February 2009, the International Monetary Fund (IMF) decided to restore Zimbabwe's voting rights after a seven-year suspension over failure to pay the US$1.3 billion it owes the organization and other creditors. The IMF has indicated that Zimbabwe has started reducing the US$140 million it owed at the end of 2009. Meanwhile, foreign aid is slowly trickling in. The United Kingdom's Department for International Development had allocated £60 million for humanitarian and development assistance in the country in 2009–10.

Nevertheless, the GNU faces an uphill battle regarding its security and socioeconomic challenges. As the unity government attempts to resurrect the country economically and politically, it will look to its neighbors in southern Africa and to the international community for much needed political and financial support and humanitarian assistance. Equally important is the potential role the private sector could play in fostering socioeconomic development as part of the government's economic reconstruction efforts. If the political landscape is managed properly by the state, accompanied by macroeconomic reforms and prudent management of the economy, the private sector could be a catalyst in driving the reconstruction efforts currently under way in this southern African state.

Conducting business in Zimbabwe has its own peculiar complexities and challenges that need to be critically addressed by both business corporations and government. Zimbabwe stands by a new controversial law requiring major foreign firms to sell 51 percent of their stakes to locals, but will allow companies to choose their own partners. Meanwhile, critics have often complained that operating multinationals in Zimbabwe is tantamount to propping up Mugabe's regime. While the involvement of foreign governments, multilateral institutions, nongovernmental organizations (NGOs), and the private sector is essential for the strengthening of good governance and economic reconstruction, much hinges on whether the MDC and ZANU-PF could work together in an atmosphere of peaceful cooperation for the sake of the country and its people.

The coalition has been rocked by differences over how to share power. Prime Minister Tsvangirai has being pressing for reform of the security forces, which he had accused of being used by Mugabe's ZANU-PF to stifle dissent. Mugabe, who was endorsed in December 2009 to lead his ZANU-PF part for another five years, had vowed to resist demands by the international community and the country's opposition to reform the country's security forces. The MDC accuses Mugabe of stalling on political reforms and continuing to launch attacks and intimidate its supporters. The Zimbabwean Human Rights NGO forum continues to stress those cases of political violence and human rights violations continue unabated. The other concerns deal with allegations that Mugabe's ZANU-PF continues to act in bad faith over a range of issues connected to the power-sharing agreement. Meanwhile, international organizations and governments point out that governance, provision of basic services, and human rights are still falling well below the needs of the Zimbabwean people.

Nevertheless, internal economic and political pressure in Zimbabwe is coinciding with increasing efforts by the Southern African Development Community (SADC) as well as by the international community to put pressure on Mugabe's ZANU-PF. A sound and inclusive economic recovery and reconstruction plan would facilitate efforts by those responsible for reform in Zimbabwe, as well as efforts by the international community to achieve a successful outcome. It would help to prevent the worst-case scenario of civil conflict, instability, and regional destabilization from becoming a reality during any further attempted political and economic transition.

The Purpose and Plan of the Book

In light of the ongoing discussion surrounding Zimbabwe's economic recovery and political transition, this volume chronicles the country's options on key governance issues. It examines the current state of Zimbabwe and takes stock of efforts underway by regional and international actors to address the various economic, political, and social challenges it currently faces. *Zimbabwe: Picking Up the Pieces* includes experts' advice from and on the region on the way forward for Zimbabwe, including what conditions are necessary to initiate stakeholders in reconstruction, development efforts, and good governance practices. It takes a particular look at the private sector efforts and donor mobilization strategies required to initiate a sustainable recovery effort for Zimbabwe.

The book is divided into three sections: peace building and strengthening institutions for good governance; economic recovery strategies for sustainable development; and foreign direct investment and donor engagement for socioeconomic reconstruction.

In chapter two, Zondi traces the domestic political terrain in Zimbabwe since independence, illustrating a history of conflict and mutual distrust between competing groups and a calculated mission by the ZANU—and subsequently the ZANU-PF—for political hegemony across Zimbabwe. Repression, subversive agendas, and stagnant processes of reform are entrenched in the country's political culture, and Zondi argues that external actors, such as the SADC, are needed to shift institutional reform out of its stalemate and mediate cooperation between the ZANU-PF and the MDC. Focusing on the waves of instability in the past few years, and how the crisis has shifted from static to dynamic, Zondi uses the constitutional amendment and the outcomes of the Global Political Agreement (GPA) to contend that real power-sharing has not been translated from rhetoric to action. Reforms encouraged by the SADC have been intended to promote political tolerance and shift the normative framework toward dialogue and human rights, but Mugabe continues to spoil these efforts—acting unilaterally, resisting fundamental change, and envisioning the GPA as a means to co-opt or subordinate the MDC rather than accepting the need for genuine cooperation. These underlying tensions have created a dependence on external actors to continuously oversee and intervene in the political developments.

The chapter by Werner and Chitiyo analyzes the potential for security sector reform in Zimbabwe, detailing evidence of the overwhelming politicization of the security sector and the militarization of the political and socioeconomic landscape, and arguing that reform, as it was in the aftermath of independence, must be a vital component of reconstruction. According to Werner and Chitiyo, this transformation is rendered nearly impossible by an underlying ethos of hard security and the state-security-business nexus, which the ZANU-PF has fine-tuned to terrorize opposition supporters, contain the MDC, and militarize the political economy. Despite the power-sharing agreement, the MDC boasts only soft power and little leverage against the security sector, which still acts as the guardian of the ZANU-PF. Asserting that security sector transformation is still possible in the Mugabe era, Werner and Chitiyo consider entry points that the MDC and the international community can take advantage of: momentum from the opening up of domestic political space; the GPA, whose terms can be used as leverage; reforms in other sectors that can advance incremental progress; and the formulation of a white paper on security, which would outline the roles and responsibilities of the security sector in the context of a new Zimbabwe.

In chapter four, Moore cites a Gramscian analysis to argue that the Zimbabwean media has served as a venue for state-civil society relations, tensions between public and market forces, and debates over narratives of Western hegemony and African anti-imperialism. Although the GPA was supposed to usher in a fair and open press and the return of independent newspapers, media reform has been a microcosm of the difficult transition from authoritarianism to democracy as the ZANU-PF continues to corrupt the flow of information and suppress opponents. Through selective appointments to the Zimbabwe Media Commission, the press remains an arm of the state whereby free media is vilified as part of the machinery of external intervention—therefore strict regulations are enforced and audiences are persuaded that Western ideas of liberal democracy and human rights represent imperial efforts to demobilize African unity. Moore's ideological and discursive analysis of Zimbabwean, and also South African, news reports is the foundation of his argument that developmental journalism—that is, the direct penetration of media by the state—invariably leads to a reining in of criticism, the insertion of political campaigns to delegitimize opponents and portray a false reality, and the erosion of democracy. Zimbabwe must find a formula that maintains the media as a public good, yet prevents it from insulating the regime and serving the state's antidemocratic objectives.

Robertson's chapter is a criticism of Zimbabwe's land reform process as the precipitator of the economic collapse that the country is now faced with recovering from. According to Robertson, commercial agriculture, at one time the strength of the Zimbabwean economy, was built on the innovations introduced by colonialism, in which private property ownership stimulated the development of skills and advanced techniques and facilitated investment and access to capital through loans.

Robertson argues that commercial agriculture upheld the nation's prosperity and stability by assuring food security, foreign exchange, employment, and government revenues to invest in social services. But the government's misguided resettlement and indigenization programs, in pursuit of redressing past injustices, yet plagued by patronage and corruption, have tried to reinstate obsolete and unproductive traditional structures, which has acted as a bulwark against progress—driving modern innovation and skill into exile and undoing private-public cooperation and business successes. Robertson suggests that the formalization of individual property rights and a return to large-scale commercial farming (including in communal and smallholder lands) can reestablish agriculture as the primary generator of wealth, thus bringing back food self-sufficiency, cash incomes, and export earnings. Economic recovery should not be conflated with political contestation or concerns for compensation for historical injustices, and the imperative must be market reforms that add value to land and remove unnecessary state intervention and the disincentives to efficiency.

Balancing the costs and benefits of official dollarization, Makochekanwa and Kambarami conclude in chapter six that the conditions in Zimbabwe are conducive to this policy alternative as a solution to rein in out-of-control hyperinflation, and they recommend randization as being most appropriate. Zimbabwe's myopic and often contradictory monetary decisions have propagated hyperinflation and delegitimized policymakers, and therefore dollarization would not only lower inflation, but also bring discipline and credibility to the financial sector, as well as attract investors and eliminate the government's costs of maintaining a national currency. Makochekanwa and Kambarami detail a host of factors making Zimbabwe a good candidate for dollarization, the most prominent being that semiofficial and unofficial dollarization already characterize 95 percent of the economy (thus making the transition less shocking), with foreign currencies operating as a unit of account and means of payment. Makochekanwa and Kambarami believe the political costs to be greater than the economic ones because of the implications for sovereignty and foreign policy. While they acknowledge there are distinct economic drawbacks to dollarization, including erosion of monetary autonomy and increased risk during financial crises due to the loss of seigniorage, these costs can be mitigated by other policy channels if the government responsibly undertakes dollarization, a step for which Makochekanwa and Kambarami believe Zimbabwe is ripe.

In chapter seven Moyo offers a criticism of how most scholars have analyzed Zimbabwe's agricultural collapse and prescribes a set of policy recommendations to make rural agricultural recovery the centerpiece of broad-based development and poverty alleviation. He argues that a heterogeneous set of structural factors such as the legacies of a discriminatory and racialized tenure system, developments in the global political economy, and the withdrawal of donor support have as much contributed to the fall in production as has land reform, which mainstream scholars have labeled as being the unilateral cause. Moyo's conclusions are social justice-based, as he reminds readers that despite the ills of the fast-track land-reform program, it has been effective in reducing inequities and empowering small farmers, and it came out of a time in which market land reforms were unsatisfactory, bilateral and multilateral donors had abandoned support, and social pressure from disadvantaged groups for land acquisition was mounting. Moyo is critical of state policies that did not target small and medium farms for access to inputs and infrastructural improvements, but he also links this to the political and economic isolation caused by the retreat of Western investment and aid, the impact of sanctions, and the adoption of liberalization policies. Showing that smallholders have been historically responsible for the majority of national food production, Moyo argues that the new agro-industrial development model must prioritize the rural and urban poor and honestly mediate class struggles to ensure an equitable allocation of resources that promotes food sovereignty and expands the productive capacities of the poor through subsidies and extension services.

In chapter eight, Pazvakavambwa charts the causes of Zimbabwe's major food security problems, electing to widen the scope of analysis beyond the land reform program and focus instead on a series of misdirected, short-sighted, and, at times, dishonest policy choices that were intended to boost agricultural production, but that actually damaged the agricultural sector severely. Zimbabwe's past proclivity as a food self-sufficient nation always relied upon state support and well-planned interventions, but Pazvakavambwa traces a series of policy failures over the past decade, namely the Government Input Scheme and the Champion Farmers program, that show a poor assessment of food security and the agricultural sector on the part of the state. Much of the inadequate performance of recent agricultural support mechanisms is attributable to the broader economic crisis itself—funding could not keep up with inflation, and it was nearly impossible to design a formula for increased production with a shrinking supply of affordable inputs—but the state's policies were also careless and reactive as, for instance, they delayed importing inputs until prices had soared, and failed to appropriately target subsidies where they could result in increased production. Bureaucratic issues also contributed to the country's agricultural collapse as commercial lending became cumbersome and unsatisfactory for farmers, agricultural experts ceased to be consulted, and decision-making power became centralized within the Reserve Bank of Zimbabwe, thereby marginalizing and compromising the traditional roles of the Ministries of Finance and Agriculture. Pazvakavambwa recommends a more proactive and sustainable agricultural strategy in which resources are distributed with food security, and not patronage networks, in mind and advocates policy choices that restore farmer initiative (by halting the free provision of inputs), target rural areas, and best use the competencies of relevant NGOs, CSOs, and ministries.

In chapter nine, Helen Moatshe suggests a prominent role for private-public partnerships (PPPs) in addressing an often-ignored consequence of Zimbabwe's political and economic collapse—the exodus of skilled workers and the deterioration of human resources and social infrastructure. Structural adjustment, political repression, hyperinflation, and events such as Operation Murambatsvina not only scared investment and foreign aid, but they also caused an outflow of the qualified professional class (doctors, teachers, managers, and engineers), who also happened to be attracted to the stability and wage opportunities available in South Africa—wanting to make themselves candidates for black affirmative action programs. Because the GNU has failed to accumulate the necessary donor pledges from the international community, Moatshe argues that the SADC, through state-owned enterprises and the private sector, should reassert its support to Zimbabwe by setting up the institutional arrangements for attracting FDI and implementing service delivery projects. South African PPPs can serve as models as Zimbabwe's southern neighbor, through programs such as Siyenza Manje, has successfully launched groundbreaking municipal projects focused on increasing technical capacity building, improving health and education conditions, and developing/attracting social capital. Moatshe contends that a concerted effort from civil society, NGOs, public agencies, and private institutions should be anchored to the expertise of regional development finance institutions (e.g., DBSA), which have extensive experience in leading development projects. The Zimbabwean government too needs to create an enabling environment for business success by removing the constraints imposed on investment (costs and risks), deepening trade relations, and facilitating a larger role for the private sector in rehabilitating infrastructure.

In chapter ten, Games examines the toxic relationship between state and business in Zimbabwe, deconstructing their dysfunctional interactions and elaborating on the reasons why some multinationals felt compelled to continue their Zimbabwean operations, while other foreign investors decided to stay far away. According to Games, the operating environment for business and investment has been completely chaotic since 2000: in addition to the overarching problems of economic contraction in every sector, currency devaluation, and resource and skill shortages, the state has placed an onerous burden on multinationals through insidious policies, punitive regulations, harassment, and seizure of properties, in addition to summarily blaming the private sector for problems of its own doing, which in total have nearly destroyed the formal economy. The eruption of violence during the 2008 elections is the centerpiece for the thorny nature of the state-business relationship. The public response to the pressure to disinvest combined concern for the livelihoods of abandoned Zimbabwean workers and a desire to be part of the reconstruction process, but Games criticizes the silence and complicity of business actors, who were largely silent on government despotism and human rights violations and who often provided indirect loans to the regime. She acknowledges, however, that fear, survival, and government strong-arming influenced corporate behavior, and that a number of firms chose to leave in 2008, citing moral and political reasons. Continuous political uncertainty, as a result of Mugabe's obvious attempts to spoil the GPA, and controversial legislation, such as the Indigenization program, which many feel is geared toward elite empowerment rather than black empowerment, have undermined business confidence and led potential investors of all stripes (Chinese, Indian, Western) to adopt a "wait-and-see" approach and in many cases withdraw their interest. For Games, multinationals, through the creation of downstream benefits, private-public partnerships, and cross-sectoral linkages, have a major role to play in reconstruction, but donors and the state must facilitate the renewal of their economic activity, credibility, and corporate governance structures, all of which have been systematically eroded.

In the following chapter, Naidu assesses the challenges facing the South African private sector as it positions itself to take a leading role in the economic revival of Zimbabwe. Unlike the majority of foreign investment operating in the troubled country, many South African businesses were able to remain active in Zimbabwe during the political and economic turmoil, owing to deep historical and commercial linkages, surviving Mugabe's nationalization, monopolization, and indigenization policies. Naidu notes that South Africa should clearly be interested in pursuing multisectoral market-led development opportunities, especially given its similar role in reconstruction elsewhere in the region, but as the subcontinent's hegemon, other countries, including Zimbabwe, are suspicious that South Africa is undertaking an imperialist agenda, seeking to liberate South African capital rather than forge genuine development partnerships. Naidu also considers South Africa's main challenger for market dominance in Zimbabwe, China, which has already profited from the West's reluctance to engage with Zimbabwe. The financial muscle and political willingness of China's "go global" strategy, along with Zimbabwe's "Look East" policy, have created a strong partnership, and Naidu finds that China's willingness to engage with the GNU as a whole gives it a distinct advantage over South Africa, which has closer ties with Tsvangirai and whose African renaissance project is still looked upon skeptically as being economically self-interested. Despite the obstacles, Naidu does see a lot of potential for South African business in Zimbabwe, due mainly to its commercial reputation in the region, but investors will also rely on politicians to ensure that the investment climate is stable and secure.

In chapter twelve, Hansen examines the evolution of the aid framework that Western nations have applied to Zimbabwe, arguing that donors must look for alternative solutions to the traditional model—beset with carrots, sticks, and conditionalities—that are based on government-to-government support and long-term poverty alleviation, in addition to responding to the country's unique and pointed state of instability. The aid debate is convoluted to begin with, a balancing act between the terms of the Paris Declaration, recipient ownership, and normative donor guidance in terms of human rights and good governance principles. But as Hansen argues, implementing a salient development policy is further complicated in Zimbabwe by an obstructive environment in which aid disbursement is hijacked and politicized, clampdowns on rights and freedoms are increasing, and accusations of neocolonialism are fertile. Despite a worsening humanitarian situation and what he labels a "Potemkin democracy," Hansen applauds donors, especially Denmark, for fine-tuning their aid strategies and exploring new approaches to proactively engage with Zimbabwe, through the Humanitarian Plus initiative, for example, in a manner that shifts beyond short-term relief toward long-term regeneration, development, and reform. Hansen sees potential for more effective aid arising out of the MDC's authority over the "soft" portfolios of health and education within the GNU, and he notes recent efforts by like-minded donors to reorient aid according to updated agendas that consider the political realities (e.g., Mugabe's reuse of violence and defiance of the GPA) and the need for holistic democratic change. The Multi-Donor Trust Fund and a refocus on system change, which encompasses elements such as power-sharing and security sector reform, rather than regime change, stand out.

In the last chapter of the book Gruzd, Sidiropoulos, and Katito contend that it is in South Africa's self-interest to put Zimbabwe near the top of its foreign policy agenda by taking the lead in the reconstruction process, which would not only serve as an instructive case study for its new coordinated development assistance approach, but also serve its goals of regional political stability and economic prosperity and integration. To date, South Africa's aid system has been fragmented and diffused among different government agencies, lacking coherence and institutional memory, but with internal reform and initiatives such as the Pan-African Infrastructural Development Fund, South Africa is promoting not only a more coordinated outreach effort, but an African renaissance that would see South African capital spread and entrenched across southern Africa. Different elements within the government prioritize commercial self-interest or altruism, but it is clear from policy documents such as the Polokwane Resolutions that South Africa wants to use its economic and political muscle in Zimbabwe without being perceived as an imperialistic hegemon, instead emphasizing development "partnerships." South Africa has made a number of attempts to increase its authority over the reconstruction effort, taking the lead in SADC mediation efforts and setting up an agricultural task team to oversee comprehensive food security interventions, but Gruzd, Sidiropoulos, and Katito see other opportunities to enhance its role, including integration into the Southern African Customs Union and the use of South African private firms and parastatals to catalyze economic rebirth in Zimbabwe. The authors conclude that South Africa will have to delicately and pragmatically utilize its leverage—through skilful diplomacy and strategic development assistance—to overcome the GNU's paralysis, but pulling Zimbabwe out of crisis is necessary for South Africa to achieve its regional objectives.

Notes

1. Reuters, "Zim Unemployment Skyrockets," *Mail & Guardian online,* January 29, 2009, http://www.mg.co.za/article/2009–01–29-zim-unemployment-skyrockets.
2. Sandra Nyaira, "Three Out of Four Zimbabweans Living in Poverty, Hungry; Many of Them AIDS Orphans," *Voices of America,* April 12, 2010, http://www1.voanews.com/zimbabwe/news/food-agriculture/Zimbabwe-Poverty-Hunger-Widespread-12Apr10–90647654.html.
3. Bob Herbert, "Zimbabwe is Dying," *The New York Times,* January 16, 2009, http://www.nytimes.com/2009/01/17/opinion/17herbert.html.
4. "UK Aid Delivers in Zimbabwe But Violence Threatens Progress, Say MPs," parliament.uk, March 26, 2010, http://news.parliament.uk/business/news/2010/03/uk-aid-delivers-in-zimbabwe-but-violence-threatens-progress-say-mps/.

Part I

Peace Building and Strengthening Institutions for Good Governance

Chapter 2

ZANU-PF and MDC Power-Sharing

Zimbabwe Still at a Crossroads?

Siphamandla Zondi

Introduction

For nine years Zimbabwe descended into an abyss of a political-cum-economic crisis. This led to a gradual decline of the economy, political polarization, and the disintegration of the state. During all this time, neither loud diplomacy by the West, nor "quiet" diplomacy by African states could lead Zimbabwe out of the conflict. With the signing of the Global Political Agreement (GPA) between the Zimbabwe African National Union-Patriotic Front (ZANU-PF) and the two Movement for Democratic Change (MDC) factions in September 2008, Zimbabwe finally edged closer to finding the long-elusive political settlement and a formula for establishing a new political and economic dispensation. Four months earlier Zimbabwe had witnessed relatively free and fair elections for the first time in many years, only for the situation to degenerate again into an orgy of political violence and intolerance in the run-up to the presidential runoff elections in June 2008.

Thus, the positive atmosphere of the run-up to the March 29, 2008, elections gave way to political conflict, prompting the Southern African Development Community (SADC) to intensify its diplomatic moves to get the two sides of the conflict to find a negotiated political settlement. As the SADC envoy, former South African president Thabo Mbeki, pushed the parties in intensive talks behind closed doors, the economy continued to sink into an abyss, with inflation and the prices of consumer goods rising fast to the detriment of livelihoods in villages and townships. The humanitarian situation also worsened with the continued collapse of the social and physical infrastructure and over 80 percent unemployment. The cholera epidemic, which broke out in October 2008 and continued well into early 2009, infected thousands and killed hundreds of Zimbabweans.

Yet, the peace negotiations remained on course, and some progress was registered with the formation of bipartisan monitoring mechanism and the decision by the MDC faction led by Morgan Tsvangirai (the MDC-T) in late January 2009 to join the inclusive government. Both factions of the MDC are active drivers of the Government of National Unity (GNU), and trust amongst the parties has grown with the passage of time.

This chapter provides a comprehensive overview of the evolution of the peace process in Zimbabwe. It argues that although the negotiated process of conflict resolution through mediation has stalemated a number of times and even collapsed on some occasions, it can be a useful basis for lasting peace and democracy in Zimbabwe. This chapter argues that positive outcomes of the protracted progress are due partly to the skill of the SADC facilitation team and partly to the fact that the conflict was ripe for a negotiated settlement; the stalemate is no longer bearable for the political elite because it erodes both their privileges and legitimacy before significant constituencies.

Dynamic Stalemates: A Conceptual Framework

The fundamental conceptual point underpinning this chapter is that conflict resolution and the onset of peace are facilitated by the ripening of the conflict and political stalemate, and the damage that it causes to the interests, resources, and standing of the parties involved. This draws largely from the work of William Zartman who, in his book *Ripe for Resolution* (1985), argued that the timing of the resolution of conflict is just as important as the quality of the proposals.[1]

This chapter argues that after a decade of bruising battles, economic meltdown, socioeconomic decline, and popular discontent, the Zimbabwean parties realized, with the help of the SADC facilitator, that a negotiated settlement was a more attractive option than military victory or a popular revolution. The situation was also ripe following the failure of successive attempts by international actors to push parties toward some form of conflict resolution, including a regime change.[2]

The roots of the Zimbabwean conflict are complex. They include structural distortions in its political economy shaped during the colonial period, such as a dictatorial state and the racial structure of the economy, with a small white minority controlling the bulk of economic resources and a black majority languishing in poverty. These distortions were further intensified by the failure of the postcolonial state to transform the political economy and the manner in which the state handled newly found political authority. The austerity program imposed by the International Monetary Fund (IMF) and the World Bank (WB) during the 1990s helped to cement the structural abnormalities and to entrench the ZANU-PF's one-party state agenda.

The confrontation between active portions of civil society and the state escalated with the formation of the MDC in 1999 out of a coalition of critical interests that included trade unions, nongovernmental organizations (NGOs), and advocacy groups. The new party intended to be the opposition to the ZANU-PF. The conflict also worsened as the MDC increased its powerbase and posed a serious threat to the ZANU-PF's long-held state power.

Toward a One-Party State: Suppression of ZAPU, ZUM, and MDC

The ruthless suppression of decent opposition started in the 1980s as part of the ZANU-PF agenda to create a one-party state. The absorption of the Zimbabwe People's African Union (ZAPU) into its rival, the ZANU, after a truce between Joshua Nkomo and Robert Mugabe in 1987 was an important part of this concentration of power project. This was the culmination of a cold-blooded suppression of the ZAPU by the ZANU after years of bloody streets fights between the combatants of the two old liberation movements.

The tensions between the two organizations can be traced back to the 1960s when a split in the Ndabaningi Sithole-led ZAPU precipitated the formation in 1963 of ZANU under Mugabe, ZANU's erstwhile general secretary. Followers of the two parties fought fiercely over which of the two parties controlled the Chimurenga/ Umvukela (struggle against colonial rule). This led to the loss of many lives in an estimated 4919 acts of political violence in 1963 alone.[3] The colonial government took advantage of this and arrested some leaders of the warring political organizations, causing the rest to escape into exile, from where they launched a particularly violent chapter of their struggle, the so-called second Chimurenga.

There were several failed attempts before 1987 to unite the two organizations. For instance, the Front for the Liberation of Zimbabwe (FROLIZI), which was a united front between the two organizations, only lasted two years—between 1971 and 1973—before it collapsed due to the failure of the two parties to show commitment to unity. Herbert Chitepo's Joint Military Command of 1972 was ineffectual because of a lack of political will from the ZANU and ZAPU. Unity attempts by the Frontline States Initiative in 1975 also floundered. But when confronted with a need to present a common front in response to proposals by the then U.S. secretary of state Henry Kissinger, ZANU and ZAPU formed an effective "Patriotic Front" in 1976 through the mediation of Mozambique's president Samora Machel. The front lasted until the Lancaster Agreement was signed in 1980, after which it collapsed because the two parties decided to campaign for the first postindependence elections separately.

The violent suppression of ZAPU by the new ZANU government in the mid-1980s, which led to an orgy of violence and deaths of thousands, was part of a long history of conflict. Having acquired control over the state's instruments of force, ZANU thought it could annihilate its long-standing nemesis at the slightest irritation. The conflict began with clashes between the two parties' armies—Zimbabwe People's Revolutionary Army (ZIPRA) of ZAPU and Zimbabwe National Liberation Army (ZANLA) of ZANU—from 1980 to 1981. This escalated into a violent confrontation as the ZANU government descended on Matabeleland, ZAPU's base, with strong-arm tactics. It dismissed ZAPU leaders from the unity government and arrested others. Seeing ZAPU as an extension of apartheid South Africa's onslaught on the southern African region, the ZANU government unleashed the ruthless Fifth Brigade on the people of Matabeleland in 1983 in a bloody suppression that lasted until 1987.[4]

Peace talks between ZANU and ZAPU led to a truce in 1987, which saw the merciless Fifth Brigade withdrawn from Matabeleland and the granting of amnesty to ZIPRA combatants involved in the war. However, the truce also sought to achieve a long-standing ZANU pursuit for total political hegemony and the assimilation of the ZAPU into its ranks. Indeed, the two parties merged under the terms of the Unity Accord signed by Mugabe and Joshua Nkomo in the same year. For this reason, instead of a merger, the ZANU saw the Unity Accord as a means of liquidating the ZAPU. ZANU-PF was thus meant to be a reincarnation of ZANU.[5]

However, just how this idea was to be achieved created tensions within the ZANU-PF, leading the party's Politburo to vote against the idea in 1989 and again in 1990. Mugabe's close ally and the party's general secretary Edgar Tekere was among the most vocal critics of the one-party state idea. He publicly opposed the constitutional changes that saw Mugabe assume full executive powers and become an imperial president.

As a result, Tekere was summarily expelled from the party, compelling him to establish a new political platform in opposition to the ZANU-PF: the Zimbabwe Unity Movement (ZUM). The party surprised everyone by getting 20 percent of the vote and two parliamentary seats during the 1990 elections. These results also suggested that the ZANU-PF's hegemony could be challenged. The ZANU-PF panicked and embarked upon a ruthless clampdown of political dissent through arbitrary arrests of members of the ZUM, violent responses to strikes by university students and unionized workers, and the disappearance of activists under the hands of the notorious Central Intelligence Organization (CIO).[6] It did not allow the young ZUM to grow, leading to its collapse by the time of the next elections in 1995.[7]

With the ZUM successfully repressed, the Zimbabwe Congress for Trade Unions (ZCTU) became the vehicle for political opposition to the mighty ZANU-PF. It led the formation in 1997 of an alliance of critical civil society organizations (CSOs) seeking wide-ranging democratic change under the name National Constitutional Assembly (NCA), with the fiery trade unionist Morgan Tsvangirai at its helm. The NCA helped popularize the struggle for democracy in Zimbabwe through extensive civic education and campaigns for a new constitution to replace the Lancaster House Agreement. In response to immense pressure for the NCA and ZCTU to enter into active politics, the latter convened what it called the National Working People's Convention in February 1999 to map out a broad political agenda for civil society. Having resolved that Zimbabwe's problems stemmed from a crisis of governance, the convention decided to establish a popularly driven and organized movement for democratic change. Thus, the MDC was established, with Morgan Tsvangirai as its president.

Unlike previous opposition movements, the MDC was born into an organized and widespread mass base, with the militant labor federation and constitutional reform forum as its engines. But the strong focus on the removal of Mugabe from government led to a narrow political focus in the MDC's agenda. This narrow agenda was informed in part by influences from business interests, organized white commercial farmers, and external donors.[8]

Following the MDC's strong showing in both the constitutional referendum and parliamentary elections of 2000, and with prospects of an even stronger showing during the 2002 presidential elections, the ZANU-PF regime unleashed a merciless campaign to suppress and destroy the MDC. This included fiddling with the electoral system in favor of the ZANU-PF; a clampdown on independent media; and the unleashing of ruthless war veterans against its enemies. This vicious campaign coincided with a period in which the new movement contended with the challenges of transforming from a broad church of class interests into a coherent political party.

The reign of terror combined with internal disagreements to weaken the MDC, culminating in a split into two factions—a moderate one led by Arthur Mutambara, and the main faction under Tsvangirai's leadership. The SADC and regional powers like South Africa did not have an effective response to these developments, and were unable to persuade or pressure the ZANU-PF to allow democracy to flower in Zimbabwe. The SADC's attempts to persuade the ZANU-PF to negotiate an amicable solution with the MDC failed.

The Crisis of Expectations, Land Reform, and Conflict

Seeds of the Zimbabwean crisis were sowed very early on in the ZANU-PF's reign. As previously noted, these included the inherited structural distortions from colonialism, which were allowed to deepen after independence. The economy also failed to grow strong enough to enable the new government to sustain its increased spending on social services by which it projected itself as a caring government. The inflation started to rise as early 1983; the Zimbabwe dollar exchange rate fell, while the deficits in the current and capital accounts increased.[9] This meltdown coincided with a bad drought and a combination of military incursions and trade blockage by apartheid South Africa, all of which negatively affected the economy. Neither the fiscus, nor donor funding could cover the costly willing buyer, willing seller-based land reform program.

The state's crisis management response incorporated a self-imposed stabilization program of 1982, which included the devaluation of the Zimbabwean dollar, restrictions on new non-concessionary foreign borrowing, balance of payment controls, price controls, a wage freeze, and export incentives. This was followed by even more severe austerity measures imposed by the IMF and the WB, until ideological differences with the Zimbabwean government led to an abrupt closure of the program.[10]

As socioeconomic conditions deepened, the plunder of state resources, nepotism, and kleptocracy worsened. Polarization between the state and the increasingly militant civil society also deepened. In this context, trade unions, students' organizations, and social movements became even more militant and politicized.[11]

The engagement of the IMF, which led to the Economic Structural Adjustment Programme (ESAP) of 1991, meant more tightening of the belt, with big cuts to social spending and the downsizing of state and industry. This led to deeper poverty and retrenchments, further angering the militant civil society. By 1995, the budget deficit had risen to over 8 percent, while economic growth rate had shrunk to 0.8 percent.[12] The ensuing hostile relationship between the IMF and the government culminated in the IMF's withdrawal in 1999. Indicative of popular discontent, the number of strikes and protests over socioeconomic conditions increased dramatically between 1990 and 1998.[13]

The historically and ideologically important process of land redistribution had failed in this context. A major thrust of the postcolonial agricultural policy was to achieve redress of inherited inequalities through the reallocation of land, the development of marketing infrastructure, and extension services. But there was actually very little land redistribution in the first decade of independence. By 1990, the land reform process had only yielded three million hectares of land for black beneficiaries, 40 percent of which was not conducive for farming.[14] The economic climate, restrictions imposed by the Lancaster Agreement, state mismanagement of the process, and profit-seeking by landlords had conspired in this failure.[15] The United Kingdom's pledge to provide funds toward land resettlement was not fully and consistently honored. According to a former U.K. high commissioner to Africa, the United Kingdom gave forty-seven million pounds between 1981 and 1988, but there is no indication of how these amounts were used, or what happened after 1988.[16] The Zimbabwean government became complacent, while the United Kingdom started to show a loss of interest as the second decade approached.

As a result, only 14 percent of the total land targeted for resettlement was acquired between 1986 and 1990. Furthermore, 27 percent of households were resettled compared to 70 percent during the preceding five-year period. The communal land reorganization program slowed down. Between 1986 and 1991, plans had been drawn up for only four out of ninety villages in the UMP (Uzumba-Maramba-Pfungwe) district.[17]

A Confluence of Problems: The Current Crisis since 1997

By 1997, the Zimbabwean government had failed on a number of fronts. Primarily, it had failed to articulate and translate the aspirations of its citizens into practical policies and programs, choosing rather to embrace the neoliberal economic agenda and enjoy the privileges handed down by its colonial predecessor. It emulated the colonial state in its use of crude force to suppress dissenting masses and in advocating economic policies that advance elite interests.

Unhappy that only a few ZANU-PF elites were benefiting, former liberation fighters organized themselves into the Zimbabwe National Liberation War Veterans Association and other pressure groups to call for radical land redistribution and affirmative action.[18] In 1999, the government joined a SADC military expedition in the Democratic Republic of the Congo (DRC) in support of Laurent Kabila, sending some eleven thousand soldiers and several helicopters and attack aircrafts at huge costs to the state coffers. This caused a major budget deficit as millions of U.S. dollars were spent outside of the budget.[19]

In response to the NCA–MDC push for a comprehensive constitutional reform process from 1999 to 2000, the ZANU-PF government introduced a closely controlled constitutional reform process via a hastily assembled Constitutional Commission of four hundred persons. After five thousand public meetings throughout the country, the commission submitted a draft constitution to President Mugabe on November 29, 1999. While the draft made provisions for a bill of rights and international law, emphasized participatory governance, established a prime minister position, and enhanced the role of parliament, it failed to reduce the excessive powers of the presidency. This led to a boycott of the constitution-making process by many groups, describing it as a sham designed to legitimize Mugabe. The ZANU-PF decided to go ahead on its own, presenting its draft constitution in a referendum.[20] The MDC successfully mobilized civil society against the draft, resulting in a resounding *no* vote (55 percent versus 45 percent *yes* vote).

The government was shocked. Fearing that this had set a bad precedent for the impending 2002 presidential elections, it began a crackdown on the MDC and the radical civil society movement. It established the Joint Operations Command (JOC), headed by security chiefs with sweeping powers to use force against all threats to state. On January 9, 2002, chiefs of armed forces issued a joint statement ahead of the presidential elections, declaring that they would not submit to a commander-in-chief who lacked "liberation credentials."[21]

The strategy of intimidation worked. Alternative parties were denied space to campaign, and their constituencies were intimidated. Thus, the ZANU-PF averted defeat and forced its way back into power. It was a contested victory though, with Mugabe garnering 56 percent to Tsvangirai's 42 percent.[22]

Having worked once, this became the main strategy of the ZANU-PF for subsequent elections. Hence, the run-up to the 2005 parliamentary elections was also marred by violence and other forms of state brutality against the opposition, including a clampdown on the independent media, strict control over donor funding, and arbitrary arrests of critics. Opposition activists, and even critical journalists, did not escape the brutal hand of state security offices. The preelection violence was orchestrated to intimidate two major constituencies of the opposition: the urban middle class and the restless peri-urban poor.[23]

Another part of the strategy was to divide the opposition by offering false concessions on constitutional and state reform. Just before the 2005 elections, the ZANU-PF regime introduced constitutional amendment no. 17 to create a lower house of parliament that would be filled with chiefs and a number of senators appointed by the president. The Senate was given powers to review laws and policies proposed by the National Assembly.

Although the change failed to excite the angry public, it helped to precipitate an acrimonious debate within the MDC over whether the party should endorse this move and use its seats in the Senate strategically to contest state power. Finally, the MDC split into two, with those in favor of using the Senate forming an MDC faction led by former student activist, Arthur Mutambara, and those opposed remaining in the bigger MDC faction under Tsvangirai.

With the MDC in tatters and voters largely apathetic to yet another managed elections, the ZANU-PF won 59.6 percent of the vote to the MDC's 39.5 percent in the 2005 elections. In the newly created Senate, the ZANU-PF won a whopping 73 percent to the MDC's 20 percent.[24] Thus, the MDC had fallen into a ZANU-PF trap designed to keep them divided ahead of crucial elections, a distraction from the ZANU-PF's own internal challenges.

The African Responses to ZANU-PF Brutality

The police attacks on Morgan Tsvangirai and other leaders of the opposition and critical civil society in March 2007, which precipitated the SADC intervention, were part of the deepening authoritarianism and an attempt to annihilate the MDC before the 2008 elections.[25]

Many analysts have taken the cue from the United Kingdom and the United States by believing that it was the ZANU-PF alone that was to blame for the crisis in Zimbabwe. They overlook the impact of the inherited structural constraints to land reform and transformation. For them, the Lancaster House Agreement is in the past and has no bearing on developments of the past decade. They even ignore the resistance of white commercial farmers and landowners to land reform. They also overlook the failure of donors to honor their pledges of financial support toward land reform and economic recovery in both the 1981 and 1998 donor conferences.[26] But this chapter demonstrates that the reasons for the crisis are more complex and multifaceted than is often assumed.

African leaders saw that the situation in Zimbabwe was ripe for a concerted SADC–African Union (AU) mediation of interparty negotiations toward a political settlement. It was clear to the region that the Zimbabwean economy had been badly battered by the political stalemate of the past seven years. Some SADC leaders were also motivated by national interests, seeing that Zimbabweans were fleeing in droves into neighboring countries, thereby precipitating a regional humanitarian crisis. The resistance had taken its toll on the MDC leadership, along with the violent suppression by government, the internal fissure, and donor fatigue. Former South African president Thabo Mbeki calculated that the "time was now," referring to the propitious conditions for a negotiated settlement.[27] The time was ripe for a negotiated resolution.

The SADC Mediation

The SADC mandated Thabo Mbeki to facilitate negotiations between the ZANU-PF and the MDC factions. The protracted process of negotiations culminated in the signing of the power-sharing deal on September 15, 2008. The deal represented a major departure from suppression and resistance of the past and began a road toward a peaceful settlement of Zimbabwe's problems. The establishment of an inclusive government in early 2009 provided an institutional vehicle for the process of shaping this new future, as it was the result of a mediation in which both Zimbabwean parties were involved in, rather than an imposed change. The SADC Double Troika Summit[28] in Dar es Salaam in late March 2007, which appointed South Africa as a mediator, was preceded by a visit to Harare by Tanzanian president Jakaya Kikwete, in his capacity as the chair of the troika of the SADC Organ on Politics, Defence, and Security Cooperation.[29] There were many behind-the-door engagements among members of the Double Troika. In the preceding weeks, Kikwete had had discussions with leaders of the European Union (EU), briefing them on SADC diplomatic efforts to arrest the Zimbabwe crisis, and even earlier, the Zambian president Levy Mwanawasa indicated that backroom shuttle diplomacy was taking place between willing neighbors who were talking about a constructive engagement with the Zimbabwean leadership.

So indications are that the initiative had full backing from key states in the region and the powerful Double Troika of the SADC, whose integrity and authority was at stake in the tricky peacemaking process. Thabo Mbeki brought a wealth of experience in peace diplomacy, having been involved in brokering peace in Burundi, Cote d'Ivoire, the DRC, and Lesotho. South Africa also brought the diplomatic prestige that it continues to enjoy throughout the world to help manage the international dimension of the Zimbabwean conflict, constantly assuring the international community of its commitment to finally bring an end to the mayhem in Zimbabwe.

The SADC mediation enjoyed tacit support from key international role-players; however, many opted to wait and see the prospects of a negotiated settlement in Zimbabwe before openly backing the mediation. In turn, the facilitator skillfully used the threat of further punitive action by the West to keep the parties negotiating until agreement was reached. He told them that the failure of the SADC mediation and the onset of an international process would almost certainly leave the parties very limited space to stake their claim to the outcomes of a peace process, as seen in Cote d'Ivoire and Sudan. This helped force Harare to adhere to SADC rules, although on a few occasions, such as the presidential runoff elections and the continued maltreatment of Morgan Tsvangirai, the Mugabe government breached the SADC agreement. But the government of Zimbabwe understands that it has a better chance of protecting its interests by staying in the peace process rather than allowing for an international intervention, such as the one in Kenya after the 2008 electoral violence.

When the SADC mediation began in May 2007, the mediator allowed both sides to table proposals on the agenda and the framework of the mediation itself, both in terms of substance and process—the harmonized agenda was finally adopted on June 19, 2007. The positions put on the agenda by each party showed that both the ZANU-PF and the MDC factions were narrowly focused on creating conditions for the next round of elections, which were a few months away. This meant that, for the moment, the aspirations of Zimbabweans for freedom from fear, want, and oppression were neglected as the competition for state power became the main focus of the negotiations. While the matter of future political, constitutional, and developmental dispensation was raised by the MDC-T, it was not at the center of discussions. The fundamental question of security sector reform was also underemphasized. From the onset, parties tended to see the facilitated talks as an end in itself rather than as a mini-dialogue that should culminate in a fully inclusive national dialogue on the modalities of the creation of a new Zimbabwe.

First Milestone toward a Settlement: Constitutional Amendment No. 18

Yet, the dialogue did not take long before positive outcomes were registered. The Eighteenth Constitutional Amendment, which sought to clear the way for harmonized elections (i.e., simultaneous presidential, legislative, and senatorial elections) in March 2008[30] was adopted in October 2007, barely five months after the beginning of talks. The amendment altered the presidential term of office from six to five years, making it coterminous with the term of national parliament. While it kept Mugabe's term to 2008 intact, the parliamentary term was cut short by two years. The amendment also changed the method of election of a new president in the event of death, resignation, or removal from office by allowing a joint sitting of both houses of parliament to elect a new president.[31] This was designed to allow Mugabe to resign and let a ZANU-PF-controlled parliament appoint his successor. The dilemma for the former ruling party was that it did not have a strong alternative candidate to lead it to an election victory, and thus had to hold on to Mugabe and then choose a successor. But this plan did not anticipate that the ZANU-PF would lose the March 2008 elections by getting ninety-nine parliamentary seats as opposed to the MDC-T's one hundred seats.[32]

The amendment also altered the composition of the House of Assembly—which is the higher house, with full powers to make laws and policies—and the Senate—the new lower chamber with a mandate to scrutinize laws and policies referred to it by the Assembly. The Senate increased from sixty-six to ninety-three members.[33]

The number of members for the National Assembly increased from 150 to 210, whereby 200 would be elected by voters in 200 parliamentary constituencies and 10 would be appointed by the president. The number of appointees had been reduced from 12 under the old constitution. The amendment also empowered the Zimbabwe Electoral Commission (ZEC) to re-delineate the boundaries of the 200 National Assembly constituencies and 60 senatorial constituencies, and required the ZEC to publish results on a board outside each polling station.[34] It also created a Human Rights Commission of eight independent citizens and formally introduced the positions of deputy chief of justice and a public protector.[35]

Milestone Two: The Harmonized Elections in March 2008

As a result of the headway made during facilitated talks between the ZANU-PF and the two factions of the MDC, the run-up to the March 29 elections was generally smooth. With negotiations, political violence dramatically declined. By the time that the aforementioned amendment was passed by parliament in October 2007, the MDC factions were able to hold huge rallies without much intimidation.[36] Somehow unruly youth and war veterans vacated the streets and stopped harassing peri-urban and rural villages thought to be pro-MDC.[37] The conditions were such that even the MDC could conduct door-to-door campaigns openly and relatively freely.[38] The watchful eye of the AU, SADC, and the mediation team helped guarantee these much improved election conditions.

Under these conditions, one of the ZANU-PF reformists and its former minister of finance and economic development Dr. Simba Makoni also entered the elections in February 2008 by standing as an independent candidate for the presidency. Makoni sought to take advantage of grave divisions within the ZANU-PF over the results of the primary elections to launch a reformist front from outside the party. Although he had hoped to run without losing his membership in the ZANU-PF, the party expelled him and forced him to contest as an independent candidate.[39] As the energies of ZANU-PF were directed at Makoni, Tsvangirai was allowed space to push ahead with his campaigns for several weeks without much challenge.

The promising preelection conditions and peaceful election day helped make it possible for the MDC to narrowly defeat the ZANU-PF in the March 29 parliamentary polls. The slow release of the electoral results sparked fears that the governing party was manipulating them to ensure that it did not lose the presidential campaign. It was not until April 15, more than two weeks after the elections, that the ZEC released the final House of Assembly results. These showed that the MDC-T had narrowly won the contest with one hundred seats to ZANU-PF's ninety-nine, while the MDC-M received ten seats. There was one seat won by an independent candidate, Jonathan Moyo. The ZANU-PF and the MDC-T had thirty seats apiece in the senatorial vote.[40]

After a poorly explained one-month delay, the ZEC finally released the results of the presidential election on May 2, 2008. It is suspected that the delay was a strategy by the ZANU-PF meant to influence the ZEC into announcing a tie in the tight electoral contest. The delay caused fear of post-electoral violence, similar to what happened in Kenya and with dire consequences for the region. The SADC held an emergency meeting on April 12, 2008, to consider its response to the looming postelection crisis. The meeting concluded with a commitment to a negotiated solution in Zimbabwe.[41]

The final results of the presidential race showed that Tsvangirai had won the elections by garnering 47.9 percent of the votes to Mugabe's 43.2 percent, while Makoni got only 8 percent. Tsvangirai's failure to surpass the 50 percent threshold forced him into a run-off vote against Mugabe, hastily scheduled for June 27, 2008. But the run-up to the run-off was in complete contrast to the calm environment prior to the March elections. There was a sudden resurgence of violence, unleashed mainly by ZANU-PF youth militia and state security forces against opposition members, leaders, and supporters. MDC rallies were disrupted and its bus campaigns were hindered by illegal roadblocks and arbitrary arrests. The brutality was so bad that it forced Tsvangirai to withdraw from the run-off in early June, leaving Mugabe to run as a sole candidate in elections that both the AU and SADC advised should be cancelled.

Milestone Three: The Power-Sharing Deal

Following the run-off elections, the SADC expressed dismay and called for a political settlement through its mediator, Thabo Mbeki. The AU effectively refused to recognize the results of the June 27 elections when the July 1 summit in Egypt called for a government of national unity.[42] Several African leaders spoke openly and loudly about the unacceptable actions of the ZANU-PF and its hunger for power. This included the presidents of Botswana and Zambia, the prime minister of Kenya, and various other prominent Africans.

Although the MDC victory in the parliamentary elections, narrow as it was, ushered in a new era in the legislature with the election of its member of parliament as the first opposition speaker, the controversies surrounding the presidential elections dominated Zimbabwean politics. On July 10, 2008, the parties were back to the proverbial square one as they started negotiations toward a GNU. The three party principals met on July 21 to officially launch the negotiations by agreeing to a framework for talks. They signed a memorandum of understanding (MoU; figure 2.1) by which they committed their respective parties to "a dialogue with each other with a view to creating a genuine, viable, permanent and sustainable solution to the Zimbabwean situation."[43]

It would take another painstaking six weeks of intensive talks in secret locations in South Africa for the parties to produce the GPA. Hostilities between the ZANU-PF and the MDC-T surfaced many times in the course of talks. Several times Tsvangirai threatened to pull out of talks because of the continued harassment of members and activists, and because of the bully tactics used by the ZANU-PF

It set out the framework agenda as follows:

a) Economic stability
- Economic stabilization
- Sanctions
- Land questions

b) Political
- New constitution
- Promotion of equality, national healing and cohesion, and unity
- External interference
- Free political activity
- Rule of law
- State organs and institutions
- Legislative agenda priorities

c) Security of persons and prevention of violence

d) Communication
- Media
- External radio stations

Source: Memorandum of Understanding at www.newzimbabwe.com

Figure 2.1　The MoU between ZANU-PF and two formations of the MDC.

in negotiations and an alleged uneven handling of the heated dialogue by the mediator.

The agreement was formally launched, with much ceremony, on September 15, 2008. It was similar to other power-sharing agreements in Africa, notably the Kenyan, Ivorian, and Sudanese deals, in that it was primarily about the sharing of executive power, although it made provisions for political and economic reforms on a grand scale. The agreement provided for a two-tier executive—one being a Cabinet of Ministers responsible for the overall strategic direction of government and chaired by Robert Mugabe as the president, and the other a Council of Ministers charged with overseeing the implementation of policies and programs of government under the chairmanship of Morgan Tsvangirai as an executive prime minister. The president would be assisted by two vice presidents, while the prime minister would also have two deputies, one of whom would be Arthur Mutambara, the leader of the smaller faction of the MDC. It was later agreed that the second deputy prime minister would be Thokozani Kupe of the MDC-T.

In the terms of the agreement, the formula for the composition of both the cabinet and the Council of Ministers was similar in that the thirty-one members of each would be comprised of fifteen ministers from the ZANU-PF, thirteen from the MDC-T, and three from the MDC-M. The detailed breakdown of the corresponding mandates of the two bodies demonstrates the will of the parties to ensure greater collaboration on the basis of a neat distinction of duties and clear lines of interface between institutions controlled by either of the parties.[44]

The agreement retained some powers of the president, including: the power to chair the cabinet with the prime minister as a deputy chairperson; powers to approve laws brought to him by cabinet and sign treaties on behalf of Zimbabwe; the authority to declare war and conduct national ceremonies; and powers to appoint the cabinet and persons proposed for diplomatic posts. The responsibility to direct the national effort to address the needs of the people through economic, social, and political programs was ceded to the prime minister, whose duty it was to supervise the entire government and to oversee coherent efforts by various departments and organs of state to achieve national goals. In a sense, therefore, the president lost significant powers that Mugabe had held on his own for three decades. The prime minister position was also given significant powers to actually run the government. In this way, Mugabe was to become the head of state, while Tsvangirai would become a head of government. This delicate balancing was designed to ensure that power-sharing in the new government would be serious. Further provisions on the functions of the various segments of the executive show an intention to force the president to consult and work with the prime minister in running the affairs of the state.

Although most of the analysis and public commentary on the agreement tends to focus on the executive power arrangement, the deal was also significant in what it said about other matters important for effective political change. Principal among these are provisions in the agreement that set the framework for a more fundamental transformation of politics and society in Zimbabwe. This includes the provision for a structured and inclusive process of constitutional reform.

The parties agreed that it was the fundamental right of the people of Zimbabwe to play an active part in the drafting of a constitution in a transparent and democratic process, so that they would own it. The expectation was that this would take a year to complete. The parties agreed to set up a Select Committee of Parliament, which would appoint multiparty subcommittees to draft various sections of the constitution for public comment. The draft constitution would be put through a referendum three months after the signing of the agreement. The agreement imposed no preconditions other than to give practical expression to the common values of national reconciliation, national unity, national sovereignty, human rights, and the rule of law.

The agreement also made provisions for a concerted effort, led by the new government, to bring about national healing and unity, cohesion, and equality. The idea was that the new government would promote the equality of all Zimbabweans and equal development of all regions of Zimbabwe. Such a government was mandated to set up mechanisms to advise and assist it in promoting national healing, national unity, and political tolerance after years of polarization and violence. It would also put measures in place to attract Zimbabweans who had fled the country to come back and help rebuild its shattered economy, and society in general.

The power-sharing agreement also pronounced in detail how the new government and society would be built on a human rights framework. Several articles of the agreement elaborate how the new government will promote freedom of political activity, freedom of association, the rule of law, and respect for the constitution. Article 18 has a long list of measures to be taken to eradicate the culture and infrastructure of violence built over two decades of misrule. These include stopping the use of violence for political goals and promoting the culture of political tolerance, nonviolence, and dialogue. This was a significant shift of the normative framework governing the conduct of politics and human behaviour in a new Zimbabwe away from authoritarianism, militarism, and elitism.

The third major thrust of the agreement is the transformation of both the economy and development, which has a number of elements. The very first substantive article of the agreement (Article 3) is actually about the restoration of economic stability and growth through the development and implementation of an economic recovery strategy and plan. This plan, to be developed by all parties working together, was meant to address urgent short-term problems of economic production, food security, inputs, and seeds for the agricultural season of 2008–2009, and the medium-term challenges of high inflation, interest rates, and the exchange rate. The plan would also address long-term systemic challenges of the economy, such as deep poverty, high unemployment, and disinvestment.

The agreement provided for the establishment of a National Economic Council comprised of political parties, as well as key economic sectors, such as manufacturing, mining, agriculture, tourism, commerce, financial, labor, and academia, to formulate economic plans and advise the government in its management of the economic recovery; however, it is not clear if this council will have a legal and formal standing like other oversight structures. The parties also agreed to provide space for the implementation of SADC ideas on economic recovery, including support that SADC member states committed to provide once a peace agreement was signed and a new government established in Zimbabwe. Finally, the agreement mandated the parties to reengage the international community in order to stop sanctions and the economic isolation of Zimbabwe. This has not yet happened, partly because the inclusive government is still setting its policies in place and consulting with the SADC on economic recovery. The hope was that if this international reengagement was made as a joint call by internal parties, with the support of guarantors of the agreement—the SADC and the AU—it could assist the region in beginning an economic recovery support program for Zimbabwe.

The question of land reform is also given special prominence, with a full article dedicated to this matter. The agreement acknowledges that the land question is part of the colonial legacy, with pre-independence patterns of land ownership having persisted into the post-independence period. It recognizes that land reform was a major goal for which the liberation struggle was fought. It also expresses the desirability of a comprehensive land reform process, thus acknowledging that the ZANU-PF government's land expropriation programs were not comprehensive. However, the details on how this reform program would be designed, and how it could be implemented, are not included in the agreement. They remain a subject of further negotiations by the parties.

The Stalemate Over Power-Sharing

From the outset, the agreement was signed amidst underlying protest. The negotiations were somewhat rushed, with the SADC hoping to have the agreement finalized by its annually scheduled summit in August 2008. The old problem of *agreements for their own sake* had thus somewhat resurfaced in this regard. During the launch of the agreement and in the subsequent days, Tsvangirai was cautious about the prospects of this agreement because, in his view, power-sharing arrangements are by nature undemocratic pacts by self-interested political elites. He was also worried about being part of a growing trend on the African continent in which election losers use their control over the means of violence to force winners into an executive political power-sharing arrangement.

Political games and grandstanding aside, Tsvangirai was aware of the general unease surrounding these power arrangements. These long-held concerns had been heightened in the aftermath of the signing of a similar agreement in Kenya after terrible postelection violence. The Kenyan deal was mediated by former UN secretary general Kofi Annan after postelection violence in December 2007. There was a lot of media analysis pointing out these underlying weaknesses of power-sharing politics. This attracted many public misgivings about the willingness of Africa to sacrifice the expressed will of the people in order to return unwanted rulers back into power through some elite pact. Tsvangirai must have picked up this sentiment and realized the negative bearing it would have on the MDC's moral high-ground political stance in Zimbabwean politics.

On the other side, the ZANU-PF was at pains to defend the power-sharing deal. Their discomfort was epitomized by the ambiguity displayed by Mugabe in his speech during the formal signing ceremony in Harare; the ZANU-PF too was less than willing to make power-sharing work unless strictly on its own terms. Mugabe saw the accord as opening a new chapter in the history of Zimbabwe, one in which Zimbabwe would be governed by means the ZANU-PF was unaccustomed to, most notably represented by a loss of full ZANU-PF control. He pointed out that there were many provisions that he and his party were unhappy with, but praised Mbeki for his persistence and creativity. He suggested that they had been persuaded and forced by the skill of the mediator to agree to each term of the agreement. Mugabe, as if his was still the ruling party despite the March 29 election loss, warned opposition parties not to act as if they were governing.[45] He committed the ZANU-PF to a position in which it would be a senior party to the agreement.[46]

Upon closer examination of ZANU-PF statements and general conduct, it seems to see power-sharing deals as a way of co-opting its nemesis into power as a junior party so as to neutralize it once and for all. Its attitude was that it would take what it wanted from the new government and leave the rest to the MDC as a junior partner. Indeed, that is how the ZANU-PF has approached the implementation of the GPA. Its rhetoric shows that the ZANU-PF understands the agreement as being about ceding elements of its power, rather than as being about sharing the power given to them by the people of Zimbabwe. This is a fundamental problem in Zimbabwe at the moment.

On the first bone of contention, the ZANU-PF wanted to take all cabinet portfolios it considered important and give the remainder to MDC factions. The MDC-T position was that the three parties should share the ministries equitably in each of the three clusters of government: security, administration/social cluster, and economy. On this basis, if the ZANU-PF took control of the defence ministry, the MDC-T would take the home affairs ministry, which controls police, and the MDC-M would control internal security. The same would then apply to trade and industry, mining and resources, and finance ministries. The MDC-M kept an open mind, preferring to allow negotiations to find the best formula for the apportionment of ministries. This was calculated to give the MDC-M the power to broker the impasse between the two stronger parties. In turn, the party saw the agreement as the easiest route to power-sharing.

The war of words that followed the ZANU-PF's media release of their own list of ministers was resolved with the help of facilitators in a marathon of meetings in October and November 2008.[47]

The government failed to issue Tsvangirai's passport to enable him to attend an emergency SADC summit in Swaziland in October 2008. He was instead issued with a temporary travel document valid only for the duration of the meeting, a deliberate ploy to ensure that he did not have time to mobilize the region or Africa against ZANU-PF. Even this document was issued after SADC leaders protested and had to postpone the meeting. After the meeting, Tsvangirai refused to return to Zimbabwe until he was issued with a full passport. While he waited for the passport, Tsvangirai mobilized support using South Africa's wide media platform and later relocated to Botswana, an outspoken critic of the ZANU-PF.

To pile pressure up, and as part of an assertive element of its policy, the South African government withheld R300 million (US$30 million) meant to fund agricultural activities until an inclusive government was in place.[48] It used this figure as a carrot to get the Zimbabwean parties to resolve all the remaining challenges on the table.

At the continental level, support for the SADC mediation led to the appointment of a reference group, which consisted of the UN secretary general's representative, the SADC executive secretary, and the AU Commission chairman Jean Ping.[49] This helped provide significant political support for the much-vilified mediator Thabo Mbeki at a time when he was under political pressure to concentrate on the domestic situation in South Africa.

In December 2008, Mugabe formally invited Tsvangirai and Mutambara to take up the positions of prime minister and deputy prime minister, respectively. This followed an intense ZANU-PF national congress that agreed to a party strategy on power-sharing. Indeed, subsequent to the meeting, the ZANU-PF-controlled administration finally issued Tsvangirai with a passport, thus bringing to an end several weeks of controversy. Then on January 2, 2009, Mugabe fired nine ministers and three deputy ministers to make way for MDC candidates. In response, the MDC-controlled speaker of parliament decided to convene on January 20, 2009, to approve the formation of the new government and begin its part in the implementation of the agreement, the clearest indication that some progress had been made in the interparty dialogue. Tsvangirai returned to Zimbabwe in mid-January 2009 and had a one-on-one meeting with Mugabe to finalize some details about the dialogue.

The government was subsequently established with the swearing in of MDC ministers and deputy ministers. But the MDC's treasurer, who was nominated for the position of deputy minister of agriculture, could not be sworn in because he was arrested for what some think were trumped up charges by the ZANU-PF-controlled police. There was also tension over Mugabe's unilateral changes to the portfolios of information and communication, moving the powerful information (which is used in political propaganda) element to the ZANU-PF's Webster Shamu, and leaving the original minister, the MDC-T's Nelson Chamisa, with only communication.[50]

A Perpetual Movement from Change to Status Quo: Static Dynamism in Zimbabwe's Peace Process

It remains to be seen whether the establishment of the inclusive government under the watchful eye of the SADC and the rest of the international community will translate into long-lasting peace and fundamental change in the culture of politics in Zimbabwe. The protracted peace process has over the years been characterized by many missed opportunities and a number of near-breakthroughs. There is mutual mistrust amongst the parties, as shown by the speed with which they refer matters of difficulty to the mediator and guarantors.

There has been a tendency for the crisis to move from static to dynamic and back to static. This creates a sense of movement toward peace and democracy, but in essence, the fundamental reality is that there is no movement. The developments that followed the signing of the agreement in September 2008 suggest that there is a lot of progress being achieved. In fact, the results of the March 2008 elections meant that the power balance on the ground had swung in favour of the MDC factions at the expense of the ZANU-PF. It is safe to read out of this that the latter was left with no choice but to follow the advice of the SADC regarding a negotiated settlement. The very fact that Mugabe shares his seat with Tsvangirai at SADC and AU summits is indicative of this shift in power balance.

It is not unlikely that the ZANU-PF is buying time by making half-hearted concessions in order to avoid losing the support of the southern African region, without actually making progress toward peace. The party makes superficial changes and raises the peace rhetoric as part of the calculated strategy to deceive its domestic opponents, external critiques, and the region into false hopes. It announced certain changes even before the new government was formed to suggest that it was capable of changing on its own. But it also did so in order to preempt the changes that MDC ministers were bound to make, thus robbing them of credit for beginning the change. For instance, it was the ZANU-PF cabinet that dropped price and exchange controls and began the dollarization of the economy in late 2008 when it was clear that the MDC-T would get the finance portfolio in cabinet. This was also an attempt to minimize the amount of power that this and other portfolios would have in the name of deregulation. It seems that the former ruling party is intent on maintaining the status quo, allowing changes it can live with and resisting fundamental changes that would alter the power balance and the political culture in Zimbabwe.

The disputes over the allocation of ministries in December 2008, the allocation of provincial governors until February 2009, and subsequent conflict over the appointment of the attorney general and reserve bank governor suggest deep-seated mistrust between the ZANU-PF and the MDC factions. It is also a sign of difficulties inherent in the shift of the balance of power away from the ZANU-PF that the March 29 elections demonstrated. They also illustrate the difficulties that power-sharing confronts when signed by two mutually suspicious parties.

Finally, the new government was formed with the swearing in of members of the new cabinet from all three parties, according to the agreed formula in the September accord. Keen to demonstrate that they had been ready to run Zimbabwe, MDC ministers moved quickly to outline their plans, especially on economic rejuvenation, international relations, and public services, including the payment of salaries to disgruntled public servants. Prime Minister Tsvangirai and Deputy Prime Minister Mutambara also demonstrated visible leadership, visiting hotspots of political conflict and social disintegration. They spoke firmly against continued invasion of farms and harassment of farm workers by ZANU-PF-aligned groups. They traveled the region assuring neighboring states of their intention to make this government work at any cost. They also moved quickly to avoid internal rebellion within their own parties because of differences over how enthusiastically the multinationals should participate in the inclusive government.

The willingness of Mugabe to give the inclusive government a chance, and political leadership helped isolate ZANU-PF hardliners who wanted to undermine the power-sharing agreement from the outset. Mugabe toned down his anti-Western and anti-MDC rhetoric, allowing for a new kind of language to emerge in Zimbabwe's political platforms—a discourse of reconstruction and reconciliation. While he has not helped resolve the ongoing dispute over the reserve bank governor and attorney general positions, even Tsvangirai has publicly declared that Mugabe has become a positive influence in the implementation of the power-sharing agreement. But the GNU has had to refer matters time and again to the mediator because of the ZANU-PF's reluctance to cooperate on anything without putting up a fight.

While Mugabe's soft touch might be motivated by his eagerness to leave a positive legacy after a decade of misrule, the ZANU-PF as an institution is still geared toward a one-party regime scenario. This means that until the crisis seriously hurts the ZANU-PF, the process of change will be slowed down by frequent stumbling blocks placed mainly by this party. For as long as the ZANU-PF sees other ways of achieving its interests, the power-sharing deal will either be manipulated or ignored. The party continues to believe that it can use the transitional power-sharing arrangement to weaken the MDC's power on the ground by ensuring that its participation does not make a difference. The ZANU-PF is constantly sending messages, both domestically and externally, that the MDC factions have failed to help Zimbabwe get rid of Western sanctions, suggesting that the MDC has had no political influence on its sponsors.

The stalemate will persist until the MDC factions manage to galvanize all key internal and external players, including active civil society, organized business, and youth formations, as well as regional states, continental organizations, and global institutions, in support of a thorough implementation of the agreement. As long as the perception persists in the region that the MDC is fighting to protect its narrow sectional interests and an external political agenda, its struggle will remain weakened in the region.

Conclusion

Another long meeting of the SADC heads of state in Tshwane, South Africa, on January 27, 2009, produced a firm undertaking by the ZANU-PF and the MDC to forge ahead with the implementation of the September accord. This led to the establishment of a three apiece Joint Monitoring and Implementation Committee (JMIC; figure 2.2) to oversee the implementation of the agreement, receive and process progress reports, resolve disputes, and promote continuous dialogue between the parties.

The new cabinet was sworn in on February 13, 2009, after last-minute horse-trading under the guidance of the SADC mediator President Motlanthe of South Africa, Minister Dos Anjos of Angola, and SADC executive secretary Tomaz Salamao.

The process of implementing the peace agreement has proved complex because of a history of political acrimony and mutual mistrust between the ZANU-PF and the MDC-T, and entrenched political cultures that will take a long time to overcome. While it is still at a crossroads with an inclusive government in place, Zimbabwe looks set to turn the corner toward an enduring democracy, provided the parties

<u>Members of the JMIC</u>

MDC-M

Professor Welshman Ncube (Co-Chairperson)
Mr Frank Chamunorwa
Mr Edward Mkhosi and
Ms Priscilla Misihairambi-Mushonga,

MDC-T

Mr Elton Mangoma (Co-Chairperson),
Mr Elias Mudzuri,
Ms Tabita Khumalo
Mr Innocent Changonda

ZANU PF

Mr Nicholas T. Goche (Co-Chairperson)
Mr Patrick A Chinamasa
Mr Emmerson Mnangagwa
Ms Oppah Muchinguri

Source: http://www.info.gov.za/speeches/2009/09013016451004.htm

Figure 2.2 Members of the JMIC.

succeed in making peace and democratization attractive, isolate spoilers, and create an inclusive national process of nation building and change. The role of the SADC and other regional organizations in support of this process of change will be critical as a factor between dynamism and inertia.

Notes

1. See I. William Zartman, *Ripe for Resolution* (New York: Oxford University Press, 1985). The transition from conflict and mistrust to peace and mutual trust happens when effective mediation happens at a moment ripe for resolution. One key ingredient of ripeness is that conflict begins to hurt the core interests and resources of the parties to the conflict; the other is when unilateral means of exiting conflict, either suppression or resistance, are blocked and parties feel they are in a costly and uncomfortable predicament. So, realizing or even catalyzing the ripeness of time for conflict resolution is the basic essence of diplomacy because good diplomacy is about doing the right thing at the right time.

   The underlying assumption is that parties in conflict are rational actors who, when their unilateral pursuit of satisfactory results is blocked, seek alternative ways out of the impasse. Mediation, arbitration, and other diplomatic interventions are attractive alternatives to perpetual and mutually hurting stalemate and conflict. In this perspective, a skilful mediator is able to persuade parties that time is ripe for negotiated settlement by demonstrating the stalemate is hurting the strategic interests of the parties or their key constituencies [I. William Zartman, "The Timing of Peace Initiatives: Hurting

Stalemates and Ripe Moments," *The Global Review of Ethnopolitics* 1, no. 1 (2001): 3]. For this reason, the argument is that while ripeness is a necessary condition for conflict resolution, it is not sufficient without skilful mediation.

2. These include the efforts by former presidents Joachim Chissano of Mozambique, Benjamin Mkapa of Tanzania, and Bakili Muluzi of Malawi on behalf of the SADC between 2003 and 2006. The governing ZANU-PF resisted the efforts of the Commonwealth Troika of Mbeki, President Olusegun Obasanjo (Nigeria), and Australia's prime minister John Howard in 2002.

3. Africa Institute of South Africa, "Terrorism in Southern Africa," Occasional Paper no. 28 (date), 4.

4. Dumiso Dabengwa, "ZIPRA in the Zimbabwe War of Liberation," in *Soldiers in Zimbabwe's Liberation War,* eds. N. Bhebhe and T. Ranger (London: James Currey, 1995), 24–35; and Jocelyn Alexander, Joanne McGregor, and Terence Ranger, *Violence and Memory: A Hundred Years in the Dark Forests of Matabeleland* (London: James Currey, 2000).

5. Alois Mlambo, "The Ambiguities of Independence, Zimbabwe 1980–1990," in *Unfinished Business: The Land Crisis in Southern Africa,* eds. Margaret Lee and Karen Colvard (Pretoria: Africa Institute of South Africa, 2003), 195–222.

6. L. Sachikonye, "Between Authoritarianism and Democracy: Politics in Zimbabwe since 1990," in Lee and Colvard, *Unfinished Business,* 97–132.

7. Alexander, McGregor and Ranger, *Violence and Memory,* 188.

8. Sachikonye, "Between Authoritarianism and Democracy," 112.

9. John Robertson, "The State of the Economy," paper presented at the Zimbabwe at the Crossroads Seminar, Tshwane, South Africa, October 2007.

10. Ibid.

11. Sachikonye, "Between Authoritarianism and Democracy," 102–104.

12. D. Ndlela, "Zimbabwe's Economy Since 1990," in Lee and Colvard, *Unfinished Business,* 133–58.

13. Robertson, "The State of the Economy."

14. S. Moyo, "The Political Economy of Land Acquisition and Redistribution in Zimbabwe, 1990–1999," *Journal of Southern African Studies* 26, no. 1 (2000): 5–28.

15. Comments at South African Loan Originators meeting, Johannesburg, March 1, 2008.

16. Paul Boateng, Zimbabwe Broke the Land Deal," *newzimbabwe.com,* December 15, 2008. http://www.newzimbabwe.com/pages/farm59.16552.html.

17. Ibid, 12.

18. When the war veterans disrupted Mugabe's speech in a rally in August 1997, the government panicked. It acceded to their demand for a once-off payment of Z$50,000 for each of the 50,000 ex-combatants by December 1997, an amount that was not budgeted for (the US$ was equivalent to Z$50 in 2000).

19. Justin Pearce, "Mugabe's Costly Congo Venture," *BBC News Online,* July 25, 2000. http://news.bbc.co.uk/2/hi/africa/611898.stm.

20. Author's interviews with constitutional experts, Harare, May 20–26, 2007. See also Amnesty International, "Zimbabwe: Constitutional Reform—An Opportunity to Strengthen Human Rights," February 2, 2000. http://www.amnesty.org/en/library/info/AFR46/001/2000.

21. Chris Maroleng, "Zimbabwe: Increased Securitization of the State," Institute for Security Studies Situation Report, Pretoria, 2005, 5.

22. See Electoral Institute of Southern Africa, "Zimbabwe: 2002 Presidential Election Results," http://www.eisa.org.za/WEP/zimresults2002.htm.

23. Bertha Chiroro, "Apathy, Fatigue or Boycott? An Analysis of 2005 Zimbabwe Senate Elections," EISA Occasional Paper No. 38, November 2005.

24. Ibid.

25. See "Zimbabwe: SA Government Holds on the Line," *Business Day,* March 22, 2007. This was preceded by the installation of senior security officers in leadership positions of parastatals, and in other key position in the public sector. Retired general Nyambuya was appointed minister of power and energy; retired brigadier general Chiwenza is on the board of Zimbabwe Electricity Supply Commission; Brigadier General Nyikayaramba is chairman of the National Railways Board; Air Commodore Karakadzai is National Railways' general manager; retired colonel Muvhuti is general manager of the Grain Marketing Board; retired major general Mbewe heads National Parks and Wildlife; Major General Rugeje directs Zimbabwe Broadcasting radio programs; and Colonel Mutize headed Operation Maguta, the military supervision of agriculture. Many of these appointments were widely reported in the state press, *The Herald,* and debated in the independent media as well.

26. This point is made by various analysts including Issa Shivji.

27. See "Solve Zimbabwe or risk blight on World Cup," April 2, 2007, http://www.monstersandcritics.com/news/africa/news/article_1285840.php/Tsvangirai_warns_Mbeki_Solve_Zimbabwe_or_risk_blight_on_World_Cup.

28. The Double Troika consists of the Troika of SADC and Troika of the Organ on Politics, Defence, and Security Cooperation.

29. The Organ is the security arm of SADC responsible for managing conflicts and wars in the region.

30. See party responses to this amendment in http://www.newzimbabwe.com/pages/parly30.16937.html (accessed February 2008).

31. Thokozani Khupe, MDC Deputy Head, speech on the Constitutional Amendment 18. http://www.newzimbabwe.com/pages/parly30.16937.html.

32. "Zimbabwe Senate and Assembly Results," *Reuters,* August 22, 2008.

33. Ibid. Six from each of the ten provinces, ten provincial governors, two to be president and deputy president of the Council of Chiefs, sixteen chiefs, and five to be appointed by the President

34. Ibid.

35. Khupe, speech.

36. This was the view of most observer mission reports including the very critical Pan African Parliament and SADC observer missions.

37. Ibid.

38. Author's observations.

39. "Mugabe Says Challenger Makoni is a 'Prostitute,'" *Mail & Guardian online,* February 22, 2008. http://www.mg.co.za/article/2008–02–22-mugabe-says-challenger-makoni-is-a-prostitute.

40. "Zimbabwe Senate and Assembly Results," *Reuters,* August 22, 2008.

41. "Summit Delivers No Quick Fix to Zimbabwe Deadlock," *AFP (IOL),* April 13, 2008. http://www.iol.co.za/index.php?art_id=nw20080413082805446C362265.

42. "African Call for Zimbabwe Unity," *BBC News,* July 2, 2008. http://news.bbc.co.uk/2/hi/africa/7484165.stm.

43. See copy of the MoU, www.issafrica.org.

44. See the Global Political Agreement.

45. Mark Ellis, "Robert Mugabe Signs Historic Powersharing Deal With Bitter Political Enemy," September 16, 2008. http://www.mirror.co.uk/news-old/top-stories

/2008/09/16/robert-mugabe-signs-historic-powersharing-deal-with-bitter-political-enemy-115875–20738423/.

46. Ibid.
47. Chris McGreal, "Tsvangirai Threatens to Quit Zimbabwe Deal After Mugabe Seizes Cabinet Posts," *guardian.co.uk,* October 12, 2008. http://www.guardian.co.uk/world/2008/oct/12/zimbabwe1.
48. "South Africa Withholds Aid," *Business Day,* November 27, 2008.
49. See transcripts of SABC interviews with Thabo Mbeki at www.dfa.gov.za.
50. "The New Cabinet," *Zimbabwean Independent,* February 26, 2009.

Chapter 3

Reform of the Security Sector in Zimbabwe
Challenges and Opportunities
Karolina Werner and Knox Chitiyo

Introduction

The establishment of Zimbabwe's Government of National Unity (GNU) in February 2009 inaugurated a fragile power-sharing process between the Zimbabwe African National Union-Patriotic Front (ZANU-PF), the Movement for Democratic Change-Tsvangirai (MDC-T) party, and the smaller MDC-Mutambara (MDC-M) group. The GNU has undoubtedly helped to revive Zimbabwe's economy. However, although there has been some power-sharing and interparty cooperation in some sectors, the GNU has also become an arena for intense interparty power-struggles and conflict. In essence, the GNU is a two-government structure, with the MDC-T wielding power in the economic and infrastructure sectors, while the ZANU-PF controls the "hard power" sectors, including the military, mines, agriculture, and the media. (The MDC-M is often dismissed as being either an irrelevance within the GNU, or a proxy for ZANU-PF. In fact, it has become clear that the MDC-M has played a useful mediatory role between their larger rivals within the GNU) On a positive note, a multisectoral transformation process has begun, and the establishment of national commissions is a major step; but, as of yet, there has been little attempt to reform the security sector. In the long term, reforming Zimbabwe's security institutions and establishing the rule of law is essential for reconstruction and sustainable development.

Zimbabwe's security sector is an integral part of the country's political, ideological, economic, and military life. The Zimbabwe Defence Forces (ZDF), which is comprised of the Zimbabwe National Army (ZNA), the Air Force of Zimbabwe (AFZ), the Zimbabwe Republic Police (ZRP), the Central Intelligence Organisation

(CIO), and the Zimbabwe Prison Service (ZPS), are the *managers of hard security* in Zimbabwe. Since 2000, the Zimbabwe National Liberation War Veterans Association (ZNLWVA) and ZANU-PF Youth League have been incorporated into a de facto tripartite alliance with the ZDF and ZANU-PF.[1] This alliance has two clear goals: the retention of Robert Mugabe as president of Zimbabwe and the preservation of the ZANU-PF as the dominant force in state politics.

However, the emergence of the MDC as a nationally based opposition group, and, more recently, as a key partner in the coalition, has resulted in the exponential encroachment of the security sector into politics. It has also led to an ambiguous and often uneasy relationship between securocrats and politicians, as the ZANU-PF and the Joint Operations Command (JOC) jostle for state power. The JOC, which consists of service chiefs of the formal security sectors, has had sway over Zimbabwean politics since 2000. Initially modeled on the Rhodesian JOC, which was primarily employed at a tactical level for purely military purposes, the new JOC has operated on a much grander strategic scale over the last decade.[2]

During this period, Zimbabwe's political and socioeconomic landscape was been heavily militarized, with soldiers taking over the running of key state institutions by holding high-level positions in ministries such as Energy and Power Development, Industry and International Trade, Foreign Affairs, and the Ministry of Prisons, among others (more recently, large swathes of the business sector have also been securitized, with serving or retired senior officers appointed to the 2010 Indigenisation committees).[3] Over the past decade, the security sector itself has been politicized and de-professionalized, with serving or former security service personnel taking on a large number of state jobs and focusing on political and military goals, often at the expense of professional values. As a result, the security elite has become a *politocracy* rather than a meritocracy. Zimbabwe's power-sharing agreement[4] among the ZANU-PF and the MDC-T and the MDC-M[5] is a major step forward on the road to resolving the nation's crisis; but it is a fragile partnership between two political entities united only by mutual distrust.

Amidst the plethora of practical and conceptual issues that threaten to derail the agreement, one factor stands out—without the consent and constructive participation of the security sector, the GNU, and post-GNU Zimbabwe ,will fail. In addition, reform of the security sector (and the political sector) is critical to ensure positive and sustainable transformation in Zimbabwe. In this regard, the security sector is both the problem and the solution. The soldiers, and the militarist culture they exemplify, can block reform, but if they become part of the process, they can play a vital role in the transition. Over the next eighteen months, Zimbabwe will undergo a crucial constitutional reform process and national elections. During the past decade the military has undergone an extreme process, not of reform but of politicized transformation. The ongoing electoral-constitutional process will again highlight the military's role in Zimbabwe's politics and is already giving impetus to calls for SSR. With the security sector's grip on power continuing unabated, it is likely that the process will focus on more modest, but achievable SSR goals. The grand SSR ideal of a of a comprehensive overhaul remains a long term objective, but in practice, a more modest (negotiated) goal of reducing or removing military control and political violence from the process may be a starting point for wider SSR. No one can speak with certainty about Zimbabwe's political future, but it is safe to say that reforming the military is vital.

Historical Background

Zimbabwe, known as Southern Rhodesia prior to independence, like Angola, Mozambique, and Namibia, traces its independence to the armed struggles of the 1960s and 1970s against settler minority rule (and metropolitan rule in the case of Angola and Mozambique). The Rhodesian Police had been the dominant player in Rhodesia's security sector. It operated as both a traditional police force against criminals, and also as a trained paramilitary force capable of army-style operations. When the Federation of Nyasaland (what is now modern-day Malawi) and the Rhodesians (Zambia and Zimbabwe) were dissolved in 1963,[6] it was Southern Rhodesia that inherited the federation's armory, to which it had vastly contributed. It was this munitions windfall and the start of the Chimurenga[7] war of liberation in the 1960s that forced the Rhodesians to create a large standing army for the first time. The CIO was also expanded to encompass not just covert military intelligence, but also active paramilitary operations by operatives in the field. By the end of the war, the Rhodesian JOC was coordinating the war effort across the various military sectors. It also ensured that Ian Smith's Rhodesian Front (RF) party would remain as the dominant political stakeholder, even during the short-lived Internal Settlement of 1978 and the United African National Council (UANC) government that followed in 1979.[8]

In the meantime, the Zimbabwe African National Liberation Army (ZANLA) and Zimbabwe People's Revolutionary Army (ZIPRA), the military wings of the ZANU and ZAPU nationalist parties, respectively, had, after a shaky start, emerged as formidable guerrilla forces that achieved a qualitative equilibrium to bolster their quantitative superiority over the Rhodesian security forces. Both armies were also well indoctrinated and often acted as political recruiters with easy access to the population, particularly in rural areas.

1980–1997

Following the overwhelming victory of ZANU in the 1980 elections, the new government called for reconciliation and integration of military and paramilitary personnel, in the hopes of avoiding any coups. Operation Merger—the fusion of ZANLA, ZIPRA, and the RSF to create the ZDF—was highly successful because of the political will on all sides to make it work, and also because all three armies were already professional forces, despite propaganda claims by the Rhodesians throughout the war that the guerrillas were "terrorists" who invariably ran away at the first shot. Approximately twenty-three thousand soldiers became active reservists, with ministries and other state and local institutions encouraged to draw on this pool for staffing purposes.[9] The creation of the ZNA—Zimbabwe's first truly representative national army—was the engine for national reconstruction. If the operation had failed, the country would certainly have reverted to civil war.

What is important to note here is that Operation Merger and the complementary 2000–2003 demobilization, demilitarization, and reintegration/rehabilitation (DDR) exercise were transformative. From late 1979 and into 1980, a Joint High Command was established, which brought together the commanders of the three rival forces. The JHC was a conduit for integration process. The British Military Advisory Training Team (BMATT) also played an important role in training the nascent ZNA in modern warfare. The guerrilla forces were incorporated into a professional, traditional army; in turn, the new army abandoned the race-based Officer Selection Board (OSB) system in favor of a system based on supporting individuals selected by the guerrilla leaders through training and other types of support.[10] Moreover, the ZNA incorporated the lessons on insurgency into its military brief. But the transformation, although broad, was not deep; the new ZNA, like its predecessor, had an underlying ethos of hard security, based on institutional loyalty, competence, and fealty to the state.

There has never been an apolitical military in Zimbabwe's history. The raison d'être of the Zimbabwean military has always been national security, which is defined as protecting the territorial integrity of Zimbabwe, and the sovereignty and survival of the state. The methodology has always included a mixture of violence and persuasion. Post-1980, the political transformation of the security sector occurred in two major surges. The first surge was from 1981 to 1987 with the Gukurahundi war in Matabeleland,[11] and the simultaneous overlap with the ZNA deployment in Mozambique (as an ally of the Liberation Front of Mozambique [FRELIMO] in the war with RENAMO)[12] to protect rail and road links to Mozambican ports. These events strengthened the re-politicization of the military and the power of the security sector in the nation's politics. The second surge was from 1997 to the present.

1997–2008

The period from 1997 to 2008 has seen the Zimbabwean state develop an approximation of South Africa's apartheid-era *total strategy* to counter a perceived total onslaught from internal and external opposition. Major components of the strategy include the institutionalization of presidentialism, the entrenchment of the ideologies of patriotic history and patriotic blackness to retain regional and continental support, and the retooling of the military and political architecture of Zimbabwe. This has entailed the merger of the party and the state, blurring any past distinctions; the formalization of a political/security/business compact; the emergence of the security sector in the form of the JOC as a "shadow state" in parallel to government; and the creation of a war economy, with many state institutions becoming militarized and politicized, reportedly to counter disinvestment and economic collapse.

There has always been a close relationship between the Zimbabwean military and the state, and after 2000, the role of the military shifted from defending national sovereignty to ensuring regime survival by denying the MDC access to state power, amongst other tactics. This has resulted in the systematic politicization of the security sector and the militarization of Zimbabwe's political economy. Since 2000, the JOC has formalized the methodology of violence in response to the opposition's political challenge. The majority of both larger and smaller military operations that took place post-2000 coincided with national elections.

Zimbabwe has been categorized as an operational zone, with the struggle for the survival of the state a military operation in itself.[13] This is contested by both the ZANU-PF and the MDC. Since 2000, and as a continuation of a guerrilla war strategy, Zimbabwe has been divided into "liberated zones" (the ZANU-PF heartland of Mashonaland, Masvingo, and parts of Manicaland); "contested zones" (the urban areas); and "enemy" zones (Bulawayo and Matabeleland, which have always been hostile to ZANU-PF). The post-2000 strategy has been to consolidate the ZANU-PF's hold on the liberated zones, retake the contested zones, and disrupt the enemy's hold in the enemy zones. The principal methodologies used by the security-state nexus are violence, liberationism (the ideology of [black] African liberation), and patronage networks. Activities undertaken included forcibly taking over farms of white commercial farmers, running of national elections under military auspices, and awarding taken farms to military and other officials.

The security sector (which includes paramilitary groups such as the ZNLWA and ZANU-PF Youth League in alliance with the ZDF) has developed a political-military strategy of survival. This strategy aims at containing and rolling back the MDC by terrorizing people into voting for the ZANU-PF, forcing them to flee the area and, thus, be unable to cast a vote, or through indoctrination sessions during which traitors are tortured and killed. This was particularly evident after the MDC victory in the 2008 national elections when the violence escalated to a point where the MDC was forced to withdraw from further elections. A combination of poor intelligence on the ground, a highly effective strategy of mobilization by the MDC, and overwhelming popular demands for change caused the ZANU-PF and the security sector to seriously underestimate opposition support and lose the March 2008 elections. The MDC victory (in the ZANU-PF heartland in particular) was a major shock to ZANU-PF. However, the political-military alliance then used violence, on an unprecedented scale, to force the MDC to negotiate away any dreams of sole power.

From June to December 2008, the MDC-T and ZANU-PF were locked in a deadly contest of political gamesmanship. The MDC-T knew that without their participation in a coalition government, a sole ZANU-PF government or a ZANU-PF/MDC-M coalition would not get legitimacy even from traditionally sympathetic SADC states. On the other hand, a continued refusal by the MDC-T to join a coalition would have resulted in further military crackdowns and, possibly, the physical annihilation of the MDC-T. In addition, many Zimbabweans were now beginning to blame the MDC's recalcitrance for the worsening economic situation. The MDC thus risked losing core support if it waited any longer. For ZANU-PF, the continued stalemate risked heightening disaffection within the military, who were also affected by the economic collapse. For the MDC-M, a junior role in a coalition government was their only salvation after a dismal showing in the March 2008 elections. Thus, and for differing reasons, all sides needed a deal. The GNU was a reluctant coalition based on mutual need, not wants.

2009–The Present

Time and again, Zimbabwe's military and political nexus has proved to be highly adaptive and resilient. Following the creation of the GNU in February 2009, the security sector retreated a few paces from the frontline of Zimbabwe politics. This time out allowed the military to assess whether the GNU and the MDC-T offered a significant threat to their power; it also offered the military a chance to regroup, restrategize, and retool for a changing environment. By mid-2009, it was clear that although some of their influence in the peripheries was under siege, in broad terms, the coalition government offered little threat to their power. The MDC-T had proposed a program of action to reform the military and reduce military influence in politics; but the ideas received short shrift in cross-party discussions. Nor were there any prosecutions of the perpetrators of political violence (however, the post-2009 period has opened up a space for members of the public to sue senior politicians and military commanders for abuses and legal infringements).[14] The emphasis on reconciliation and peace since 2009, although laudable and necessary, has also played into the hands of the security sector as a conduit for soft power and as a diversion from the contentious issues of justice and compensation. Thus, by mid-2009, the security sector, which had been briefly unnerved by the establishment of the GNU, had regained its composure. The military's control of the diamond fields in Marange in eastern Zimbabwe, has also ensured ready access to finance to oil the wheels of power.[15]

The military has thus consistently used adaptive strategies of force and persuasion to reduce the MDC-T's ability to translate its popular political support into hard political power. Although the MDC has now won major power-sharing concessions from the ZANU-PF on paper, several strategic ministries, such as defense, local government, and justice and legal affairs,[16] are allocated based on a unilateral endorsement by Mugabe,[17] with the MDC having only slight leverage through the control of financial state institutions in Zimbabwe. The security sector, the ultimate guardian of state power, continues to be well within ZANU-PF control. The fear of loss of power and potential prosecution for various abuses provides ample motivation for various securocrats to veto any reforms that would allow for a more unified transitional government.[18]

The military has thus emerged as a parallel government that competes with both the ZANU-PF and the MDC for political space. According to the Global Political Agreement (GPA), Morgan Tsvangirai will sit in on security sessions of the renamed JOC (now the National Security Council [NSC]), which is to manage and oversee the activities of the army, police, and central intelligence agencies. Members of the JOC are meant to be committee members of the new council, but with no voting powers. The idea behind this is to give civilian oversight to the security sector, leading ultimately to a dilution of the security sector's powers and making it more accountable. It remains to be seen, however, whether the MDC will be able to make any significant inroads on changing the power of the military. The role of the NSC continues to be highly contested, having currently more of a review role rather than managerial oversight. The NSC has now begun to hold monthly meetings that include the participation of the Prime Minister and representatives from the three GPA parties. This is a promising development, but there are still doubts as to whether the NSC will be able to assert its civilian oversight role over the military when it does meet. Furthermore, the JOC has not suspended its regular meetings, which include ZANU-PF officials, but no MDC members.[19]

Challenges

The fundamental challenge to serious security sector reform (SSR) in Zimbabwe is that key personalities, such as Robert Mugabe, and institutions, such as the JOC, which have presided over the post-2000 negative security sector transformation, are still in power. While moderates exist, SSR will only be possible if the political economy of the country is demilitarized and the military becomes depoliticized. This is not to say that Zimbabwe's military is homogenous—there are many within the security sectors who wish to see a return to a professional, non-politicized value system. But hardliners within the military elite, and also some mid-level officers who entered the military after serving with the Youth Brigades, remain keen to retain the military as a purely ZANU-PF reserve. They see the MDC and other groups as "anti-Zimbabwean" and envisage national security purely in terms of state/party survival against internal opposition. It is thus highly problematic and hypothetical to assume that there exists a genuine political will to affect political sector reform (PSR) and SSR. This is not simply the result of the hardliners' determined resistance to change; it is also a result of the MDC and other groups' lack of leverage over the military. The power-sharing agreement and unity government are open-ended. Despite having popular support, the MDC groups have no hard power capability to compel the ZANU-PF to concede power in the key strategic sectors, such as the defense and justice sectors.

The Challenge of Definition

There is the conceptual challenge of defining what we mean by SSR and of integrating universalist theory and practice within local realities. There are different schools of thought on SSR. The *professionalism* school contends that SSR should be based solely on the professionalization of the military, and that the reform process should not be involved in politics or ideology since it is felt that a professional military is an apolitical military. This is countered by the *developmentalist* school that insists the purpose of SSR is not just to professionalize the military; it is to ensure that the military is a partner in a national process of development and democracy. They feel that the guiding rationale of SSR must be human security.

Admirable as the latter value system is, within Zimbabwe, partnering with the security sector in SSR means that the concept has to amalgamate traditional "hard security" norms with "soft security" ideals. A "wide tent" definition would be less threatening to the security sector and they would be less inclined to block reform. A partnership between the security and civil sector becomes more realistic as professionalization is restored.

The Challenge of History

Zimbabwe does not have a tradition of SSR, certainly not in the modern meaning of the term. The creation of the ZNA was certainly transformative, and for a time, the ZNA was indeed a people's army that pursued a developmental as well as military agenda.

Activities such as Operation Seed (Soldiers Employed in Economic Development—which saw the military helping to plant crops) and Operation Kudzidza (the building of schools) continued the "swords into ploughshares" theme. But the developmentalist mission of the ZNA was corrupted by a permanently adversarial political landscape and the growing power of the military in the affairs of state. The military has only sporadically been an agent of developmental change in Zimbabwe. It always reverts to its default position as the guardian of state as force continues to be a powerful tool in the arsenal of the ruling party. Changing this historically ingrained ethos and reversing the post-1997 negative transformation of the security sector will be a major challenge.

Asymmetry

Despite the power-sharing agreement, the military under the JOC and the military-political covenant between the security sector, Robert Mugabe, and the ZANU-PF remains unbroken, although it is fraying at the seams. There is, as of yet, no real counterweight to the power of the military in Zimbabwe. In 1980, the three competing military forces (ZANLA, ZIPRA, and the RSF) counterbalanced each other. The shared heritage of combat ultimately bred a level of mutual respect, and this eased the integration and transformation process. However, the counternarrative of anti-integrationism and rising state intolerance led to the "dissident" war in Matabeleland, and the persecution of ZAPU.

t was a very different situation in 2009. Although the MDC has internal and international support and could use the collapsed economy as leverage against the ZANU-PF, this was soft power. The MDC has no military roots, but rather stemmed from trade unions. The ZANU-PF had an overwhelming advantage in hard power. The military believes that its hard power advantage will always reverse any political gains made by the MDC. This means that Zimbabwe's military sees little reason to negotiate with the MDC and no reason to negotiate in good faith, particularly considering that these negotiations may infringe upon some of the vast powers the military currently holds.

Not only does Zimbabwe's security elite believe that military power will always neutralize the MDC, many in the JOC feel that that the unity agreement can be subverted to either incorporate the MDC as a junior partner, or force the MDC to abandon the agreement and take the blame. The security sector is still at the apex of power and, thus, sees little need for SSR, and the MDC has few real levers to compel or persuade the military elite to accept reform. Officials in the sector see SSR as being unnecessary and a threat to their power. Thus the challenge will be to bring in Zimbabwe's security sector as partners in the positive transformation of Zimbabwe's security sector. The NSC is one of many steps that may lead to this transition if it fulfils its core mandate of bringing accountability and civilian oversight to the security sector. Other potential avenues include drafting a national defense and security strategy, implementing SSR in phases, rather than all at once, revisiting the electoral system to ensure free and fair elections, and providing an opportunity for reconciliation through institutions such as a truth and reconciliation commission, among others.[20] Naturally, not all of these will be easily implemented or successful right away, and may need the support of the international community or regional actors.

Robert Mugabe, and the Military-Political Nexus

During the ZANU-PF congress in December 2009, Robert Mugabe stated categorically that there is no need for SSR in Zimbabwe.[21] The strategic alliance between the President and the military remains intact and has been bolstered by the MDC's inability to make any real inroads into the military's territory. With the military ensuring ZANU-PF hold on key state organs and with the continuation of the covenant between Mugabe and the military, the security sector thus sees no need for SSR. Indeed they see SSR as a euphemism for regime change. Given its position of strength and with Presidential support, the military sees no reason to overhaul itself. Secondly despite problems of desertion and "minor" mutinies over the past decade, Zimbabwe's military is still a relatively efficient force. The ZDF is also playing a major role in the establishment of the regional SADC Standby Force Brigade which is due to be operationalized in late 2010. But the fact that the ZDF plays an important part in SADC operations is also seen by the security sector as regional legitimization of both their capabilities and behavior. This in turn, increases their determination to resist reform despite local and regional civil society demands for SADC to make Zimbabwe's military accountable for continuous human rights abuses. Many of the hardliners believe that a form of SSR has already occurred; the politicization and "patriotization" of the Zimbabwe's security sector, which "weeded out" non –ZANU-PF elements, is seen from their perspective, as a reform process. However the security sector is not monolithic; many junior officers and some long-standing professionals resent the coercive and politicized culture which now operates . Given that the security sector cannot be coerced or legislated into SSR, it is clear that only internal dialogue on security (with regional/continental assistance) can break the deadlock. A variety of conversations have to take place; these include intra-sectoral discussions, talks between the security sector and all the political parties, and civil society-security sector discussions. Zimbabwe's security dialogue has to be a locally owned, indigenous exercise. SSR in Zimbabwe, if it is to occur, needs to be put in the context of national reconstruction and as a partnership between military and civilians.

Until the psychological barriers are broken, the military stalemate will continue. Since the establishment of the GNU, the MDCs have found little support from ZANU-PF for "hard" SSR. Instead any headway which has been made, has been made in "soft" reforms, that is, reforming institutions such as the judiciary and media, which includes the military, but which is not their direct preserve. Meanwhile the MDC has continued to press for substantial SSR, including training on governance and human rights for military officers.[22] (Ironically, democracy and human rights are a long established part of the curricula at the army and Police Staff Colleges.) But the SSR debate has been subsumed into wider disputes between ZANU-PF and the MDC-T over sanctions and the GPA. ZANU-PF has linked the two issues and refused to implement certain agreed-upon items within the GPA until the MDC is able to convince the West to lift the various travel bans and asset freezes against key ZANU-PF members.

There is, however, no guarantee that ZANU-PF Mugabe-ism will not continue after he has left the scene. Although the December 2009 congress confirmed Mugabe as party leader for the next five years, the tensions within were also plainly visible. The members did not agree on a number of matters related to the party's constitution, which will have a bearing on the selection of Mugabe's successor.[23] The ZANU-PF is divided along factional lines between Emmerson Mnangagwa (defense minister), who controls the state bureaucracy, and Joice Mujuru (current vice president), who holds sway over the party's grassroots following. While Mnangagwa is a presidential hopeful and has been nurturing ties to the security sector, Mujuru has taken the more pragmatic approach of establishing some lines of communication with the MDC-T.[24]

Therefore, the fundamental question we ought to be asking is whether SSR can really commence while Mugabe is still in power. The post-Mugabe discourse implies that no meaningful SSR can begin while he is still on the scene; but this argument for conditionality is deeply pessimistic and condemns SSR to an indeterminate future—its logical conclusion is that SSR is impossible in the foreseeable future.

The real challenge is not to begin SSR in a post-Mugabe Zimbabwe. Rather, the task is to lay the groundwork and begin the SSR process now, during this admittedly flawed power-sharing transition, and to consolidate the process in a post-Mugabe Zimbabwe. Although the military still retains enormous power and comprehensive SSR remains on Zimbabwe's wish list, the ongoing reform of other sectors (including justice, the civil service, and the media) is important. The military is also embedded in these sectors, and the processes of depoliticization and re-professionalization is thus prying open the military's grip from the outer rim of security sector influence. Over time, it may be possible to proceed in stages to the inner core of the security sector's domain.

Entry Points

The military perceives the MDC as being "unpatriotic" and hostile to the security establishment. Some suspect SSR in Zimbabwe as being a euphemism for the dismantling of the security sector. The MDC, therefore, has to find an entry point into the military sector to avoid becoming an irrelevance. Knowing and understanding the structures and personalities of the military system is key; only when the GNU gains a level of trust from the military can real SSR commence. The challenge is to make alliances with the military professionals who resent the politicization of their profession, thus making reform a common cause. Promoting a return to professional military values is one way of doing this. In this regard, the GPA, which stipulates a return to the rule of law, is the key entry point. The MDC, civil society, and the SADC have made strategic use of the GPA (which was signed by all parties) to pressure Robert Mugabe and the ZANU-PF to corral the military and to genuinely share power, although struggles over the implementation of several items from the GPA continue. The GPA is undoubtedly a flawed document, but its provisions have created a transformational space in Zimbabwe; it has also given the MDC and civil society some leverage against ZANU-PF machinations. In addition, as has been mentioned earlier in this chapter, the multisectoral transformation that has been initiated will have an impact on the security sector and will create pressure on the military to avoid being the lone holdout against compromise and change.

Another entry point may be through the Defense Forces Commission, which both the MDC and members of the army have shown interest in supporting to make it a more active body in overseeing issues of morale and conditions of service in the military.[25] The Police Commission that was established in May 2010 has proved to be divisive politically because of composition of its membership. Nevertheless, in the long-term if agreement can be reached on the mission and membership of the Police Commission, it has the potential to speed constructive change.

As mentioned earlier, another key entry point will be through the electoral-constitutional process. In 2000 this political cycle provided an entry point for the military into national political economy; it also proved to be a generator of cycles of violence. Only internal and external discussions and agreement on security in Zimbabwe will prevent a repeat of history during the 2010–2012 as the military again turns Zimbabwe into an operational zone. In this regard it is important to discuss the military's withdrawal from the process not in terms of Western SSR formulas but in the context of the Police Ac and ZNA Constitution, both of which stipulate that the military should be nonpolitical forces that protect the people.

Professionalism and conditions of service also possible entry point. Politicization is not the only issue facing the ZRP—there is also a growing problem of criminal activity. In October 2010 Deputy Police Commissioner General Innocent Matibiri acknowledged the "shocking number of cases of indiscipline being recorded" by the Police Support Unit. (The Zimbabwe Independent 8 October 2010.) The problems of indiscipline and criminality are linked to conditions of service so this is an area in which it may be possible to broker a general stakeholder consensus on the need for change.

The Challenge of Holistic Reform

Security sector reform in Zimbabwe is vital, but it cannot be done in isolation; it must be done as a holistic, comprehensive reform process that complements PSR. The political sector has been corrupted and militarized at the same time as the security sector has been politicized and de-professionalized. Thus, SSR and PSR are symbiotic and complementary; the overall objective is to re-professionalize the institutions and place democracy in the forefront.

Opportunities

Widening of Political Space

The GNU is very fragile, and there are doubts as to whether and for how long it can hold. It is a transitional government and is meant to lead to constitutional reform and new democratic elections. It is clear that the ZANU-PF's monopoly over power is finite. Although the ZANU-PF will continue to be a major factor in Zimbabwe's future for the foreseeable time, there has been an opening up of political space, and this breach in the ZANU-PF's hegemony is an opportunity for serious debate on SSR. Indeed, since the creation of the GNU, there have been ongoing debates in various forums across the country on the rule of law and the role of the military.

What has emerged from these consultations, which have been conducted in the rural and urban areas, is that the majority of Zimbabweans, including many in the military, want SSR.

Regional and Global Momentum for SSR in Zimbabwe

The regional, continental, and international communities also have a major role to play in pressing for the rule of law and SSR in Zimbabwe. Zimbabwe is expected to be actively involved in the establishment of the regional Africa Standby Force (ASF) brigades in 2010. These are intended to be standing forces that will conduct peace and stabilization operations as, and where, needed. There is increasing pressure on South Africa and the SADC to ensure that Zimbabwean forces do not promote peace abroad while promulgating political warfare at home. Having long been involved in the negotiation of the GPA, the SADC, with South African president Jacob Zuma leading the mediation, is attempting to address the SSR issue in part by dealing with the securocrat problem. Military officials from South Africa and other SADC countries, and the SADC Peace and Security Organ, are regularly meeting with Zimbabwean officers to discuss the role of the military in a civilian-led government. Over the past decade, the Zimbabwe crisis has polarized the regional, continental, and global communities and led to the emergence of mutually hostile pro-ZANU-PF and pro-MDC blocs. There is, however, a growing consensus amongst the regional, continental, and global community that investment in Zimbabwe and sustainable development are directly linked to the rule of law and the trammeling of the powers of Zimbabwe's military. The MDC and local and regional civil society have repeatedly called on South Africa and SADC to ensure the Zimbabwe's Constitutional Referendum (due in June–July 2011) are carried out in a free and fair manner. The May–October constitutional consultations were marred by violent attacks from the youth militias, war veterans, and the military that launched Operation Vara Muromo ("Shut up!") across the country. International pressure is likely to increase and it would be highly damaging to South Africa and SADC if they recognized a violent process that was run by the military. This, and a likelihood of possible regional divisions over Zimbabwe, may spur SADC to reexamine the military's role in Zimbabwe's forthcoming elections. This consensus, and the momentum for security transformation that it will create, may lead to SSR in Zimbabwe.

Incremental Reforms

As previously mentioned, it may be unrealistic to expect a comprehensive transformation of Zimbabwe's security sector anytime soon. However, there is a process of transformation occurring across other sectors—some associated with the military—in Zimbabwe. This in turn creates the space for incremental progress on security reform. The factors that will push the agenda for security reform include: first, the reemergence of the Prime Minister's Office in managing the Council of Ministers (and the performance appraisal of ministers by the prime minister through the Government Work Programme, which was launched in March 2010).[26] Second, the establishment of Commissions on Human Rights and on Media,[27] amongst others, is a major step forward, particularly since commissioners have not been chosen on grounds of political loyalty, but for their professional competence. Third, a number of legislative reform bills are awaiting ratification. If passed, bills that amend or repeal repressive legislation, such as the notorious Public Order and Security Act (POSA), would begin to curb the powers of the military. POSA, for instance, gives the police force almost untrammeled powers of arrest and detention. Fourth, the constitutional reform process may also help to loosen the grip of the military in the political domain, and it would reestablish the separation of powers between party, government, and the military.

There is, therefore, an opportunity for incremental SSR by making big changes in associated sectors such as justice and the media, and by making small, sequenced changes in the security sector. This process of change, leading to eventual transformation, has to be something that all sides can agree on before tackling the big issues. For instance, agreement on reviving the military civil service and bringing back qualified personnel would be a useful first step and a mutual confidence-building measure. Also, a dialogue needs to be established on issues of defense and security. This should be led by Zimbabwe, but allow for input from international experts and analysts. Lessons can be learned from other African countries that undertook SSR, such as South Africa, Eritrea, and Sierra Leone, keeping in mind that each country is unique.

Defense/Security Sector White Paper

Discussion of SSR in Zimbabwe has been on a very limited, ad hoc basis. Therefore, it is of paramount importance for Zimbabwe to have a guiding document that articulates the role of Zimbabwe's military and SSR transformation in the twenty-first century in a structured, comprehensive way. Now is the time to have a document showing that the military needs to have both hard and soft power capabilities, but also capacities that serve a developmental rather than purely militaristic agenda. The military should be the defender of the people as well as the state. Zimbabwe needs a white paper on security and political sector transformation that puts SSR in the context of a national political and socioeconomic transformation. The 1990s South African White Paper on National Defence could offer some pointers on what the Zimbabwe paper would cover, although Zimbabwe's context is politically and militarily different.

There is not the space in this chapter to itemize everything that a Zimbabwe white paper on security and political sector reform would cover, but a few points can be mentioned. The paper would:

- articulate the role of the military in a multiparty, democratic Zimbabwe;
- be the result of a multistakeholder consultative process that includes the military, civil society, parliament, political parties, and other stakeholders;
- serve as a living document and as a confidence-building measure;

- although serving as a stand-alone document, ideally be part of a political/constitutional white paper that also articulates the constitutional and political reform process;
- seek to address the challenge of transforming and reforming the military in Zimbabwe, both incrementally and exponentially;
- seek to embed the role of the military in the context of a revised constitution;
- embed discussion within the context of civil-military relations—the aim would be to reestablish civilian oversight on defense and to reestablish military professionalism and also to bring institutional reform to the military while transforming the outlook of the security sector from militarism to humanism;
- aim to underscore the need to re-professionalize and depoliticize the military and suggest ways in which this could be done;
- discuss military command-and-control and the conditions under which the military can be deployed and how it should be deployed, internally and externally;
- discuss the role and structure of the police in twenty-first-century Zimbabwe;
- discuss the primary and secondary roles of the security sector;
- discuss the question of militia groups and how they could be formally integrated into the professional military, or permanently demobilized and retrained;
- discuss budget transparency;
- discuss the security sector's role in development and democracy;
- discuss methods for reestablishing trust in security forces as well as reconciliation; and
- avoid being perceived as a punitive document.

There would be much else besides but, overall, the paper would outline the need and process that would transform the security sector from a private fiefdom into a security sector that truly represents and acts on behalf of all Zimbabweans. Much of the paper would, of course, be an inspirational wish list, but it would be a valuable start in reconceptualizing and reconstructing Zimbabwe.

Triggers for Violence, Catalysts for Reform

Zimbabwe is currently undergoing a constitutional reform process, and there is the possibility of national elections in 2011. In 2000, the constitutional referendum and March elections were triggers for the reemergence of the military and for a new wave of state-sponsored political violence that continues to this day. Without a return to the rule of law, there is every chance that the constitutional referendum/electoral cycle in 2010–2011 will trigger a repeat of the intense political violence of 2000. Militia groups are threatening civilians in rural and urban areas (particularly in the former ZANU-PF strongholds in Mashonaland East), with dire penalties imposed if they do not approve the draft constitution.[28] There are also concerns that the ZANU-PF and the military are rearming for a final climactic electoral battle with the MDC for political power. It is thus imperative that the electoral process and the justice system are depoliticized, and that the military be removed from politics before the elections. If the military controls the electoral process, as has been the case for the past decade, then the elections will trigger a return to violence and national decline.

On the other hand, the constitutional process and elections are also an opportunity for transformative change in the security domain. Indeed the prospect of elections in 2011 or 2012 has already triggered an intriguing discourse between the ZRP and the electoral community. Currently the Attorney-General's Office is preparing a new Electoral Amendment Bill, which, if passed by Parliament, would allow for the implementation of electoral reforms agreed to by the GPA. The reforms are aimed at preventing electoral malfeasance and minimizing control by the army and police (the reforms would also bar the police and army from "camping" in the polling booths)..The constitutional process is currently being overseen by parliament and a professional Constitutional Commission. The ZEC and other electoral organizations should have the mandate to manage Zimbabwe's elections without interference from the military. In addition the presence of election observers from the SADC, the African Union (AU), and the global community would enhance the chances for a credible, nonviolent electoral process. A multinational civilian security force could also be deployed as a deterrent against political violence. If these steps are taken, there will be a greater chance that the electoral/constitutional process will be a "circuit breaker" rather than a "circuit maker" of political violence. What is certain is that the constitutional process and the elections will determine the sustainability of Zimbabwe's economic recovery.

Conclusion

Each country that undertakes SSR has a unique environment with its own challenges. As noted by an Organisation for Economic Co-operation and Development (OECD) report in 2005,[29] the approaches have to be tailored to the country's circumstances and needs. This naturally does not exclude learning lessons from other countries in the region.

There is no doubt that the establishment of the GNU has changed the political and economic dynamics of Zimbabwe. All three coalition parties have found a space in which to regroup; it has also energized civil society and a plethora of smaller political parties. The dollarization of the economy has brought increased stability, and given new opportunities for entrepreneurship and public-private sector partnerships. But there has been little perceptible change in the security sector, and the challenge of encouraging the military to be partners in national transformation and reconstruction remains. The question of the security sector's role in national development has been slightly muted since 2009, as the GNU concentrated on holding the fragile coalition together and rebuilding the economy. However, within the next eighteen months, the combination of the constitutional review process, national elections; increasingly fraught intra and inter-party dynamics; and the land and justices issues will return the military question, and

SSR to centre-stage. There is a definite need for the transformation of the political and security sector in Zimbabwe, but there can be no illusions about the magnitude of the task. As exemplified by the SSR process in South Africa, it will take a great deal of political will from all sides. The process will have to be an incremental partnership, but it can be done. In a country where the very guardians of order and human life were at one point also those who brought death and terror to communities, reconciliation will also play a large part in moving the process ahead and reestablishing public trust and credibility of the security system, including the police and prisons. Other stakeholders, such as parliament and civil society, will have to be brought into the process, functioning as public oversight mechanisms. The region and South Africa in particular stands to play a key role in Zimbabwe's security sector transformation. Donor governments can also invest in training and exchange programs that would benefit the sector based on its strengths and weaknesses. Perhaps, most importantly, discussions and process have to be based on realism. Grand SSR is unlikely to occur in Zimbabwe anytime soon; but the looming post-GNU period and the electoral-constitutional cycle are triggering a renewed focus on the role of the military in this process. Returning the process to civilian management is a smaller, but more focused and tangible, goal than grandiose schemes for grand SSR.

The security sector, which we now understand to include the human rights dimension as well, is key to nation building and sustainable development. Zimbabwe's economy and development has improved significantly since the desperate months of 2008. The country's environment remains both challenging and dynamic; ultimately, only the security sector can decide whether Zimbabwe's national transformation occurs *because* of the military's support; or *despite* the military's reluctance. There are no simple or quick solutions but if Zimbabwe is to have sustainable security and development, the role of the military, and SSR needs to be addressed now.

Notes

1. The ZNLWVA and the Youth League are highly politicized militia groups often acting as "shock troops" for attacks particularly in smaller towns and rural areas. The ZNLWVA numbers approximately thirty thousand. The Youth League has around fifteen thousand members, and was created as part of the national Youth Training Service in 2001. For further details, please see Knox Chitiyo, "The Case for Security Sector Reform in Zimbabwe," *RUSI Occasional Paper*, September 2009.
2. For further reference, please see ibid.
3. The March 2010, Indigenisation Law require foreign owned firms to cede 51 percent of shares to local Zimbabweans. The law required the process to be done within 45 days; but after protests from various sectors that the law would hamper investment the process was modified. The percentage of shareholding is now variable, not fixed, and inclusive Indigenisation committees were established to oversee the modalities.
4. In February 2009 a power-sharing agreement was signed between ZANU-PF, MDC-T, and MDC-M, forming the Government of National Unity (GNU).

5. The MDC-T, the larger of the two MDC factions, is led by Prime Minister Morgan Tsvangirai. The MDC-M is a faction led by Deputy Prime Minister Arthur Mutambara, which originally broke away from the MDC in 2005. MDC-M has maintained its relevance by joining the GNU, and now plays an important power-broker role between the two larger parties.

6. The Federation of Rhodesia and Nyasaland, also known as the Central African Federation, was established in August of 1953. The major argument for the Federation was the hope that it would provide a framework for the economic development of British Central Africa, and of racial cooperation, ironically established against the protests of the African opposition. See Carl G. Rosberg Jr, "The Federation of Rhodesia and Nyasaland: Problems of Democratic Government," *Annals of the American Academy of Political and Social Science* 306, Africa and the Western World (July 1956): 98–105. Plagued by political differences between the European and African parties, the Federation officially dissolved in 1963, with Northern Rhodesia gaining independence as Zambia, Southern Rhodesia becoming Rhodesia and then Zimbabwe, and Nyasaland becoming Malawi.

7. The Second Chimurenga War, also known as the Rhodesian Bush War or the Zimbabwe War of Liberation, took place from 1966 to 1979. It was a guerrilla war fought between the white minority regime of Ian Smith's Rhodesian Front, and the ZANU led by Robert Mugabe and ZAPU led by Joshua Nkomo. It is considered a war of liberation from colonialism and racism, and resulted in the formation of Zimbabwe under the leadership of Robert Mugabe.

8. The Internal Settlement was signed between the Rhodesian prime minister Ian Smith and Abel Muzorewa of UANC, who became prime minister following elections. The UANC government lasted only until 1980 when another election resulted in the rise of Robert Mugabe to power. For further background, please see William Cyrus Reed, "International Politics and National Liberation: ZANU and the Politics of Contested Sovereignty in Zimbabwe," *African Studies Review* 36, no. 2 (1993): 31–59; or Robert O. Matthews, "From Rhodesia to Zimbabwe: Prerequisites of a Settlement," *International Journal* 45, no. 2, Managing Regional Conflict (1990): 292–333.

9. Please see Martin Rupiah Lecturer, "Demobilization and Integration: 'Operation Merger' and the Zimbabwe National Defence Force 1980–1987," *African Security Review* 4, no. 3 (1995), 52–64.

10. Norma Kriger, *Guerilla Veterans in Post-War Zimbabwe: Symbolic and Violent Politics 1980–1987* (Cambridge: Cambridge University Press, 2003), 111.

11. Following the success of ZANU, there was an upsurge of violence in the Midlands and Matabeleland, which were predominantly occupied by followers of Joshua Nkomo (ZAPU). Between 1982 and 1985 thousands of people were victims of torture, massacres, human rights abuses, and killings. When in 1985 ZAPU continued to win the election in Matabeleland, it was banned. Mediation between the parties finally led to the Unity Accord of 1987 in which ZANU and ZAPU became ZANU-PF, de facto creating a one-party state. Please see Chitiyo, "The Case for Security Sector Reform in Zimbabwe"; and Brian Raftopoulos and Tyrone Savage, eds., *Zimbabwe: Injustice and Political Reconciliation,* (Cape Town, South Africa, Institute for Justice and Reconciliation, 2004)

12. ZANU-PF remained friendly toward FRELIMO after FRELIMO allowed ZANU to operate from a base in Mozambique on the border of Zimbabwe in 1972. For more information, see Mathew Holden, Jr, ed., *The Changing Racial Regime, t* (New Jersey, USA, Transaction Publishers, 1995)

13. Knox Chitiyo and M. Rupiya, "Tracking Zimbabwe's Political History: The Zimbabwe Defence Force from 1980–2005," in *Evolutions and Revolutions: A Contemporary History*

of Militaries in Southern Africa, ed. M. Rupiya (Pretoria: Institute for Security Studies, 2008).

14. In September 2010, Zimbabwe courts began to hear the cases against ZANU-PF ministers and senior security sector officials. These cases were brought by MDC activists and civilians who are suing for abuses committed during 2008; and after. (See "ZANU-PF torture trial begins" *SW Radio Africa*, September 13, 2010.) In addition, civil society group Women of Zimbabwe Arise (WOZA) wrote to Home Affairs Co Ministers Kembo Mohadi and Theresa Makone, stating their intention to sue the Ministers for the abuse the suffered and "inhumane" conditions at Harare Central Prison cells. (See "Zim women sue Ministers over Deplorable Prisons", *Radio VOP* 13 September 2010.)

15. In August 2010, the Kimberley Process (KP) allowed Zimbabwe to have auction its diamonds in the international market. Although the KP has put limits and conditionalities on Zimbabwe diamond sales, human rights groups have criticised the KP for endorsing what they see as the militarisation of Zimbabwe's mineral resources.

16. Chitiyo, "The Case for Security Sector Reform in Zimbabwe."

17. International Crisis Group, "Zimbabwe: Engaging the Inclusive Government," *Africa Briefing* no. 59, Harare/Pretoria/Nairobi/Brussels, April 20, 2009.

18. International Crisis Group, "Zimbabwe: Political and Security Challenges to the Transition," *Africa Briefing* no. 70, Harare/Pretoria/Nairobi/Brussels, March 3, 2010.

19. Ibid.

20. Chitiyo, "The Case for Security Sector Reform in Zimbabwe."

21. Never Chanda, "Mugabe, Zuma Clash Looms," *The Zimbabwean*, December 14, 2009.

22. Ibid.

23. Kitselpile Nyathi, "ZANU-PF's Congress Shows Mugabe Days Numbered," *Daily Nation,* December 13, 2009.

24. International Crisis Group, "Zimbabwe: Political and Security Challenges to the Transition" *Africa Briefing No 70*, 2010.

25. Chitiyo, "The Case for Security Sector Reform in Zimbabwe."

26. Kholwani Nyathi, "Tsvangirai Now in Charge," *The Standard,* March 20, 2010.

27. Tichaona Sibanda, "Media Commission Finally Begins Work," *SW Radio Africa,* March 19, 2010.

28. Caiphas Chimhete, "ZANU-PF's Terror Campaign Threat to Constitution," *The Standard,* January 30, 2010.

29. OECD, Security System Reform and Guidelines, DAC Guidelines and Reference Series, 2005.

Chapter 4

Zimbabwe's Media

Between Party-State Politics and Press Freedom under Mugabe's Rule

David Moore

Introduction

Toward the end of March 2010, the Zimbabwean Media Commission (ZMC) announced that it would issue licenses to private newspapers; by July the street-corner vendors had a large variety to sell.[1] Thus was fulfilled a promise of Zimbabwe's Government of National Unity (GNU), which in February 2009 allowed the Zimbabwe African National Union-Patriotic Front (ZANU-PF) to rule alongside the Movement for Democratic Change-Tsvangirai (MDC-T) and the smaller Movement for Democratic Change-Mutambara (MDC-M) rather than accept defeat in the 2008 elections, judged invalid by most observers due to improper counting and excessive violence. Appointed in December 2009, the ZMC's mandate included registering mass media operations (for which many applicants had been waiting), promoting and enforcing good media ethics, ensuring wide and equitable access to information, and establishing a media council comprised of civil society representatives ranging from journalists to youth.

The ZMC symbolized the Zimbabwean interim government's shortcomings. The press' liberalization was announced at the end of South Africa's president Jacob Zuma's two-day Harare visit, which was credited with reviving the moribund arrangement. This suggests little internal commitment to mutual governance, thus the need for external pressure—especially on ZANU-PF—to move toward liberty at the transitional tunnel's end. Besides the ZMC's appointment process overstepping GNU rules, its representative mix of party-political and "neutral" appointments symbolized the GNU's political and ideological dimensions: haltingly democratic and stalemated between party-statism and liberal ideas of freedom. Thus, the ZMC was a microcosm of the GNU—its functions and members born of the compromises in a regime transitory between authoritarianism and fuller democracy, working in a semi-corporatist mode and trying to include civil society alongside the ZANU-PF's efforts to maintain dominance and sinecures amidst its own fracturing.[2]

The ZMC, like the media, reflected its society's historically structured social and political realities and would change shape in the new era of constitutional democracy. The ZANU-PF's deeply rooted despotism would not disappear quickly, and neither would a hundred flowers bloom in private and state media overnight. This chapter blends past and present perspectives on the Zimbabwean media, including the ideological imbrications thereof, to indicate some difficulties in "picking up the pieces" of Zimbabwe's public sources of information and debate. Some South African media responses to Zimbabwe's crisis suggest similar issues south of the Limpopo are not far from the fore.

To the chagrin of many democrats believing that parties democratically winning elections should take control of the relevant state structures, Zimbabwe's main opposition party, the MDC,[3] gained no power in any of the elections it contested for nearly a decade since it entered the political scene on September 11, 1999. Zimbabwe's contest for parliament in June 2000, the presidential election in February 2002, and another parliamentary one in March 2005 were all stolen through a combination of intimidation, gerrymandering, deliberate miscounting of ballots, and the complicity of neighboring countries,[4] amongst other means of electoral chicanery (including less than liberal media strategies since 2002) employed by Robert Mugabe's ZANU-PF.[5] ZANU-PF schemes for cheating at elections mirror the cynical options for those forced unwillingly to resort to elections to maintain power, outlined contemptuously by Paul Collier in the countries inhabited by his "bottom billion." Democracy is impossible there, he says, thus justifying limited intervention until the problems of accountability and security are solved by those with the responsibility to protect.[6] Without this, dictators with democratic veneers, such as Mugabe, resort to many techniques to win elections; if the media is under control, lying is one.[7] Others include scapegoating minorities or foreigners, bribery, intimidation, keeping opponents out, and miscounting ballots. If recent events following flawed election results in Kenya and Zimbabwe are indicative, Collier—along with an increasing number of academics[8]—could add "create a government of national unity" to the list.

Yet Zimbabwe's harmonized (presidential, parliamentary, and municipal) electoral battles on March 29, 2008, were almost different. Each polling station's results were posted outside upon closing so that the ZANU-PF's handpicked vote counters would not be able to manufacture results in Harare easily; thousands of cell phone photos of the results broadcasted the results before the official count.

By early April 2008, the MDC's long-awaited victory appeared certain. Yet a hitch became apparent: even though many observers attested to a 57–58 percent victory for the MDC in the presidential contest,[9] just a few days after the poll, a prominent election-observing nongovernmental organization (NGO) announced just under 48 percent for Tsvangirai and over 43 percent for the incumbent (a late entrant, former ZANU-PF minister Simba Makoni gained more than 8 percent).[10] The rules demanded 50 percent plus one for the new president. In parliament, the MDC-T gained ninety-nine seats, the MDC-M ten, and the ZANU-PF won only ninety-seven. The official presidential tally took more time: the ZANU-PF-dominated election commission counted for five weeks, but its numbers could not rise beyond the NGO's tally.

The expected runoff was called.[11] The ZANU-PF pulled out all its repressive machine's plugs—so much so that Morgan Tsvangirai stopped campaigning rather than see his supporters (and even ZANU-PF voters who had voted for their parliamentary candidate, but not Mugabe for president) subjected to more brutality than had been meted since the horrific *Gukurahundi* in the 1980s, when up to twenty thousand residents of Matabeleland and the Midlands were killed by the ZANU-PF's "Five Brigade."[12] From January to September 2008, the Zimbabwe Human Rights NGO Forum reported 107 politically inspired murders, 118 kidnappings, 703 cases of torture, 6 rapes, and 1815 assaults at the hands of the ZANU-PF and its militia. Most of these—carefully targeted at the MDC's security activists such as Tonderai Ndira, whose corpse, found in the morgue a week after he had disappeared, could only be identified by a bracelet[13]—were executed from April to the end of June, when the ostensible presidential election was held with only one candidate.

Not even the historically supine Southern African Development Community (SADC) leaders, united in seeming eternity for the preservation of sovereignty's privileges, and so supporting Robert Mugabe for almost as long, could claim such an election was free or fair. Thus, the SADC mediator, South Africa's president Thabo Mbeki—better known for supporting his northern comrade through thick and thin—was mandated to revive the task of banging Tsvangirai's and Mugabe's heads together to create a GNU. By July 21, 2008, there was a Memorandum of Understanding (MoU) to that effect. By September 15, the Global Political Agreement (GPA) paved the way for Constitutional Amendment No. 19 to be added to Zimbabwe's oft-changed constitution. The transitional inclusive government was slated to begin in February of 2009.[14] For at least eighteen months, although many pundits predicted the transition would last until 2013, the two MDC formations were to share state power with Robert Mugabe's powerful machine. A new constitution and elections would follow. It appeared that the ZANU-PF could no longer trick and brutalize its way out of free and fair elections, so deigned to sign up to a power-sharing pact, perhaps in the hopes it could regain full measure powers shortly thereafter. Yet on paper, at least, with the new constitution, the GNU would usher in media freedom; an open press and broadcasting regime was built into the GPA, paving the way toward shared government.

Along with the GNU's preparations for freedom, the media would also experience liberty again: perhaps, practitioners and pundits prognosticated, the heady days of the *Daily News*—which emerged along with the party of hope, but after consistent bombings of its offices and presses and failed assassination attempts on its editor was shut down by the state in late 2003[15]—would return. The weekly *Zimbabwe Independent* had printing presses ready for a daily, as did Thursday's *Financial Gazette*. Some signatories to the GPA were so hopeful that they agreed to stop the broadcasters (notably SW Radio Africa, the Voice of America, and Studio 7) signaling from outside Zimbabwe.[16] Amendment 19 made it clear that all signatories were, in solemn constitutional tones, "aware of the emergence of foreign based radio stations broadcasting into Zimbabwe, some of which are funded by foreign governments," and concerned that "foreign government funded external radio stations broadcasting into Zimbabwe are not in Zimbabwe's national interest."[17] Agreeing that these external radio stations might have located abroad because of "the failure to issue licences under the Broadcasting Services Act to alternative broadcasters"[18] the signatories concurred they were "desirous of ensuring the opening up of the air waves and ensuring the operation of as many media houses as possible." Thus, Amendment 19 stated that the GNU would persuade supporting governments and donors to "cease such hosting and funding"—and that the new Zimbabwean state would "encourage the Zimbabweans running or working for external radio stations broadcasting into Zimbabwe to return to Zimbabwe; and [take] steps...to ensure that the public media provides balanced and fair coverage to all political parties for their legitimate political activities."[19] Such clear ZANU-PF versus MDC positions ran throughout the GPA's various versions—the ZANU-PF changing some after signing—indicating the precarious balancing act to come. As the crowning touch to the GPA's media mandate, the hope that "the public and private media shall refrain from using abusive language that may incite hostility, political intolerance and ethnic hatred or that unfairly undermines political parties and other organisations" was written into the GPA: most of the time honored in the breach by the state-party media.

In mid-October 2009, eight months into the GNU, the MDC-T disengaged because of the ZANU-PF's procrastination on many features of the GPA. A year after the GPA's signing, on "suspending participation" in cabinet, the MDC complained that of the thirty-four items agreed-to in the GPA, only four had been fully implemented. The most important problems included:[20]

- failure to appoint provincial governors and the irregular appointment of the central bank governor and attorney general;
- failure to review ministerial positions and the GPA despite pledges to do so by the SADC, the broker and guarantor of the GPA;
- lack of progress on the democratization of the media, the constitutional process, land audit, and rule of law[21];
- extensive militarization of the countryside through military deployment and the reemergence of bases of violence similar to those following the March 29, 2008, elections;
- imposition of sixteen thousand ZANU-PF youths on the government payroll;
- selective application of the rule of law, resulting in seven MDC members of parliament (MPs) being convicted on shadowy charges while others remained on remand; and
- the public media's—especially the Zimbabwe Broadcasting Corporation (ZBC) and *The Herald*—treatment of the MDC, with claims that its government ministers were acting in the interests of Western powers.

Perhaps the October 15 continuation of Roy Bennett's—the MDC's treasurer and (not appointed) nominee for deputy minister of agriculture—terrorism trial was the straw that broke the MDC's back. The MDC's challenge was met on October 24 by fifty police officers raiding an MDC house, ostensibly in search of weapons, and by Minister of State for Presidential Affairs Didymus Mutasa stating that the ZANU-PF would pay no attention to the MDC's "going on strike like little babies."[22] Three prominent civil society activists were arrested after their October 26 "summer school," on suspicion of holding a political meeting, still banned without permission under the January 2002 Public Order and Security Act (POSA). Additionally, an al Jazeera crew, filming the first GNU cabinet meeting without the MDC, was imprisoned for three hours. State media journalists were ordered not to cover opposition politicians, and two senior MDC members were nearly abducted.

The foreign ministers of Mozambique, Angola, and Zambia visited Harare on October 29 and 30 to discuss the MDC's complaints, not surprisingly advising the MDC to keep inside.[23] Simultaneously, Zimbabwe's foreign ministry cancelled the visit of the UN torture investigator Manfred Nowack, arranged over a period of two years by Morgan Tsvangirai and ZANU-PF justice minister Patrick Chinamasa.[24] This symbolized Zimbabwe's new governmental mode: international interventions were easily dispelled while Zimbabwean citizens were powerless in the face of elite pacting gone sour.

Yet the disengagement did appear to spur the SADC and its hegemon, South Africa, into action. A special summit in Maputo on November 5 set a thirty-day deadline for clear resolution to the GPA's hitches. President Jacob Zuma of South Africa put together a special team to hasten progress, led by his political adviser Charles Nqakula, with Special Envoy Mac Maharaj (seen by progressive South Africans with Zimbabwean concerns as a positive choice, given his antipathy to former president Thabo Mbeki, whose facilitation role ended with this team's formation) and international relations adviser Lindiwe Zulu.[25]

Amidst speculation that the parties would be pushed to an election in early 2011 if they could not agree on the modalities for the GNU's progress, international media reported the apparent results of President Zuma's Harare visit in March 2010 with palpable glee. The Zimbabwean parties were said to have agreed to appoint new provincial governors to replace the Reserve Bank of Zimbabwe (RBZ) chair Gideon Gono and Attorney General Tomana, and to remove the charges on Roy Bennett (if he would take a deputy ministry other than agriculture). At the same time, representatives of the three parties would approach the European Union (EU) to lobby for the end of sanctions, which were extended for a year due to the GNU's lack of progress.[26]

In the middle of Zuma's visit, the ZMC met and announced that it would license the private newspapers queuing up since mid-2009.[27] Perhaps, one could have speculated, it took just a little more than South Africa's traditional "quiet diplomacy" to push the transition along.[28] Yet a few weeks later, despondency set in once again: nothing had moved. Indeed, in early April 2010, Julius Malema, the nearly demagogic leader of the ANC Youth League, visited his counterparts and Robert Mugabe in Zimbabwe. He ignored the MDC pointedly, later calling the party "mickey-mouse."[29] It seemed—aside from the media commission and its siblings, regarding human rights and elections being formed, albeit devoid of action—that nothing had changed. Rumors of elections within a year circulated with intensity, whilst other voices cautioned against a repeat of June 2008's violence.[30]

Regulating the Media during the GNU: Ideologies and Politics At An Impasse

In the meantime, the media, like all other temporarily inclusive institutions, was hovering between increasingly militarized modalities and the long deferred dream of democratic opening.[31] Whilst the appointments to the ZMC were in abeyance after the Parliamentary Committee on Standing Rules and Orders interviewed twenty-seven candidates in August, appointments to media boards, ranging from Kingstons book distributors to Zimpapers (the party-state controlled press), were made in late September. Tafataona Mahoso, whose leadership of the Media and Information Commission during the worst years of the Mugabe regime earned him a reputation as a "media hangman" and the "biggest threat to free media in Zimbabwe," undoubtedly contributing to his rating last in the parliamentary interviews, was reported to have been appointed chairman of the Broadcasting Authority of Zimbabwe (BAZ), on which several ZANU-PF military retirees sat. Critics claimed Mugabe had made the appointment, advised by Information and Publicity Minister Webster Shamu, without consulting the GNU partners.[32] Yet, soon after the November 2009 Maputo summit, and just before the Zuma-Zimbabwe team visit in early 2010, Prime Minister Tsvangirai announced that Mahoso had never been appointed to that post.[33] A few days later, it was reported that the former journalism lecturer—who called journalists opposing him "part of the global conveyor belt of lies,"[34] and penned long diatribes in the state newspapers against Western "media terrorism"—had taken half of a farm in the Eastern Highlands from its white owner, repeating a ZANU-PF elite trend renewed since the GPA's signing.[35] In listing the members of the ZMC, along with some indications of their ideological and political proclivities—and comparing them with Mahoso's—one can gain an indication of the balance (or better, stalemate) within the GNU.

Just before Christmas 2009, the ZMC, along with commissions for elections and human rights, was announced.[36] Its chair Godfrey Majonga, deputy-director of a charity for the disabled (on which Robert Mugabe's wife Grace was a board member) and once a popular ZBC television personality, had been wheelchair-bound since falling from a Harare Avenue apartment window. Rumors claimed that he was pushed by men hired by Emmerson Munangagwa—said to be second in the running to replace Mugabe as ZANU-PF leader—as punishment for being involved with one of Munangagwa's mistresses. The ZMC's deputy chair was Nqobile Nyathi, a lecturer at Bulawayo's National University of Science and Technology (NUST), formerly an editor at the *Daily News* and the *Daily News on Sunday* while they were shut down in 2003 (before which she was jailed briefly for publishing a cartoon perceived by the Mugabe regime as insulting to the president) and news editor of the weekly *Financial Gazette*. Nyathi is on record as saying in a lecture for the Commonwealth Journalists Association's World Press Freedom Day that media associations, not governments, should develop codes of ethics for the media, and that "by having a stranglehold on the country's access to information, [the Mugabe regime had] been destroying democracy in Zimbabwe."[37]

Another member Henry Muradzikwa, formerly a University of Zimbabwe sociology lecturer trained in Egypt, had been fired in March 2008 as chief executive officer of the ZBC because the ZANU-PF told the ZBC that he had handled "national issues" improperly. He had disobeyed the party-state's instructions to deny favorable broadcasting coverage to the opposition and to give positive coverage to Mugabe. He had lost his editorship of the state-run *Sunday Mail* in 1987 when the president was displeased with a story he published about Zimbabwean students being deported from Cuba. Some reports suggest Muradzikwa's experience with print media would have made him the preferred chair, but Mugabe refused.

The member chosen but not recommended by the parliamentary committee interviewing the candidates was Christopher Mutsvangwa, also a former chief executive officer of the ZBC and recent ambassador to China.[38] Dr. Lawton Hikwa, considered politically neutral by Zimbabwean journalists, was also not recommended by the committee. He was the dean of NUST's Communication and Information Science faculty, formerly a Zimpapers board member, and currently a board member in the National Youth Development Trust. Hikwa was also a member of the National Library and Documentation Service Council, established in July 2009 by the minister of education MDC-M MP David Coltart to breathe life into Zimbabwe's library system.

Miriam Madziwa, once a *Bulawayo Chronicle* journalist but at the time of appointment a media consultant and author of many feminist articles about the difficulties faced by women during Zimbabwe's crisis, was also appointed. So too was Chris Mhike, a lawyer active in human rights and media issues, previously a journalist for both *The Herald* and the *Daily News*. For many journalists, and apparently the parliamentary committee, Mhike was the preferred chair. Some claim that another member Matthew Takaona, president of the Zimbabwe Union of Journalists (ZUJ) from 1998 to 2009, was a Tsvangirai supporter; however, the way in which he was alleged to have manipulated his succession to the ZUJ's leadership in December 2009 led independent journalists to accuse him of ZANU-PF sympathies. Simultaneously though, he threatened to take the Zimpapers chief executive to court for attempting to stack the ZUJ's leadership election with the latter's supporters, which indicated conflict within the party-state ideological apparatuses. Furthermore, the fact that he lost his Zimpapers job when, as ZUJ president, he supported *Daily News* reporters and was beaten and robbed by Zimbabwean soldiers just before the 2008 elections does not suggest complete acquiescence to the status quo.

The ninth member of the board, former radio broadcaster Dr. Millicent Mombeshora, was divisional head of Special Projects and Strategic Planning in the RBZ, notorious under the chairmanship of Gideon Gono for leading Zimbabwe into such inflation that it lost sovereignty over its currency. She was under Australian travel sanctions and was implicated in grain-smuggling attempts with her husband, the ZANU-PF deputy minister of health and child welfare.

This line-up indicates the nature of the impasse recognized by the very formation of the GNU itself: it took at least four months for the commission to be formed, and its membership was made up of roughly equal numbers of oppositional, "neutral," and ZANU-PF political types. It blended liberals, leftists, party-state-accumulators, and technocrats, some appointed through parliament and some by "the president in consultation," and it was given the task of creating more freedom for the media whilst simultaneously relying on the less than democratic GNU. As Antonio Gramsci put it about another interregnum in which the old was dying and the new not yet born, "the gap is full of morbid symptoms."[39]

To assist the diagnosis of those symptoms, Mahoso's philosophy warrants some examination, given his tenure as director of the ZMC's predecessor and his profuse and ponderous writings in the Zimbabwean state media. This ideology reflects the fate of what at one time appeared to be the ZANU-PF's "progressive" ideology and its installation into the state apparatuses that became instruments of repression rather than transformation. Contrasting it with the ideology of *state-less freedom* is also instructive. As Morgan Tsvangirai stated at the meeting, when he said that Mahoso was not the chair of the BAZ:

> I do not support the argument that due to the potential power of the media, the state has obligation to ensure it is properly regulated...I do not believe in regulation of the media. Instead I am a strong proponent of the view that due to its very power and inalienable right of freedom of information, freedom of expression, the state should play no role in its regulations...The media, like so many other professions, should operate largely on the basis of self regulation.[40]

To those accustomed to the fixations of Zimbabwe's state media, personified by the tedious Mahoso, blended with the vindictive diatribe of Jonathan Moyo, once ZANU-PF's minister of state for information and publicity in the Office of the President and Cabinet,[41] such words must imply a breath of fresh air. However, the media market will likely only assist the construction of freedom for a few if its regulation is completely stateless—only those who can afford it will have access to public information and debate. Unless foreign funding through NGOs continues supporting such initiatives (such as the Media Monitoring Project of Zimbabwe's Public Information Rights program),[42] media activists struggling to make media accessible to the poor and rural areas will have to consider state support. The dilemma for democrats involved in this little bit of socialism, however, is the tendency for state support to be accompanied by state control. In Zimbabwe, this has historically meant ZANU-PF command; therefore, those advocating new media legislation tend to balk at this prospect.

Thus, in reading Tafataona Mahoso pontificate, one questions the pedigree of developmental journalism prevalent in the 1970s and 1980s, when the ZANU-PF's pretensions toward Marxist-Leninist-Maoist thought were part of a worldwide movement incorporating progressive ideas of a "new information order." This school of thought proclaimed that the free media was dominated by imperialists and that a media leading to wider socioeconomic freedoms would need state and society mobilization around anticapitalist developmental ideals. If Mahoso's contemporary rendering of this discourse holds for many of its other adherents, observers could be excused for thinking that the language of developmental journalism was but an excuse for authoritarianism.

An interview with *The Herald*, Zimbabwe's party-state newspaper (albeit with a 23.8 percent share owned by South African-based Old Mutual and just over 25 percent held by other not entirely state-owned businesses) illustrates some of these traits. In it, Mahoso claimed that Scandinavian development agencies were trying to "reinvent [the] minority media to make it mainstream again"[43] by supporting opposition media, and thereby the puppets of the West. For him, the craft of journalism itself was "part and parcel of the machinery of foreign intervention" epitomized by Henry Morgan Stanley in any case; ever since the likes of Stanley, Africans have waged a "struggle between the external foreign voice embedded among us, and the African voice."[44] The latter only came into Zimbabwe from the liberation movement's exiled days during the liberation war of the 1970s, and is still "establishing itself and has not yet fully overcome the obstacles created by the minority [i.e., white] media, and one reason is that Zimbabwe is a neighbour to a country where the minority voice is still mainstream—South Africa."[45] Thus, journalists should be educated so they can lead the transformation necessary for real development. Mahoso proposed that media educational programs—producing far too many graduates, he said—be monitored more closely by the Media and Information Commission to adhere to a curriculum that would develop this African voice, in addition to educating the audience itself.

Presumably that education would convince them that the notion of human rights is the result of an American-led plan "intended to demobilise the African revolution in its infancy and to save white capital and white settlers while appearing to be advancing a form of "human rights" for everyone, a new form of human rights far superior to the demands of the African liberation movements themselves."[46] Quoting Mahmood Mamdani on the history of human rights discourse to that effect, Mahoso compiled a list of Zimbabwean writers, journalists, and activists who were

> the frontline troops for white "soft power" and the "Rhodie core of MDC-T". Jenny Ellis, Peta Thorncroft [*sic*], Peter Hain, Mike Auret, Georgina Godwin, Gerry Jackson, George Feltoe, Cathy Buckle, Roy Bennett and so many other former white settlers emerging in the 1990s as champions of human rights and Press freedom for Africans…a new myth of human rights and democracy was created in which the Anglo-Saxon oppressors became the teachers once again.[47]

Even al Jazeera is included in this claim, originating in Mahoso's unpacking of "the West's" racism since the days of slavery, always justifying "economic genocide" in the name of white superiority.

Albeit highly functionalist and derivative, such writing has clear roots in the radicalized sections of the post-1960s Western academy in which Mahoso studied in the United States of America,[48] contributing to the thinking of a wide array of scholarly activism during the liberation struggles in southern Africa. It was not unpopular then to criticize the writings of Walt Whitman Rostow, and Mahoso did so in this typical passage. However, when this radical dependency material turned into the rhetoric of regimes such as Zimbabwe's, it lost its critical edge regarding *comprador elites.* Its anticapitalist rigor and vigor became rote and ritualized, its anger replaced by only a racism justifying the ZANU-PF's stay in power to participate in an accumulation process benefiting the new ruling classes. Perhaps this could be called "primitive accumulation with a racial twist."[49]

Other journalistic ideologues have also taken on these tendencies. Reason Wafawarova (alleged to have been a director of the Green Bombers program through which ZANU-PF youth militia were trained but studying in Australia for a masters degree in international relations in 2009[50]) wrote copious opaque essays attempting to marry rationality and rabid ZANU-PF defense. For example, in a piece entitled "Unity is the Best Enemy Repellent," posted by the Pan-African News Wire, he wrote:

> It must be understood in the context that whatever conflict we had among ourselves as Zimbabweans from 1999—that conflict was a fight to repel an external enemy. It was never a conflict to express a quest for tyranny or the love for self-inflicted suffering. That is the propaganda we have heard from the enemy and it is time we earnestly engaged ourselves in the national healing process that will help us rebuild a country we helped shatter by allowing ourselves to collaborate with those external forces that sought to strangulate our economy. The denunciation of President Mugabe has become a secular doctrine in the West, and that fulmination is all rooted in the imperial commitment to world domination and the establishment of client states in place of the fallen colonies…it is not going to retreat just because we have decided to rebuild our shattered country as one family.[51]

Wafawarova suggests that the national healing process in Zimbabwe should take into account those "who succumbed to death as the economy of the country was shattered by the ruinous Western sanctions onslaught."[52] They "should be viewed as having fallen on the field of honour" but also "each of us Zimbabweans must make an effort to surmount all feelings of hate, rejection, bitterness and hostility toward our fellow citizens" while uniting to "repel…the real enemy behind this confrontation…it is only the Western community that stands opposed to the inclusive Government and our efforts to rebuild our nation. We have the blessing and good will of all members of the family of nations but the West."[53]

It is not clear if this is a call against quick elections—which in early 2010 seemed to be advocated by some in the west, but also by the predictably pro-Mugabe *New African*,[54] or a tactical feint to the GNU's National Healing Commission to advise amnesty for Zimbabwe's state-centered human rights abusers. In an article for *The Herald* a few days before, Wafawarova suggested that:

> Hindsight justice and witch hunting may be palatable options for purposes of pleasing external donors and the forces behind them, and perhaps for the goal of extinguishing our own bitterness, but there is no healing that comes with retribution. Those that have suffered violence and those that have lost lives in this moment of our extremism have indeed paid a price for our peace. Their suffering, and even death; must not inspire us for more conflict.[55]

It should be noted too that the re-invocation of "nation" is an attempt to be bipartisan. All party members are invited to rejoin in a unity that was never really sundered, although the imperialists tried: "Each of us…must win the ultimate victory by killing all seeds of hostility and enmity within us toward fellow citizens. This is an important victory to win—bigger than any election victory."[56] Yet the sting in the tail remains: if the "seeds of genuine love and oneness in our hearts—a love capable of withstanding the murderous assault of ruinous sanctions and isolation"[57] are not planted by all, then those who refuse must still be in the hands of the imperialists.

Of most interest, however, and deserving much more ideological and rhetoric analyses is the lineage connecting writings such as Wafawarova and Mahoso's with the publications and speeches of Robert Mugabe. Could the president of Zimbabwe have created a distinct style, influencing Zimbabwe's intelligentsia forever? The pious religiosity and seemingly sincere gestures toward reconciliation convinced much of the West, many white commercial farmers, and the left in the 1970s and 1980s of Mugabe's good intentions, carrying right through the Gukurahundi massacres.[58]

A brief exegesis into the history of this discourse, along with an example of how the press in South Africa, too, is sometimes subject to similar pressure as that exerted in Zimbabwe can contribute toward an understanding of the seemingly benign nationalism in southern Africa that can lead immeasurably to the ability of parties such as the ZANU-PF to continue their rule.

The Media Divide: Historical and Regional Perspectives

The days of the *Bantu Mirror, Chapapu, African Home News,* the *African Daily News Bulletin,* the *African Daily News, Venture,* the *Central African Examiner,* and later, the nationalist movement's many magazines, such as the *Zimbabwe Review* and *Zimbabwe News,* indicate long simmering divides between those wishing to open vigorous debate about the direction of Zimbabwean society, and those hoping to close the debate.[59] The early days of African journalism in Rhodesia were marked by a stark contrast between the well-educated elitists who took on all the appearances of liberals in alliance with the varieties of white liberalism (e.g., promoting a qualified rather than open franchise), and those less-educated political activists who, in the opinion of what one elitist called the "eggheads," were only too willing to employ "spivs and loafers…people who hardly understand what the [leaders] are driving at [and who] become restless and the result is always the same: lawlessness and hooliganism."[60]

As these struggles moved from mass actions (such as bus boycotts) to more cohesive, union-led strikes and to the liberation war, this division would be maintained, albeit in many mutations. As history marched on, the elitists realized that they would have to ally with the masses to gain power. Their discourse—in media, as in politics per se—vacillated enormously to incorporate tropes ranging from anti-imperialism to homophobia. There would be little apparent empirical logic behind such public utterances. For example, while moving toward an apparent anti-imperialism, Robert Mugabe, for example, made many lasting alliances with American and British practitioners.[61] Ironically, the elitists of that age are the ruling group now, and they are still employing "spivs and hooligans" in their efforts to maintain power. The continuing thread is the desire to repress the voices and actions of the majority of the population, in other words, to restrain democracy. Of course, when engaged in armed struggle against white minority rule, the nascent ruling class had to employ spivs and hooligans to be their soldiers; anti-working class language would not do for that task.

Not all of the recruits were easily fooled, however. In the mid-1970s, a group of them challenged the old guard, including its relatively new member Robert Mugabe, and its propensity to make deals with the international powers keen to moderate the advance of majority rule in Zimbabwe. The Zimbabwean People's Army (ZIPA) was whisked away to Mozambique's prisons as soon as it was seen as a threat to Mugabe's rise to power, and thus on the left of the Cold War divide.[62]

One of the most interesting milestones in the history of the political and ideological calcification of ZANU-PF is a 1977 version of *Zimbabwe News* that marks the rise of Mugabe to power within his party and the elimination of the ZIPA "threat," just after Robert Mugabe and former Mozambique president Samora Machel had thrown the best liberation fighters in the jails where they would remain until 1980. The indications that this new leader was not about to bide dissent, either in the party or in civil society, are present in the article "Comrade Mugabe Lays the Line at Historic Chimoio Central Committee Meeting." The words—published for liberation struggle supporters around the world—foreshadowed the future of dissent in the nascent ruling party. Mugabe spoke of the destructive forces in the party:

> Those amongst us who arduously strive in any direction that militates against the party or who, in any way, seek, like the rebels of 1974 and 1975/6, to bring about change in the leadership or structure of the party by maliciously planting contradictions within our ranks. We must negate them in turn. This is what is referred to as the negation of the negation…the ZANU axe must continue to fall upon the necks of rebels when we find it no longer possible to persuade them into the harmony that binds us all.[63]

Those worried about too much of the so-called left in the ZANU-PF were likely pleased by Mugabe's efforts to rid the party of the negative side of the Cold War.[64] The point is, though, that the party was already well on its way to developing a pattern of repressing opposition within its ranks, no matter the ideological persuasion, and publicizing its tendencies quite openly through its media outlets.

In the late 1980s, well entrenched in power and with Gukurahundi under its belt, the ruling party found itself challenged by another contingent of youth, and the response was well reported in the media. When students at the University of Zimbabwe demonstrated in favor of the idea of multiparty democracy in 1989, Mugabe called them a "bunch of rapists, drunkards and drug addicts who could not be allowed into the city because they were given to violence…They are our children. We will discipline them our way."[65] By 2009, one of the students leading those demonstrations was the deputy prime minister in the interim government. Along the way to Arthur Mutambara's position beside him, though, Mugabe had demonstrated to the country and the world that he was not the sort of leader pleased with freedom of expression, or the institutions that would allow it to flower.

Yet, for reasons unfathomable to the West, where such freedoms are taken for granted, the state expected to be a bulwark of such values, South Africa, aided and abetted the ZANU-PF regime as long as it could.[66] Here too, the free media were seen as a mixed blessing, to be handled carefully by the state and influenced in the correct way by "revolutionary intellectuals." In the wake of Zimbabwe's 2008 elections, two cases of attempts to influence the South African media illustrate how elements of the South African state and its revolutionary intellectuals can be easily tempted to sway public opinion in an antidemocratic direction.

As discussed earlier, the ZANU-PF found it hard to digest the results of the March 2008 poll and thereafter spent an inordinate amount of time counting and recounting the ballots. The extended vote counting—which included a ZANU-PF appeal of twenty-three constituency results—created consternation among the SADC's members. Zambia and Botswana were openly chafing at Zimbabwe's denial of democracy, while Tanzania and even Mozambique were less quiet than usual. An extraordinary summit was called in Lusaka for April 12, but Robert Mugabe refused to go. Thabo Mbeki visited Harare on his way to Lusaka and declared, hand in hand with Mugabe, that there was no crisis in Zimbabwe.

This nonchalance bothered many South African newspapers: the Independent chain's *Sunday Argus* in Cape Town, for example, wrote of "handshakes and smiles" in Harare that "appeared to say it all."[67] In response, a few weeks later Frank Chikane, director-general of the president's office and a participant in the negotiations over Zimbabwe's fate, stormed into the editorial offices of Johannesburg's *Star*—the lead paper of the Independent group. He lectured the editor and the foreign affairs editor on the rectitude of the South African stance on Zimbabwe and told them their papers were writing lies about that country. He demanded that they print something more amenable to the South African president. On May 5, they did. The leading story "Quo Vadis, Zimbabwe?" opined that "there is no basis to believe the Zimbabwe Electoral Commission's presidential vote count has been compromised."[68] It continued to proclaim:

> The MDC has shown little maturity in its handling of the political crisis. It has made wild claims of victory, exaggerated the violence and now fears ZANU-PF's rallying of its grassroots support could legitimately reverse the presidential result in a runoff. The globe-trotting Tsvangirai has spent little or no time in Zimbabwe itself, leaving his party with little direction on handling the problem. And there seems to be a lot of truth in Mugabe's claims that Tsvangirai gets his instructions from Washington and London. The British and U.S. governments have played an undermining role in the SADC mediation process led by South Africa. They simply want regime change similar to Iraq regardless of the consequences. South Africa and SADC must aim to mediate a government of national unity that could begin the reconstruction of Zimbabwe.[69]

It would be difficult to replicate the words of the country's president and the SADC's facilitator of the Zimbabwean dialogue more accurately.[70]

South Africa's "revolutionary intellectuals" did not have to be told by the president's office what to write. Apparently worried by aspirant president Jacob Zuma's April 2008 visit with British prime minister Gordon Brown,[71] where Zimbabwe was discussed, South African scholars (with PhDs in history and sociology from Western universities) Eddy Maloka and Ben Magubane penned a twenty-two-page essay entitled "Zimbabwe: An International Pariah—What are the Revolutionary Tasks of the South African Democratic Movement?" for circulation within the ANC.[72] Their document—which also went to the *City Press* on Sunday, May 4, 2008—in language familiar to veterans of struggles and their histories, called for "all genuine revolutionaries" to defend Robert Mugabe's regime from those in the United Kingdom so desperate to achieve regime change in Zimbabwe "that they are ready to do anything and everything to accomplish their goal, including turning the President of the ANC into their agent!"[73]

The essay continues to repeat the South African state's perspective on Zimbabwe. What were the "revolutionary tasks of the South African democratic movement" regarding Zimbabwe? "Defend ZANU-PF in Zimbabwe": the imperialist campaign to "defeat [it] is but a curtain-raiser to what will inevitably follow—a sustained offensive to defeat our very own movement!" As for the South African press record-ing atrocities in Zimbabwe, it is "bourgeois... with its pliant black and white scribes [and] reactionary members of the national intelligentsia." The essay—nearly a quar-ter of which consists of material copied from British anti-imperialist writings in newspapers such as *The Guardian*—concludes with the exhortation that "no one but us can defend and save the African revolution, acting together with all other like-minded forces in our country, our region and Continent, and everywhere else in the world!" One presumes that the last call, reminiscent of *workers of the world unite* would be thankful for internationalist workers' defense of a trade union-based political party, but the defense of sovereignty trumps calls for global solidarity.

By May 11, 2008, erstwhile pan-Africanist trade unionist, then Investic Business Development director Cunningham Ngcukana penned a piece interesting for its attempt to chart the real history of the president's efforts.[74] Simultaneously, the daughter of the Pan-African Congress (PAC) leader wrote an op-ed article in South Africa's most popular Sunday paper decrying Western schemes to remove Mugabe from his legitimate place in Zimbabwe's hierarchy.[75] It shared Maloka's and Magubane's penchant to quote British writers condemning imperialism, thus demonstrating divisions in the West's intelligentsia and its vigorous contestation over imperialism's meaning.

These two cases illustrate that the South African state sometimes penetrates the media through direct intervention, or with selected or self-appointed intellectuals' help. They indicate that the media is far from an independent sector in a civil society floating between the political and economic parts of society.

Back to the Future

Before closing on such a negative note, however, it should be noted that aside from the lack of daily papers and private broadcasters—all lined up for accreditation in 2010—during Zimbabwe's dark decade of the 2000s, and in spite of all the ZANU-PF's attempts to muzzle the country's flow of information, the well-resourced urban classes had access to relatively independent media. Since the closure of the *Daily News* in 2003, there remained weekly newspapers—*The Financial Gazette, The Zimbabwe Independent,* and *The Standard*—with varying degrees of autonomy from Zimbabwe's ruling classes (e.g., *The Financial Gazette* was owned partly by the RBZ chairman, Gideon Gono). From outside, there is *The Zimbabwean* and the South African-based, but Zimbabwean-owned, *Mail and Guardian* (with Zimbabwean sales subsidized by a democracy-promoting NGO).

Anyone with access to the electronic media could read a score of webzines—from *ZimOnline* to the *Zimbabwe Times* to *newZimbabwe.com*—along with other sources of news. From Toronto, former Canadian University Services Overseas (CUSO)[76] volunteer Bill Sparks broadcast daily emails of selected news stories globally, and the Australian-based *Zimbabwe Situation* collected even more on its website. Bloggers filled their sites with Zimbabwean news and commentary. A "zimbabwe-fight-on-dont-mourn" discussion group flourished among youth, and the more pristine *Zimbabwe Democracy Now* website promoted more democracy and satirized ZANU-PF pundits such as Mahoso. The MDC's *Changing Times* wound its way through cyberspace, while paper copies were distributed to block-long queues outside Harvest House, its Harare headquarters. Hundreds of newspapers originating from Washington, D.C. to Beijing were available on the web too. What the ZANU-PF called "pirate" radio stations broadcasted from outside Zimbabwe regularly on the radio and the web. Satellite television allowed relatively wealthy suburbanites to avoid the boring diet of ZBC news and entertainment.

NGOs such as Human Rights Watch, Physicians for Human Rights, Solidarity Peace Trust, and the International Crisis Group covered Zimbabwe intensely. The Media Monitoring Project's Weekly Media Update—run by the former editor of *Horizon*, a magazine that opened a lot of space in the late 1980s and 1990s—is available to those with email interested in charting the many biases of the ZANU-PF media (and its competitors), while the Media Institute of Southern Africa also chronicles Zimbabwe's press and broadcasters.

All of these media constitute sources of vigorous contestation and debate and employ some of the estimated two hundred journalists who graduate from Zimbabwean media training institutions every year.[77] To be sure, they are limited in breadth due to difficulties of access and cost, but they are deep in that they facilitate and inform political debate within Zimbabwe's "organic intellectuals,"[78] and, thus, should be taken seriously. Indeed, when Information Minister Professor Jonathan Moyo was fighting them off, he lambasted the "ghost internet sites," Western think-tanks, "writing NGO and opinion mendicants," and the "partisan" United Nations as imperialists trying to remove his president.[79] The new media forms clearly worried him: he could not ban them as he did the *Daily News*, or control them as he did the ZBC and its many offshoots privatized to ZANU-PF members. The best the ZANU-PF could do was to launch some websites itself. For the contending factions in Zimbabwe's political elite—in the ZANU-PF, the MDC parties, and the professional end of civil society—the minor matter of a few independent daily newspapers may not be that important. Government attempts to clog the internet are not nearly as effective as the ZANU-PF's mentors in China. Limited bandwidth and poor electricity supply only serve to slow down the spread of information, opinion, and intrigue. The intricacies of the ZANU-PF's infighting are known to all who care; so too is the extent of disease and starvation suffered by the masses.

The latter clause is the one that matters, of course. Media freedom is only half-consummated if it benefits the relatively rich, while the masses starve and die of cholera. The public space it creates is then only half-full, and towers to transmit microwaves are easier to build and fund in times of crisis than the nitty-gritty of public goods, such as sewers and water pipes. Yet in spite of the public's limited access to the media, a recent attempt to survey public opinion in Zimbabwe found that propaganda, rather than fear and starvation, served to convince most Zimbabweans to believe the ZANU-PF's messages instead of the MDC's.[80] In 2004 *Afrobarometer*, a well-funded surveyor and purveyor of opinions about democracy in Africa, gained this admission from 354 interviewees with access to the state newspapers. Of those, 220 rated the president highly. From this statistical base, the mass opinion surveyors informed the world that Robert Mugabe was winning a propaganda war—not the battles of coercion and fear.

Afrobarometer's findings were heralded by the likes of Jonathan Moyo.[81] Electoral "successes" may have confirmed their belief, but only if one discounts the theft and intimidation. This sort of social science indicates two things: first, it is very difficult to measure the impact the media has on electoral and other political behavior and second, without due consideration of the effect of brutality and violence on the political scene, one can only see through the narrowest of lenses.

Theorizing a Conclusion

To theorize the contradictory relations imbricating southern African media complexes, it is useful to turn once again to Gramsci. Gramsci is a good antidote to liberal theories of civil society, which posit all sorts of voluntarily entered associations as the realm of freedom against the repressive terror of the state (and somehow also free of the market, although it is never explained how this break is made).[82] As confusing as he is on the notion of civil society, Gramsci at least realized that it can never be fully separated from political society. One of the realms of freedom enjoyed by those partaking in civil society is that of forming political parties: state formation germinates with this move. It was present when the liberation parties in Zimbabwe were fighting on the ideological front (Gramsci's war of position), as well as the military one (his war of maneuver). Did the former consist of the fora for the construction of consent or hegemony (the making of the moral and intellectual leadership of the ruling class), and the latter the other end of the stick? Let us just say that there is a continuum between political society and civil society and relations of force within the "political."

The media's relative autonomy from these political pursuits depends on the strength of the market (i.e., of capitalists), of the institutions set up by states, and of active civil society in capitalist societies to be able to insulate the media from over-reliance on market forces—in other words, to preserve the quality of the media as a public good rather than have it completely privatized. In societies wherein neither market nor polity are fully developed in the capitalist sense of the word, the nature of the means by which new classes are gaining power and holding on to it conditions the media. The state constitutes the most important end of these means. The ends of the pursuit of hegemony, through the state and the media necessary for it, will never be declared as "building up the bourgeoisie," but instead as "development," and in some cases "freedom from imperialism."

The pursuit of political correctness should not allow us to forget what Gramsci said about the possibilities of the trenches of bourgeois hegemony and the freedoms bolstering it existing in "the east,"—or what could be called the unevenly developed state-society complexes in the third world. He did not see many possibilities for consensual hegemony. In "backward countries or…the colonies…the State was everything, civil society was primordial and gelatinous…forms which elsewhere have been superseded and have become anachronistic are still in vigour."[83] Civil society did not have the strength to challenge feudal states, yet new ideologies come into colonial and postcolonial societies, along with the other aspects of uneven capitalist development. When ideologies "born in a highly developed country [are] disseminated in less developed countries, impinging upon the local interplay of combinations" they create "new, unique, and historically concrete combinations."[84] Thus it is with civil society, which is as much an ideological expression of a political desire to create a liberal society as anything else.[85] When looking at the idea of civil society and its expression through various media

> one must…distinguish between historically organic ideologies, those, that is, which are necessary to a given structure, and ideologies that are arbitrary, rationalistic, or "willed." To the extent that ideologies are historically necessary they have a validity which is "psychological;" they "organize" human masses, and create the terrain on which men move, acquire consciousness of their position, struggle, etc. To the extent that they are arbitrary they only create individual "movements," polemics and so on (even though these are not completely useless, since they function like an error which by contrasting with the truth, demonstrates it).[86]

The question is, in Zimbabwe and the rest of Africa too, who is willing what ideology? Is a consortium of Western liberal imperialists imposing civil society, multiparty democracy, and the rest in advance of the ability of social formations to absorb them? Or are the kleptocratic sovereigntists, such as Mugabe, the ones who are trying to will their outdated world on a modern liberal, or even democratic socialist, set of ideologies? Both currents are at play, but most important are the ones emerging organically from the ordinary people, as they articulate explanations for the crisis hitting them all. In South Africa too, the tensions are all over the media landscape, although the strength of the private media and the absence of a very visible party-state organ makes the struggles appear more muted than in its northern neighbor.[87] Yet, as the aforementioned cases illustrate, the party-state and its faithful hacks make every attempt to spread its word when it feels threatened.

In Zimbabwe, the future of a free media is contingent upon contending forces within the state and the emerging market, coming to a *modus vivendi* on a strategy for accumulation that takes public goods (including a freedom that can only be guarded by a judicious state) as seriously as private accumulation (which in the conditions of capitalism's origins is sometimes criminalized).[88] With the unfolding of the GNU, the efforts to combine state, market, and international donor forces that crisscrossed the Zimbabwean media landscape during the 1980s and early 1990s will be reinvented. A judicious combination of state and market in this realm, as in most, can be aspired to. The state must protect, and even promote, a notion of public readership that the market can never accomplish. However, the excesses of ZANU-PF tutelage are a warning to any future attempts to craft developmental journalism. One can only hope that the ZANU-PF's surfeit of statecraft has not turned everyone in Zimbabwe into the sort of libertarians who allow capital to rule all realms. Governments of national unity seem, to twist Samuel Beckett's words, to fail again: in so doing, the lessons learned can be used to push harder for real democracy. Gaining from the mistakes of the past, the failures will be smaller, and thus better, in the media, as in the society they reflect and shape.[89]

Notes

1. At the time of the last revisions to this chapter, September 14, 2010, a number of new newspapers were being published in Zimbabwe. However, radio and television were still solely in the hands of the government and dominated by ZANU-PF. Restrictions on media content, e.g., severe penalties for insulting the president, were still in force. Furthermore, few newspapers other than the state's reach rural areas.

2. See also Richard Saunders, "Zimbabwe: Liberation Nationalism, Old and Born Again," *Africa Files* (August 2010): 6; and his "Geologies of Power: Blood Diamonds, Security Politics and Zimbabwe's Troubled Transition," in *Legacies of Liberation: Postcolonial Struggles for a Democratic Southern Africa,* eds. Marlea Clarke and Carolyn Bassett (Toronto and Johannesburg: Fernwood and HSRC Press, forthcoming), for similar thoughts vis-à-vis the exploitation of diamonds.

3. Until October 2005, the MDC was one party. Then a group within the MDC split and by early 2006 formed the MDC-M under Arthur Mutambara's leadership. Mutambara was deputy prime minister in the GNU, having gained ten seats in the 2008 elections and thus the balance of power. Technically, the party led by Prime Minister Morgan Tsvangirai is the MDC-T, but in this chapter "MDC" and "MDC-T" will refer to the party led by Zimbabwe's prime minister, while "MDC-M" will refer to the "splinter" group. For details, see Brian Raftopoulos, "Reflections on Opposition Politics in Zimbabwe: The Politics of the Movement for Democratic Change (MDC)," in *Reflections on Democratic Politics in Zimbabwe,* eds. Brian Raftopoulos and Karin Alexander (Cape Town: Institute for Justice and Reconciliation, 2006), 6–28. On the 2008 elections see Susan Booysen, "The Presidential and Parliamentary Elections in Zimbabwe, March and June 2008," *Electoral Studies* 28, no. 1 (2009): 150–154; and Susan Booysen, *EISA Election Observer Mission Report No. 28: Observer Mission Report: Zimbabwe—The Zimbabwe Harmonized Elections of 29 March 2008, Presidential, Parliamentary and Local Government Elections with Postscript on the Presidential Run-off of 27 June 2008 and the Multi-party Agreement of 15 September 2008,* Electoral Institute of Southern Africa, Richmond, 2008.

4. Southern African Liaison Office (SALO), "Country Focus: South Africa's Relations with Zimbabwe," Johannesburg, 2009, http://cage.dcis.gov.za/documents/pdf/SALO_Country_Focus_Paper-Zimbabwe_FULL.pdf.

5. For one small example, the 2002 presidential elections had so few urban polling booths that voters had to queue for days to mark their ballot; even after the voting period was extended by a day, many missed their chance at electoral democracy. See Patrick Bond and David Moore, "Zimbabwe: Elections, Despondency and Civil Society's Responsibility," *Pambazuka,* April 7, 2005.

6. Paul Collier, *Wars, Guns and Votes: Democracy in Dangerous Places* (New York: Harper Collins, 2009). One wonders how seriously this cavalier economist should be taken. On page thirty-nine he spells the name of South Africa's last president incorrectly, illustrating that for many economists, names don't really alter the nature of the data. As always, Alex de Waal's *Famine Crimes: Politics and the Disaster Relief Industry in Africa* (London: James Currey, 1997) provides an alternative argument that does not fall into a Mugabeist "anti-imperialist" trope.

7. In Zimbabwe of course this is not quite the case: as will be discussed, there is a plethora of other media for well-resourced social groups.

8. Roland Paris, *At War's End: Building Peace after Civil Conflicts* (Cambridge: Cambridge University Press, 2004) and Anna K. Jarstad and Timothy D. Sisk, eds., *From War to Democracy: Dilemmas of Peacebuilding* (Cambridge: Cambridge University Press, 2008). These indicate that the once *liberal-democracy-at-any-cost* academics on Africa are being replaced by those with disenchanted second thoughts: too much democracy too soon can exacerbate conflict rather than serve the cause of peace. Of course, when their GNUs were created Kenya and Zimbabwe were not quite at war, but their instances of institutional order may be seen as preemptive. Samuel Huntington's *Political Order in Changing Societies* (New Haven: Yale University Press, 1968) has returned by stealth. Less democracy is approved as long as benevolent foreigners are behind the interventions.

9. Interviews with anonymous sources close to the counters and watchers; see also Stephen Chan, "Zimbabwe's Tense Countdown," *New Statesman,* April 3, 2008; and "Exit Mugabe," *Prospect Magazine,* 145, April 2008; and R. W. Johnson, *South Africa's Brave New World: The Beloved Country since the End of Apartheid* (London: Allen Lane, 2009), 366.

10. Zimbabwe Election Support Network, "ZEC Announces Final House of Assembly Results," April 3, 2008. The MDC announced it had won 50.2 percent in the presidential election, while Mugabe gained 43.8 percent. Stephanie Nolen, "Mugabe Loses Control of Harare Legislature," *The Globe and Mail,* April 2, 2008.

11. David Moore, "Make Mugabe an Offer He can't refuse," *The Globe and Mail,* April 9, 2008. The last two chapters of Douglas Rogers, *The Last Resort: A Memoir of Zimbabwe* (Johannesburg and Cape Town: Jonathan Ball, 2009) cover the elections, with a Manicaland focus, as well as other reportage.

12. Shari Eppel, "'Gukurahundi' The Need for Truth and Reparation," in *Zimbabwe: Injustice and political reconciliation,* eds. Brian Raftopoulos and Tyrone Savage (Cape Town: Institute for Justice and Reconciliation, 2005).

13. Peta Thornycroft, "Zimbabwe: Ndira Body Found," *Association of Concerned African Scholars Bulletin: Special Issue on Zimbabwean Election* 79 (Winter 2008): 46–8.

14. See SALO, "A Decade of Diplomacy," in "Country Focus," 1–17. Alastair Sparks, "At Home and Abroad: It's Time Zuma Stood Up for Tsvangirai," *Business Day,* October 27, 2009, argues that by January 2009, Morgan Tsvangirai was reluctant to continue on the path to the inclusive government, but was led to believe that imminent South African president Jacob Zuma would be tougher on Mugabe, due in part to his assumed strong relationship with the South African Congress of Trade Unions (SOCATU) and the SA Communist Party, which during the Mbeki era expressed strong disapproval of the ZANU-PF. Zuma's inaction at a key SADC meeting in Kinshasa in mid-September

2009 suggests, though, that either South African diplomats were outmaneuvered by their elders, or simply did not care enough. See Japhet Ncube, "Kabila Rescues Mugabe," *City Press*, September 13, 2009, 10.

15. Geoffrey Nyarota, *Against the Grain: Memoirs of a Zimbabwean Newsman* (Cape Town: Zebra, 2006).

16. Stephanie Nolen, "Independent Radio a Lifeline for Zimbabwe's Opposition," *The Globe and Mail*, March 26, 2005.

17. Government of Zimbabwe, " Article XIX: Freedom of Expression and Communication," *Constitution of Zimbabwe Amendment No. 19*, Harare, 2008.

18. Amendment 19 could have added that independent radio stations and newspapers in Zimbabwe had been bombed in the early 2000s, but the document is notable for its decorum. See Peta Thornycroft, "Bomb Destroys Studio of Zimbabwe Independent Radio Station," *Voice of America*, August 29, 2002.

19. Government of Zimbabwe, *Amendment No. 19*.

20. Media Monitoring Project, *Weekly Media Update 2009–41*, Harare: October 12–18, 2009.

21. The Access to Information and Protection of Privacy Act (AIPPA), implemented March 15, 2002, was responsible for media restrictions in all spheres, through its controls on registration to media outlets and accreditation of journalists. The AIPPA was modified in early 2008 to ostensibly allow more media freedom in advance of the March elections, but remained essentially unchanged until June 2009, when the Media and Information Commission, which had been implementing the AIPPA, was ruled null and void. POSA, adopted on January 10, 2002—famous for ruling that any meeting of more than five people was "political" and therefore requiring police permission—is similarly restrictive and unchanged in spite of Amendment 19's Article X call for "free political activity throughout Zimbabwe within the ambit of the law in which all political parties are able to propagate their views and canvass for support, free of harassment and intimidation." More positively, by July 2009, the BBC and CNN were allowed to enter Zimbabwe. As for the constitutional drafting process, Amendment 19 charted a clear route with civil society organizations involved in the relevant subcommittee, replete with stakeholder conferences and a referendum to be called, all in less than eighteen months. By October 2009, public meetings had been broken up by war veterans mobilized by the ZANU-PF. Civil society organizations feared the *Kariba Constitution* of September 2007, drawn up by MDC and ZANU-PF politicians as a template, would end up becoming the real thing, depositing far too much power in the executive, and parliament was finding it difficult to raise money for the process. By April 2010 the donors had decided to press the process forward, possibly to hasten an election—setting a *per diem* rate of $US15, instead of the U$50 desired by the parliamentarians.

22. Bill Corcoran, "Zimbabwean Police Raid MDC House," *Irish Times*, October 23, 2009; and Violet Gonda, "Hot Seat: ZANU-PF Minister D. Mutasa and MDC's Gordon Moyo," *SW Radio Africa*, October 23, 2009.

23. Chris Chinaka, "Tsvangirai under Pressure to End Cabinet Boycott," *Swissinfo.ch*, October 30, 2009.

24. "UN Expert Denied Zimbabwe Entry," *BBC*, October 28, 2009.

25. "Zuma Appoints Zimbabwe Team," *Radiovop.com*, November 24, 2009, www.radiovop. com/index2.php?option=com_content&do_pdf=1&id=7498.

26. Bill Corcoron, "Zimbabwe Rivals Agree Some Details on Powersharing," *Irish Times*, March 20, 2010, http://www.irishtimes.com/newspaper/world/2010/0320/1224266708380 pf.html; "Zuma Breaks Zim Deadlock," *TimesLive*, March 21, 2010, http:// www.timeslive.co.za/africa/article365911.ece?service=print; and Gertrude Gumede,

"Zimbabwe's Reluctant Election Drama," *Zimbabwe Telegraph,* March 20, 2010, http://www.zimtelegraph.com/?p=6505, all accessed March 23, 2010.

27. Nelson Banya, "Zimbabwe Commission to Licence Private Newspapers," *Reuters,* March 19, 2010.

28. David Moore, "Now Onus is on SA to Deliver: Power-sharing Arrangement Makes Regional Sovereign Responsible for Building a Decent Dispensation," *Cape Times,* February 3, 2009, 10. On one source of South Africa's diplomacy vis-à-vis Zimbabwe, see David Moore, "A Decade of Disquieting Diplomacy: South Africa, Zimbabwe and the Ideology of the National Democratic Revolution, 1999–2009," *History Compass,* 8, no. 8 (2010): 752–767.

29. David Smith, "ANC's Julius Malema Lashes Out At 'Misbehaving' BBC Journalist," *The Guardian,* April 8, 2010.

30. Solidarity Peace Trust, "What Options for Zimbabwe?" Johannesburg, March 31. 2010., http://www.solidaritypeacetrust.org/download/report-files/what_options_for_Zimbabwe.pdf.

31. Readers are warned that this writer is not a media expert. They are advised to read Richard Saunders, *Zimbabwe: Politics, the Press and Hegemony* (London: Merlin, forthcoming) for a comprehensive analysis of the political economy of the Zimbabwean media from its Rhodesian days to 2008.

32. Tamuka Ngwenya, "Mahoso Bounces Back," *ZimDaily,* October 1, 2009.

33. "P.M dismisses Mahoso Comeback," *Media in Zimbabwe,* November 19, 2009, www.mediainzimbabwe.com/?p=2430.

34. Caesar Zvayi, "We Welcome Self-Regulation: Mahoso," *The Herald,* July 30, 2005.

35. "Mahoso Did Not Give Farmer 48-Hour Eviction Order," *The Zimbabwean,* December 5, 2009.

36. Information for the next two paragraphs is from: Tangai Chipangura, "Zim Journos Celebrate Media Freedom," *City Press,* December 22, 2009; "Appointments to Commissions Announced," *Zimbabwe Times,* December 22, 2009; Tichaona Sibanda, "Zanu PF Apologist Smuggled Back Onto Media Commission: Indications that Major Changes Have Been Made to the Original Lists Sent to Mugabe in August," *SW Radio Africa,* December 18, 2009; "Mtambanengwe Tipped to Head ZEC," *Zimbabwe Times,* December 18, 2009; Violet Gonda, "Journalists Take Journalist Union to Court," *SW Radio Africa,* December 17, 2009; "Takaona Threatens to Sue Mutasa," *The Zimbabwean,* December 9, 2009; Edwin Mlambo, "RBZ Schemes Structured to Loot State Coffers," *The Zimbabwe Telegraph,* April 21, 2009, www.gonogonow.com/?p=587; Caiphus Chimhete, "Fertilizer Saga: Heads Likely to Roll," *Zimbabwe Standard,* November 19, 2006, http://www.zimbabwesituation.com/nov19_2006.html; Lebo Nkatazo, "Gono's Adviser Linked to Wheat Bust," *Newzimbabwe.com,* February 15, 2006, www.newzimbabwe.com/pages/gono18.13737.html; Guthrie Munyuki, "Independent Journalists Have Been Excluded from ZUJ," *Journalism.co.za,* December 10, 2009; "ZUJ President Vies for Sixth Term of Office," *Zimbabwe Times,* March 25, 2009; Miriam Madziwa, "Zimbabwean Women Forced to Give Sexual Favors to Survive," *Pambazuka,* November 11, 2007, http://pambazuka.org/en/category/comment/44716; and "No Joy for Pregnant Women during Economic Crisis," *Genderlinks,* January 28, 2008, www.genderlinks.org.za/article.php?a_id=894.

37. See www.zoominfo.com/people/Nyathi_Nqobile_370248525.aspx.

38. Mutsvangwa was also a "graduate" of an ideological college, set up by a group of radicals in Zimbabwe's war of liberation, that was eliminated by Robert Mugabe in early 1977 as he removed all suspected challengers on his way to power. As such, he is more aware than most of how the ZANU- PF treats difference of opinion. See David Moore,

"Democracy, Violence and Identity in the Zimbabwean War of National Liberation: Reflections from the Realms of Dissent," *Canadian Journal of African Studies* 29, no. 3 (1995): 375–402.

39. Antonio Gramsci, *Selections from Prison Notebooks* (New York: International Publishers, 1971), 276.

40. "PM Dismisses Mahoso Comeback," *Media in Zimbabwe,* November 19, 2009, www.mediainzimbabwe.com/?p=2430.

41. Professor Moyo was once a liberal political scientist at the University of Zimbabwe. After scandal-ridden spells at the Ford Foundation and the University of the Witwatersrand, he was taken on in 1999 by the ZANU-PF as the media advisor for its constitutional reform campaign, followed by the post of election campaign director in the 2000 election (when he informed this writer in an interview that only "alienated urban intellectuals" did not support the ZANU-PF) and then information minister (during which time he penned "Nathaniel Manheru" columns in the Harare papers as well as "Mzala Joe's" in Bulawayo). He was expelled from ZANU-PF for being too close to a party faction threatening Robert Mugabe's choice as ZANU-PF vice president in late 2004. In October, 2009, while an independent MP, he rejoined the party. By April 2010 he had not gained a powerful position, however. More detail up to 2007 is found in David Moore, "'Intellectuals' Interpreting Zimbabwe's Primitive Accumulation: Progress to Market Civilisation?" *Safundi* 8, no. 2 (2007): 201, 203–205.

42. Africa Governance Monitoring and Advocacy Project, *Zimbabwe: Public Broadcasting in Africa Series* (Johannesburg: Open Society Institute Network, 2009), 91–2.

43. Caesar Zvayi, "We Welcome Self-Regulation: Mahoso," Interview with Mahoso, *The Herald,* July 30, 2005.

44. Ibid.

45. Ibid.

46. Tafataona P. Mahoso, "Africa Focus: Material Bases for Anglo-Saxon Demonisation of the African," *Sunday Mail*, January 3, 2010.

47. Ibid.

48. Archives containing Mahoso's letters, poetry, curricular, and other academic material can be found in the collection of a murdered radical American woman who cohabited with Mahoso whilst he was in the United States, at the Iowa Women's Archives at the University of Iowa in Iowa City: Ruth Laughlin (1954–1986) Papers, »1956–1997, http://sdrc.lib.uiowa.edu/iwa/findingaids/html/LaughlinRuth.htm.

49. David Moore, "Zimbabwe: Twists on the Tale of Primitive Accumulation," in *Globalizing Africa,* ed. Malinda Smith (Trenton: Africa World Press, 2003), 247–69.

50. Apparently Wafawarova has been under investigation for deportation by Australian immigration authorities since 2007. See Raymond Mhaka, "Pressure Mounts for Australia to Deport Reason Wafawarova," *Zimbabwemetro.com,* September 4, 2008; and Muckraker, "Why is it that All the Losers are the Loudest?," *Zimbabwe Independent,* November 26, 2009.

51. Reason Wafawarova, "Unity is the Best Enemy Repellent," *Zikker: International News Forum,* online at http://zikkir.com/content/22727, accessed January 4, 2009.

52. Ibid.

53. Ibid.

54. Mabasa Sasa, "Zimbabwe: Are Fresh Elections Inevitable?" *New African,* December 2009, 44–5.

55. Reason Wafawarova, "Zimbabwe: Imperialism—Chief Enemy of Zim's Revolution," *Herald*, December 24, 2009.

56. Ibid.

57. Wafawarova, "Unity is the Best Enemy Repellent."

58. James Kilgore, *We Are All Zimbabweans Now* (Cape Town: Umuzi, 2009) is a novel in part attempting to explain why the left was enchanted with Mugabe for some time—and how disenchantment evolved.

59. For a fascinating memoir taking in these days, by a man intimately involved in the African nationalist movements in the Rhodesias and Nyasaland, see Peter Mackay, *We Have Tomorrow: Stirrings in Africa 1959–1967* (Wilby Hall: Michael Russell, 2008).

60. *African Daily News Bulletin*, September 18, 1956—this editorial was in response to a bus boycott organized by Harare's City Youth League. It is cited in David Moore, "The Contradictory Construction of Hegemony in Zimbabwe: Politics, Ideology and Class in the Formation of a New African State" PhD, York University, Toronto, 1990. The author who coined the term "eggheads" was Nathan Shamuyarira, writing "Revolt of the Intellectuals: Eggheads Join the NDP," in the *Central African Examiner*, 4, no. 2 (1960): 10–11. He was noting the long-awaited engagement of intellectuals such as Herbert Chitepo with the nationalist movement. However, Shamuyarira was holding his own political guns until later. As Ian Hancock's *White Liberals, Moderates and Radicals in Rhodesia: 1953–1958* (London: Croom Helm, 1984), 27 notes, Shamuyarira "lasted longer in the multi-racial societies than many who became nationalists but... overcame this slow start and a later political indiscretion to take an important ministry under Robert Mugabe." The indiscretion was to abandon the ZANU in 1971 to form a new party, the Front for the Liberation of Zimbabwe (FROLIZI)—along with, ironically, George Nyandoro and James Chikerema, two of the men he claimed to despise as "radicals" in 1956. Shamuyarira joined Mugabe's faction during the Geneva conference in 1976, at which Robert Mugabe pulled together various strands of Zimbabwe's intellectuals to form the basis of the ZANU-PF today, and has remained loyal to him ever since.

61. See the results of Timothy Scarnecchia's careful archival sleuthing in his *The Urban Roots of Democracy and Political Violence in Zimbabwe: Harare and Highfield, 1940–1964* (Rochester: University of Rochester Press, 2008), 135–8 and 128–33, wherein it is clear that people such as Herbert Chitepo and Ndabaningi Sithole were requesting assistance from Americans for their planned split from Joshua Nkomo's Zimbabwe African People Union (ZAPU), and that if they did not have direct support, they received help from "private American sources of funds" steered in their direction by officials such as the deputy assistant secretary for Africa of the State Department J. Wayne Fredericks (p. 128). See David Moore, "ZANU-PF and the Ghosts of Foreign Funding," *Review of African Political Economy* 103 (2005): 156–62; and "Today's 'Imperialists' were Those Who Nurtured Mugabe," *Sunday Independent*, January 20, 2008, for evidence of support for Mugabe from elements of the British state.

62. On the mid-1970s, see, in particular, Luise White, *The Assassination of Herbert Chitepo: Text and Politics in Zimbabwe* (Harare and Bloomington: Weaver and Indiana University Press, 2002); on Zipa, see David Moore, "Democracy, Violence and Identity in the Zimbabwean War of National Liberation: Reflections from the Realms of Dissent," *Canadian Journal of African Studies* 29, no. 3 (1995): 375–402; and "The Zimbabwe People's Army: Strategic Innovation or More of the Same?" in *Soldiers and the Zimbabwean Liberation War*, eds. Ngwabi Bhebe and Terence Ranger (London: James Currey, 1995), 73–86. It is not yet clear how involved the West was in squashing Zipa, but Henry Kissinger's September 27, 1976, letter to British secretary of state Anthony Crosland, who was trying to make a conference at Geneva ease the white minority out of power, made it clear that "radical Africans" (Zipa) were feared because if their demands were met, the *Russians* would "meddle," thus "chaos" would ensue. Kissinger warned: "this whole enterprise after all only makes sense as a firebreak to African

radicalism and Soviet intervention." Crosland Papers, London School of Economics and Political Science Library, HK-AC 21/10/76.

63. "Comrade Mugabe Lays the Line at Historic Chimoio Central Committee Meeting," *Zimbabwe News*, 5–6 (July–December 1977), p. 13.

64. Relatedly, because of Zimbabwe's strategic importance in Cold War struggles after 1980—the Zimbabwean regime was notably cool toward the supposedly Soviet-aligned ANC—the Western media, and certainly its states, were reluctant to take much interest in the ZANU-PF's murderous campaign in Matabeleland. The ANC's closeness to the ZAPU meant that pressure on one was pressure on the other. To be sure, complications entered the scene when some South Africans saw it fit to assist the "Super-ZAPU," or "dissident" efforts.

65. "The Unnecessary Embarrassment," *Moto,* November/December 1991, 4–5; and Donatus Bonde, "Student Politics—Sense and Nonsense," *Moto,* December/November 1991, 5–6.

66. On South Africa's disquieting diplomacy, in addition to SALO, "Country Focus: South Africa's Relations," see R. W. Johnson, *South Africa's Brave New World: The Beloved Country Since the End of Apartheid* (London: Allen Lane, 2009), 340–60, for a Western, or perhaps cynical liberal, view of South Africa's foreign policy vis-à-vis Zimbabwe. A more sympathetic view is Mark Gevisser, *Thabo Mbeki: The Dream Deferred* (Johannesburg: Jonathan Ball, 2007), 431–46.

67. "Crisis? What Crisis? Mbeki Drops In for Harare Handshake," *Sunday Argus,* April 13, 2008.

68. "Quo Vadis, Zimbabwe?" *The Star,* May 5, 2008, 12.

69. Ibid.

70. For Thabo Mbeki's writing on Zimbabwe, see his, "The Mbeki-Mugabe Papers: A Discussion Document," *New Agenda,* 2nd Quarter (2008), 56–75; and his "Mr. Morgan Tsvangirai," letter dated November 22, 2008, www.talkzimbabwe.com/news/117/ARTICLE/3818/2008-11-28.html.

71 As Zuma was approaching power, there was much hope in Zimbabwe and South Africa that he would take a tougher stance on Robert Mugabe. By October 2009, however, it appeared that such anticipation was misplaced. See Alastair Sparks, "At Home and Abroad: It's Time Zuma Stood Up for Tsvangirai," *Business Day,* October 27, 2009.

72. Copies can be found on *The Zimbabwe Situation* website or *Amandla,* www.amandla-publishers.co.za. Eddy Maloka has stated that the authors intended to keep the document within the ANC as confidential.

73. This section probably refers to Jacob Zuma's visit to Gordon Brown, which Eddy Maloka said inspired the writing of this piece.

74. Cunningham Ngcukana, "Mbeki is On the Right Track," *City Press,* May 11, 2008. Zimbabwe watchers in South Africa claim that Ngcukana "writes at Mbeki's bidding."

75. Mohau Pheko, "The West is Conspiring to Unseat that Valiant Warrior, Mugabe," *Sunday Times,* May 11, 2008.

76. In the 1970s, Canadian University Service Overseas (CUSO) volunteers were very close to the Zimbabwean African People's Union. Indeed, a CUSO teacher married Edward Ndlovu, the ZAPU head of external affairs, who much later was imprisoned in Zimbabwe on suspicion of plotting a coup by an increasingly paranoid ZANU-PF. Mary Ndlovu remains in Bulawayo, still a stalwart in the struggle for human rights.

77. Tangai Chipangura, "Zim Journos Celebrate Media Freedom," *City Press,* December 22, 2009.

78. Antonio Gramsci, *Prison Notebooks,* ed. and trans. Joseph Buttigieg (New York: Columbia University Press, 1996).

79. Cited in Media Monitoring Project Zimbabwe, "Power of Propaganda," August 16–22, 2004.

80. Annie Chikwana, Tulani Sithole, and Michael Bratton, "The Power of Propaganda: Public Opinion in Zimbabwe, 2004," Afrobarometer Working Paper no. 42, Institute for Democratic Alternatives, Centre for Democratic Development, Michigan State University, August 2004. This report is also published as Michael Bratton, Annie Chikwana, and Tulani Sithole, "Propaganda and Public Opinion in Zimbabwe," *Journal of Contemporary African Studies* 23, no. 1 (2005): 77–108. For criticism, see David Moore, "A Reply to 'The Power of Propaganda: Public Opinion in Zimbabwe 2004,'" *Journal of Contemporary African Studies* 23, no. 1 (2005): 109–19.

81. Nathaniel Manheru, "Afrobarometer: Stubborn Facts versus Preferences," *Saturday Herald*, August 21, 2004, 8.

82. John Hoffman, *The Gramscian Challenge: Coercion and Consent in Marxist Political Theory* (Oxford: Basil Blackwell, 1984), remains the best effort to interrogate Gramsci on the relation between consent and the coercive imperatives of the market *and* the state.

83. Gramsci, *Prison Notebooks*, 238, 242–3.

84. Ibid., 182; and Joseph Femia, "Gramsci, Machiavelli and International Relations," *Political Quarterly* 76, no. 3 (2005): 343, adds, quoting the same page, hegemony "occurs not only within a nation, between the various forces of which the nation is composed, but in the international and world-wide field, between complexes of national and continental civilisations." Femia is critical of the overly enthusiastic application of Gramsci to the field of international political economy, noting that these passages are "isolated." However, he somehow manages to equate the neo-Gramscians with Kantian advocates of easily applied universal notions of international human rights, which is pushing things a bit too far.

85. Bjorn Beckman, "The Liberation of Civil Society: Neo-Liberal Ideology and Political Theory," *Review of African Political Economy*, no. 58 (1993).

86. Gramsci, *Prison Notebooks*, 367–8.

87. R. W. Johnson, *South Africa's Brave New World: The Beloved Country Since the End of Apartheid* (London: Allen Lane, 2009), 305–12, attempts to use Gramsci's ideas to discuss the ANC's attempts to create hegemony in South Africa. The ANC and Johnson seem to share the mistaken belief that a party anchored in little but the state can gain hegemony. Thus, both are bound to fall on the reality of a "Bonapartist" situation of stalemated class relations, wherein, absent of full hegemony, Gramsci's morbid symptoms are most likely to permeate society. If Zimbabwe's fate is thus a chronicle of a death foretold, what is South Africa's?

88. David Moore, "The Second Age of the Third World: From Primitive Accumulation to Public Goods?" *Third World Quarterly* 25, no. 1 (2004): 87–109.

89. David Moore, "Zimbabwe: Failing Better?" *Association of Concerned African Scholars Bulletin: Special Issue on Zimbabwe II* 80 (Winter 2008): 59–64.

Part II

Economic Recovery Strategies for Sustainable Development

Chapter 5

A Macroeconomic Policy Framework for Economic Stabilization in Zimbabwe

John Robertson

Zimbabwe is now a struggling economy that can no longer produce enough food for its population. In 2008, it also suffered the highest inflation in the world, which peaked at about seven sextillion percent[1]; the most rapidly falling currency; the world's worst credit rating; and the most serious skills exodus, with between three million and four million people leaving the country (table 5.1).

Zimbabwe's Gross Domestic Product (GDP) is estimated to have fallen by 57 percent to approximately US$3 billion. The country also achieved a budget deficit estimated to be in excess of 200 percent of GDP; the most rapidly falling life expectancy, currently about thirty-seven years for men and thirty-four for women[2]; the steepest fall in foreign earnings, down from US$3.6 billion in 1995 to US$1.3 billion in 2008; and the most rapidly falling standard of living in the world.

Nearly all of these difficulties are the direct outcome of the choices made by the ruling political regime since the end of 1997, but they were not the intended results. The government's stated intention was to transfer wealth to black Zimbabweans, although a considerable amount of evidence shows that the political hierarchy ensured that their own names headed the redistribution list. However, the forced changes of ownership of economic resources have not achieved the expected transfer of wealth.

In the agricultural sector, it is certainly true that white Zimbabweans' hold on economic resources has been broken. However, the transfer of these resources to black Zimbabweans has not led to prosperity, but instead to unemployment, deprivation, malnutrition, and poverty. Two issues are of immediate and growing concern: the government's continuing defense of the policy decisions that led directly to these

Table 5.1   Zimbabwe's exchange rate changes in 2008

$Z per $US	January 2008	December 2008	Percentage Change
Official market	322,500	48,941,670,000,000,000	15,175,711,627,807
Black market	10,000,000,000	350,000,000,000,000,000,000, 000,000	3,500,000,000,000,000,000

Note: The ten zeroes dropped from the currency notes on August 1, 2008, are still shown in these figures. At the end of February 2009 another twelve zeroes were dropped. As three zeroes had been taken off on August 1, 2006, this brought the total to twenty-five.

problems and the repercussions of these actions, which are generating increasingly widespread dissatisfaction.

Overwhelming evidence now supports the view that the policy choices affecting commercial agriculture were made on the basis of mistaken beliefs about the nature of this sector. To Zimbabwe's authorities, the large-scale commercial farms appeared to be manifestations of colonialism simply because in precolonial Zimbabwe there was no such thing and the concept of individual freehold title to land did not exist.

No attempt will be made here to justify the colonial process; this would pose the same problems as would any attempt to justify the colonization of the Americas. However, the colonization of Africa's interior began after medical breakthroughs permitted colonizers to survive a range of tropical diseases, and profound technological and geopolitical changes created previously undreamed of instability in Europe. The capacities of the industrializing nations were so far beyond those of indigenous populations that the question of whether or not their territory should be colonized never arose. The only concern of the competing countries was to claim the area ahead of their rivals.

Zimbabwe's pioneer settlers were allocated tracts of land by the first colonial administrator, the British South Africa Company, but the land acquisition process was formalized into a property market for the settlers who followed. They had to buy their land, but the collateral value of their land meant that buyers could borrow against the value of the title deeds to pay for it, and could also borrow more to carry out their farming activities. The revenues from these sales went toward building roads and bridges to assist the farmers.

With this access to capital, farmers were able to adopt and adapt to rapidly developing technologies and acquire the skills needed to farm successfully in very uncertain tropical conditions. They also managed to preserve their soil and to improve upon good results. During Rhodesia's ninety-year existence, these advantages helped to create a reasonably prosperous commercial farming community, but after independence, the Zimbabwean government chose to resent both its success and its economic leverage. To Zimbabwe's politicians, it seemed right and proper that in order to break the influence of the colonial past, the countryside should be purged of large-scale commercial farms and all of the institutional structures that supported them. In effect, the latter were the development-supporting structures that were themselves upheld by freehold property rights.

After a messy start to the land reform program, the white farmers targeted for dispossession successfully petitioned the courts with several class-action lawsuits that sought acknowledgment that the Constitution of Zimbabwe protected their property rights. By mid-1998, the government was forced to admit that it did not have the legal power to dispossess landowners of their lands.

As a result, the government set about changing the constitution in ways that permitted it to remove farmland from the market. The process took several years and ended with an all-encompassing amendment in 2005. Constitutional Amendment No. 17 claimed that all farmers who had received an acquisition order at any time through the previous eight years were now forced to accept that their land was the property of the state (see figure 5.1). Effectively, this meant that commercial farmland ownership rights were abolished and that the nationalization of commercial farms was completed. Large-scale commercial farms could then be "legally" confiscated and broken up, and small allotments typical of precolonial agriculture would be given to resettlement farmers.

These changes were supposed to fully restore precolonial conditions under which land was collectively owned and allocated. Additionally, land could not be sold, and so it effectively remained under the ownership and control of the political authorities. Under these basically feudal conditions, the authorities laid claim to powers that could not be interfered with by those claiming property rights, because no such rights existed.

The government's error of judgment arose from its unwillingness to consider how conditions had evolved from precolonial times. In trying to revert to traditional governance structures, they were attempting to set aside history and ignore the profound transformations experienced in the past century, not just by the economy of Zimbabwe, but by economies throughout the world.

In order to offer suggestions on how Zimbabwe might now pick up the pieces and rebuild its economy, it is important to focus on issues that make abundantly clear the differences between preindustrial and industrializing economies. The key issue in any discussion on this subject is investment. The fact that is clearest of all is that investment in economic enterprise of every possible kind is made very much more likely and more successful with property ownership rights.

Where they existed, these rights made a major and vital contribution toward Zimbabwe's economic transformation, even if success was patchy and the successes of the few were resented by the much larger numbers who, for whatever reason, did not adopt the more advanced methods. What separated these groups can be described in many different ways, but the fundamental difference was whether the individuals in these groups had property rights.

For those who had such rights, bank loans were more readily available, and these individuals could more easily tap into the rapidly changing world technologies since they could fund their ambitions. Small in number as they were in relation to the rest of the population, their investments made Zimbabwe the second most industrialized economy in sub-Saharan Africa. Table 5.2, taken from *Africa at a Glance* and published by the Africa Institute of South Africa (1992) and *The Economist*, shows Africa's top fifteen countries in 1989. While Zimbabwe may only have had

> The important paragraphs in this Act read as follows:
>
> (a) all agricultural land-
>
> (i) that was identified on or before the 8th July, 2005, in the *Gazette* or *Gazette Extraordinary* under the proviso to section 5(1) of the Land Acquisition Act [*Chapter 20:10*] and which is itemised in Schedule 7, being agricultural land required for resettlement purposes; or
>
> (ii) that is identified after the 8th July, 2005, but before the appointed day, in the *Gazette* or *Gazette Extraordinary* under the proviso to section 5(1) of the Land Acquisition Act [*Chapter 20:10*], being agricultural land required for resettlement purposes; or
>
> (iii) that is identified in terms of this section by the acquiring authority after the appointed day in the *Gazette* or *Gazette Extraordinary* for whatever purpose, including, but not limiting to –
>
> A. settlement for agricultural or other purposes; or
>
> B. the purposes of land organization, forestry, environmental conservation or the utilization of wild life or other natural resources; or
>
> C. the relocation of persons dispossessed in consequence of the utilization of land for a purpose referred to in subparagraph A or B;
>
> is acquired by and vested in the State with full title therein with effect from the appointed day or, in the case of land referred to in subparagraph (iii), with effect from the thirteenth day after the date it is identified in the manner specified in that paragraph; and
>
> (b) no compensation shall be payable for land referred to in paragraph (a) except for any improvements effected on such land before it was acquired.
>
> (3) The provisions of any law referred to in section 16 (1) regulating the compulsory acquisition of land that is in force on the appointed day, and the provisions of section 18 (9), shall not apply in relation to land referred to in subsection (2)(a) except for the purpose of determining any question related to the payment of compensation referred to in subsection (2) (b), that is to say, a person having any right or interest in the land -
>
> (a) shall not apply to a court to challenge the acquisition of the land by the State, and no court shall entertain any such challenge;

Figure 5.1   Constitution of Zimbabwe Amendment (No. 17) Act, 2005.

the seventh highest GDP, the country had the highest manufacturing level as a percentage of GDP.

What was needed in Zimbabwe was adoption of this successful recipe by the entire population; instead, the government chose to focus on its resentments of past imbalances and injustices. Evidence of this was all too easily assembled, but the government had no intention of remedying the root causes of the apparent disparities, which included the more deeply seated structural differences. These can be most easily described as cultural or traditional relationships, such as the chief's authority to allocate scarce resources. The government assumed the powers of the paramount

Table 5.2   Africa's top fifteen countries, 1989

	Total GDP in $US	Manufacturing as percent of GDP	Manufacturing value in $US
South Africa	88,870	24	21,329
Zimbabwe	5,250	25	1,313
Cote d'Ivoire	7,170	17	1,219
Zambia	4,700	24	1,218
Nigeria	28,920	4	1,099
DRC	9,610	10	961
Senegal	4660	20	932
Kenya	7,130	12	856
Ghana	5,260	10	526
Mauritius	1,740	24	418
Congo	2,270	9	204
Malawi	1,410	11	155
Tanzania	2,540	4	102
Botswana	2,500	4	100
Namibia	1,650	5	83

Source: Africa at a Glance.

chief and wielded them through patronage. But to give effect to these powers, it needed to create access to assets with which it could reward loyalty and support. For the government, the acquisition of these assets was made easy by empowering themselves to simply take from the rich. The Zimbabwean government rejected offers of advice on how it might, instead, elevate the poor by introducing them to and installing them into the systems that had delivered proven results.

In trying to understand why they spurned these offers, the evidence shows clearly that the government's core objective was to strengthen its authority. Because it viewed the economically strong business sector as a competitor rather than a partner, the government felt the need to restrict businesses. Furthest of all from their thoughts was any plan to actually empower the rest of the population.

When commercial farmers tried to use their economic strength and constitutional rights to challenge government plans, this was viewed as a contest that the government could not afford to lose. However, in the ensuing battle, the government's decision to brush aside all the major institutional structures that gave this sector its economic strength caused just as much damage, since commercial agriculture had become the most important pillar supporting the entire economy.

The architects of this chaos focused exclusively on the relatively small number of farmers they displaced. Wider social issues were dismissed as irrelevant, even though the destruction of about four thousand large-scale farming businesses impacted directly upon approximately four hundred thousand permanent or seasonal employees, many more suppliers and customers, and indirectly upon every other member of Zimbabwe's population.

In essence:

- In the process of reclaiming land, about forty-five hundred farming companies were nationalized and dismantled, causing the direct loss of three hundred and fifty thousand full-time farm jobs and sharply cutting production of export crops, as well as crops for local consumption.
- The loss of property also meant the loss of accommodation, and many elementary schools, clinics, and high schools, as well as incomes that supported the workers' families—a total of several million people.
- Almost all of these people became destitute, and assessments suggest that up to 30 percent of this population subsequently died of hunger and exposure.
- Inexperienced small-scale and peasant farmers soon made up the majority of the farming sector.
- Since Zimbabwe's agricultural land lost its collateral value, the new farmers could not use their holdings as security for bank loans.
- The government was forced to support the new small-scale farmers with massive subsidies, which had not previously been needed by the former large-scale farmers.
- As the subsidies were beyond Zimbabwe's financial means, the payments served to contribute to the very high rates of inflation that eventually reached world record levels.
- The loss of foreign earnings from the export of crops and other products drastically reduced the country's ability to import essential goods.
- The need to import food (that Zimbabwe had in the past exported) further reduced the foreign currency available for other industrial and commercial imports.
- The closure of large-scale farms severely damaged the viability of thousands of other companies that depended on them.
- In the hands of less experienced farmers, the land and farm assets captured had only a fraction of the value and earning capacity that they had in the hands of the dispossessed, highly skilled farmers.
- The rapidly deteriorating services infrastructure and frequent fuel shortages generated severely critical press reports that caused, and then accelerated, the decline of Zimbabwe's tourist industry;
- The state-sponsored attack on property rights arrested productive investment, job creation, and export growth, which consequently prevented access to international credit and project finance.
- Far from being the success claimed by the government, the land reform program was an unmitigated disaster.

The authorities did not recognize that the commercial farming sector had become much more than a collection of farms; by independence in 1980, these farms represented the primary generator of wealth and the principal assets of large and successful companies, with these formal businesses making up Zimbabwe's most important industry.

This industry was the envy of Africa and it led the way in many other areas of economic activity and investment. In demolishing it, the government also destroyed the country's most important contributor to the viability of other sectors. In terms of GDP per person per year, the International Monetary Fund (IMF) statistics show that Zimbabwe's economy has shrunk so much that its GDP per capita has now been overtaken by Mozambique, Tanzania, and Zambia, all of which had economies that were smaller than Zimbabwe's ten years ago.[3]

When the Zimbabwe government started its land reform program in 1997, the linkages between commercial agriculture and the manufacturing, mining, commercial, transport, construction, tourism, and banking sectors were not appreciated or even recognized. Neither were the linkages between commercial agriculture and employment, tax revenues, investment and international credit, export revenues, and the country's ability to pay for essential imports acknowledged.

Each of these areas of activity has suffered considerable damage since the launch of the land reform program. Figure 5.2 illustrates the effects felt by the manufacturing sector, and statistics on activity levels in most other economic sectors show similar trends.

Commercial agriculture's former successes also supported scientific research in a wide range of areas, including hybridization and hybrid seed production, tsetse control, livestock disease control, dam-building techniques, and irrigation, all of which further improved the industry's prospects. Advancements led to more dependable harvests, more productive livestock, increased food security, and export surpluses. These surpluses were derived from production volumes well in excess of Zimbabwe's

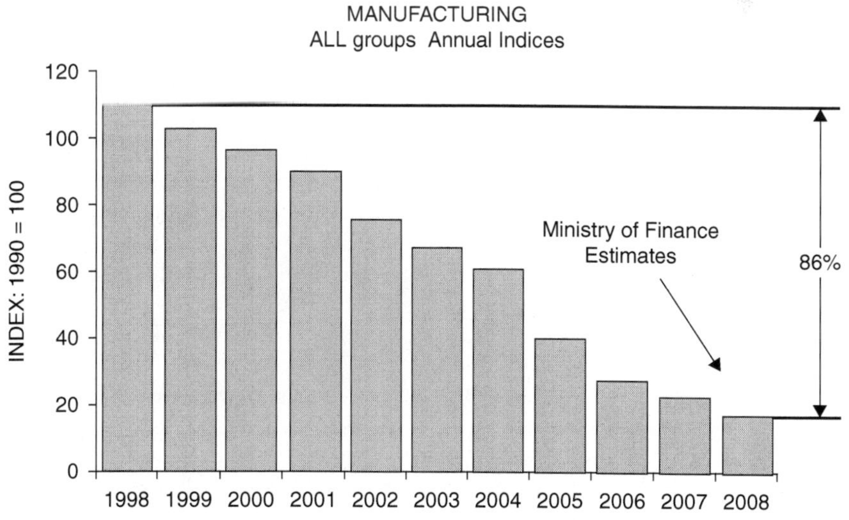

Figure 5.2 Manufacturing: annual indices of all groups.

needs, especially for sugar, tea, coffee, soya, beef, poultry, citrus, deciduous fruit, fresh vegetables, flowers, and cotton, with tobacco attaining by far the largest surplus. On many occasions, Zimbabwe was also able to export maize, milk, and stock feed.

At the same time, the large-scale farming industry's successes reinforced commercial activity in the smaller towns across the country and supported agricultural training institutions, as well as schools and clinics, for hundreds of thousands of farm workers and their families. Zimbabwe's tobacco training facilities were considered the best outside the United States, while schools built by farmers had enrolments of junior school pupils numbering more than one million. Almost every commercial farmer offered primary health care facilities, and the community as a unit itself was the country's foremost supporter of acquired immunodeficiency syndrome (AIDS) awareness education.

Unfortunately, every one of these facilities has been badly affected by the government's policy changes. Most of the schools built on commercial farms have been closed, with some even demolished by people scavenging for building materials. Almost all of the clinics have ceased functioning, and the future of the tobacco training school is threatened by the small number of enrolments.

Because of the importance of commercial agriculture, this accelerating deterioration soon began to affect tax revenues so badly that the delivery of services by the public sector, as well as parastatal and municipal departments, soon began to falter. Road maintenance has been so inadequate on the national, as well as urban, road networks that the road surfaces have disintegrated in many areas. Water supplies are also inadequate in the major cities due to lack of maintenance, for example, in Harare, many of the suburbs have not received municipal water for more than a year. With falling standards affecting electricity supplies, water, rail, road, and air transport, telecommunications, education, health, and social services, damage has been caused to the quality of every facet of life in Zimbabwe.

Each of these declining output volumes has had its own separate and serious impact on employment, export volumes, import substitution, tourist inflows, and the abilities of other service sectors, such as the petroleum fuel sector, to function efficiently.

The fuel sector was targeted for political reasons, with the government claiming that the multinational "fuel majors," including Caltex, Shell, Total, BP, Mobil, and Engen, constituted a threat because they could hold the country to ransom. The decision was made to offer fuel import licenses to indigenous Zimbabweans, and more than a hundred licenses were issued. Low fuel import volumes were already a problem because of foreign exchange shortages, but supplies suffered further shrinkage as the large number of new players struggled to acquire or create service station capacity. Many failed, and some years passed before the survivors of the challenges could function with any degree of efficiency.

Almost all of those who succeeded owed their success to their early adoption of a foreign currency-based coupon system, which required buyers to pay for coupons in advance. With U.S. dollars accompanying their orders, the dealers were able to obtain supplies, which were mostly delivered by road tankers. These procedures, mostly involving small traders, seldom permitted the use of the more efficient delivery of fuel via the pipeline from Beira to Mutare.

As with the development of manufacturing and mining, the growth and success of large-scale commercial farming could not have happened in Zimbabwe without the enormously important advances in science and technology that were taking place in the world's developed countries during the period from 1890 to 1980. By adopting and adapting to the rapidly changing techniques that were made possible by the development of agricultural machines, Zimbabwe's commercial farmers started off on a track that would inevitably take them deeper into the need for capital-intensive methods, and, therefore, into the need for training in the use of these technologies and for the money to pay for them. Because the collateral value of their title deeds gave commercial farmers security of tenure and access to finance, they could make the most of Western developments, and their successes quickly set them apart from other African nations.

While these developments did coincide with the colonial period, they were driven by far-reaching advances that were completely independent of the politically driven scramble for Africa. Colonialism had nothing to do with the fact that new ideas were eagerly accepted, or that these ideas helped farmers to achieve levels of efficiency never previously dreamed of in Africa.

When this land was confiscated from commercial farmers and allocated for free to resettlement farmers, these new farmers moved into an extremely limiting business environment. Without title deeds to their land, they had neither the inclination to make the commitments to succeed, the means to purchase the equipment, nor even the ability to pay regular wages to staff in the months prior to receipt of payments for crops.

However, in Zimbabwe, as elsewhere, the costs involved made the rates of assimilation of new ideas very uneven across different social groups. The Zimbabweans who were best positioned to benefit quickly from the innovations were those who had the confidence to spend the time needed to learn how each new technique, each scientific innovation, and each new machine might be applied to their needs. Inevitably, the farmers possessing both this requisite confidence and access to the money needed were the farmers who made the most progress. They were also the farmers who had title to land.

With the help of bank financing that was available because of their property rights, these farmers could take advantage of the opportunities offered by new ideas. They were supported by academics, researchers, engineers, bankers, and other businesses, all of whom were keen to build active working arrangements to serve the markets opened up by new discoveries. These farmers, with the support of the aforementioned group, often found themselves leading the way in field trials and research. These soon made the commercial farmers' direct investments some of the most powerful of the economy's driving forces.

An example of this is the transformation of the formerly dry, tsetse fly-infested southeast lowveld area of Zimbabwe into an extensive and highly productive sugar-producing area. A complex infrastructure of dams, weirs, and canals permitted the growers to irrigate thousands of hectares and to ensure that water could be moved from any storage dam to any area that needed it.

The creation of water storage dams was one of the more important forms of investment in other areas as well, given Zimbabwe's highly uncertain rainfall. Building these dams involved civil engineering design teams, thus providing major contracts to civil engineering companies and suppliers of earthmoving equipment. Funding for these projects came from longer-term loans, made on the strength of claims that high-yielding crops would be delivered no matter how erratic the weather patterns. Many of the techniques involved in earth-wall dam construction that are now in use around the world were developed in Zimbabwe.

In the tobacco sector, Zimbabwe made its mark with the production of flu-cured Virginia tobacco, and research by individual farmers led to the development of more cost-effective tobacco-curing procedures. These made possible the efficient regulation and sequencing of changes to temperature and humidity, and the delivery of quality second only to the United States. Many of these ideas were successfully patented and are now in use in many other countries.

Commercial farmers in Zimbabwe were also responsible for the recovery of very large herds of antelope and other animals, a field of investment that led to the recognition of Zimbabwe's wildlife conservancies as some of the best in the world. Many of the farmers built facilities to cater to the tourist trade, offering camera safaris and adventure-trail holidays to hundreds of thousands of visitors. Techniques were developed for the capture and relocation of animals, such as elephants, giraffes, and rhinos, to better-protected areas. Before the land reform program, Zimbabwe was developing into one of the world's most attractive eco-tourist destinations. With the subsequent breakup of those farms and the allocation of plots to thousands of resettlement farmers who had neither the skill nor the funds to grow food crops or to preserve the wildlife, most of the animals were slaughtered. Estimates place the loss at about 83 percent of the herds that had been rebuilt by 1997.[4]

Prior to the land reform disaster, intricately balanced business successes were being built upon earlier successes, and these further strengthened the farming enterprises and consequently the whole economy. These successes also deepened the dependability of, and interdependence between, the economic sectors; between private sector and government institutions; and between regional and overseas markets.

Since the entirety of this farming-based development helped to promote growth in every other sector, it also supported and even aided Zimbabwe's vigorous population growth. From 1890 to 1990, while the world population increased by 3.6 times and the population of Africa as a whole increased by 5.7 times, Zimbabwe's national census statistics show that the country's indigenous population expanded twenty-fold, from five hundred thousand to ten million, during this period. This increase made Zimbabwe's growing prosperity ever more dependent on the continued success of the business sector, including commercial farming.

Ideally, communal land farmers should have just as readily taken up all the new ideas of industrialized agriculture. However, the new methods demanded not only access to considerable sums of money, but a very sizeable personal commitment as well. These characteristics could be found in, and justified by, only those farmers who had land tenure security, essentially meaning that only those with property rights were capable of taking up or initiating new ideas.

Without the benefit of these property rights, the communal farmers were inevitably left behind while the successful commercial farmers saw their enterprises go through a significant growth phase. Communal farmers actually faced severe disincentives: for example, in a farmer's claim for a piece of land, he or she might have been able to win recognition from the local chief, but if their farming efforts were unusually successful, an envious but more important neighbor would have no difficulty persuading the chief to reallocate that plot to him and accommodate the displaced farmer somewhere else. With no security of tenure, communal farmers wishing to be left alone have had to strive not for success, but for mediocrity. Currently, decades after independence, communal farmers are still being denied the individual property ownership rights they need to protect themselves from being penalized for succeeding.

At the core of the problem has been the handicap of traditional constraints. Science, technology, engineering, banking, and legally supported contractual arrangements have long since rendered traditional land management structures obsolete, yet very few efforts have been made to accelerate the adoption of the clearly more successful modern systems. However, as politicians were determined to prevent the dilution of their authority by preventing the growth of economic power among the masses, they found no motivating reason to promote modern methods. Undeniably more successful modern methods were needed. Well before the 1990s, Zimbabwe's much larger population, and therefore more extensive requirements, meant that the country needed more efficient and productive farms. It no longer had the option to revert to the farming practices of precolonial times.

Unfortunately, all of the intricately balanced linkages and business relationships that had helped to deliver success and food security were damaged or broken by the land reform program. Now that the big farming businesses had been closed and all the big farms broken up, the accumulated skills and experiences of farmers were displaced, the commercial services infrastructure dislocated and incapacitated, the vast body of knowledge acquired over many years driven into forced retirement or exile, and the vitally important corporate memory lost.

Estimates of the number of farmers that left the country vary, but most suggest that more than half of the forty-five hundred who were dispossessed have had to relocate to other countries.[5] Others were able to move into new business ventures or develop activities that were formerly sidelined. More than a thousand of the farmers are thought still to be resident in Zimbabwe. Every one of these farmers is still needed. Now, in any efforts that are made to rebuild this sector, the government and international bodies wishing to assist the country must face up to—and change—the fact that the country was forced to adopt systems that do not meet the requirements of a larger, better educated, and much more demanding population, and do not deliver the tax revenues needed to run the country.

In trying to bring about the needed changes, Zimbabwe should not be looking for advice on how to make its badly chosen policies work better. Donor countries and development agencies should ensure that they are not trying to offer such advice. In essence, the disbursal of assistance in any form should be made conditional upon Zimbabwe showing the needed willingness and determination to make radical changes and to adopt acceptable policies. The primary, nonnegotiable condition should be the empowerment of ordinary citizens through the acceptance and promotion of individual property rights, and that these rights are given protection in the proposed constitution.

Today, Zimbabwe's agricultural sector consists largely of small farms created through the breaking up the large farms acquired by the state. As state properties that cannot be sold, these farms have no market value, and therefore no collateral value, so the new farmers cannot pledge their allocations of land in support of bank loans.

Despite subsidies and state funding, very few farmers have been able to move away from peasant farming methods, and since the land reforms, harvests have been extremely disappointing. Furthermore, every year since land acquisitions started in earnest, Zimbabwe has had to import food. Much of this has come into the country as direct imports by the commercial sector, but the Crop and Food Supply Assessment mission of the World Food Programme (WFP) estimated that five million Zimbabweans would need food aid in the early months of 2009.

An Urban Food Security Assessment study[6] carried out by the Zimbabwe Vulnerability Assessment Committee of the Food and Nutrition Council in January 2009 shows that 58 percent of the individuals in their sample survey had eaten only two meals on the day before participating in the study, and that another 18 percent had eaten only one meal that day. Moreover, only 22.6 percent of the sample had eaten three meals on that day. The figures are compared to the results of a survey carried out in November 2006, when 54.1 percent of those questioned had eaten three meals, 37.4 percent had eaten two meals, and only 4.2 percent had only one on the day before completing the questionnaire.

The two distinctly different sets of arrangements inherent in freehold individual ownership and collective (or state) ownership yield distinctly different results. They can be classified as two economic systems that make very different demands on farmers and generate widely different prospects of success. These are the same essential differences that lie between South Korea and North Korea today, and they were the main differences between the separate countries formerly known as the Federal Republic of Germany and the German Democratic Republic. The populations of these countries belonged to the same race and spoke the same language, but the different property ownership structures imposed upon them led to completely different levels of success.

In Zimbabwe, two different systems were applied to the farming practices of two different races, again with very different results. However, as the Korean and German examples show, the race of the farmers is not the relevant issue: it is the ownership rights and whether open markets exist for the properties that make the difference.

In many other countries, racial as well as a host of cultural differences have been readily accommodated within forward-looking technological, financial, and economic structures. Property rights and market systems have made this possible simply because, as developments and as intellectual breakthroughs, they have been among the most important of the modern age.

At a practical level, the need for functional links between farmers and their suppliers reinforces the requirement for legally enforceable property ownership rights and the transferability of such assets through the market. These, in turn, provide bankers with the security needed to permit the release of funding.

This vital property ownership rights link between producers and bankers has, in all economically successful countries, also developed between bankers and their clients in every other sector. Property ownership rights, supported by open market structures, greatly empower the participants involved in every other sphere of activity in the economy, particularly the manufacturing, mining, commercial, construction, transport, and property development sectors.

By destroying the collateral value of agricultural land in Zimbabwe, the government has effectively disempowered the people and disabled the land. In the process, it has also debilitated the farmers to whom the land had been given. In exercising its claimed right to control every individual and every enterprise, the government has shouldered the unmanageable burdens of subsidies, grants, and supervision. But in trying to deliver on these obligations, the government has inflicted upon the population the certainty of restricted supplies, recurrent crop failures, and high inflation.

An unfortunate component of official party policy has been its effort to promote, or sustain, contrived resentment against the levels of success achieved by the former commercial farmers, all with the apparent purpose of placing any thought of their reengagement absolutely beyond the pale. This is rationalized by claims that others must be given a chance to succeed; however, this is a deeply flawed argument. The success enjoyed by commercial farmers never precluded the adoption of their methods by others, and these farmers' conduct did not crowd out competition. As no one was competing against anyone else, they had no need to wait to be "given" a chance.

By 1997, commercial farmers occupied about 30 percent of the country's agricultural land, or 11.8 million hectares of the total 39 million hectare total. The successful methods used by commercial farmers could have been adopted and applied by the people on the remaining 70 percent, but after twenty-seven (now thirty) years of independence, the farmers on this land were still denied individual ownership rights and lacked tenure security, as well as the access to finance needed to apply more efficient methods. They were therefore rigidly bound to the less successful system.

Traditional social structures also stood in the way of change. The authority of the chief in every area was tied to his right to allocate land and to ensure that individuals with no claim to family connections not be permitted to settle within his jurisdiction. Concerns about freehold ownership rights included the fears of incursions by people from other tribal areas, but the concerns most often expressed were that peasant farmers would be left landless and destitute after being persuaded to sell to wealthy urban businesspeople. The limitations of the system held in place by these traditions prevented the adoption of more efficient, larger-scale farming practices, and explained poor performance in the past, but these limitations have not been removed by the land reform process.

These limitations include the lack of freehold title, the lack of security of tenure, the lack of personal motivation, the farmers' poor access to funding, and the small scale of their farming operations. Even very experienced farmers can do very little in such an environment, and even the best of the commercial farmers would have achieved very little if they had been restricted by the same handicaps. Hopes that experience on its own will eventually overcome these limitations are certain to be frustrated.

The constraints are so severe that the less-experienced farmers and those with no experience at all, to whom most of the land was given, had no chance of succeeding. However, as land was allocated to a great many such people, usually because of their political connections, and as they could use their political leverage to extract support from the state, they were able to hold on to this land.

In desperate attempts to improve results, the state has become increasingly generous, but despite handouts of free seed, fertilizer, fuel, and agricultural machinery, together with subsidized power, transport, and marketing services, most of these farmers have failed. Regrettably, the government's performance has not been recorded as failure because its prime objective, the displacement of white commercial farmers, was accomplished successfully. The very disappointing harvests, therefore, have not led to replacement on farms by people with better prospects of success as farmers.

If Zimbabwe is to achieve important economic objectives, its authorities need to abandon their apparent contention that they possess the authority and sovereign right to insist on certain preferred systems, and demand the results that are delivered by more exacting and demanding systems. But they do make such claims, and they go further to demand that any differences that show up should be squared-off by handouts of aid.

Penalties have costs, but even advantages have costs. In this context, the cost of achieving greater prosperity for the population as a whole would be the government's relinquishment of controls over the scope of citizens' productive activities, and their choice of the methods needed to achieve them. Zimbabwe can only restore the needed productive capacity investment flows in other sectors by reengaging investors, prime examples of whom were the country's commercial farmers. Furthermore, the prerequisites for productive investment of any kind include property rights and confidence.

By enlisting the support of the many exceptionally skilled Zimbabwean farmers who know how to do the work, Zimbabwe would be able to greatly accelerate the recovery process and would more easily attract investors to other business sectors. Alternative political policies are now within reach, following the power-sharing agreement between the Zimbabwe African National Union-Patriotic Front (ZANU-PF) and the Movement for Democratic Change (MDC), but the ZANU-PF needs to abandon its attempts to prevent or slow the process of change.

The right policy changes would go a long way toward generating interest and restoring confidence among new investors, as well as those who would willingly return to Zimbabwe if they could be assured that their rights would be respected. However, the country's recent history dictates that these assurances, particularly with respect to property rights, will have to be firmly entrenched in a new constitution, the preparation of which should be given the highest priority.

Many other issues also need urgent attention, and all of them should receive consideration. However, their importance and urgency should not be allowed to dilute or undermine the efforts to restore property rights. The subjects of civil rights, compensation, investment policies, and the variety of other issues that will have to be tackled to restore Zimbabwe's capacity, as well as its international credibility, all need special consideration. But, these issues should be the subject of other papers and other initiatives. No matter how significant these issues are, they should not be allowed to deflect attention away from the core issue of property rights. In particular, demands for compensation should not be allowed to become a precondition for the acceptance of other proposals. Zimbabwe is virtually bankrupt, and therefore incapable of making such payments, even if they were awarded by international courts. At the same time, no other country has been persuaded that it has an obligation to pay compensation for the conduct of the Zimbabwean government.

Several important advantages would flow from efforts to concentrate on restoring property rights. Legal requirements with far-reaching consequences in many areas would have to be met at the same time, which would consequently help rebuild the foundations of civil rights, contract law, investment flows, investor confidence, and respect for market mechanisms. These, in turn, would help rebuild intricate business relationships that would automatically initiate restorative work in a host of other areas of concern in the recovery process.

In other words, the quickest way to start the process that would ease all of the country's economic problems would be to rebuild the foundations of commercial agriculture. Peasant, or small-scale, farming methods are typically adequate to only meet the needs of small communities, and even then, only when they have the advantage of good rains. Population growth in Zimbabwe has made the country dependent on much larger output volumes that cannot be delivered by the traditional farming methods of small populations.

Concerning food security, Zimbabwe needs to avoid having to spend substantial amounts on food imports and a dependence on charity. One way to do this would be to reinstate its large-scale, capital-intensive farms. The ability of commercial farms to make use of more efficient mechanized cultivation methods would dramatically improve yields and offer the assurance of good crop delivery, even in seasons that are badly affected by the weather.

The easing of the remaining political problems presents further challenges, all of which deserve careful thought and special attention, but that could also easily deflect or derail the economic recovery. To ensure that political debates do not interfere with economic recovery, these problems must be addressed by distinctly separate programs and discussions. Resentments about past injustices are currently fueling corrosive forces that are working against the interests of everyone, even of those who feel most keenly that they have suffered ill treatment. However, clear distinctions must be drawn between what is needed to make amends for past failings and what is needed to ensure future success. Undiluted attention has to be focused on proposals that can deliver future recovery and growth, allowing others to concentrate their undivided attention on the challenges caused by past errors in judgment.

The adoption of market mechanisms and the acceptance that participants at every level should meet certain market requirements should form the basis of new arrangements. People prepared to work with the knowledge that they can have anything they can pay for, and who show that they can keep to loan repayment commitments, become sound contributors. They, in turn, set high standards for others. Performance alone determines who succeeds, and arbitrary decisions made by people with political influence cease to have any bearing on business relationships.

The many people occupying land that they received for nothing should be persuaded that land with no market value is land that cannot support bank loans. It represents nothing more than "dead capital," to use the phrase of Hernando de Soto, the most articulate of those scholars who have sought to promote individual property rights.[7] These farmers should, therefore, be persuaded that to keep the land, they must pay for it, and those without funds could be offered loans to do so. As failure to meet the loan repayments would lead to foreclosure, the farmer would be strongly motivated to make the land productive. Those who succeed would retain ownership rights, and those who fail would have to release their land back into the market.

Zimbabwe, as a developing country, cannot afford subsidies, but subsidies are being paid out regardless. To fund them, the government has had to borrow or print most of the money. Budget statements have shown the development of substantial budget deficits, particularly for the years since 2005; but nonetheless, the subsidies were funded by enforced treasury bill sales to financial institutions and from Statutory Reserves demanded by the Reserve Bank of Zimbabwe (RBZ) from the banking sector. Normally, the statutory reserve ratio is of the order of 12–15 percent of total deposits, but with declines in tax revenues and rising expenditures, the government chose to extract much larger sums from the banks. By 2006, the ratio was 60 percent of deposits at an interest rate of 0 percent. This money was used to fund farmers' subsidies as well as the subsidies paid to loss-making parastatals,[8] such as the Grain Marketing Board (GMB).[9]

Various loan schemes were also introduced, but as the RBZ had no interest to pay on the funds, it could lend the money at very low rates—a figure of 25 percent applying to most of them. With annual inflation rising from 500 to 1400 percent during 2006, the RBZ was effectively confiscating the bulk of the nation's corporate and personal funds and then giving virtually all of the money to the companies most threatened by financial losses.

Subsidies that rescued farmers from inadequate performance, if not bankruptcy, also relieved them of the need to improve their operating techniques. As a result, subsidies helped perpetuate low yields at high costs, thereby generating even more inflation. As government finances became further stretched, more shortages and climbing inflation became inevitable.

Employing this strategy, the country made no progress, but 24 Zimbabwean commercial farmers were welcomed into Nigeria in 2005 after 140 had moved to Zambia in 2004. These developments were reported by the *Christian Science Monitor,* *The New York Times, BBC,* the US National Public Radio, and other media at the time. Other farmers went to Mozambique and several other countries to restore their agricultural earnings, and the rural areas in Zimbabwe became patchworks of derelict farms.

Nigeria's Kwara State recently reported on the transformation of agriculture in its Shonga district as a result of land concessions being given to Zimbabwean farmers.[10]

Looking to other countries that have seen similar declines suggests that Zimbabwe might expect its increasingly impoverished farming areas to become competing fiefdoms run by warlords, each of whom will be trying to capture increasing amounts of the scarce land. Early indications of this have become evident in the deforestation of resettled farmland, as new farmers are enlisted by local chiefs to cut down trees for fuel wood. This wood has proved to be a more immediate revenue source than crops, which require planting and tending. The activities of gold panning in river beds and those searching ancient alluvial beds for diamonds have also come under the restrictive control of local politicians, who capitalize on the system's rejection of individual rights.

If the policy decisions that caused these problems are not changed, towns will continue to suffer from declining food security and business opportunities, and these pressures will carry Zimbabwe into worsening chaos, increasing conflict, and deepening political instability.

Hopefully the increasingly obvious failures of ZANU-PF policy choices will permit the adoption of better alternatives during the coming months, and the improving performances will help accelerate change for the better. However, some of the more deeply seated problems, such as the severely damaged power, transport, health, education, and financial services sectors, will need to receive specialized assistance and concessional financing if they are to be prevented from slowing the process of change. If Zimbabwe cannot break free of central-planning concepts, another possibility is that the state will force its new farmers to be productive under the discipline of state-run central planning authorities. If such ideas are followed, the country will depend upon the considerable involvement of the military and other uniformed forces. At best, Zimbabwe might see these management methods lead to gradual improvements in output, but subsidies would remain essential, and a deficit in the still-needed skills would see the country maintain its floundering pace in thirty years' time. However, the former Soviet Union, China, and North Korea tried these command economy ideas for considerably more than thirty years, and they all failed.

The preferred option should be to restore respect for civil rights and market forces. A good start is to encourage the experienced farmers to return to the land. Meeting these farmers' requirements will be difficult, but assistance (which would certainly be denied under the first two options) would undoubtedly become available if the third route is chosen. The farmers' requirements are the reinstatement and constitutionally guaranteed protection of property rights, as well as access to finance. These requirements call for the adoption of appropriate constitutional provisions as well as the recapitalization of Zimbabwe's banks, but such improvements are better described as the removal of disincentives, rather than the creation of incentives.

To establish the requirements that are taken for granted in well-run economies, Zimbabwe has only to reassemble the components of the commercial farming sector that made it successful before, and to ensure that the same market mechanisms and structures are made available to the whole population. Improved profit prospects and working conditions will enable existing suppliers in the agricultural sector to respond with their own recovery and expansion plans. Given the right political and business environment, Zimbabwe's many attractions as a place to work and live will readily be recalled by the thousands who are eager to return.

With these issues at the top of a new agenda, the government should be invited to accept a new direction for the land reform program that will help rebuild Zimbabwe's total economy in the shortest possible time.

The essential requirements for the recovery of successful and dependable commercial agricultural production are themselves interdependent. They all imply significant shifts in government thinking, each of which reinforces the effectiveness of every other change.

- Restoration of the rule of law.
- Restoration of land titles and the market for land.
- Restoration of land tenure security.
- Reengagement of skilled farmers.
- Access to finance to help rebuild lost capacity, funded in part by the privatization of parastatals, by loan finance raised from the sales of syndicated loan stock on international capital markets, and by obtaining concessionary finance from international development organizations.
- Access to loan capital from the banking sector once it has been recapitalized by injections of equity finance.
- Confidence to commit to medium to long-term investment plans.
- Access to farm labor on the basis of restoring and improving on the incomes, training, housing, and social amenities for employees and their families.
- Access to the needed farm inputs, following upon the restoration of capacity in the seed, fertilizer, agricultural machinery, and crop chemical sectors, as well as the needed efforts to improve electricity supplies, the condition of the roads, and the quality of administrative services in farming districts.
- Access to acceptable markets for agricultural output, ranging from crops and livestock for food industries to nonfood products, such as tobacco, cotton, and timber.
- Exemption from income tax and import duties during the recovery phases to compensate producers for the loss of equipment and the deprivation of earnings during the period of the land reform program. These special concessions should be made available for the same number of years.
- Supportive investment conditions that assure investors of clear-cut and corruption-free procedures for registering businesses and meeting statutory requirements.
- Restoration of capacity for suppliers of farm machinery.
- Restoration of capacity to produce agro-inputs.
- Restoration of capacity in service sectors, particularly engineering, construction, transport and banking services, training, and legal advice.
- Restoration of efficient and cost-effective research services to meet ongoing requirements for disease and pest-resistant seed; updated rainfall, temperature, and humidity charts to track possible climate changes; expert advice on agronomy, animal husbandry, and wildlife management; and other extension services.

- Restoration of agricultural training programs, including support for the tobacco training facility and the creation of similar institutions for specialists in livestock and other food crops, forestry, and wildlife.
- Restoration of crop and livestock disease control programs, particularly with regard to foot-and-mouth disease, tick-borne diseases, poultry diseases, and tsetse-fly control.
- The formation of a new Lands Commission to take over the functions of the former Natural Resources Board—the new body would be empowered to ensure that measures were enforced to prevent soil erosion and the siltation of dams, to study and advise on the suitability of certain crops for areas under observation, to advise on crop rotation and cultivation procedures, and to prevent overstocking and other environmental damage. In addition, the Land Commission would be empowered to ensure the efficient and sustainable use of land, water, and other natural resources.

Before the land reform program was launched, Zimbabwe had all of these requirements in place. The justification for restoring and improving upon them lies simply in the fact that their contributions are vital to the recovery of the whole economy. The hope of a recovery without them is far too uncertain.

Estimates expressed at public meetings of farmers suggest that perhaps only 10 percent of the displaced skilled farmers could be immediately persuaded to return to their farms by the adoption of the suggested policy changes. If the sincerity of the authority's policy change intentions stands up to scrutiny, many of those farmers who relocated to regional countries might be expected to follow suit. If these assessments prove true, it is likely that Zimbabwe will achieve self-sufficiency in maize production within three years and recover up to half of its tobacco output of 2000 in about the same time. If electricity supplies can be improved by restoring the efficiency levels at Hwange and Kariba Power Stations, wheat and barley production might be expected to double from its current low base in two years. The achievement of crop volumes of pre-1999 levels will require more time, particularly in the dairy and beef industries.

Confidence would be restored most rapidly by assurances that each of the farmers would be permitted to return to the land over which they claimed, and could again claim, title. A high proportion of this land currently lies idle, so this should pose no problem for the authorities in many parts of Zimbabwe. Resettlement farmers that accept the challenges of having to pay for their land, and of having to accept market prices without guarantees of subsidies, are excellent candidates for students of training schools. Thousands of these candidates have already acquired technical and management skills by working on commercial farms before their employers' businesses were closed down by the confiscation of their land, and, thus, many of them will be able to present themselves to the authorities and the banks as ideal candidates for material and financial assistance.

To meet these financing challenges, Zimbabwe's returning commercial farmers also need considerable assistance, primarily in foreign exchange. While a high proportion of the essential work can be accomplished by these farmers without help, their ability to respond would be much more effective with assistance, in the form of soft loans or grants, enabling them to re-equip their farms and rebuild an effective workforce more quickly. As the early success of these farmers would help place every other business sector in Zimbabwe back onto a recovery path, the effective leverage of funding made available by development organizations or donor countries on concessional terms would have an impact vastly greater than funding offered in any other form.

Due to the far-reaching effects of the adoption of these policies, the many advantages that would rapidly follow would include:

- restoration of food self-sufficiency and export surpluses;
- employment growth in every economic sector;
- restoration of regular cash incomes and secure accommodation for many hundreds of thousands of farm workers and their families;
- restoration of exports of nonfood agricultural products;
- restoration of demand for requirements from manufacturing companies;
- restoration of production volumes from manufacturing companies that add value to agricultural output;
- restoration of wildlife conservancies and tourist resorts that would help recapture Zimbabwe's excellent reputation as a first-class tourist destination;
- reestablishment of industrial, commercial, and service industry capacities in Zimbabwe's rural towns, better serving the communal, as well as commercial, farming areas;
- increase in government revenues from profits and personal income taxes and import and excise duties;
- increase in foreign exchange inflows that will support all other industrial and commercial activity;
- increase in foreign reserves that will eliminate fuel and power shortages and greatly increase business efficiency;
- rapid decline in inflation by reducing scarcities of goods and foreign currency; and
- investor interest in new manufacturing, mining, commercial, and infrastructural developments.

The amount of time these advantages will take to materialize will depend directly on the number of experienced farmers who can be reinstated on their land, the amount of money and inputs they can assemble, and the number of people they can employ, all of which will affect the output volumes they can generate. However, the success of commercial farmers will directly address one of Zimbabwe's more serious problems: the country's low gross national product per head of population. IMF statistics show that this has fallen from about US$2 per day to less than US$1 per day since the start of the land reform program.

With the improved outlook for investors that would flow from the restoration of property rights and the application of Zimbabwe's existing investment promotion legislation, the policy changes would quickly lead to poverty alleviation through:

- direct and indirect job creation;
- the cautious promotion of individual property rights in communal areas;

- accelerated communal area developments of stored water, marketing structures, banking services, technical and managerial advisory services, and transport and communications services;
- the establishment of equal property ownership and inheritance rights for men and women;
- lifting current maize yields from below one ton per hectare to figures five times higher, or more, through the adoption of better cultivation techniques that would preserve the land as well as release land for other crops;
- the development of a symbiotic relationship between commercial and communal agriculture through the promotion of commercialization of all communal land activities; and
- through an end to the forced migration of work seekers to neighboring countries and the return of many of those who left in recent years.

Within this framework of restored property ownership rights, many options and possibilities will present themselves for accommodating the claims of those who have been allocated A1 and A2 farms.[11] Simply by recognizing and accepting that land empowers its owners by having a market value, the government would be encouraging all new farmers to purchase the land they want. To further assist them to make this transition, government and private sector banks could offer mortgage bond finance to help farmers make their purchases over a period of years.

Having had their deposit base and their accumulated capital reserves demolished by the combined effects of hyperinflation, interest rates at fractions of the rate of inflation, and RBZ decisions to set the statutory reserve ratio at up to 60 percent of deposits, the banks themselves are among the country's more serious casualties. Before they will have any prospect of assisting the recovery, they will need to be recapitalized; however, the funding available seems unlikely to be enough to recapitalize the twenty-eight institutions currently registered, fifteen of which are commercial banks.[12] The cautious approach from investors seems likely to result in a significant shrinkage of the number of banks.

However, modest levels of success will themselves add momentum to the recovery process. Earnings and payments could become bank deposits, which could then begin to support the lending from which banks derive their income. Once started, with assistance and injections of equity finance where possible, the recovery process would become self-sustaining. The requirements that are in need of support are those that will prime the pumps, or assist the capital accumulation process to make a start.

The effective restoration of commercial agriculture offers the best prospect of recapturing, and then exceeding, the country's former broadly based gross earnings from all productive sectors. However, having sustained damage every year for the last ten years, the economy is very unlikely to move onto a recovery process that restores former levels of production and employment in less time than that. A large proportion of the skilled workforce, the capital equipment, the nation's savings, and even the services infrastructure have been rendered inadequate by the destructive policies. These are the variables that have been under attack for the past decade, severely damaging, if not demolishing, decades of development. Almost all of the billions invested by all players over those years are needed again to restore that capacity; unfortunately, Zimbabwe must now compete for these funds in much more difficult circumstances. That said, it is also true that very significant progress can be achieved in a short amount of time compared to other developing countries.

To attract the levels of investment and loan capital needed, Zimbabwe will have to considerably improve the rate at which it is rebuilding confidence in its short-term, as well as longer-term prospects. Unfortunately, the recent political changes, with the formation of the Government of National Unity (GNU) and the release of several key ministries to MDC political direction, have been forced upon the reluctant ZANU-PF party as much by the failures of their own policies as by the vote count. It is equally unfortunate that in the months that followed, the ZANU-PF's reluctance has been more strongly in evidence than its willingness to accommodate change.

Issues affecting the rate at which those still wielding political influence are prepared to relinquish power include concerns for their personal safety, as well as for their previously assured income flows. They have no wish to see a weakening of their long-established impunity, nor do they accept that need for changes that erode their embedded privileges. These have proved to be very severe impediments to progress and are seen to be beyond the scope of what now passes for administrative authority or due process of law in Zimbabwe.

In summary, the executive authority of the president still completely overwhelms the authority of the rest of the governmental structure, the new prime minister included. Until more decisive pressures can be brought into the mix, whether from internal or external sources, Zimbabwe will remain on a very slow path to recovery, with the pace set by low expectations of investors and the resulting severe limitations on capital inflows.

Notes

The author of this chapter is a leading and respected Zimbabwean economist based in Harare. Due to a lack of reliable economic figures on Zimbabwe, the author sourced much of his information directly from his own economic consultancy firm, Robertson Economic Information Services.

1. Professor Steve Hanke, Johns Hopkins University, various publications.
2. World Health Organisation (WHO), *The African Regional Health Report*, http://www.afro.who.int.
3. Statistics derived from IMF website, www.imf.org.
4. Zimbabwe Conservation Task Force, "Wildlife Horror Stories," http://www.zctf.mweb.co.zw/page2.html.
5. Justice for Agriculture unpublished research.
6. Zimbabwe Vulnerability Assessment Committee, "Urban Food Security Assessment," Zimbabwe, January 2009.
7. Hernando de Soto, *The Mystery of Capital: Why Capitalism Triumphs in the West and Fails Everywhere Else* (New York: Basic Books, 2000).

8. Reserve Bank of Zimbabwe (RBZ), "Monetary Policy Review Statement, First-Half," 2006.

9. Ibid.

10. "Kwara State, Nigeria's Garden of Eden," advertisement in *The Economist,* March 13, 2010.

11. Two resettlement models, A1 and A2, were proposed in the first phase of the Land Reform and Resettlement program. These are still being followed and are defined as follows:

> Model A1: This is described as the decongestion model that permits the relocation of people from overcrowded communal farming areas and the allocation of plots to landless peasants. Two types of small-scale farms are described under the scheme, one being the self-contained variety and the other the villagized variety in which cooperative activities are promoted. As the government amended its original target of five million hectares—to eleven million hectares of formerly commercial farm land—it increased the number of intended A1 plots to two hundred and fifty thousand. At the outset, it declared its intention to allocate 20 percent of all A1 plots to war veterans.

> Model A2: This model is intended for the peri-urban, small-scale commercial, medium-scale commercial, and the large-scale commercial farmers who have some knowledge of farming, and have access to finance and other resources. The size of A2 farms can range from 20 to 250 hectares in the high rainfall areas, and from 240 to 2,000 hectares in low rainfall ranching areas. State farms were also to have been subdivided for A2 farmer occupation.

12. RBZ, "Monetary Policy Review Statement, First-Half," 2006.

Chapter 6

Zimbabwe's Hyperinflation
Can Dollarization Be the Cure?

Albert Makochekanwa and Prosper Kambarami

Executive Summary

This chapter results from a study of the main features of four possible monetary system options that can be potential solutions to Zimbabwe's current hyperinflationary trend. The system presented and analyzed here is dollarization, which occurs when a country makes a foreign currency (currencies) full legal tender and reduces its own currency, if any, to a subsidiary role—issued only in coins having small value. For this system, the practicality of Zimbabwe adopting and/or implementing dollarization is also explained. The conclusion of the research is that, generally, the country is ready to adopt official dollarization; however, several issues specific to Zimbabwe need to be seriously considered, otherwise implementation of any of these systems may be both fruitless and a waste of resources.

Introduction

Although for a number of years after independence in 1980, Zimbabwe's economic health status was generally considered sound for a developing state, more recently, the country's economic performance has been both tumultuous and disastrous to say the least. The fact that Zimbabwe is currently under severe and chaotic hyperinflation is common knowledge, both to the country's citizens and the world over. Although the latest inflation rate released by Zimbabwe's Central Statistical Office (CSO)[1] is from July 2008 when the country's month-on-month rate was estimated at 231.2 million percent, the International Monetary Fund (IMF) estimates the hyperinflation rate to be 489 billion percent as of September 2008.[2] Independent analysts, for instance, Steve Hanke, put the inflation rate at 6.5 quindecillion novemdecillion percent (i.e., 65 followed by 107 zeros) as of December 2008.[3] In comparison with other countries, currently the second highest inflation rate is found in Burma, whose inflation rate is approximately 39 percent. Relative and in comparison to other African countries and Southern African Development Community (SADC) countries in particular, where the average annual inflation since 2000 has been below 20 percent, Zimbabwe's inflation rate is by far an extreme outlier.

The country has been ravaged by hyperinflation for a considerable period to such an extent that even the use of the local currency, the Zimbabwean dollar (Z$), has been estimated to have lost more than 99.99 percent of its value within a space of less than two years, between 2007 and 2008.[4] In the local context, the Zimbabwean dollar has been playing a more minor role in comparison to other currencies, such as the US dollar (US$), the South African rand (ZAR), the Euro, the British pound, and the Botswanan pula—credible currencies used in almost all transactions in the country. The use of these currencies gained ascendancy as far back as 2006, although their widespread use began in the early part of 2008 throughout the country, with even rural people selling their livestock in US$ and ZAR. Currently, transactions are conducted in the aforementioned currencies, with the US$ and the ZAR dominating most transactions.

A combination of hyperinflation and the central bank's monopoly over the production of currency over the past two or so years has forced the entire Zimbabwean economy to use the government-issued currency *under duress,* with no recourse for the populace to address their dissatisfaction with the currency's value. Zimbabweans have felt the bitter brute as they have had to cope with recurrent currency transitions, from denomination notes of Z$5, Z$10, and Z$20 maxims (at independence in 1980), to a currency whose denominations have rapidly shifted from thousands, to millions, to billions, to trillions, to quadrillion, to hextillion, and, currently, to octillion.[5] There is the further possibility of denominations shifting to nonillion, decillion, and other higher families of "-llions."[6]

The presence of both semi- and informal dollarization has forced the current government to allow use of multiple currencies in a situation where the Z$ remains the legal tender alongside other currencies, such as the rand, British pound, pula, and the euro.[7] This piecemeal policy was announced recently during the presentation of the country's 2009 national budget on January 30, 2009.[8] Allowing multiple currencies was, however, a correct and long-overdue government admittance of the fact that the country's local currency had, for all intents and purposes, been rendered useless. From an economic point of view, it is important to point out that this multiple use of currency, as announced, may not provide a permanent solution to inflation unless underpinned by local production increases.

Zimbabwe's Hyperinflationary Trend

Hyperinflation is considered to be out of control inflation—a condition in which prices increase rapidly as local currency loses its value. Cagan defines hyperinflation as "beginning in the month the rise in price exceeds 50 percent and as ending in the month before the monthly rise in prices drops below that amount and stays below for at least a year."[9]

The history of hyperinflation in Zimbabwe can be said to date back to early 1999. Although data from civil society organizations (CSOs) demonstrate that the country's monthly inflation rate reached the 50 percent mark in February 1999, this monthly rate was above 100 percent by November 2001, before jumping to rates higher than 200 percent by January 2003. By December 2003, the rate sat at 600 percent, though it temporarily declined through 2004 and into 2005, reaching the trough of 124 percent in March 2005. Since April 2006, the monthly rate has been above 1000 percent, with the upward trend reaching 2200.2 percent in March 2007. This inflation rate was estimated at 231.2 million percent by the end of July 2008,[10] with the IMF's 2009 estimates putting the hyperinflation rate to be 489 billion percent as of September 2008.[11] This hyperinflationary trend and other economic indicators are depicted in table 6.1.

Factors that have been among the major causes of hyperinflation in Zimbabwe include money printing (seigniorage), foreign currency shortages (with its resultant black market premium), demand-pull inflation (due to disrupted production activities, especially in the agricultural sector), and imported/cost-push inflation.[12]

With respect to money printing, the Zimbabwean government has been good at using the money machine print. For instance, the unbudgeted government expenditure of 1997 (to pay the war veterans' gratuities); the publicly condemned and

Table 6.1 Zimbabwe's economic performance

Year	GDP		GDP per capita (US$)	Annual inflation (%)
	US$ (billions)	% growth		
1980–1998	7.0	3.9	740.4	20.5
1999	6.0	–3.6	508	56.9
2000	5.7	–7.3	489	55.2
2001	5.7	–2.7	490	112.1
2002	5.6	–4.4	478	198.9
2003	5.1	–10.4	433	598.7
2004	5.0	–3.6	430	132.7
2005	5.0	–4.0	427	585.8
2006	4.9	–5.4	417	1,281.1
2007	4.7	–6.1	403	108,844.1
2008	3.2	–14.1	265[a]	489,000,000,000[b]

[a] Taken from Government of Zimbabwe's Fiscal Mid Year Review of July 2009.

[b] Taken from IMF's Consultation Mission on Zimbabwe addressed to Zimbabwe's minister of finance, March 23, 2003.

Sources: IMF online database; Government of Zimbabwe online database; and IMF, 2009.

unjustifiable Zimbabwe's intervention in the Democratic Republic of Congo's (DRC) war in 1998; the expenses of the controversial land reform (beginning in 2000); the parliamentary (2000 and 2005) and presidential (2002) elections; the introduction of senators in 2005 (at least sixty-six posts) as part of "widening the think tank base"; and the international payments obligations, especially since 2004, all resulted in massive money printing by the government.[13] Above these highlighted and topical expenditure issues, the printing machines have also been the government's solution for such expenses as civil servants' salaries.

With respect to cost push inflation, whilst wages were generally reviewed twice a year (in January and July), both in the public and private sectors before hyperinflation started, the situation has since changed. Even though up to now the public sector unshakably continued to review its salaries as before (i.e., in January and July), as if nothing happened (of course at the expense of high labor turnover and loss of skilled personnel), the private sector has since changed the review process. Since 2000, most private companies have been reviewing salaries on a quarterly basis and upwardly in line with inflation trends, with some other private companies reviewing them on monthly bases. These labor costs have contributed to the higher market prices, as companies have been putting higher markups to recover their costs.

On demand-pull inflation, the Zimbabwean situation has been compounded by shortages of basic commodities (i.e., mealie-meal staple diet, cooking oil, flour, fuel, and sugar), thus resulting in pent-up upward pressure in the overall prices. These shortages were in turn caused by reduced production in the agricultural sector following the 2000 farm inversions, which resulted in serious productive farmers being chased away from their farming businesses.

Whilst the government, through the Reserve Bank of Zimbabwe (RBZ), has introduced some impulsive "policies" to deal with the situation, the major shortfalls have been that the policies have been devised in a straightjacket and myopic manner, addressing the symptoms, and leaving (and unwilling to deal with) the real underlying causes of runaway inflation. Two of such policies are the "zeros chopping" policy and the "money printing and oozing" policy. For instance, the RBZ has twice chopped off the zeros from the local currency to make it easier for both bank computers to cope with numbers, and the majority of the population to be able to read and transact. On August 1, 2006, three zeros were chopped along with this so-called chopping of zeros policy, and again on August 1, 2008, a whooping ten zeros were chopped off. In total, thirteen zeros have been removed from the Zimbabwean dollar in a space of three years.[14]

On the money printing policy, a total of twenty-seven new Zimbabwean dollar denominations have been printed and introduced in 2008, and six new denominations (Z$10 billion, Z$50 billion, Z$10 trillion, Z$20 trillion, Z$50 trillion, and Z$100 trillion) in January 2009.[15] All these attempts and efforts, as expected from an understanding of basic economic principles, have not improved anything as far as inflation reduction is concerned, the main reason being that neither attempt was backed by real supply side fundamentals, especially production.

Although RBZ monetary policy statements since 2003 through to the end of 2008 have suggested policy measures to deal with hyperinflation, incredible actions by the same institution have discouraged the majority in the war against hyperinflation. That is, actions such as money printing to finance government expenditures have led the public view of any hyperinflation stabilization policy from the RBZ as a joke. As such, hyperinflation persisted until end of January 2009.

The RBZ governor vowed in October 2008 to continue propagating hyperinflation by printing money, as evidenced by an unequivocal and publicly announced statement that said: "I am not afraid to print money and I will continue doing so."[16] The powers to carry such a deadly economic threat have been curtailed by changes in the political real of the country. Whilst the developments after January 31, 2009, are not analyzed in this chapter, suffice it to say that following the formation of Zimbabwe's Government of National Unity (GNU) on February 13, 2009, which resulted in the ministry of finance (under which the RBZ falls) being given to the opposition party, both the RBZ and the governor's wings were clipped. Also, a combination of the RBZ's limited power, the use of multiple currencies, and the suspension of the Zimbabwean dollar for at least a year resulted in the immediate cessation of money printing.[17]

Reversing this inflationary trend requires some radical and serious tailor-made inflation-fighting measures. A possible measure that the country should consider implementing is dollarization,[18] among others. A general positivist view is that Zimbabwe is not new to any of the four possible options. For instance, between 1892 and 1940, the country's banking system operated through a combination of free banking, dollarization, and monetary area. The last two systems were in place because South Africa's coins were legal tender in Zimbabwe due to a profit-sharing agreement for revenue seigniorage between the two countries.[19]

From 1940 until 1956, the country operated a currency board system, before shifting to a central bank system under the Central African Federation (CFA), which consisted of Northern Rhodesia (now Zambia), Nyasaland (now Malawi), and Southern Rhodesia (now Zimbabwe).[20] These four systems represent monetary arrangements that have all proven records of success in providing reliable and low inflation currencies wherever they have been instituted. The main motive behind instituting any one of these systems, or a combination thereof, in the Zimbabwean economy is that such a system has the ability to halt the hyperinflationary trend and ensure a stable currency—both conditions are necessary for economic growth and development.

Main Characteristics of Possible
Anti-Hyperinflation Options

Dollarization

Dollarization is used in a number of countries. Specifically, on an informal basis, the U.S. dollar has circulated alongside national currencies in a number of countries, both in the developing and developed world. It is only formal dollarization that seems to prop up much interest, especially in highly inflated countries such as Zimbabwe. Thus, to have a clear understanding of dollarization, three types of dollarization will be distinguished in this section.

Definitions of Dollarization

Official or *full dollarization* occurs when a country makes a foreign currency (currencies) full legal tender and reduces its own currency, if any, to a subsidiary role—issued only in coins having small value. Generally, under such an arrangement, there will be no risk of domestic currency, no currency risk, and, therefore, no risk of currency crisis.[21] With official dollarization, the foreign currency (currencies) adopted will not only be a legal tender for use among private parties, but it will also be used by the government. According to Borenszstein and Berg, one of the main features of full dollarization is that once adopted it will be permanent or nearly permanent.[22] Comparatively, full dollarization will be relatively more difficult to reverse than doing away with or modifying a currency board.

A variation of official or full dollarization is called *semiofficial* dollarization or implementing a *bimonetary system*, which exists when a foreign currency (currencies) is adopted as the legal tender dominating bank deposits, but which still plays a secondary role to the local currency in payments of such costs as wages, taxes, and day-to-day transactions, such as transport, groceries, and so forth. Under this arrangement, the semiofficial dollarizing countries have their own central banks, or monetary authorities, thus possessing vested authorities to champion their own monetary policies. An example of this arrangement is the Common Monetary Area (CMA), whereby Lesotho, Namibia, and Swaziland have allowed the South African rand to circulate in their territories as legal tender alongside their respective local currencies.

Unofficial dollarization occurs when residents of a given country hold a large proportion of their financial wealth in foreign currency-dominated assets, even though foreign currency is not a legal tender according to the country's financial or monetary laws. In this setup, the dollar (or any other foreign currency) is widely used in private transactions as a medium of exchange, as a unit of account, and as a store of value.

According to Bogetic, official dollarization may constitute the holding of foreign currency in a variety of forms, such as the holding of: (1) foreign currency bonds or other noncash assets; (2) foreign currency cash, whether possessing it is legal or illegal; (3) foreign currency deposits in domestic banks; and (4) foreign currency deposits in foreign banks. In the case of Zimbabwe, the majority of citizens have managed to unofficially hold their foreign currency in a variety of forms of cash.[23] This has been necessitated by a number of factors. First, most goods and services since 2006 have been priced in foreign currency, so having foreign currency (US$ or Z$) has been a daily prerequisite for any transaction. Second, up to end of January 2009, laws pertaining to opening and operating foreign currency accounts (FCAs) were tightened up, making it very difficult to even withdraw foreign currency in any local bank once deposited, which made it prudent for people to hold the foreign currency in cash and not deposit it into local banks.[24] Last, given the severe and acute shortages of foreign currencies in the country, for one to decide to part ways with his or her hard-earned foreign currency through deposits into the local bank is inconceivable, as withdrawing it has become a fruitless exercise because in 99 percent of cases there will be no foreign currency cash in the bank.

It is important to note that the term dollarization is no longer the sole preserve of the U.S. dollar, but now includes the use of other foreign currencies, such as the euro (where the term "eurorization" may apply), the South African rand (where the terms "randization" or "randify" may apply), and the British pound, among other currencies.

Advantages of Dollarization

Low Inflation
Dollarization, especially when constituted at the right conversion rate, is likely to ensure low inflation in the dollarizing country. This arises from the fact that the dollarizing country's inflation will be closely related to the anchor country's inflation rate, since these two countries will be using the same currency and applying relatively similar monetary policies (devised by the anchor country). For Zimbabwe, this will be one of the most important advantages should the country dollarize, given that hyperinflation has had unbearable social ramifications, with the majority of citizens being pushed below the poverty datum line.

Reduced Administrative Expenses
With dollarization there will be reduced administrative expenses. The reasoning here is that the government of the dollarizing country will not incur the cost of maintaining an infrastructure dedicated solely to the production and management of another country's national currency. For a country like Zimbabwe, these savings (especially at a time like this when the country is bedeviled by hyperinflation) will be significant given that the country is currently using a lot of resources—for example, money printed to purchase foreign currency on the parallel market—in chasing the little amounts of foreign currency in the hands of exporters, banks, and individuals.

Establishment of a Sound Financial Sector
Dollarization can also provide a firm basis for the recreation of a sounder financial sector. In this case, dollarization will go beyond the mere adoption of a foreign currency, but will also entail financial integration with the anchor country, which will force domestic financial institutions to improve their efficiency and the quality of their services. Also, dollarization implicitly implies a supposedly irreversible institutional change,[25] which can act as a signal for permanent commitment to low inflation, fiscal responsibility, and transparency. Such a scenario would be an asset for Zimbabwe given that it has not enjoyed a consistently good reputation for price or fiscal stability.

Lower Interest Rates
With dollarization there could be a substantial reduction of interest rates for local borrowers. Dollarization establishes a stable relationship with a currency whose

reputation is already well established and secure, thus lowering the level and volatility of domestic interest rates (real and nominal interest rates) by eliminating the risk of devaluation. This also eliminates the devaluation-risk premium in local currency interest rates. Through dollarization, instead of investing heavily in efforts to build market confidence in its own monetary policy, a government can achieve instant credibility by "hiring" the respected anchor country's central bank policy.[26] Given that Zimbabwe's interest rates[27] are currently much higher than the average rates applied in other neighboring southern African countries, any policy that reduces interest rates is likely to be viewed as positive for the future prosperity of the country.

Stimulate Domestic Long-Term Capital Markets

Dollarization spurs the development of domestic long-term capital markets by eliminating the risk of high inflation and currency devaluation. This comes from the fact that in a dollarization system, the dollarizing country cannot devalue the anchor currency it has adopted.[28] The confidence brought about by a stable adopted currency (among other factors) will motivate investors, both domestic and foreign, to participate in the country's long-term capital market.

Lower Transaction Costs

Since the country will be using an anchor currency, which in most cases will be highly traded and convertible (for instance, the U.S. dollar or the South African rand), when compared to the local currency, transaction costs in international trade and investments will be lowered—because there will be a reduced need for currency conversions. Currently, because of the nonconvertibility of the Zimbabwean dollar, transaction costs of doing international business are very high. For instance, if a buyer from Zimbabwe wants to import from Japan, the buyer first must convert the Zimbabwean dollars to U.S. dollars, and those U.S. dollars will then be converted into Japanese yen. Because of hyperinflation and a shortage of U.S. dollars in Zimbabwe's banks, the buyer will have to seek the U.S. dollar from the expensive foreign currency black market, and this will imply huge transactions costs. On the other hand, in the case of dollarization with the U.S. dollar as the anchor currency, the Zimbabwean buyer will simply pass through one conversion, from U.S. dollar to yen, thus reducing transaction costs (of importing in this example).

Possible Disadvantages of Dollarization

The disadvantages of dollarization are demarcated into two categories: economic and political drawbacks. Cohen argues that, in reality, the more critical disadvantages of dollarization are *political*, not economic, and claims that the former drawbacks "are in fact the costs that are likely to matter most in practice."[29]

Economic Costs

Forfeiture of autonomous monetary authority   Adoption of dollarization implies the forfeiture of independent and autonomous monetary policy since the dollarizing country will no longer exercise unilateral control over its own money supply or exchange rate. There were will be an inherent hierarchical relationship as such authority is ceded to the U.S. Federal Reserve (if the U.S. dollar is the adopted currency) or the South African Reserve Bank (if the South African rand is the adopted currency), with little promise that the dollarizing country's specific circumstances would be taken into account when monetary decisions are made in the anchor country.

Nevertheless, in most cases when a country considers instituting dollarization, it is likely that much of the country's monetary autonomy will already have been greatly eroded—as is the case with Zimbabwe, which is currently 99 percent dollarized (informally, and semiofficially) as of end of January 2009.[30] Had this not been the case, the country would not even be considering dollarization in the first place. Generally, the greater the degree of currency substitution that has already occurred due to informal dollarization (reflecting market pressures and preferences), the greater is the degree of constraint already imposed on a government's ability to manage macroeconomic conditions, and, hence, the smaller will be the actual loss of monetary autonomy if the local money is eliminated formally in the future. For Zimbabwe, informal dollarization has rendered monetary pronouncements useless; thus, formal adoption of dollarization may not bear much difference because the country has already implicitly forfeited its monetary authority independence.

Loss of seigniorage revenue   One huge cost of dollarization, especially to a country like Zimbabwe that has generated revenue through money printing for economic survival, is forfeiture of a potential tool for underwriting public expenditures—that is, the forgoing of the capacity to create money. Seigniorage is the interest income a central bank earns by issuing noninterest bearing money to purchase interest-bearing assets.[31] A country's central bank is part of its government; hence the income described is part of the government's revenues. When a country officially dollarizes, its central bank has to withdraw the local currency from circulation and replace it with the anchor currency. To get those U.S. dollars, the central bank will have to sell some of its assets—normally interest-bearing, U.S. dollar-denominated assets. The result is that the central bank's interest income declines.

In other words, seigniorage can thus be considered as an alternative source of revenue for the state beyond what can be raised via taxation or by borrowing from financial markets at home or abroad. What cannot be paid for with tax receipts or borrowed funds can be paid for, in effect, by money printing. Dollarization automatically terminates this revenue unless explicitly offset by some kind of agreed formula for seigniorage sharing with the anchor country. But once again, in reality, the greater is the degree of prior informal dollarization, the more likely the negative impacts of seigniorage loss will be reduced. In the case of Zimbabwe, with widespread informal dollarization, this loss will thus be very small.

Loss of the ability to use inflationTtax   Although somewhat similar to the just discussed drawback, with dollarization, a country will lose its ability to use the inflation tax ("revenue of last resort") by printing money in a national emergency. Normally, a government levies an implicit inflation tax when it issues so much new money that it generates inflation. With inflation, the real value of money will diminish over time, thus, inflation behaves like a tax levied on those who hold the local money.

When a country officially dollarizes, its government can no longer issue new money, so it can no longer use the inflation tax.[32] Zimbabwe has been using this inflation tax consistently since 2008, and adoption of dollarization will surely be a cost.

Loss of lender of last resort   Dollarization relinquishes the formal lender of last resort function of the dollarizing country (through its central bank) since in adopting a foreign currency, the latter country also gives up a central bank capable of discounting freely in times of financial crisis. Theoretically, it follows that domestic banks might become more exposed to potential liquidity risks. In practical terms, however, this alleged cost could be rather easily offset by a number of channels. First, dollarization normally eliminates or minimizes the overall need for international reserves, given that a share of external transactions that previously used to involve foreign currency can now be treated as equivalent to domestic transactions. Thus, a percentage of the central bank's dollar assets could then be devoted to a public stabilization fund that will bail out domestic financial institutions under stress. Another possible channel is that a contingency fund could be built up over time from tax revenues. Furthermore, flexible credit lines with foreign banks or monetary authorities could be negotiated, using future tax revenues or seigniorage sharing as collateral. Thus, in reality, this disadvantage is not a serious drawback for Zimbabwe should it consider adopting dollarization.[33]

Inability to adjust exchange rate in critical circumstances   The country will be unable to adjust its exchange rate in the peculiar circumstances when such a decision would be helpful to its economic activities. In effect, the fact that the economies of the anchor and dollarizing countries generally differ requires that appropriate policies, including exchange rate adjustment, be tailor-made to suit the dollarizing country's scenario. This loss of control over exchange rate policy may expose the country's economy to external shocks, such as primary commodity and food price volatility, especially given that the world trading system is likely to open up further due to globalization.

Political Costs

Loss of nation symbol   Among the most tangible national symbols that differentiate one country from the rest are flags, national anthems, postage stamps, public architecture, and money, the latter being one of the most potent ones. According to Cohen, the ability of money to symbolize the uniqueness of national identity stems from two sources.[34] First, since the government, or its central bank, issues its preserved currency notes, money plays the role of reminding citizens on daily basis of their loyalty, connectedness, and oneness with the country. Second, because it is pervasively used on daily transactions, a currency highlights the fact that everyone is part of the same social entity. Thus, adoption of foreign currency through dollarization entails a loss of these prerogatives. Specifically, given the current government's foreign policy thrust of sovereignty, this will be a major blow not only to its national symbol but also to its sovereignty.

Loss of insurance against risk   For the government of Zimbabwe, whose budget has, over the past few years, depended heavily on money printing, preservation of a national currency acts as a kind of insurance policy against risk, whereas seigniorage is a marginal source of revenue for the state. Although money printing has wreaked havoc in accelerating hyperinflation in Zimbabwe, it can, however, serve as an emergency source of revenue in the face of genuine problems, thus providing an option for finding needed purchasing power quickly when confronted with unexpected contingencies. With seigniorage, needed resources can be gathered together instantaneously without being forced to wait for tax returns to be filed or loans to be negotiated. Referring to seigniorage, Keynes noted that "a government can live by this means when it can live by no other."[35] Thus, adoption of another currency means this privilege will be completely eroded.

Foreign policy and diplomacy   From a foreign policy and diplomatic perspective, the ability of any sovereign state to have its own national currency reduces the risk of external dependence and threat. Autonomous national monetary authority ensures that a county does not have to rely on external sources for its most vital economic resources. With full dollarization, this insulation is lost. At the same time, the anchor country, whose money is used to dollarize, gains an authoritative device, which it can employ to influence the dependent dollarized economy. For instance, in the CMA, South Africa's monetary policy and changes in exchange rate influence monetary policy and exchange rate changes in Namibia and Lesotho. Given that these countries use the South African Reserve Bank (SARB) as their lender of last resort, when interest rates are changed in South Africa, CMA member countries automatically and instantly change their rates to reflect the changes enacted by South Africa.

Factors to be Considered in Assessing Zimbabwe's Readiness for Dollarization

Given that Zimbabwe is currently under severe hyperinflation and that dollarization stands as a possible panacea to this problem, it is important to digest the various criteria and assess the extent to which the country is ready to dollarize. To this end, this section provides some factors that need to be considered.

Monetary Factors

Policy Credibility

Countries where historical evidence, especially in the monetary area, shows that policymakers have suffered from a lack of policy credibility are potential beneficiaries of a rule-based monetary regime, such as a currency board or dollarization, given these systems' imposed discipline. Lack of policy credibility is normally measured by looking at some of the following variables:

- the country's experience with inflation—Zimbabwe's current inflation rate being astronomical;

- a past history of exchange rate instability and crises—Zimbabwe has to deal with over seven exchange rates, ranging from the official, bank, parallel market, gold, tobacco, and import/export rate, among others[36];
- the existence of previous financial and banking crises—Zimbabwe has placed at least five banks[37] under curatorship since 2004;
- the degree of unofficial dollarization—since 2007, use and application of foreign currency in any transaction was a street choice free for any scenario;
- the country's inability to borrow long term in domestic currency—borrowing from any bank or microfinance institution is a major liability in Zimbabwe as interest rates are both unreasonable and unmanageable; and
- a defunct fiscal record characterized by high budget deficits—Zimbabwe's deficits have been averaging more than 6 percent of the country's GDP since 1999, according to figures from the RBZ.

In a nutshell, all these variables perfectly suit Zimbabwe's situation over the past five or so years. Hence, judging by these criteria, Zimbabwe is ripe for either formal dollarization or a currency board.

History of Monetary Instability

Generally, countries needing the most stringently imposed rules, for instance, through adoption of dollarization, are those that have had a history of monetary instability. Specifically, dollarization is considered as the most appropriate solution for countries that have had high monetary instability, but that now either possess a competent and stable government, or are in the process of instituting such a government. There should be deep popular support for a commitment to rigid monetary rules that maintain long-run policy stability. Zimbabwe's situation portrays this description, and as such, it is a suitable candidate for dollarization.

Current Exchange Rate Regime

Although a country can adopt dollarization starting from any exchange rate regime, a successful past experience with credibly fixed exchange rates is a step forward. Past experience with fixed exchange rates, according to Roubini, indicates three things. First, it signals that the country has already shown its commitment to a stable currency.[38] Second, it indicates the country's willingness to pay any costs associated with fixed exchange rates, and last, it is a sign to indicate that the country will unlikely experience further large costs from giving up altogether a national currency.

Another advantage of previous implementation of fixed exchange rates is that the additional transitional costs associated with moving to dollarization from fixed rates are lower than when starting from more flexible exchange rate regimes. Zimbabwe, although its previous and current fixed exchange rates regimes have not been successful, has nonetheless implemented these policies in the past with the intention of stabilizing its currency. Thus, by inferring from this requisite factor, Zimbabwe is a potential candidate for dollarization.

Reserve Coverage of Monetary Base

Theoretically, literature points out that another criterion for dollarization is that the foreign exchange reserves of the implementing country should at least cover the monetary base (or the currency in circulation).[39] Nevertheless, one branch of literature suggests that potential countries for dollarization that do not satisfy this requirement may consider borrowing the necessary reserves from official or private creditors.[40] These reserves are needed to convert the money base into U.S. dollars (after dollarization).

Currently, Zimbabwe's foreign currency reserves have been exempt for a number of years to such an extent that the country struggles to buy (or import) essential products such as medicine and electricity, among other imports. IMF figures show Zimbabwe gross official reserves at US$58 million and US$5.8 million for 2007 and 2008. respectively.[41] At the same time, no rational officials or private creditors are currently willing to lend to the Zimbabwean government. However, international creditors[42] have indicated a willingness to provide credit lines only to business entities in cases in which they are assured of getting profitable returns at mutually agreed upon rates. Thus, by considering this criterion, dollarization in Zimbabwe may be successful.

Soundness of the Banking System

Existence of a sound, competitive, well-supervised, and well-regulated banking system is an important ingredient for the successful implementation of dollarization. A weak banking system may lead to financial panic and serious economic distress in cases where the banking sector experiences systemic crises that are fiscally costly, especially given the absence of a strong lender of last resort facility under dollarization. However, this weak banking system might be helped by the presence of foreign banks[43] in a dollarizing economy, and in the case of Zimbabwe, the presence of foreign banks will also go a long way in stabilizing the country's financial sector. Foreign banks must play the important roles of reducing the risk of banking crises and providing implicit lender of last resort support through home country's head offices. Currently, foreign banks operating in the country include Barclays, Standard Chartered, and Stanbic, among others, and these may act as stabilizers. Thus, in consideration of the presence of foreign banks, Zimbabwe is a potential candidate for dollarization.

Extent of Informal Dollarization

The greater is the magnitude of current unofficial dollarization, the smaller will be the benefits of exchange rate devaluation, and the greater will be the potential benefits of formal dollarization. In a situation where the U.S. dollar (or another currency) is already used as a unit of account, means of payment, and store of value, the costs of a transition to formal dollarization will be minimized. Zimbabwe is currently believed to be more than 95 percent unofficially and semiofficially dollarized, and any formalization will just cement the current situation. Thus, according to this requisite fact, Zimbabwe is currently the most ideal candidate for dollarization.

Ability to Provide Lender of Last Resort Functions after Dollarization

Although dollarization limits a country's central bank's ability to provide lender of last resort services to its banking system, such a function can be performed even in a dollarized economy through a variety of channels. First, in the case where foreign reserves are in excess of what is normally needed to cover the monetary base, such excess reserves can be used to cover some components of monetary aggregates, including demand deposits and other longer-term liquid liabilities of the banking system. For Zimbabwe, this option is not available given that its foreign currency reserves have long dried up. Second, the country instituting dollarization can build liquid reserves through borrowing, either from the private sector (private contingent credit lines), or from international financial institutions. Such international institutions include the IMF and the African Development Bank (AfDB), among other potential institutions. Again, this option may not be available for Zimbabwe given that no rational lender is currently willing to lend money to Zimbabwe because of the current government's mismanagement.[44] Third, changes in reserve requirement ratios[45] might provide further liquidity to a banking system under pressure. This may be an available option for Zimbabwe if it dollarizes. Fourth, in the situation in which there is provision of seigniorage revenue-sharing arrangement with the anchor currency's country, the discounted value of the stream of future seigniorage payments could be used as collateral for lines of credit with private and/or official creditors. This option is to be debated between Zimbabwe and the country whose currency is to be adopted in case Zimbabwe decides to formally dollarize, and, as such, we consider it not available at present

Revenue Cost of Seigniorage Loss

Dollarization that occurs without seigniorage-sharing with the anchor currency implies a revenue cost in the form of seigniorage revenue loss. For countries in which seigniorage accounts for a significant fraction of government revenues, such loss has serious fiscal consequences and needs to be compensated by an increase in non-seigniorage revenues. If seigniorage revenues are significant, this switch in sources of revenue may require tax reforms to reduce a structural reliance on seigniorage. In the absence of revenue sharing, the seigniorage loss is partly reduced if the dollarized country imposes non-remunerated reserve requirements on its banking system (essentially another form of taxation of banks), and, thus, the central bank can earn the interest rate on the non-currency component of the monetary base. To mitigate this potential revenue loss, the Zimbabwe government can impose the non-remunerated reserve requirements.

Central Bank Solvency in the Absence of Seigniorage Sharing

Another version of seigniorage loss to be well-thought-out is how such a loss affects the solvency of the central bank of a dollarizing economy. Under normal circumstances, the discounted value of future seigniorage is considered as an asset for central banks, which does not appear in their current balance sheets. This generally means that central banks often officially have negative net worth, but this will not be a worry when a country has its own currency—since the discounted value of the stream of seigniorage revenues is a substantial asset that is not shown in such balance sheets. In the case of Zimbabwe, its central bank's balance sheet shows negative net worth, a situation that indicates insolvency of the RBZ. This apparent insolvency of the RBZ becomes a larger hurdle if Zimbabwe decides to dollarize, especially in the case where seigniorage will not be shared with the anchor country. In this instance, a negative net worth of the RBZ will become a real form of insolvency. Thus, the ability of the RBZ to provide credible lender of last resort services (if authorized to do so by dollarization-imposed rules) might be further undermined. Using this criterion, implementation of dollarization by Zimbabwe may not be a successful adventure.

State of Public Finances

The greater the budget deficit and the stock of public debt, the risk increases that dollarization might fail. This comes from the fact that unsustainable fiscal conditions may eventually tempt policymakers to reverse dollarization and return to a domestic currency so as to be able to resume printing money and regain access to the inflation tax. At the same time, acute fiscal problems may also weaken the public's confidence in fiscal authorities and lead to a foreign debt-related financial crisis, whereby the country might stop honoring financial creditors.[46] Zimbabwe is currently one of the countries with a very high budget deficit and significant stock of public debt, as well as severe fiscal problems caused by, among other things, persistent hyperinflation in the past few years. According to this criterion, implementing dollarization may not achieve the desired end result.[47]

Supply-Side and Trade Related Factors

Ability to Successfully Pursue Countercyclical Monetary Policies

Literature on the subject matter has suggested that some small open economies with a history of high inflation and high exchange rate volatility are normally unable to use monetary policy for countercyclical purposes.[48] Generally, the presence of a combination of unofficial dollarization, lack of policy credibility, and wage indexation[49] are some of the complex issues that may render monetary policy ineffective against countercyclical shocks.

The ability of Zimbabwe on this factor is difficult to assess, especially given that ever since the high inflationary period, there have been a number of factors bedeviling the country—to the point that its monetary policy has been reduced to printing money and instituting some caveat policies to chase the few U.S. dollars earned by exporters. By and large, the country has not shown any ability to pursue countercyclical monetary policy to date, although there is a higher possibility of such policies being implemented in the near future, especially with the new GNU.

Correlation of the Business Cycle with the Anchor Currency's Country (South Africa)

In a situation where the dollarized country's business cycle is highly correlated with that of the anchor country, there will be no need for exchange rate adjustment. With such synchronization, any shock hitting a common currency area will be common to all economies in the area. As such, there will be a reduced need (if any) for currency adjustment. In such a situation, the monetary policy of the anchor country will likely be appropriate for the dollarized economy. The extent of business cycle synchronization between the dollarizing and anchoring countries, in turn, depends on real and structural factors, such as the degree of trade integration and the similarity in production structures between the two countries. As alluded to in the previous paragraph, due to chaotic structural changes happening in Zimbabwe since 1999, there has not been any serious business cycle to talk about because production has been dwindling year after year. Thus, under this criterion, one can safely say that the country's business cycle is not synchronized to either of the potential two anchor countries, the United States and South Africa.

Trade Integration With the Anchor Country's Currency

Chances of succesfull dollarization are higher if a larger share of the dollarizing country's exports and imports are traded with the anchor country. This is important as it will ensure that the dollarizing country is economically linked to the anchor country; hence, in such a case, adopting the latter country's currency will likely work for the former part. Financial and capital integration also correlate with trade integration. Although Zimbabwe does not contribute much in terms of volume to these variables, the country is highly integrated with South Africa, and not the United States, in its trade interactions.[50] Considering this criterion, one can conclude that Zimbabwe is a potential candidate for dollarization using South Africa as the anchor country and the South African rand as the chosen currency with which to dollarize.

Vulnerability to Terms of Trade Shocks

Vulnerability to terms of trade shocks is normally greater for countries whose exports are concentrated in a narrow range of primary commodities. A small country, and therefore a price taker for imports and exports in the market,[51] may not be able to modify its terms of trade. Under such circumstances, the benefits of dollarization will be potentially larger for such a small open economy.[52] Zimbabwe's main exports (though they are currently at minimum levels) are primary commodities, including tobacco, sugar, and cotton. Thus, inferring from this criteria, the country is a suitable candidate for dollarization.

Other Factors

Flexibility of Labor Markets

Enough flexibility in labor markets implies that any external shocks requiring a change in real wages and/or mobility of labor across sectors will not have lasting effects on the rate of unemployment. This flexibility may include the following types: (1) downward flexibility of nominal wages (to induce a reduction in real wage if so required); (2) labor mobility across sectors and regions if changes in relative prices require a reallocation of factors of production; and (3) low hiring and firing costs to ensure labor market flexibility.[53] Although there are some rigidities in Zimbabwe's labor market, generally, the country has relatively enough labor market flexibility, and judging by this factor, the country is ready for dollarization.

Degree of Labor Migration

Although free labor mobility between the country considering dollarization and the anchor country is an important consideration, such free mobility is generally ruled out since there are restrictions on crossnational labor migration. Nevertheless, in practice, the degree of labor mobility may be significant as there will also be a significant number of legal (and illegal) temporary and permanent migrant workers who can move between the anchor country and their country of origin. This is the present situation between Zimbabwe and South Africa. It is believed that there are currently more than three million Zimbabweans (a quarter of the population) living and working in South Africa, both on a legal and illegal basis, with the latter migrants being the majority. Thus, one can safely say that there is relatively less-restrained labor mobility for Zimbabwe moving into South Africa. More significantly, South Africa has suspended visa requirements for Zimbabweans seeking to enter or work for a period of ninety days or less.

Degree of Capital Mobility

The success of dollarization is also enhanced by a higher degree of capital mobility into the dollarizing economy, with capital mobility measured by flows of inward foreign direct investment (FDI). Currently, there is no meaningful inward FDI into Zimbabwe due to a number of factors, including political instability, hyperinflation, and general mismanagement of the economy. Thus, according to this criterion and as of now, implementation of dollarization may not be successful.[54]

Implicit or Explicit Fiscal Federalism and Income-Insurance Schemes

In a domestic currency union, for instance, the U.S. federal system, misfortunes experienced in one region are squarely (or partly) compensated by a federal (or central) system of tax and transfers. With dollarization, such an automatic insurance scheme disappears as monetary integration will not be associated with fiscal integration, since the dollarizing and anchor countries will possess different fiscal policies. However, there may be some implicit forms of income insurance still at work. For instance, if a dollarizing country has a large number of migrant workers in the anchor country, worker remittances could be an important source of income for the dollarizing economy.

Table 6.2   Zimbabwe's readiness for dollarization

Factors	Ready
Monetary, financial, and fiscal	
1 Policy credibility	Yes
2 Inflation experience	Yes
3 Current exchange rate regime	Yes
4 Reserve coverage of monetary base	No
5 Soundness of the banking system	Yes
6 Extent of informal dollarization	Yes
7 Ability to provide lender of last resort functions after dollarization	No
8 Revenue cost of seigniorage loss	Yes
9 Central bank solvency in the absence of seigniorage	No
10 State of public finance	No
Supply-side and trade related	
11 Ability to successfully pursue countercyclical monetary policy	No
12 Correlation of the business cycle with the South Africa (or United States)	No
13 Trade integration with South Africa (or United States)	Yes
14 Vulnerability to terms of trade shocks	Yes
15 Openness to trade	Yes
Others	
16 Flexibility of labor markets	Yes
17 Degree of labor migration	Yes
18 Degree of capital mobility	No
19 Implicit or explicit fiscal federalism and income insurance schemes	Yes
20 Political factors	No
Overall readiness	**YES**

Source: Author's summary from the analysis presented in the chapter.

Zimbabwe is fortunate to have a sizeable proportion of its working population (nearly 50 percent of its labor force) working in the diaspora, including such countries as South Africa, the United Kingdom, and Botswana, to mention just a few countries. Although these people send remittances, they have neither been sending them through the formal bank, nor through money transfer channels, due to the perennial RBZ's fixed exchange rate, which individuals have rationally evaded for its unfairness.[55] Most have been sending money through bus drivers (especially those in South Africa), relatives, and other money transfer agencies—whose exchange rates were closer to the prevailing rates of black market foreign exchanges at the time of transfer. Nevertheless, if the country formally dollarizes, there will not be any problem with exchange rates, and there is 100 percent probability that these remittances would come into Zimbabwe through formal bank channels.

Political Factors

The success of dollarization requires a high level of majority support. Normally, countries entangled in deep political divisions (with a history of political turmoil) and lacking stable democratic institutions, with significant political minorities opposed to dollarization, may not be good candidates for dollarization. In such a situation, there might not be any political support for dollarization, and there would be a greater probability that those groups opposed to dollarization could at some point reverse it should they come to power. Zimbabwe, at present, is caught up in a dilemma in which confidence in the use of the local currency has been eroded. Business and industry are pressuring for dollarization. Opposition to adoption of dollarization might come from politicians who have been direct beneficiaries of the skewed predicament of hyperinflation, obtaining the foreign currency at close to ridiculous, subsidized exchange rates.

Based on the analysis presented here, table 6.2 provides a summarized version of the country's readiness for dollarization.

Conclusion and Policy Recommendations

The analysis presented in this chapter shows the advantages and disadvantages of dollarization as a possible solution to Zimbabwe's current hyperinflation environment. Although, like any system, there will be negative consequences, the positive advantages of this system indicate that overall Zimbabwe is a potential candidate for this system.

The Zimbabwean government is therefore recommended to consider adopting dollarization as a possible way of taking the country out of hyperinflation. Although the choice of the anchor currency could logically be between the U.S. dollar and the South African rand, the latter seems to be the most appropriate.

Notes

1. CSO is the collector and custodian of the country's formal statistics on socioeconomic issues.
2. International Monetary Fund (IMF), "Preliminary Conclusions of the IMF Article IV Consultation Mission," Facsimile addressed to Zimbabwe's minister of finance, March 23, 2009.
3. Steve Hanke, "Zimbabwe: From Hyperinflation to Growth," Cato Institute, Centre for Global Liberty and Prosperity Development Policy Analysis, 2008. Steve H. Hanke is a professor of applied economics at Johns Hopkins University in Baltimore. He has written extensively on monetary issues, including dollarization and currency boards in general, and has also written a number of briefs and papers, in particular on Zimbabwe's hyperinflation scenario.
4. Ibid.
5. Zimbabwe's highest money denomination as of January 2009 is Z$100 trillion. Adding back the thirteen zeros Zimbabwe's central bank has lopped off since August 2006 (three zeros were chopped off on August 1, 2006, and further ten on August 1, 2008)

as a means of trying to make the country's currency somewhat more manageable, the total number of zeros would be twenty-seven.

6. One million has six zeros, one trillion has twelve, one hextillion has twenty-one, one octillion has twenty-seven, one nonillion has thirty, and one decillion has thirty-three.

7. It is important to note that the country's use of multiple currencies is not legal, and neither is formal dollarization from the government of Zimbabwe's point of view as pointed by the RBZ's governor. See "Reintroduce Zim dollar: [RBZ governor]," *The Herald*, August 18, 2009, http://www1.herald.co.zw/inside.aspx?sectid=8782&cat=1

8. Government of Zimbabwe, Ministry of Finance, 2009, http://www.kubatana.net/docs/econ/min_fin_budget_2009_090129.pdf.

9. Phillip Cagan, "The Monetary Dynamics of Hyperinflation," in *Studies in the Quantity Theory of Money*, ed. Milton Friedman (Chicago: University of Chicago Press, 1956), 25.

10. Central Statistical Office.

11. IMF, "Preliminary Conclusions."

12. Albert Makochekanwa, "A Dynamic Enquiry into the Causes of Hyperinflation in Zimbabwe," Working Paper Series no. 9, Department of Economics, University of Pretoria, 2007.

13. Ibid.

14. "Economy's Dollarisation A Quick Fix," *Independent Online*, January 27, 2009, http://www.int.iol.co.za/index.php?click_id=68&set_id=1&art_id=nw20090127052719343C403802.

15. "RBZ Unveils 100 Trillion," *The Herald*, January 16, 2009, http://www.herald.co.zw/inside.aspx?sectid=153&cat=1.

16. "I'm Ready to Quit [RBZ Governor]," *Radio VOP*, October 1, 2008, http://www.thezimbabwean.co.uk/index.php?option=com_content&view=article&id=15526:im-ready-to-quit-gono&catid=31:top%20zimbabwe%20stories&Itemid=66.

17. "Zimbabwe Suspends Own Currency for 12 months," *South African Press Association (SAPA)*, April 14, 2009, www.thezimbabwean.co.uk/index.php?option=com_content&task=view&id=20402&Itemid=103.

18. Besides dollarization, the country can also consider any of these three: currency board, free banking, or joining the Common Market Area (CMA).

19. Hanke, "Zimbabwe: From Hyperinflation."

20. Ibid.

21. Zeljko Bogetic, "Official Dollarization: Current Experiences and Issues," *Cato Journal* 20, no. 2 (2000): 179–212.

22. Eduardo Borensztein and Andrew Berg, "Full Dollarization: The Pros and Cons," Economic Issues no. 24, IMF, Washington, 2000, http://www.imf.org/external/pubs/ft/issues/issues24/.

23. Bogetic, "Official Dollarization," 2000.

24. Since the introduction of multiple currencies in the beginning of February 2009, FCAs have been liberalized, that is, anyone can open an FCA.

25. Whether dollarization is on a permanent or temporary basis is not the most important issue. The idea or assumption is that once institutions are set to manage dollarization, even if the local currency is brought back in future, those institutions will maintain the low inflation principles they might have learned during dollarization.

26. S. Meyer, "Dollarization: An Introduction," paper presented at the Philadelphia Council of Business Economics, Philadelphia, Pennsylvania, December 6, 2000.

27. Zimbabwe's interest rates are above 400 percent, compared to SADC's rates of below 20 percent.

28. Devaluing any currency is the privilege of only one country—the owner of the currency. Thus, if Zimbabwe adopts the U.S. dollar or South African rand, only the U.S. government can devalue the U.S. dollar, and the South African government can devalue the rand (and not Zimbabwe in either case).

29. B.J. Cohen, "Dollarization: Pros and Cons," prepared for the workshop "Dollarization, Democracy and Trade: External Influences on Economic Integration in the Americas," 2000.

30. Following the introduction of multiple currencies, the country has been at 100 percent dollarization since February 2009.

31. R.C. Burdekin, "Currency Boars vs. Dollarization: Lessons from the Cook Island." *Cato Journal* 28, no. 1 (2008): 101–114.

32. Meyer, "Dollarization: An Introduction."

33. Losing the lender of last resort capacity in an arrangement like a monetary union is slightly different than losing this capacity when a country dollarizes. In the former, regional monetary policy to be implemented in signatory member states is normally crafted by all participating regional members, and there likely will be clearly laid-out rules regarding the function of lender of last resort.

34. Cohen, "Dollarization: Pros and Cons."

35. John Maynard Keynes, *The Economic Consequences of Peace* (London: MacMillan Press, 1920).

36. Since 2004, these rates have been especially applied, but at different time periods.

37. According to the RBZ, the following banks have at one time been (or are currently) under curatorship: Barbican Bank, CFX Bank, Royal Bank, Time Bank, and Trust Bank.

38. N. Roubini, "Factors to be Considered in Assessing a Country's Readiness for Dollarization," Stern School of Business, New York University, New York, 2001.

39. Ibid. Whether this will be sufficient or not will depend of the country's import basket.

40. Meyer, "Dollarization: An Introduction."

41. IMF, "Preliminary Conclusions."

42. These include creditors from South Africa and China.

43. It is important to note that these foreign banks, besides having good capital, will also bring best practices for risk management into the country. The assumption is that their positive contribution will outweigh their negative contribution to the overall economy and financial sector.

44. However, some countries, such as China, have indicated a willingness to lend to Zimbabwe despite the latter country's mismanagement. China's willingness might be strategic given its interest in Zimbabwe's mining and infrastructure projects.

45. Reserve requirement ratio (RRR) is the percentage of deposited money that a bank is required—for monetary authorities, such as the RBZ in Zimbabwe's case—to keep and not lend in the form of loans. For instance, if the RRR is 10 percent, then for a $10 deposit, a bank will be allowed only to lend a maximum of $0.90, and must keep $0.10 in its coffers (or lodge it with central bank). This RRR ensures than depositors can get their cash any time they visit the bank for a withdrawal.

46. A good example is Mexico's 1982 foreign-debt crisis. The Mexican government borrowed heavily from foreign sources to such an extent that its foreign debt was around US$70 billion in January 1982 and increased to US$80 billion by October of the same year. Because the country could not repay the foreign debt according to the agreed timelines, on September 6, 1982, it suspended all payments toward the foreign debt. See Mabry, 1982, "Mexican Financial Crisis." Available at: http://historicaltextarchive.com/sections.php?action=read&artid=330.

47. IMF, "Preliminary Conclusions."
48. Countercyclical policies are intended to go in opposite direction of trends in economic activities. A good example is the bailout packages being rolled out by European countries and the United States over the past few months. As a result of downward trends (recession) in these countries, to counteract problems such as low product demand and a rise in unemployment, these governments have instituted countercyclical policies. Under the "scrap car" scheme in the United Kingdom, citizens are given two thousand sterling pounds by the government for the purchase of a new car, aimed at stimulating the low car sales. This increased demand will encourage more production, which in turn will increase employment. The United States and Germany have also implemented similar bailout initiatives.
49. Wage indexation refers to a situation in which the percentage increase in wages reflects the percentage increase in inflation. A one-on-one indexation indicates that if, for instance, inflation increases by 20 percent, the wages will also increase by 20 percent.
50. For the five year period, 2000–2004, Zimbabwe exported an annual average of US$576 million worth of products to South Africa and US$73.4 million to the United States. For the same period, the country's annual average imports were US$917 million from South Africa and US$57.4 million from the United States. See TIPS database, www.tips.org.za.
51. Price taker in this case means that the prices for products exported from Zimbabwe are determined by the world market through supply and demand. Zimbabwe will only either take the price or leave it. It cannot set the price say for its exported goods.
52. One measure of openness used in literature is the percentage ratio of total trade (exports plus imports) to GDP. For the time period analyzed in this chapter (i.e., 2000 to end of January 2009), Zimbabwe's annual openness ratio was averaging above 67 percent, using figure from the IMF database.
53. Roubini, "Factors to be Considered."
54. This may, however, change if issues of property rights are addressed via the empowerment legislation. This was the case with post-conflict countries such as Angola and Mozambique, where there has been a surge in their respective natural resource sectors, such as and oil and gas. Zimbabwe's relatively good financial and physical infrastructure could support this trend well.
55. S. Bracking and L. Sachikonye, "Remittances, Poverty Reduction and Informalization in Zimbabwe, 2005–6: A Political Economy of Dispossession?" Working Paper 28, Brooks World Poverty Institute, 2008.

Chapter 7

Agrarian Reform and
Prospects for Recovery

Sam Moyo

Introduction

Since September 15, 2008, when the Zimbabwe African National Union-Patriotic Front (ZANU-PF) and the two Movement for Democratic Change (MDC) formations signed an interparty agreement to work together toward a peaceful democratic transition, sustainable development, and the normalization of relations, debates over Zimbabwe's economic recovery and development strategy have intensified. Various donors, including the Multi-Donor Trust Fund[1] managed by the World Bank (WB), the United Nations Development Programme (UNDP) in Harare,[2] the "Fishmongers"[3] donor group, and key "think tanks"[4] have proffered strategies. The Government of Zimbabwe's (GoZ) budget[5] and monetary statements[6] have also charted a new path of economic liberalization. A few Zimbabwean policy groups—Labour and Economic Development Research Institute of Zimbabwe (LEDRIZ), African Institute for Agrarian Studies (AIAS), and Zimbabwe Coalition on Debt and Development (ZIMCODD)—have weighed in with sectoral proposals.

The longer-term issue in Zimbabwe remains how to resolve the agrarian and national questions, with democratization being an intrinsic requirement. Zimbabwe's agrarian question today (as elsewhere) concerns its transition from a poorly developed agrarian society to an industrial society through the transformation of the roles and capacities of the various agrarian actors (including peasants, agricultural workers, landowners, and agrarian capitalists) and the state, and improvement of the social relations of production. The development of agriculture's productive forces and its enhanced contribution to national accumulation are central.[7] The immediate purpose is to "create the conditions for a rise in [agricultural] productivity, such that [the] raw materials and wage—goods needs of a growing manufacturing sector can be met, while labour is released."[8] Agrarian reform should thus entail the incremental diversification of industry and improved wage employment. Other supplementary sources and mechanisms of accumulation, however, include the mining, tourism, and services sectors. Since "national" commodity and capital flows intersect with, and are shaped by, global processes of production, and various markets—involving transnational capital,[9] agricultural trade, and related foreign financial flows (and aid)—shape the nature of the agrarian question, in terms of integration into the world economy.

The issue is how to address Zimbabwe's agrarian question, and specifically the food crisis given Zimbabwe's restructured agrarian and food systems, within the evolving global financial and food crisis. After all, the recent world food price and food aid crises have hurt Africa the most, given its poor agricultural performance and dependency on food imports.[10]

Much of the controversy over Zimbabwe's Fast Track Land Reform Program (FTLRP) since 2000 has been over how and to what extent the reforms adequately redressed inequalities and have been socioeconomically beneficial. Greater emphasis has been placed on "elite capture" in the land allocations, the abrogation of rule of law and violence in the land transfers, the marginalization of farm workers, the decline of agricultural production, and food insecurity. During the course of Zimbabwe's fast track land reform since 2000, the debate shifted from the land transfers to issues such as good governance, as well as agricultural productivity and the humanitarian "crisis."

Few scholars have recognized that the recent land redistribution had been historically progressive in so far as it yielded structural reforms in the agrarian sector, in spite of its various shortcomings.[11] Indeed, Zimbabwe's land reform has largely been discussed in terms of the problems of its democratic deficit, characterized mainly by the violence that occurred around elections since 2000, and the violence and human rights transgressions that accompanied the land redistribution.[12]

A rigorous understanding of the outcomes of the fast track land reform program is critical to any assessment of the prospects for sustainable agrarian reform within a process of democratization, for the promise of deeper forms of substantive democracy in a society pervaded by deep racial and class inequities can only be meaningfully achieved through structural changes. As we show later, despite the casualties of the land reform process, such as the economic decline (estimated at a 30 percent) experienced in Gross Domestic Product (GDP) since 2000, it has created the socioeconomic foundation and potential for broad-based development and democratization. Indeed, the focus needs to be on addressing the persistence of critical deficiencies of the land reform outcomes, particularly regarding land use and agricultural productivity, while rebuilding democratic institutions toward the goal of sustainable agrarian reform.

The complex issue of land and agrarian reform has not been handled methodically, as emotive analyses and distortions are common.[13] Some scholars label any non-mainstream views of the long term as gullible victims of Robert Mugabe's anti-imperialist script and vilify the whole land occupation movement by equating it with extreme human rights violations.[14] Moreover, debates on the pitfalls of land reform tend to be based on commonly held misperceptions about the performance of agriculture prior to 2000 (see table 7.1). There is no doubt that the economic decline was partly occasioned by the effects of land reform and the responses of capital to the increased state-interventionist policies in all markets.[15] However, economic and agricultural decline were also affected by the withdrawal of private investments and the isolation of Zimbabwe from donor funding and international financial institutions' credit. Various factors contributed to the decline of agricultural production. The result, though, is seen largely as a "collapse," or the "destruction" of agriculture, mainly due to "failed" land reform policies[16] rather than a complex set of factors.

That agricultural production has fallen below the pre-2000 average levels is not in dispute. To acknowledge this is to also recognize the unrealized potential of land reform. However, most assessments treat the so-called failure in aggregate terms and disregard the heterogeneous outcomes among the fifteen agricultural commodities, the three classes of farmers, and the five agro-ecological regions across the racial divide. The evolving nature of the outcomes (in relation to changing context: from the early acquisitions up to 2003, through the high inflation period, and then the hyper-inflationary period from 2006) tends not to be recognized. Often, inaccurate data on the scope and scale of the decline of production inputs use, forex shortages, formal agricultural job losses, and marketed crop[17] are misleadingly used. Moreover, ascribing all the economic and farming woes to the displacement of white farmers and internal policy[18] tends to promote racist Afro-pessimist teleologies.

Table 7.1 Pre-fast track land reform perceptions (1980–1999)

Common perceptions	Reality
Smallholders "subsistence" producers	• 80% national food is produced by smallholders • 70% of marketed maize, pulses are produced by smallholders
Most food supplied by large farmers	• Mainly high value foods • Smallholder high nutrition foods
Little smallholder exports	• Cotton, tobacco, paprika • Beef via large scale commercial farming (LSCF)
Rural employment mainly on large farms	• LSCF: 320,000 (50% full time) • Communal areas: 2 million+
Food production was adequate *(from "bread basket to basket case")*	• Maize output declines from 1995+ • High malnutrition levels then

Customary tenure bad–freehold tenure good	• Mixed performance results
	  – LSCF land underutilization
	  – High smallholder productivity
	• Historic state investment bias
	• Wider non-tenure financing base

Environmental "crisis" in communal areas	• Overcrowding/resilience • Low inputs system • Low water/rainfall resources

Source: Compiled by the author from various sources.

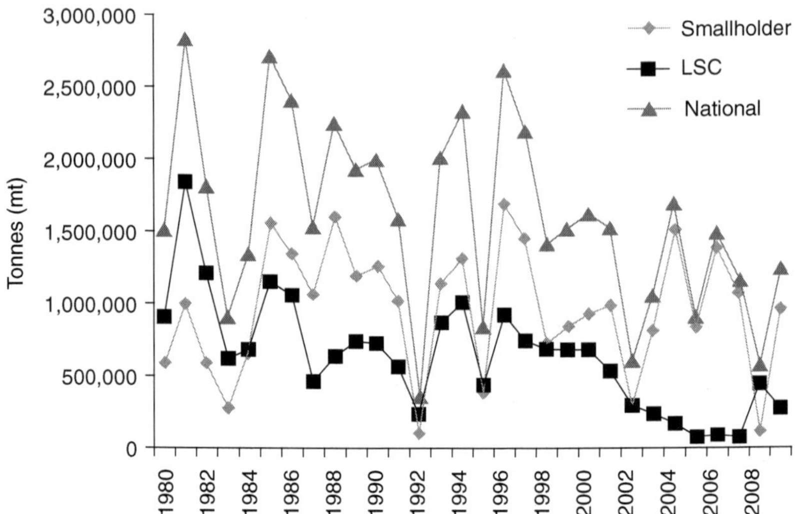

Figure 7.1   Subsectoral maize production trends (1980–2009) in Zimbabwe.

It is often erroneously alleged that almost all of Zimbabwe's agricultural production, particularly the exports and so-called marketed foods, were produced by large farmers, and that Zimbabwe was the breadbasket of the Southern African Development Community (SADC). In fact, during more than half of the years from 1980 to 1999, Zimbabwe was a food importer.[19]

This inaccurate assessment overlooks the fact that small producers supplied most of the national foods and that "peasants" were not merely subsistence producers—they contributed significantly to some exports. For instance, since 1985, 70 percent of cotton has been produced by small farmers.[20] Thus, the present agricultural decline arises from various factors, with the land redistribution being one contributor (see figure 7.1). Any credible analysis of the present agricultural production trends and their explanation needs to be founded on current factual assessments of the precise scope and intensities of production by the wide range of producers of the various crops within the changing economic context.

Zimbabwe's Land Question and Fast Track Land Reform

Zimbabwe's independence in 1980 began the democratization process by reversing settler colonialism, but fell short of addressing the historic demands for social justice, particularly with regard to land and equality. However, the Lancaster House Agreement and Constitution of 1979 had provisions that constrained land reform by requiring land acquisition to be done on a willing seller, willing buyer basis, and by demanding that compulsory land acquisition be paid for in foreign currency at market prices. This constitution would only be changed in 1990, ten years after it was signed.

The newly independent state defended privileges in landed property relations and economic participation in the name of rights, markets, and the need for economic growth, while repressing demands for redistribution through the rule of law. By 1999, Zimbabwe's deeply unequal and racialized agrarian relations remained unjust and unsustainable,[21] while strategies to resolve the land question floundered.

Zimbabwe inherited a dual, unequal, and hierarchical system of land distribution and tenure.[22] Approximately six thousand white commercial farmers, differentiated according to land holding quality and sizes,[23] held about 15.5 million hectares (45 percent of the agricultural land), most of which was located in the best agro-ecological areas. These lands were held under freehold (and leaseholds) tenure, which provided rights and duties protected by law, thus binding everybody including the state. The small-scale commercial farming sector comprised eighty-five hundred black farmers on 1.4 million hectares, holding leaseholds (with an option to buy) located mainly in drier regions (table 7.2).[24]

Zimbabwe has always had a multiform tenure system, which entailed a complex mosaic of six forms of land tenure, or access regimes, that intersected and interfaced at various levels, including: freehold, leasehold, customary, permit, statutory allocation, and license tenures.[25] Freehold tenure entails registered title deeds representing unfettered ownership of the land, freedom to sell, lease, and transfer the land through inheritance, and minimal regulation of the right to use the land. Leasehold rights are mainly regulated in terms of the conditions of use and sale. The customary land rights of the indigenous population are permissive in that they are the trusteeship of the state and cannot be freely sold. In general, the latter are not adequately protected by law, although they are recognized administratively.[26]

Table 7.2 National land distribution pattern (1980–2010)

Farm categories	1980	1999	2010
Communal areas	16,400,000	16,400,000	16,400,000
Resettlement	–	3,500,000	3,500,000
Small-scale commercial farms	1,400,000	1,400,000	1,400,000
A1	–	–	4,137,000
A2	–	–	3,497,000
Large-scale farms	15,500,000	11,725,000	3,383,000*
State farms	500,000	721,000	721,000
Urban land	196,000	250,000	250,000
Parks/forests	5,074,000	5,074,000	5,074,000
Unallocated land			708,000
Total⁺	**39,070,000**	**39,070,000**	**39,070,000**

* Includes remaining black and white large-scale commercial farms, corporate estates, institution farms, DTZ farms, BIPPAs, and conservancies.

+ Totals differ due to rounding off and some discrepancies in the data sources.

Sources: Moyo (1999); Utete Report (2003); Moyo and Yeros (2005).

The opening up of the freehold markets for land after independence led to further land concentration among white farmers, as well as among some black commercial farmers.[27] In this context, freehold and leasehold tenures were long-treated as legally superior forms of land tenure compared to customary rights,[28] although the sanctity of freehold tenure diminished after 1985 as from then on the state had the legal right of first refusal in the sale of freehold land. After the constitutional amendment in 1990, freehold agricultural land became subject to compulsory state land acquisitive powers through the Land Acquisition Act [Chapter 20:10].

The land tenure system before 2000 was, therefore, embedded in unequal and discriminatory power structures and administrative procedures that allocated land unequally on the basis of race, class, gender, and ethnicity.[29] Freehold agricultural land ownership remained predominantly in the hands of white people—at over 70 percent of the titles—while men held over 95 percent of freehold titles.[30] Political independence and resettlement entailed continuities and limited change in terms of land concentration and the land tenure system, that is, until the advent of the fast track land reform in 2000.

The roots of Zimbabwe's fast track land reforms include the fact that the colonial regime of land property rights was enshrined in the new constitution of 1979 and that the market-led land reforms of the 1980s were unsatisfactory and unworkable, particularly once external financing decreased. The three million hectares of land transferred by 1999 were well below expectations, while it was mostly the marginal lands that were transferred for resettlement by 1992 because the prices of land had escalated. The land reform program had been co-opted by the structural adjustment program in 1990. From 1990 until 1996, after having contributed forty-four million US dollars to land reform in the 1980s, the United Kingdom's conservative government and the government of Zimbabwe failed to agree on a second phase of financing. In 1997, the Blair government turned its back on the agreement on the grounds that the United Kingdom had no colonial responsibility on land matters and that its aid was shaped by its poverty reduction strategy. The donors' conference of 1998 also failed to yield progress in land redistribution, due to disagreements over the land acquisition (expropriation) strategy and over macroeconomic policy. From that point forward, external loans and aid dried up, leading to the *go it alone* strategy of the government and the incremental expansion of Western sanctions. Since 2000, the state has not had access to International Monetary Fund (IMF) or WB loans, and most grant aid was slashed after 2002. The United States imposed formal sanctions in 2002.

The FTLRP was implemented in earnest from 2000 to 2008, having begun with a failed attempt to compulsorily acquire 1471 farms (or 4.3 million hectares) in 1997. It entailed an aspect of "illegal" land occupations between 2000 and 2001 on about 1000 large scale farms, including approximately 100 black-owned properties.[31] The FTLRP then involved state expropriation of land and farm assets from about 3200 of the 4000 large scale white farmers, including those which had been illegally occupied. By 2008, about 10 million hectares of the 11.2 million hectares under freehold and leasehold tenures had been expropriated, including farms belonging to about 200 black commercial farmers.[32] Widespread landowner litigations were mounted throughout the period, leading to frequent reacquisition processes between 2000 and 2005, until the constitutional amendments of 2006 proscribed litigation on the land acquisition process.

The deep structural changes that have taken place in Zimbabwe are quite evident.[33] Scoones[34] shows that land reform was not hijacked by cronies—although some cronyism did operate; with some high ranking politicians gaining access to prime farms, it has been marginal to the whole process. The land reform has been broad based and largely egalitarian. Over 162,100 families have benefited directly, mainly among the rural poor, but also among their urban counterparts (which on average have access to 20 hectares of land), totaling 70 percent of the land acquired by government. The remaining 30 percent of the acquired land has benefited more than 16,386 new small to medium scale capitalists who were allocated an average of 100 hectares.[35] Most of the beneficiaries benefited through the A1 scheme, commonly referred to as the "social component" of the land reform program, with smallholder land sizes. Altogether, about 25 percent of Zimbabwe's entire agricultural land (including communal areas and acquired agricultural estates) is held by middle to larger scale farmers. A small segment of large scale capitalists persists, including both black and white farmers, but their land sizes have been greatly downsized to an average of 700 hectares, much lower than the average of 2000 hectares previously held by 4500 landowners on the whole of this land.[36]

The violence and violations that accompanied land reform are not in dispute, although the level of fatalities was notably low compared to rates of land reform-related fatalities in countries such as Brazil and South Africa. A maximum of six white farmers and eleven farm workers are considered to have been killed in the process of land transfer, as opposed to those killed in election violence.[37] Indeed, the recurrence of violence, including by state agents, led to the shrinking of political space and continued long after the land reform. The continued acquisition of remaining white-owned farms until 2009 has continued to focus debates on issues of violence and human rights violations. For instance, at least thirty more white farms have been acquired during 2009, and in a number of cases, the farmers have refused to vacate the farms, while those allocated the land have sought to forcibly occupy it.

In the early stages of the FTLRP (2000–2003), the leadership of the ruling party struggled to appease and co-opt the land occupation movement, and used force in defense of the landless and against the political forces allied to the white agrarian monopoly and Western interests.[38] From 2003 onward, as the land movement dissipated and the enlarged black capitalist class repositioned itself, violence was used to defend narrower class interests, as well as against forces perceived to be allied to the West (Moyo and Yeros, 2009). A series of tragedies occurred between 2005 and 2008 as economic hardship deepened. Mobilization tactics were substituted with quick-fix, military-style operations. The state evicted so-called illegal urban dwellers in an operation called Murambatsvina in 2005. Then "illegal" rural miners who had resorted to panning and smuggling for their livelihood were evicted during 2006 and 2008. Numerous small to large businesses deemed to be profiteers were subjected to a price-control blitz in 2007, but this only expanded the parallel markets. The eviction of some of the remaining white farmers escalated between 2007 and 2009. Last, during the presidential contest of 2008, opponents within and outside of the ruling party faced violence and intimidation.

The demand for land, expressed through illegal occupations and formal applications for access to land, grew between late 2000 and 2004, surpassing all previous estimations of demand for land among various classes. Over fifty thousand persons applied for A2 plots in 2002.[39] In turn, compulsory land acquisition proceeded beyond the previous five million hectare targets. Although the ruling party condoned and/or promoted the initial land occupations, it was evident that social pressures and mobilization from below had played a critical role in expanding the land acquisition and redistribution process[40] beyond the technocratic agenda of the 1998 phase two land reform plans[41]; it took the government three years (from 2000) to structure and gain full control of the land acquisition and allocation process.[42] These processes continued over eight years and led to some notable land conflicts among competing new farmers and between new and former landowners. The Utete Report[43] found that there were over two hundred multiple landholders within A1 and A2 schemes; that the sizes of land plots allocated tended to differ from the recommended size ranges; that there was extensive interference by some politicians in the land allocations; and that agro-industrial estates were subdivided for cropping on inappropriate land sizes. The committee recommended a "correction exercise," which was expected to rationalize multiple land allocations and to provide for the needy, while settling disputed land claims.

Land redistribution was soon followed by a variety of economic and agricultural policy measures and schemes intended to support (and protect) the new and existing farmers and/or small producers in the context of economic decline and falling agricultural production, as shown later. In a loosely coordinated agrarian reform program, an increased range of state interventions (including subsidies for inputs and credit and forex allocations to agro-industry) were instituted (see the following sections). At least sixteen measures were deployed in support of agriculture (see table 7.3), in addition to other sectoral interventions, such as the supply of cheaply priced fuel, electricity, and other inputs, and financing toward agro-industry.

In the wake of the abandonment in 1996 of the Zimbabwe Programme for Economic and Social Transformation (ZIMPREST; which was the proposed second phase of the Economic Structural Adjustment Program [ESAP]) the Zimbabwean state gradually initiated a heterodox economic strategy.[44] By 2002, the government eventually began intervening across all sectors of the economy, and agriculture in particular. It increased its control over prices, distribution, credit, and forex, in addition to attempts in 2006 to control minerals and to impose legislation for indigenous capital majority control over businesses in 2007. The strategy included resurrecting state-owned enterprises (SOEs) to direct the recovery and diversification of trade and investment to the East, whereby increased investment and trade with China was encouraged. This corresponded to the period of Zimbabwe's increasing isolation from the Bretton Woods institutions (i.e., decreasing access to loans), financial markets, and aid.

Factors and Sources of Agricultural Decline

Debates on the underlying drivers of Zimbabwe's agricultural collapse counterpose the external factors (such as sanctions and droughts) against internal policy factors,

Table 7.3 Policy matrix: factors affecting agricultural production

Policy arena	Constraining factor/processes	Source	Factor
Weather	• Droughts, flooding • Mitigation/irrigation	External	Technology
Land transfers	• Reduced sizes/area planted *(some crops)* • Land disputes/conflicts/security	Land policy effects	New resource endowment, production structure
INPUTS USE	• Agro-industrial supply bottlenecks *(seed, fertilizer, agro-chemicals)* • Trade credit/forex loss • Distribution bottlenecks *(markets/transport)* • Access/affordability *(credit)*	Macro-econ and agricultural policy constraint	Technology and capital
FARMER SKILLS AND ORGANIZATION	• Skills "deficit" • Extension services deficiency • New farmer organization	Micro-institutional	Extension Training

FARM INVESTMENTS AND FINANCING	• On-farm infrastructure/ irrigation deficits
	• Domestic financing models/ deficiency
	  – State *(Credit/subsidies)*: inadequate
	  – Private *(credit/sub-contract)*: inadequate
	• External financing *(BoP loss)*
	  – Retreat of merchants *(tobacco, horticulture)*
	  – Bretton Woods/Bilateral loans loss
	• Smallholder recovery aid deficits
		Macro-econ policy Deficiency and negative external policies (isolation/ ratings)	Finance system

MARKETS LOSS	• Marketing channels control/ monopolies *(capacity, incoherence, infeasible)* • Price controls: Unviable/ infeasible • External agricultural markets loss *(horticulture, beef, etc)* • Tourists (image) and multipliers loss • Trade restrictions, smuggling	External policies and economic policy incoherence	Roles of state, markets; external relations

BoP = Balance of Payments.

Source: Author's compilation.

such as the absence of property rights, the ineffectiveness of state interventions into agriculture, economic mismanagement, and the abandonment of the rule of law. The conceptual model used to explain the latter includes notions of state failure driven by theories on neo-patrimonialism, which emphasize the shortcomings of a patronage-based authoritarian political system. Domestic "market failure," global induced crises, aid-policy deficiencies, sanctions, and the deeper structural impediments to agricultural growth are rarely discussed.

Not surprisingly such analyses tend to emphasize the need to return land to former landowners as the solution to the problems, and at best, they argue for the need to promote the new type of better-off large-scale farmer. Indeed, recent policy incentives and agricultural recovery support mechanisms have prioritized the new medium to large farmers, despite the abuse of support by some, and at the same time, these measures have marginalized or excluded small-scale farmers. Furthermore, by focusing on the new farmers' behavior, many analyzes underemphasize the problems confronting the wider agro-industrial sector and domestic financial markets, as well as the role of international markets, in constraining agricultural production since 2000. Zimbabwe's agricultural deficits are related to a complex combination of factors that include: weather-induced harvest failures, the transitional effects of rapid agrarian and structural change, and economic collapse, which is partly associated with extensive sanctions and internal and economic policy deficiencies. The influence of these factors is discussed in the following paragraphs.

Various proximate and structural factors explain the decline of agricultural production among the diverse crops (table 7.3), especially when the effects that arise directly from land transfers are separated from those that arise from wider constraints facing the economy and the efforts of new farmers to establish themselves. The diverse range of producers and commodities was variably impacted because each faced distinct constraints, depending on the policies affecting the diverse capacities of the producers. This reflects wider structural factors, which have persisted to make Zimbabwe's agricultural system vulnerable, particularly in the face of the multiple shocks (land reform, droughts, policy conflict, and sanctions), that it has faced since 1997. Policies such as government control over input and output prices were counterproductive in this situation. The hyperinflationary conditions from 2007 began to affect all commodities in similar ways as agricultural input constraints deepened. The expansive monetary policy itself drove much of the hyperinflation.

Internal factors entailed the rapid replacement of large scale commercial farmers (LSCFs) and the slow establishment of new farmers. Some national policies (particularly price controls) were a direct impediment to the farming activities of those active on the land. There was a large degree of tenure insecurity felt by some of the remaining (and larger) farmers, as their farms could be acquired at any time, while a few new farmers felt their tenure security could only be achieved once they received leases. Various on-farm production constraints and off-farm infrastructural constraints (such as erratic electricity for irrigation, fuel shortages, imported inputs shortages, tillage shortages, etc.) affected production. In particular, agricultural input and output markets did not work well for most farmers, whereas limited private lending of larger farms and low levels of state investments in support of small farmers have also been key constraints.

Agricultural "profitability," which is suggested arose from inputs and outputs price controls and exchange rate distortions, was reportedly the key constraint to agricultural production and investment.[45] The fundamental issue has been that high levels of inflation, which eventuated into protracted hyperinflation, were key obstacles to the viability of agricultural production. Inputs shortages (seeds and fertilizer), which mainly affected the smallholder farmers, seemed to be the main victim of the financial constraints facing the sector, given that other financial and trading speculative activities were more competitive.

Interestingly, the large multinational agricultural estates and key tobacco and horticulture farms that account for most of Zimbabwe's exports had received the best supply of inputs, which they get through their "toll manufacture," locally or imported directly. Smallholders and their crops (maize, small grains, and groundnuts), and to a lesser extent the cotton producers, who together account for the largest cropped areas, have consistently had the least access to fertilizers.[46] New commercial large-scale (A2) producers of controlled food crops such as wheat have also had limited access to inputs. This suggests that price and marketing-controlled commodities, most of which are domestic food goods, were the least capable of self-financing inputs, given their lack of forex and lower financial returns to production.

The utilization of fertilizers among Zimbabwe's fifteen key crops[47] has always varied. Its use declined mostly among small farmer-dominated crops, such as maize and cotton, which accounted for most of the increasing cropped areas. As well, fertilizer use dropped among those formerly LSCF-dominated crops whose crop area declined: wheat, tobacco, and oilseeds. The agricultural productivity "crisis," thus, mostly affected small and medium sized farms.

Not surprisingly, between 2001 and 2008, maize and cotton yields in Zimbabwe declined—with small producer maize yields being below one ton per hectare and yields of new middle farmers being below three tons per hectare, as opposed to the dryland potential of five tons per hectare.

Agro-input firms failed to sustain their historical production levels,[48] indicative of both the impacts of the wider economic decline, as well as a failure to adapt to new agricultural production and demand structures. Initially, it seemed they resisted to adaptation and depended on cheap government forex allocations associated with inputs price controls. From 2006, the hyperinflationary and forex-short macroeconomic situation restricted the ability of firms to adapt, while they continued to produce under contract for large estates and for export.[49] Despite the emergence of new institutions importing and marketing inputs, their effectiveness was constrained by ineffective price controls, forex resource gaps, and corrupt marketing practices in a forex-short situation.

The financing of agro-industries and farmers declined, as GDP fell considerably in 2004 (about 4 percent) and 2005 (29 percent).[50] Farm lending was reduced due to combined effects of reduced internal demand and savings, as well as reduced external financing.[51] As land use patterns shifted away from exports toward low-intensity (yields) foods, occasioned by the reduced utilization of agricultural inputs, earnings and demand decreased, while agro-industrial capacity to produce and supply inputs declined. This curtailed both domestic savings and lending.

Some agricultural capital stock, such as irrigation infrastructure, processing facilities, and machinery and equipment, was disabled during the fast track process (either removed by former owners or vandalized by some occupiers), which would have had some effect on production levels. While the level of agricultural tractorization in Zimbabwe (at seventy-five per square kilometer) also varies by subsector and is generally low, cropped areas of grains (except wheat) did not decline. However, the areas cropped for tobacco, oilseeds, and wheat did decline. The new middle farmer was, thus, the most constrained by tillage capacity. But many communal farmers (40 percent) and land reform beneficiaries do not own oxen or farm machinery, or sufficient resources to acquire these. Indeed, the relationship between labor use and access to farm machinery facing new farmers illustrates that farm labor utilization rate increases with capital intensities.[52]

Public equipment and draught hire services have so far been too undercapitalized to fill the gap, while private machinery hire services were slow in developing due to a lack of technical and financial resources. Survey data indicate that affordable fuel has been limited,[53] while some subsidized fuel has been misused, a result of the fact that some people hoarded fuel and resold it for non-agricultural purposes. Since 2007, the government's agricultural mechanization program contributed to the increased supply of machinery and equipment, with over three thousand tractors imported,[54] although this figure still remains well below the requirements of over fifteen thousand new "commercial" farmers. Foreign exchange shortages and the costs of securing forex in relation to prevailing interest rates and inflationary parallel markets have remained a key bottleneck. The securing of forex on parallel markets by the state, in order to supply machinery (and other inputs and wider national needs), contributed considerably to excessive money printing and speculative activities, and thus fueled hyperinflation.[55] But this issue underlines the importance of the gaps in agricultural and wider financing that became entrenched in the context of limited access to foreign loans and trade credit.

Investments in productive assets (e.g., irrigation facilities, electrification, and farm structures such as barns, animal sheds, granaries, and fences) and machinery and equipment tended to be low.[56] The inadequacy of investments into rural and agricultural infrastructures has tended to limit the expansion of agricultural food production and marketing. This discussion suggests a trend of low levels of mechanization, fertilizer, and pesticide utilization, which in turn suggests a failing agricultural technology transition and accounts for the persistent decline in crop productivity. The ratio of farm capital intensity to farm labor use also reflects this vicious cycle.

Relations with the West heated up in the late 1990s before the fast track land reform. The government abandoned structural adjustment (in 1996) and missed fiscal targets by paying war veterans' increased pensions.[57] The Zimbabwean government then initiated extensive compulsory land acquisition in 1997, in response to demands by war veterans and the United Kingdom's shift to an unsupportive stance toward accelerated land reform. This was followed by the intervention (with Angola and Namibia) in 1998 against the invasion of the Democratic Republic of Congo (DRC), which cost Zimbabwe substantially. By the end of 1999, the Zimbabwe government had revised its neocolonial constitution's land clause, using its parliamentary majority in 2000 (before the June elections) to achieve this in the face of opposition by the emergent MDC. From 1998 onward, some IMF and WB loans were withheld, the justification being that Zimbabwe had abrogated its fiscal targets; more aid was withheld from late 2000 through to 2001 and 2002 (before the elections and during an emergent drought) on the grounds of "increased human rights transgressions."[58] The result was a gradual retreat of Western investment capital and the construction of an elaborate sanctions regime,[59] which has played a critical function in the wider economic collapse of Zimbabwe by reducing the capacity of many industries to maintain and replace machinery and equipment, and to access forex and import raw materials. This shift in the correlation of forces set the groundwork for the more radical execution of the fast track land reform—by increasing the scale of lands acquired and postponing the farm compensation issue.

The incidence of sharp falls in Zimbabwe's GDP between 1999 and 2003 (estimated at 40 percent), when loans and aid (estimated at US$500 million a year) were withdrawn, cannot be treated as accidental, nor can the effects of land reform be attributed to this, since agricultural GDP fell most sharply after 2002 (a drought year). External factors, such as Zimbabwe's political and economic isolation therefore played a role in the decline in agricultural production, mainly through reduced access to external finance, which the Zimbabwe economy so heavily depended on. It is estimated that 35 percent of Zimbabwe's forex financing requirements were from external sources such as Bretton Woods' loans and aid grants.[60] For instance, tobacco merchants fled and long-term loans dried up, as did incomes from tourism. Social aid was also lost, shifting all such costs onto the fiscus, with dwindling forex.

The provision of food aid to an average of 30 percent of the population during the drought years does not mean there were no sanctions, as some have argued.[61] Moreover, humanitarian agencies frequently decried the shortage of food aid, and timing of delivery was always an issue. Such aid also focused on the humanitarian rather than the recovery dimension, and accompanied donor refusal to channel aid to blacks settled on newly reallocated land. Moreover, had more aid in the form of inputs been provided, the main constraint facing most small producers would have been lifted, and household food security would have improved.

Weather volatility, entailing four years of extreme droughts, long dry spells, and flooding during 2001 and 2008, led to frequent harvest failures.[62] These harvest failures highlight the disproportionately low levels of investments directed into small farmer irrigation to mitigate this problem, with the national proportion of irrigated cropped land remaining at 5 percent.[63] Between 1990 and 2003, the rate of annual growth of irrigated land in Zimbabwe was at 4.7 percent, but this modest growth is dubious because the initial irrigation level was below 3 percent.[64] Furthermore, since 2001, some irrigation facilities were disabled by various landowners, land occupiers, and criminals. The "efficient" utilization of existing scarce water and irrigation resources, (e.g., through drip technology rather than large scale center pivot systems) has also not been adequately developed. Moreover, Zimbabwe's preparedness for the anticipated effects of climate change is not convincing in terms of insufficient strategies to: relocate production to areas with the agro-ecological potential to produce food, along with the provision of necessary infrastructure;

adopting technologies to adapt to reduced growing seasons in some areas and length-
ened seasons elsewhere; adapting to water losses and gains; and so forth. Much of
this reflects the wider constraints of financing agriculture, including Zimbabwe's
exclusion from critical aid-funded initiatives.

Although Zimbabwe did not face formal trade sanctions, many exporters (in
horticulture particularly) report the loss of external markets. The effects of targeted
sanctions on some individuals, firms, and banks also constrain trade in that they
limit the government's trade promotion work. Travel warnings to Western tourists,
whose numbers declined, also affected wildlife ranchers and farmers by reducing
their client and forex-derived incomes. Thus, some agricultural production suffered
from these losses.

Neither did regional partners provide enough economic support, particularly in
terms of trade and infrastructure. For instance, Namibia entered a joint venture to
finance electricity generation with Zimbabwe, which led to increased access to power
and local electricity supply; however, the region became a hub for unrecorded smuggling
of agricultural produce and food imports, which reflected weak policy responses (price,
forex, and trade controls) in relation to regional and domestic supply and demand.

Toward Sustainable Agrarian Reform

Internal Perspectives on Agrarian Recovery

A sustainable agrarian program, which contributes to broader economic recovery and
development, needs to be sovereign and socially just and enhance the reorganization
and expression of the popular will of food consumers and agricultural producers,
especially small peasants (Moyo and Paris, 2009). It also needs to be buttressed by
trade and industrial policies that enhance balanced regional (SADC) integration and
mutual development.

Changes in economic policy between July 2008 and February 2009 indicate that
heterodox economic policymaking under hyperinflationary conditions reached a
dead end.[65] Having resisted normalization with international finance, the government[66] moved toward liberalization, beginning with various measures, including:

- multi-currencying;
- the removal of price controls;
- foreign currency exchange liberalization;
- reduced tariffs;
- 95 percent foreign currency retentions for all exporters;
- current account liberalization;
- aligned interest rates;
- termination of quasi-fiscal financing (fiscal deficit control);
- privatization;
- forex taxation; and
- government salary payments.

As a result, during the first six months of the Government of National Unity (GNU), hyperinflation came to an end, and in fact, Zimbabwe was on a deflationary path, although its South African rand referenced prices were still too high.[67]

Liberalization measures specific to agriculture included the removal of commodity price and marketing control, leaving the Grain Marketing Board (GMB) as a residual buyer of grain; the granting of permission to farmers to sell products in forex; and the establishment of the rights of agricultural exporters to retain 95 percent of their forex incomes. This seems to have encouraged farmers and retailers to sell more of their goods on open markets and to increase their outputs. However, the state promised to "continue mobilising inputs for rural and resettled small scale farmers, as well as ensuring that farmers have access to finance…and to assist farmers with technical support through integrated agricultural extension services."[68] Smart partnerships between local landowners, external financiers, and investors were also being promoted.

These steps reflect the loss of government control over monetary and exchange rate policies. Apart from easing the supply of imports and price volatility, two of the specific objectives of liberalization are to improve the conditions for foreign investments and financing and to cajole domestic capital to resuscitate production. Nonetheless, this policy framework alone can hardly be socially just, given that the poor are virtually shut out of a highly iniquitous hard currency market.

In this context, the GNU seems to be refining the policy and could set the stage for a debate on the nature of reforms required for sustainable agrarian reform. Already the new minister of finance Tendai Biti[69] has pronounced the slaying of hyperinflation by forex transaction measures, following similar pronouncements on downward price movements by the Reserve Bank of Zimbabwe (RBZ). Yet, the implementation details are not yet clear, nor are they adequately assessed by analysts. Indeed, the financing of US$2.5 billion budget in 2010 is open to conjecture given limited tax collection performance so far and weak donor support.

Regarding land policy, the GNU is yet to define its actions, which are expected to be guided by the September 15, 2008, agreement that acknowledges the difference of opinion over the method of land transfer, but that ultimately agrees that the redistribution is an "irreversible" social fact. An obvious next step is to undertake the proposed land audit, which is intended to rationalize land allocations and include others deemed eligible.

The current land redistribution outcome is in the medium term most likely to be retained *groso modo*, and can thus be expected to shape future agrarian reforms, notwithstanding the continued litigation by former owners, or demands by them for access to land. Of course unpaid compensation will have to be addressed in more reasonable terms than through some speculative and punitive pricings, which are based on debatable land market indices and property valuation norms.[70] There is general agreement that there is a need to correct anomalies—such as repossessing multiple-owned farms—rather than reverse the entire outcome, and include more beneficiaries; for instance, the various disadvantaged groups and some of the excluded black and white farmers. Additionally, the new forms of property rights need to be strengthened.

The main tenure issues in contestation are the efficacy of vesting former freehold land in the hands of the state, and the implication this could have for the security of property rights, and whether the statutory leasehold and permissory land rights being assigned to land beneficiaries can offer security. Most critical is the need to improve land utilization and agricultural productivity, bearing in mind the constraints outlined earlier.

Resolving the remaining land distribution and land tenure problems, including the associated rural labor or social relations of production identified earlier, requires the mediation of specific issues rather than wholesale conversion of land to freeholds. These issues include:

- regulating intra-elite farmer land disputes (including the holding of multiple and oversized farms) and competition for state resource allocations;
- addressing inter-farmer class struggles between the differentiated larger farmers groups and the heterogeneous small scale farmers over access to land, eviction threats, and over the threat to reform through privatization of the land tenure system;
- regulating the associated issue of unequal access to natural resources, such as water, woodlands, and wildlife;
- reversing the current system of intensive labor exploitation and the manipulative labor recruitment system, which is associated with insecure labor tenancy; and
- addressing the social reproduction crisis of agricultural labor through transformative social protection.

Zimbabwe's new agrarian structure creates a promising platform for obtaining food sovereignty, something the country has never obtained before as data on food imports and malnutrition since 1980 show.[71] There also exists the potential for creating new domestic intersectoral linkages and for the formulation of a new model of agro-industrial development, with organized small and middle farmers in the forefront. Some scholars and analysts do not recognize this potential and continue to speculate that "crony capitalism" is the ailment,[72] arguing about the "destruction of the agriculture sector"[73] as if it were a voluntarist and irretrievable state of affairs. There are some who believe that agrarian recovery can only occur if there are key reversals in the land distribution and tenure system and if previous models of financing agriculture and land use are returned (see table 7.4). The CATO Institute,[74] for instance, believes recovery requires the reinstating of the former system of large scale commercial farming (whether dominated by whites or inclusive of blacks) and the abolishment of the current "experiment" based on "subsistence plots."

Many perceptions regarding the prerequisites for agrarian recovery are not based on facts regarding Zimbabwe's pre-fast track agrarian model and its results. For instance, agricultural production statistics from the 1980s and during the 2000s show that small producers dominated staple foods and cotton exports production. New farmers are increasingly producing crops such as tobacco and soya beans, which were the forte of former landowners. New contract-farming financing is driving the gradual growth of this production, including beef, although pre-2000 output levels have not been reached. The potential to increase production among new farmers, if agricultural financing and inputs supply improve, is quite promising.

Table 7.4   Common perceptions on prerequisites of agrarian recovery versus reality

Common perceptions	Emerging realities
Recovery possible only if LSCF is reconstituted	Dynamic/diverse forms of farming at play
Reproducing past output patterns is most beneficial	• Yes for food but broader outputs are low • Why continue some exports (e.g., tobacco)
Some exports are too complex for small farmers	Exports contribution curve is growing
Investment only if "title" is provided to all farmers	• Non-freehold investment occurs • Enabling new farmers works
Financing is limited by scale economies and title	• New market structures emerging • New financing mechanisms emerging
Environmental "crisis" or tragedy is pending	• Land clearing is stabilizing • New forms of environmental stewardship

Source: Compiled by author.

Agrarian reforms need to mediate existing and potential social and class struggles over land, resources, and wider development strategy. Indeed, the new agrarian bourgeoisie tends to be more influential in agenda setting (and as previously shown, they have received most of the mechanization and inputs support) to the extent that smaller farmers may receive inadequate attention. This struggle suggests that a new lobby in favor of large farms, stripped of its white farmer leadership, could take root. Rather than anoint larger farmers to lead a pre-figured, extroverted agricultural production model at the expense of small producers, the strategy needs to recognize the importance of agriculture in the initial stages of development and support its growth toward a chosen agro-industrial growth path.

The challenge is to promote the productive capacities and improve the earnings of a range of small farm producers and agricultural labor within a reformed heterodox economic and social policy framework, in order to enhance equitable and broad based-development and address poverty. The specific agricultural measures required are those that address the critical factors that have undermined production. This does not mean that larger farmers cannot also play a role, but simply that resource allocation should be balanced.

The greatest danger is that the GNU could tilt toward an elite power-sharing pact that, under the tutelage of the Bretton Woods institutions, re-subordinates Zimbabwe to parasitical international financiers and corporations, including elements of South African capital that seek investments in Zimbabwe and undermine Zimbabwe's remaining industrial capacity. Such a process would offload the costs of recovery onto the peasants and workers because of an extroverted approach and limited humanitarian aid delivery. No doubt international financial institutions have a role to play in this, but it would be more meaningful if they focused on building upon the emergent agrarian structure and prioritized domestic food and industrial production growth.

Elements of a Sovereign and Socially Just Economic Recovery Program

Food Sovereignty

The focus of economic recovery should be a socially orientated agricultural policy aimed at protecting the marginal and vulnerable members of the rural poor, most of which are small farmers, and promoting adequate food consumption among the working poor. Over 65 percent of the population resides in rural areas[75] and survives from various sources of labor incomes and products, self-employment and remittances, and various forms of exchange. Social reproduction entails combining rural and urban livelihood strategies to attain own food production and achieve incomes that cover the expenses of schooling, medical attention, and other social needs. Own food production is thus critical in this system, where the expenditure is thinly spread between farming and social services, in a context of declining incomes from farming and reduced social subsidies from the state.

A broad range of investments and support are required to improve the agricultural performance of small producers—through increasing their land and labor productivity based on appropriate inputs supply, enhancing their markets by improving the prices realized, and resuscitating wider rural livelihood activities by promoting their diverse sources of income, and through growing public investments into progressive social protection systems. The goal should be to create a more sustainable basis for rural development and poverty eradication through addressing the core interrelated problems of *income deflation* and *demand repression,*, which have ensued in the 1990s and grown since 2002.[76]

The priorities for agrarian reform are self evident. First, economic recovery requires a comprehensive framework for achieving food sovereignty for the country as a whole, and not only for rural producers, and going beyond support measures focused on subsistence. As Ben Cousins[77] has also pointed out, peasant production should be made the pillar of economic recovery through subsidized inputs, fair prices, and secure tenure, which does not require the issuing of freehold titles in order to mobilize financing. Agrarian reform requires the technical upgrading of agriculture under the control of organized small producers' associations and the revival of agro-industries, which can focus on heterogeneous producers. The aim is to expand food production at home, focusing on enhancing smallholders' productivity and consumption of self-produced foods. The approach is to improve strategies to address the high costs and environmental effects of inorganic inputs and energy, using technologies such as seeds, fertilizers and pesticides, motorized traction, and harvesting and food processing techniques, which are less energy and capital intensive, alongside the use of external inputs. This should promote remunerative labor-intensive practices that create more and better jobs and enhance local demand. This can lower the costs of food and inputs distribution, currently based on large scale storage and transportation systems across the country and SADC region, while stimulating local small trading, food processing, and other small enterprises in an integrative manner.

As part of the immediate actions required, the GNU needs to prioritize the allocation of its limited resources and external assistance and improve relevant regulations, all toward the following ends:

- to allocate a greater amount of public resources to enable small farmers to procure (on subsidy) improved seeds and fertilizers and materials to treat and grow their livestock;
- to supplement the de-control of grain prices and markets, with measures that ensure that small farmers get a better return in local grain markets, and for small producers of cotton, tobacco, and other exports to get a fairer share of the international prices;
- to strengthen the residual marketing and food reserve role and capacity of the public GMB in order to enhance competition with usurious private traders, especially in remote smallholder markets;
- to provide low interest credit to enable small producers to rebuild their assets and to enhance their savings in order to invest in more effective medium to long term land use plans;
- to strengthen the public extension and research services so as to provide better agricultural information, and to improve beneficial links between small producers and inputs suppliers; and
- to finance the formation of stronger small farmers' associations.

There is also a need, as part of a rural development agenda, to extensively subsidize the social costs (especially of health and education) of rural populations to enable them to stretch their incomes toward wider productive activities. Indeed, given the dominance of rural-urban livelihood strategies, urban food subsidies will be needed for a few years, using measures that strengthen the demand for the various products of small producers, and to enhance cash and inputs remittances to the countryside.

Achieving food sovereignty and productive rural livelihoods will also require resolving the farm worker question. Farm workers have remained an underclass of "cheap labor" within former and new farms, and they have yet to be allocated land on an equitable basis. In particular, they need to be freed from the current labor tenancy system on so-called farm compounds, and from being considered "squatters" in newly resettled and other areas. The GNU should promote the establishment of settlements for residential and other purposes, and incorporate these into the local council system. Farm workers need to be incorporated into both their autonomous cooperativist systems, and a progressive social protection system, with the full support of the state at central and local government levels. Such *hamlets* would also serve various other non-farm employees (teachers, public workers, self-employed, etc.) for their residential and SME activities.

Agro-industrial and Sectoral Integration

Addressing the agrarian question comprehensively requires that trade and industrial policy be reformulated to secure the recovery of strategic industries and their reorientation toward producing adequate wage goods and the inputs necessary to enhance the technical upgrading of agriculture. The mining sector, which is crucial to the earning of foreign exchange and public revenue, will need to be regulated to ensure that the mines are not sold to the highest briber and that the revenues are reinvested locally, thereby focusing on financing the agrarian reform (Moyo and Yeros, 2009).

State banks should be given a leading role in the agricultural recovery given that the private banking system is not playing its part, and is unlikely to do so in the short term. Required is a credit system that directs productive and compatible investments to agriculture, industry, housing, and infrastructure, which would also promote the growth of local private sectors. Such a policy would be in line with emerging trends around the world, including the repositioning of state banks (and even the nationalization of banks) in South America, and the recent state interventions into the banking systems of the United States and Europe.

International and Regional Support for the Recovery

An independently managed international recovery fund needs to be established to undergird the proposed program recovery, with the SADC as a key player. Some argue that the possibility of a recovery policy framework without the dominance of international financial institution funding, and thus the search for a new heterodox economic policy, is not realistic, since donor financing tends to follow the cue of these major global financial actors. But the external injection of finance might not be delivered to the extent promised, while new aid conditions emerge. Moreover, aid resources have dwindled, and will dwindle further, and their channeling is affected by the financial crisis and new protectionisms. It is yet to be seen to what extent Western donors are prepared to reengage Zimbabwe beyond humanitarian aid and minor support to small farmers; there has been no major shift so far.

Key donors (e.g., the EU, United States, and Canada) will need to shift from their "humanitarian aid" plus stance of not providing social and food production assistance to newly resettled areas or lending to new farmers, while Zimbabwean state policies will also need to be reconstituted to address legitimate concerns. Moreover, aid resources should move away from procuring food aid mostly from abroad, and instead provide support to the production of a range of required agricultural inputs locally, and be directed toward small farmer input subsidies. This will also require capacity building of critical state institutions involved in land and agrarian issues and the diverse farmers' associations (which are emerging from the new agrarian structure), as well as innovative production and marketing strategies.

Contrary to our heterodox framework, the UNDP,[78] for instance, has proposed that Zimbabwe should readjust to the world economy through a form of "shock therapy." This proposal is astounding since not only did the UNDP recently distance itself from IMF/WB orthodoxy, but also because shock therapy has been completely discredited worldwide, especially in eastern Europe, Argentina, and other countries.[79] Moreover, the world economy itself faces a financial crisis, and it is unclear what exactly Zimbabwe should adjust to, even if some might claim the worst is over. In a parallel process, which reflects the lack of aid coordination (despite the requirements of the Paris Declaration on Aid Effectiveness), the Multi-Donor Trust Fund arrives at relatively similar proposals, which nonetheless pay greater attention to some social, pro-poor, and governance-related issues. Its focus is selectively directed at specific sectoral reforms, rather than based upon a holistic and strategic framework. Ironically, the UNDP proposes the need for a "developmental state," but this term is stripped of the requisite interventionist capacity, the UNDP having already proposed the privatization of most state functions and entities.

The limitations of the UNDP's recovery strategy document are most evident in its analysis of, and proposals for, the future of land and agrarian reform. It suggests that land tenure security can only be obtained if the legality and justiceability of the land transfers are resolved, following an independent land audit.[80] It recounts profusely the "chaotic" process of land reform and its abrogation of the rule of law. Indeed, its chapter on land and agriculture does not even recognize, let alone interrogate, existing evidence of the social facts on the ground: namely that the redistribution of land has meant that there are over one hundred and fifty thousand new farmers who are investing their energies and savings into agricultural production. Current agricultural production trends are not adequately treated, given the weaknesses of the data used, such that the gradual northward trend of production is underplayed.

Instead, the report focuses on the reestablishment of private agricultural (landed) property rights and land markets, including land registration in communal areas, as the panacea for reversing the agricultural production decline. The report even suggests that its proposed land tenure policy would by definition lead to the outward movement of "excess" populations out of the communal (and resettled) areas; and it erroneously claims that the Communal Area Development Plan of the mid-1980s aimed to do the same but did not keep its word.[81] Population transfers toward towns and cities are said to be necessary to enhance the consolidation of land into larger farms, which it is presumed, will make farming more efficient. What employment opportunities will be presented to these migrants is not made clear.

Yet, the prospect that external support could be directed at strengthening Zimbabwe's new agricultural land property rights, in order to make these more secure, by constructively building upon the outcomes of the reforms is only partially noted, on condition that restorative measures are adopted. Establishing a more effective land tenure administration system that provides confidence to all landholders within the multiform tenure system is indeed a prime candidate for forward-looking aid disbursement. No doubt international funding for the compensation of the land acquisitions, as well as our proposed measures, is critical to a comprehensive and speedy recovery.

The question of Zimbabwe's recovery, however, has to be viewed more holistically in the context of emerging regional dynamics, including the prospect for constructing a strategically autonomous region (Moyo and Yeros, 2009). SADC regionalism remains deeply contradictory in that the SADC Free Trade Agreement exhibits critical inequities. For instance, Zimbabwe's imports from South Africa had been on the rise since the 1990s. Dependence on the importation of basic primary and secondary goods has increased during the recent crisis, while there has been an extensive transfer of semi-skilled and skilled labor resources (estimated at over one million persons) to South Africa. Trade policy and the regional integration strategy should aim to prevent the annihilation, by South African and foreign capital, of Zimbabwe's agro-industrial base, and seek measures to compensate Zimbabwe for net resource transfers. Instead, other experts, such as the CATO Institute,[82] believe that all trade restrictions should be removed because industries have already been totally destroyed, meaning that there is nothing to protect.

Indeed, the plan to create an SADC common currency in 2015 should take precedence over ongoing "randization" dialogues, within a framework of regional integration that moves beyond its current excessive reliance on market power and functionalist logic.[83] This would most likely backfire by reinforcing unequal development in the region and harming solidarity.

Rather, Zimbabwe's agrarian reform agenda requires negotiations around the SADC free trade agreement to identify compensatory measures and developmentally sensitive areas in need of regional support. This would include regional investments into domestic food production, storage, and distribution facilities, and energy and infrastructure, as well as expanding regionally collective public goods, such as research and technological applications to intensify (non-GMO based) productivity among small producers in the SADC region. The collective (regional) generation of farm input technologies and the promotion of their utilization through subsidies would be critical in order to reduce the costs of small producers' inputs and marketing and storage, not to mention lowering food consumption prices for all.

Conclusions

A sustainable agrarian reform effort must ensure national ownership of the strategy and implementation, and prevent the issue of recovery from being transferred through the aid system to the UN and Bretton Woods institutions. These actors can play a role in providing technological advice and stabilizing reserves as originally planned. Already there is a marginalization of working peoples in "transitional" policymaking processes, led by short term, and at times superficial, consultancy advice, followed by ineffective consultations with a civil society whose capacities have been weakened—leading to the process being dominated by external experts and aid technocrats. The aid and recovery program must remain under the control of Zimbabweans, particularly farmers' organizations, and involve the SADC as part of the regional integration framework.

This agenda requires more research and analysis than is so far evident. The GNU would need to revamp its agricultural research and extension services to all farmers, as well as support and guarantee new credit schemes for farmers.

Notes

1. In 2008, all the main donors (EU, Norway, the UN family, etc.) put together a trust fund to finance analytic work on Zimbabwe's key challenges, with the view to increasing the knowledge and preparations for reengaging the government of Zimbabwe.
2. United Nations Development Programme (UNDP), *Comprehensive Economic Recovery in Zimbabwe: A Discussion Document,* UNDP Zimbabwe, 2008, http://www.undp.no/assets/Other-publications/UNDP-Comprehensive-Economic-Recovery-in-Zimbabwe-2.pdf.
3. The Fishmongers is a smaller group of like-minded donors (including Sweden, Norway, Canada, and the United Kingdom), which had by 2007 been discussing conditions under which and ways in which to reengage Zimbabwe. The Institute for Democracy in Africa (IDASA) is an institute for democracy, while CATO is a U.S.-based think tank, and the Adam Smith Institute is a U.K.-based think tank. These groups have been issuing various studies on Zimbabwe and receive substantial funding from the key donor countries.
4. Adam Smith International, "100 Days: An Agenda for Government and Donors in a New Zimbabwe," *Fragile States & Post Conflict Series,* July 2007.
5. Government of Zimbabwe, *Statement on the 2009 Budget,* presented to the Parliament of Zimbabwe by Hon. T. Biti, Ministry of Finance, March 17, 2009.
6. Reserve Bank of Zimbabwe (RBZ), *Monetary Policy Statement,* issued in terms of the *Reserve Bank of Zimbabwe Act* by RBZ Governor Dr. G. Gono, 2009.
7. H. Bernstein, "Agrarian Reform after Developmentalism?" (Presentation at the conference on Agrarian Reform and Rural Development: Taking Stock. Social Research Centre of the American University in Cairo, Egypt, October 14–15, 2001); and T.J. Byres, "The Agrarian Question and Differing Forms of Capitalist Agrarian Transition: An Essay with Reference to Asia," in *Rural Transformation in Asia,* eds. Jan Breman and Sudipto Mundle (Oxford, Delhi, and New York: Oxford University Press, 1991).
8. U. Patnaik, "Global Capitalism, Deflation and Agrarian Crisis in Developing Countries," in *Agrarian Change, Gender and Land Rights,* ed. S. Razavi (Oxford: UNRISD, Blackwell Publishing, 2003).
9. Bernstein, "Agrarian Reform after Developmentalism?"
10. Between 2002 and 2008, the prices of agricultural commodities, including grain (maize, wheat, and rice) and pulses took an upward turn away from their historically downward trend, established during the 1930s. (See Wahenga, "Biofuel Production and the Threat to South Africa's Food Security," Wahenga Brief no. 11, April 2007, www.wahenga.net/node/244.) Maize prices trebled, while the others at least doubled over five years. Various reasons have been given for this: the knock-on effects of financial, oil, and agricultural commodity speculation in the Western capital markets, the diversion of grain utilization from the food to the agro-fuel markets, increased consumption in the East, decreased production in Australia, and stagnant production in Africa.
11. See M. Mamdani, "Lessons of Zimbabwe," *London Review of Books* 30, no. 23 (2008): 17–21; H. Bernstein, "Rural Land and Land Conflicts in Sub-Saharan Africa," in *Reclaiming the Land: The Resurgence of Rural Movements in Africa, Asia and Latin America,* eds. Sam Moyo and Paris Yeros (London: Zed Books, 2005); Sam Moyo and Paris Yeros, "Land Occupations and Land Reform in Zimbabwe: Towards the National Democratic Revolution," in Moyo and Yeros , eds., *Reclaiming the Land*; and Sam Moyo, "The Land Occupation Movement and Democratization in Zimbabwe: Contradictions of Neoliberalism," *Millennium Journal of International Studies* 30, no. 2 (2001): 311–30.

12. Amanda Hammar and Brain Raftopoulos, "Zimbabwe's Unfinished Business: Rethinking Land, State and Nation," in *Zimbabwe's Unfinished Business: Rethinking Land, State and Nation in the Context of Crisis,* eds. Amanda Hammar, Brian Raftopoulos, and Stig Jensen (Harare: Weaver Press, 2003); and A. Hellum and B. Derman, "Land Reform and Human Rights in Contemporary Zimbabwe: Balancing Individual and Social Justice through an Integrated Human Rights Framework," *World Development* 32, no. 10 (2004): 1785–805.

13. David Johnson, "Mamdani, Moyo and Deep Thinkers of Zimbabwe," *Pambazuka News,* February 12, 2009, http://www.pambazuka.org/en/category/comment/54039; Patrick Bond, "Lessons of Zimbabwe: An Exchange between Patrick Bond and Mahmood Mamdani," *LINKS National Journal of Socialist Renewal*, December 2008, http://links.org.au/node/815/9693; and Horace Campbell, "Mamdani, Mugabe and the African Scholarly Community," *Pambazuka News,* December 18, 2008, http://www.pambazuka.org/en/category/features/52845.

14. See T. Scarnecchia, A. Alexander, et al., "Response to Lessons of Zimbabwe," in *Letters, London Review of Books* 30 no. 1 (2009), http://www.lrb.co.uk/v31/n01/letters.html.

15. See John Robertson "A Macroeconomic Policy Framework for Economic Stabilization in Zimbabwe" in this volume.

16. C. Richardson, "The Loss of Property Rights and the Collapse of Zimbabwe," *CATO Journal* 25 (2005): 541–65.

17. J. Robertson, Zimbabwe Productivity Issues (2010), http://www.slideshare.net/AfricanisCool/productivity-issues-j-robertsonpps (accessed on September 7, 2010).

18. For example, "Zimbabwe's New Unity Government," *The Economist,* February 12, 2009.

19. See FAOSTAT, http://faostat.fao.org.

20. M. Rukuni, P. Tawonenzi, E.K. Eicher, M. Munyuki-Hungwe, and P. Matondi, eds., *Zimbabwe's Agricultural Revolution Revisited* (Harare: University of Zimbabwe Publications, 2006).

21. Mamdani, "Lessons of Zimbabwe"; Sam Moyo, "Emerging Land Tenure Issues in Zimbabwe," Monograph Series, African Institute for Agrarian Studies (AIAS), 2007; and Sam Moyo and Paris Yeros, "Zimbabwe Ten Years On: Results and Prospects," *Pambazuka News,* February 12, 2009, http://www.pambazuka.org/en/category/features/54037.

22. I.G. Shivji, S. Moyo, W. Ncube, and D. Gunby, "National Land Policy Draft," Draft discussion paper prepared for the Government of Zimbabwe by the Food and Agricultural Organization (FAO) and the Ministry of Lands and Agriculture, Harare, 1998.

23. See Moyo, "The Land Acquisition Process in Zimbabwe (1997/8)," UNDP, 1998; Sam Moyo, "The Political Economy of Land Acquisition in Zimbabwe, 1990–1999," *Journal of Southern African* Studies 26, no. 1(1999): 5–28; and *Land Reform under Structural Adjustment in Zimbabwe; Land Use Change in Mashonaland Provinces* (Nordiska Afrika Institutet Uppsala, 2000).

24. Sam Moyo and P.B. Matondi, "Interrogating Sustainable Development and Resource Control in Zimbabwe," in *Land and Sustainable Development in Africa,* eds. Kojo S. Amanor and Sam Moyo (London: Zed Books, 2008).

25. I.G. Shivji et al., "National Land Policy Draft."

26. Ibid.

27. Sam Moyo, "The Political Economy of Land Acquisition in Zimbabwe, 1990–1999."

28. Shivji et al., "National Land Policy Draft."

29. Ibid.; and Sam Moyo, *The Land and Agrarian Question in Zimbabwe* (presented at the First Annual Colloquium at the University of Fort Hare, South Africa, September 30, 2004).

30. S. Moyo, "Emerging Land Tenure Issues in Zimbabwe," AIAS monograph series, Harare, 2007.

31. Moyo, "The Land Occupation Movement."

32. Some of the Major Themes Proposed For Discussion for the Retreat, Ministry of Lands and Rural Resettlement (MLRR), June 2009.

33. AIAS, "Zvimba District Household and Whole Farm Surveys," AIAS Survey, 2005; and AIAS, "Inter-district Household and Whole Farm Surveys," AIAS Survey, 2007.

34. Ian Scoones, "A New Start for Zimbabwe?" Livelihoods After Land Reform (LALR), September 15, 2008, http://www.lalr.org.za.

35. MLRR, 2009.

36. Moyo, *Emerging Land Tenure Issues.*

37. Human Rights Watch (HRW), "Zimbabwe: Fast Track Land Reform in Zimbabwe," A Human Rights Watch Report, 14: 1(A), March 2002, hrw.org/reports/2002/Zimbabwe/.

38. W. Sadomba, "War Veterans in Zimbabwe's Land Occupations: Complexities of a Liberation Movement in an African Post-Coilonial Settler Society" (PhD diss., Wageningen University, Netherlands, 2008).

39. Press statements from senior government officials. See "Zim Land Beneficiary List 'a Work of Fiction,'" *The Saturday Star* (SA), January 19, 2002; "Mujuru Hits Out At Greedy A2 Farmers," *The Herald*, January 13, 2004.

40. Moyo, "The Land Occupation Movement"; and Sadomba, "War Veterans."

41. By mid-2001 over one thousand large scale farms had been occupied by settlers in various parts of the country (see Sadomba, "War Veterans"). Phase II of the land reform program was presented in a plan at the 1998 Donors' Conference on Land. It targeted the transfer of five million hectares to ninety-one thousand families using both market purchases of land and expropriation. This was a follow-up on the first phase of land reform from 1980 to 1997.

42. Sam Moyo, "Land Policy, Poverty Reduction and Public Action in Zimbabwe" (paper presented at the Institute for Security Studies/UNDP Conference on Land Reform and Poverty Reduction, Hague, Netherlands, February 17–19, 2005).

43. Utete Report, "Report of the Presidential Land Review Committee under the Chairmanship of Dr Charles M.B. Utete," in *Main Report to His Excellency The President of The Republic of Zimbabwe,* Presidential Land Review Committee, Harare, 2003.

44. ZIMPREST was designed by the government of Zimbabwe in collaboration with the UNDP, WB, and other donors. It proposed to continue the fiscal austerity agenda begun under the ESAP, as well as to deepen the liberalization of trade, domestic business regulation, and privatization. Regarding land reform, it focused on the initiation of a land tax, but did not set any land acquisition and financing targets.

45. World Bank (WB), "Agricultural Growth and Land Reform in Zimbabwe: Assessment and Recovery Options," Report No. 31699-ZW, Harare, 2006.

46. Ibid.

47. The fifteen key agricultural commodities include: grains (maize, small grains, and wheat); oilseeds (soya beans, sunflower, groundnuts); key exports (cotton, tobacco, paprika); horticulture (oranges and others); floriculture (various); and livestock (beef, dairy, pork, small ruminants).

48. Ministry of Agriculture, 2008. Second round crop and livestock assessment report (April 7–12, 2008). April 23, 2008.

49. See various RBZ reports from 2004.

50. RBZ, "Monetary Policy Statement," in *Terms of the Reserve Bank of Zimbabwe Act,* by RBZ governor Dr. G. Gono, 2009.

51. RBZ, "First Half 2006 Monetary Policy Review Statement: Sunrise of Currency Reform," RBZ governor Dr. G. Gono, July 31, 2006.

52. W. Chambati, "Emergent Agrarian Labour Relations in New Resettlement Areas, Zvimba District," AIAS Monograph Series, Harare, 2007.

53. AIAS Baseline Survey, "Inter-District Household and Whole Farm Surveys," 2007.

54. RBZ, "First Quarter Monetary Policy Statement: A Focus on Food, Foreign Exchange Generation, Producer Viability and Increased Supply of Basic Commodities," April 2008.

55. See Albert Makochekanwa, "Zimbabwe's Hyperinflation: Can Dollarization be the Cure?" in this volume.

56. WB, "Agricultural Growth and Land Reform."

57. By the mid-1990s, some of the effects of the ESAP were job loss, de-industrialization, and the compression of wages (see UNDP, *Comprehensive Economic Recovery*), which led to extensive industrial activities. The War Veterans Association had mobilized street protests and other actions to force the government to increase their pensions and provide them with land (see Sadomba, "War Veterans").

58. Sam Moyo and Paris Yeros, "The Zimbabwe Question and the Two Lefts," *Historical Materialism* 15, no. 3 (2007): 171–204; Sam Moyo and Paris Yeros "After Zimbabwe: State, Nation and Region in Africa," in *The National Question Today: The Crisis of Sovereignty in Africa, Asia and Latin America,* eds. Sam Moyo, Paris Yeros, and J. Vadell (forthcoming); Sam Moyo and Paris Yeros, "Delinking in Crisis: The Resurgence of Radical Nationalism in the South Atlantic" (forthcoming).

59. Mamdani, "Lessons of Zimbabwe"; G. Elich, "Zimbabwe Under Siege," *Swans Commentary,* 2002, http://www.swans.com/library/art8/elich004.html; and S. Gowans, "Cynicism as a Substitute for Scholarship," 2008, http://gowans.wordpress.com/2008/12/30/cynicism-as-a-substitute-for-scholarship/.

60. RBZ, "The Impact of Sanctions against Zimbabwe," Supplement to the Mid-term Monetary Policy Review Statement by Dr G. Gono, Governor, Reserve Bank of Zimbabwe, October 2007.

61 Bond, "Lessons of Zimbabwe"; and Scarnecchia et al., "Response to Lessons of Zimbabwe."

62. J.A. Andersson, "How Much Did Property Rights Matter? Understanding Food Insecurity in Zimbabwe: A Critique of Richardson," *African Affairs* 106, no. 425 (2007): 681–90.

63. WB, "Agricultural Growth and Land Reform."

64. Ibid.

65. By October 2008, the economy was on a dollarization path as the public now resorted mainly to U.S. dollar and South African rand transactions, and the printing of local currency was failing to catch up with hyperinflation.

66. Government of Zimbabwe, "2009 Mid-Year Fiscal Policy Review Statement," presented to the Parliament of Zimbabwe by Hon. T. Biti., Ministry of Finance, July 16, 2009.

67. Ibid.

68. RBZ, "Monetary Policy Statement."

69. "Zimbabwe Finance Minister on Mission to 'Save' Zimbabwe Dollar," *Africa News,* February 15, 2009, http://www.zimbabwesituation.com/feb16_2009.html.

70. There are various initiatives by the Commercial Farmers' Union, Justice for Agriculture (JAG), and other human rights organizations, including EU-supported activities, and SADC and international litigations (e.g., International Centre for Settlement of Investment Disputes (ICSID) etc) that highlight this question, although research and debate on this has been limited and non-transparent.

71. See FAOSTAT, http://faostat.fao.org.

72. Bond "Lessons of Zimbabwe."

73. Campbell, "Mamdani, Mugabe and the African Scholarly Community."

74. L.M. Tupy, "A Four-Step Recovery Plan for Zimbabwe," CATO Institute, 2007, http://www.cato.org/pub_display.php?pub_id=8191.

75 Government of Zimbabwe, Central Statistical Office (CSO), "Preliminary Report of the National Census 2002," 2002.

76. Income deflation is: to restrict working population's money income relative to prices. In other words, an increase in prices relative to their money income can be achieved either through a rise in prices with an unchanging money income for them (i.e., profit inflation), or through a decline in their money income with an unchanging price (i.e., a wage deflation, or more generally an income deflation for the working population). See P. Patnaik, *The Accumulation Process in the Period of Globalization*, 2008, http://www.networkideas.org/feathm/may2008/ft28_Globalization.htm.

77 B. Cousins, "Reply to Mamdani article on Zimbabwe in London Review of Books, 4 December 2008,",unpublished, 2009.

78. UNDP, *Comprehensive Economic Recovery*.

79 Naomi Klein, *The Shock Doctrine: the Rise of Disaster Capitalism* (New York: Picador, 2007).

80. UNDP, *Comprehensive Economic Recovery*; and Movement for Democratic Change (MDC), "A New Zimbabwe," Policy Paper, Harare, 2007.

81. During the 1980s the Communal Area Development Plan (GoZ, 1986) had presumed that land utilization in Communal Areas could be reorganized by re-zoning the uses and, consolidating some plots, while the growth of urban centers in these areas (based on new small industries) would absorb "excess populations" from the countryside by providing non-farm jobs. In the event, non-farm employment nationally did not grow substantially and massive retrenchments were experienced by 1996 (see UNDP, *Comprehensive Economic Recovery*).

82. Tupy, "A Four-Step Recovery Plan for Zimbabwe."

83. The SADC has regional integration targets that include: the creation of a free trade area in 2008 (which is now underway), a customs union in 2010, a common market in 2015, and finally a monetary union with common currency in 2016.

Chapter 8

Addressing Food Security
A View from Multilateral Institutions
Simon Pazvakavambwa

Introduction

The issue of food security at both the household and national levels has taken center stage in Zimbabwe due to a variety of reasons. Historically, Zimbabwe was once regarded as the food basket of the region; however, over the last eight years there has been a major transformation from being a food surplus, self-sufficient nation to a severe food deficit basket case. While various authors have expressed varying opinions as to the cause of this major negative transformation, the real reasons have yet to be identified and analyzed. The Zimbabwean government has largely blamed frequent droughts as the major cause of food deficit; however, other countries in the region do not seem to have suffered the same effects. Zimbabwe has a well-developed agricultural irrigation sector in terms of farm dams and other storage facilities, and one would have expected these facilities to mitigate the effects of the drought.

In Zimbabwe 70 percent of the population is directly dependent on agriculture. The amount of land transferred under the land resettlement program amounts to a total of 10,485,435 hectares, benefiting a total of 237,858 families.[1] Of these beneficiaries, 13.68 percent of A2 beneficiaries (1428) were women, while almost 19.80 percent of A1 beneficiaries (28,863) were women. It should be recalled that the land reform program started in 1980, soon after independence.

On the other hand, critics of the land reform program attribute the current food deficit to the manner in which the program was undertaken. They point out that, among other reasons, the decline in the agricultural sector was largely due to the poor organization of the land redistribution program in which people with very little experience in agriculture, or no interest in agriculture whatsoever, have been allowed to sit on erstwhile productive land.[2] Whatever the reasons, the fact of the matter is that Zimbabwe is now a basket case.

As previously stated, approximately 70 percent of the population depends on agriculture as a source of livelihood. The number of people dependent on food aid has been increasing since 2000. More recently in 2008, it was estimated that up to three million people depend on food aid, while projections from the World Food Programme (WFP) indicate that as many as seven million people (approximately 50 percent of the population) may be dependent of food aid in the period beyond 2009 due to continued lack of food production capacity. There has always been an element of food assistance in the country, particularly for the dry regions of Matabeleland, Masvingo, and parts of the Midlands Province. Reasons for this development need to be documented and analyzed. While both the frequent droughts and the land redistribution program may have contributed to the current situation, the policies pursued by the government must be assessed in terms of their contribution as well. Agriculture has never been successful without appropriate state support; however, the lack of support mechanisms and the inadequate interventions adopted by the government must shoulder the large part of the blame for the current crisis. The recently launched *Short Term Emergency Recovery Programme* (STERP) makes the following provisions for agriculture:

- Assistance was given to acquire 80 percent of cereals since production over the last few years has averaged 20 percent of requirements.[3]
- Financing of the 2009–2010 wheat crop and summer crops were given priority since they were regarded as critical.[4]
- Humanitarian assistance in water and sanitation was given priority.
- Capacity utilization in agriculture to ensure more jobs, disposable incomes, and savings was highly recommended.

The country is to guarantee food security and self-reliance by addressing the land issue, consistent with the Global Political Agreement (GPA) and in particular, the need for a nonpartisan land audit and attention to issues of land tenure.[5] STERP outlines plans for the 2009–2010 season. Most of these plans are running behind schedule, indicating that it will be a while before Zimbabwe can achieve food security at the household and national levels. Although the STERP document outlines an ambitious program for the recovery of the agriculture sector, indications on the ground show that the goals will be difficult to meet due to lack of funding.

One of the major shortcomings of the Zimbabwe government was its failure to guarantee basic inputs in adequate quantities, and on time. The government's input scheme, introduced in 2001, benefited a few influential people while the deserving farmers found it difficult, if not impossible, to access inputs such as seed, fertilizers, and chemicals. The few that accessed these materials diverted them into the unofficial market, where they were being sold at exorbitant prices. Untimely delivery of inputs, due to price bickering, and delayed stage-managed imports were also a major cause of crop failure.[6] Pricing of agricultural commodities, particularly the controlled cops, resulted in many farmers moving away from these crops to other more attractive crops, yet the government insisted on a price regime that was destined to fail.

It is not surprising therefore that the situation was allowed to deteriorate, the government citing lame excuses such as drought and sanctions. Multilateral institutions have been critical of some of the policies pursued by government in an attempt to address the food security situation. This chapter examines some of these policies and their pitfalls.

Causes of Food Insecurity

Some of the identified causes of food insecurity have been stated as follows:

- Low labor productivity and nonsolvent demand as the primary roots of insufficient income;
- lack of public goods, which leads to insufficient pro-poor growth;
- low level of capital endowment leading to low yields and output price instability;
- inadequate technical application in agriculture, as signified by the very low level of inputs used and lack of adequate public research;
- lack of efficient agricultural support services such as extension and credit;
- lack of adequate supporting infrastructure, such as roads and telecommunication services, to facilitate marketing and the movement of produce;
- inadequate or misdirected government support, often given through political patronage[7];
- failed agricultural policies;
- government's reluctance to promptly engage development partners and nongovernmental organizations (NGOs).

There were early indications that the country would run short of the main staple—maize. The WFP sought to engage the government early in order to procure supplies; however, the government dragged its feet while prices soared. By the time the importation and food relief program was underway, prices had more than doubled. For example, the price of maize on the world market was US$125 per metric ton at the time when the problem was initially identified. By the time the first importations were done, the price had risen to US$260 per metric ton. The STERP makes provisions for the importation of 80 percent of the national requirements in order to provide for food security.

Significance of Food Security in Zimbabwe

Food security has been a significant factor in Zimbabwe since the turn of the century when developments in nonagricultural undertakings such as mining and manufacturing started to pick up pace. There was the need to produce food for these nonfood producing entities, and in sufficient quantities to sustain new developments related to the rapid urban expansion, which was largely a result of the liberation struggle. Many people deserted their rural homes and sought refuge in urban areas despite the fact that there were fewer jobs in the cities. Thus, although there were many people who were unemployed in urban areas at independence, they still needed to be fed.

In Zimbabwe, rapid expansion of industries and urban settlements after independence, and the increase in both formal mining and informal mining (small scale) operations, increased the number of people in the non-agricultural production area. This increase, together with a general population increase of 3.2 percent per annum, placed greater demands on agricultural production. There was therefore a need to increase and maintain agriculture production at a level that would sustain the entire population.

Declining Food Security at Household and National Levels since 2000

Since 2000, there has been a discernible decline in food security at the national level. This decline was mainly due to the newly announced policy whereby the government committed itself to supplying inputs, particularly grain related inputs, to farmers for the next six years in what was popularly dubbed the Government Input Scheme (GIS). Table 8.1 indicates the percentage reduction in major food and some cash crops over the 2000–2007 period. Using average production in the 1990s as a base, maize shows a negative trend throughout, while wheat trends are positive for the first two seasons only. Other crops indicate a similar declining productivity trend, except small grains (incomplete data due to an unavailability of data) and cotton in later years. The government tried to introduce policy interventions in order to improve productivity and food security. These specific policy pursuits are briefly described here.

Specific Policy Pursuits

During the period of 2000–2008, the government pursued various policies and strategies aimed at improving food security. In the majority of cases the intentions behind the policies were good; however, implementation failures resulted in a worsening situation. Multilateral institutions believe that the pursuit of these failed policies resulted in a worsening situation.

It will be noted that since independence Zimbabwe pursued a system of price control and subsidies. Subsidies were intended to keep the price of food for the consumer affordable. But the government failed to pay for the subsidies, particularly to the Grain Marketing Board (GMB), and soon the subsidies grew to unmanageable levels. Experience shows that subsidies are effective only when they are targeted. Following the 2009 fiscal and monetary policies, Zimbabwe appears to have abandoned the subsidy policy. However, initial indications are that farmers will not be able to produce

Table 8.1 Crop productivity trends, 2000–2007

Crop	Ave. Production* in the 1990s	Production and % changes from the 1990s average (in parentheses)**						
		2000/ 2001	2001/ 2002	2002/ 2003	2003/ 2004	2004/ 2005	2005/ 2006	2006/ 2007*
I. Main grain crops								
Maize	1668.6	(–11%) 1476.2	(–70%) 498.5	(–44%) 929.6	(–37%) 1059.0	(–55%) 750.0	(–43%) 945.0	(–52%) 799.0
Wheat	219.3	(3%) 225.0	(6%) 231.7	(–11%) 195.0	(–53%) 103.0	(–38%) 135.0	(–45%) 120.0	(–38%) 135.0
Small grains	50.0	(67%) 83.5	(–25%) 37.3	(81%) 90.7	(649.6%) 374.8			
II. Traditional export crops								
Tobacco	197.6	(2%) 202.4	(–16%) 166.0	(–59%) 81.8	(–65%) 68.7	(–62%) 73.4	(–72%) 55.0	(–67%) 65.0
Cotton	214.1	(34%) 286.1	(–21%) 168.8	(7%) 228.1	(6%) 228.0	(–8%) 198.0	(26%) 270.0	(26%) 270.0
III. Oil seed crops								
Soybeans	95.5	(84%) 175.1	(–24%) 72.4	(–72%) 26.3	(–57%) 41.0	(–25%) 72.0	(–25%) 72.0	(32%) 170.0
Groundnuts	92.0	(87%) 171.8	(–36%) 58.6	(59%) 146.7	(53%) 141.0	(–47%) 135.0	(–37%) 57.7	(–3%) 89.0
Sunflower	36.4	(–57%) 15.8	(–35%) 23.6	(–87%) 4.8	(–53%) 17.0	(–45%) 20.0	(–62%) 14.0	(–43%) 20.8

Source: Compiled by AIAS from various sources.

unless some form of subsidy is put in place. The market forces now at play appear to be making life difficult for both the farmer and the consumer. There is insufficient financing capacity to warrant total removal of agricultural subsidies in Zimbabwe.

Government Role in Input Provision: The Government Input Scheme

Following the 2000 general elections, the government announced that it would be responsible for providing inputs to the farming community for the next six years (from 2000 to 2006). Requirements for inputs such as seed fertilizers and chemicals, as well as fuel for tillage, were appropriated through the Ministry of Agriculture; however, due to resource limitations, the Ministry of Agriculture never received the funding they had budgeted for. Government revenues were not sufficient to sustain allocations to ministries, hence the Ministry of Finance resorted to severe cuts in allocation, and agriculture was not spared.

Over the years the funding gap grew because the government was not able to provide allocations that took inflation into account. Increases in allocations were therefore not in real terms, and this led to severe limitations in the implementation of programs. There was no commercial lending from banks, which cited lack of collateral security; the land reform program resulted in banks not accepting land as collateral since most agricultural land was potentially earmarked for acquisition through the gazetting process. Once the properties had been gazetted for acquisition, their collateral values declined to zero.

Despite clear indications that government would never be in a position to adequately fund agriculture, the GIS continued to prevail because the state had no suitable alternative to replace it. Furthermore, the GIS itself had not been subjected to an evaluation, which would have justified its discontinuation much earlier. In 2003, the Ministry of Finance decided not to appropriate the GIS, preferring instead to treat it as an off-budget item. This development was due to an increasing budget deficit in the face of increasing demands for funding under the GIS. The government sought alternative funding mechanisms, and the Reserve Bank of Zimbabwe (RBZ) introduced the Productive Sector Facility (PSF) in 2004.

The Productive Sector Facility

The PSF was introduced by the government through Zimbabwe's central bank, the RBZ, in 2004 to take account of the government's failed input scheme as well as the government's inability to provide sufficient resources for inputs through vote appropriations. The Ministry of Agriculture was not directly involved in the planning of the PSF. Under the PSF the RBZ availed a 25 percent interest rate for food crop production.[8] Considering that the ruling rates of interest were 300–400 percent, this gesture was welcome news to farmers; however, other provisions of the PSF made its implementation difficult. A major weakness of the PSF was that it was planned and implemented with little input from the Ministry of Agriculture and relevant stakeholders. The PSF was planed and implemented on the basis of what the central bank could afford and not necessarily on what was required for an effective and sustainable program.

The facility had a six month tenor for seasonal loans and an eighteen month tenor for capital formation loans. Loans not paid up by the maturity date, or any part remaining thereof, immediately assumed commercial attributes in terms of interest. At that time commercial interest rates were ranging between 300 and 400 percent. Although lending was for individual farmers, farmers only accessed their loans through commercial banks, which were then held liable for repayment by the RBZ. Despite relentless pressure from the farming public, releases of financial resources were late, initially from the RBZ to commercial banks, and even later from commercial banks to individual farmers. Financial planning and provisioning for the summer season starts in May with the tobacco crop. Ideally farmers should have their inputs ready by August so that they can carry out their operations without hiccups. Funding from the central bank was availed to farmers in November or December, by which time the season would have been very advanced.

Although commercial banks complained about the percentage they were allowed to charge for administrative purposes, the RBZ did not heed the call. Commercial banks were allowed to charge an administrative fee of 5 percent of the total funds they handled under the PSF. They considered this as too low to cover their administrative costs under the facility. Most seasonal loans matured and were called up before financed items were ready for the market. Short-term loans had a tenor of six months, yet it takes at least nine months to grow and sell produce financed under the short-term facility. More than 90 percent of short-term loans were called up before farmers could sell the crops they had financed. As a result, some commercial banks paid up the loans on behalf of their clients, but went on to put the loans under the ruling commercial interest rate. The result put virtually all A2 farmers (approximately fifteen thousand) and up to five hundred thousand small scale and A1 resettlement farmers into a debt trap, which further compromised their ability to go back to the land. Almost 90 percent of farmers relied on funding from the central bank. Thus, although the RBZ recovered their money from commercial banks, the commercial banks later struggled to recover from the farmers. The debt incurred by commercial farmers due to default on the RBZ facilities is estimated at Z$5 billion (approximately US$2.5 billion). Some farmers, in open defiance, resorted to side marketing, and the objective of food security was never achieved.

This shows that the PSF failed to deliver in the very first year it was conceived. This forced the RBZ to go back to the drawing table, where a number of facilities later emerged. Although the limited tenor is mostly cited as the major reason for the failure of the PSF, its administrative mechanisms were too cumbersome to make a positive contribution. Under the PSF, farmers only accessed funds through commercial banks; however, commercial banks could not advance money to farmers before the central bank had transferred money to them. This delay meant that farmers got their funds late in the season and were not in a position to move with the season. The role that the Agricultural Finance Corporation (AFC)[9] had played in the past was now split into several institutions, the majority of which were not familiar with lending to the development sector. Most banks that accessed funds from the central bank had no experience in lending to the development sector. Despite this limitation, the banks went ahead to access money from the central bank because it was the only source of funding in the absence of international lines of credit.

The Agricultural Sector Productivity Enhancement Facility

The Agricultural Sector Productivity Enhancement Facility (ASPEF)[10] was mooted from the failures of PSF. The ASPEF was administered directly by the central bank. Its objective was to finance both seasonal and medium-term requirements for agricultural development. The facility had an eighteen month tenor on short-term loans and three years on medium-term ones. The facility was an improvement in many aspects, but the bitter lesson of the PSF was too recent to forget. The ASPEF was represented by various support frameworks:

- Irrigation Rehabilitation ASPEF provided funds for the resuscitation of irrigation schemes that had ceased to operate, either due to lack of maintenance or due to vandalism. Funds were provided for the purchase of irrigation equipment, such as electric pumps and motors, pipes and sprinklers, dam rehabilitation, and outlet works.

- Horticulture ASPEF funded the construction of pack sheds, grading sheds, handling trays, and crop inputs for horticulture.
- Crop and Livestock Production ASPEF provided inputs for crop production, seed fertilizer, and chemicals, as well as drugs for the treatment of livestock. There was also a cattle finance scheme for herd improvement.
- Development of new irrigation schemes, and so forth.

In the implementation of the ASPEF, further complications arose as a result of the following shortcomings:

- ASPEF programs were poorly designed. Emphasis appears to have been on financial aspects instead of farmer empowerment and viability. The program concentrated on financial management and loan recovery without taking into account the broader aspects and risks involved in agriculture. Although the major objective of the quasi-fiscal activities of the central bank was to make agriculture more productive and sustainable, the late disbursement of funds defeated this noble cause.
- There was limited consultation between the central bank and experts in the agricultural field, which would have enriched the facility and ensured the viability of the program. It was this lack of consultation and the seeming dictatorial tendency of the central bank that prevented contributions from agricultural experts.
- Implementation was too centralized, with the RBZ making all the decisions. The central bank had recruited six senior officials from the Ministry of Agriculture, who were now the sole advisers to the bank. This decision marginalized the staff in the Ministry of Agriculture, whose role was to advise the government on all matters pertaining to agriculture.
- The role of the Ministry of Finance as the provider of funding to ministries was severely compromised. The Ministry of Finance became an inactive conduit through which requests could be channeled, but had no say over the final outcome.[11]
- The role of the Ministry of Agriculture was marginalized and structures within the ministry were rendered ineffective as they depended on the whims of the RBZ.
- Ministry plans and projections were often ignored as the central bank sought to implement its own policies and strategies, often at variance with the Ministry of Agriculture.
- The RBZ became the main player, making virtually all decisions, regardless of whether they made sense. All this was done under the now-accepted theory of having to do something differently and not in a "business-as-usual" manner.

The role of the central bank in both program planning and implementation further marginalized the Ministry of Agriculture and its structures, resulting in nonachievement of the objectives of the ASPEF. The RBZ was later to blame the failure of the

ASPEF on what they published as "advice given but ignored." Although no positive lessons can be learned from this program, it must be admitted that the attempt to fund agriculture against a background of acute resource limitations is highly commendable.

If the central bank had stuck to its traditional role and left both the ministries of finance and agriculture to play their roles and mandates, the ASPEF would have enjoyed a larger measure of success. As a food security policy and strategy, the ASPEF failed largely due to the dominance of the central bank in its implementation modalities. The development sector (small scale sector) suffered considerably under the ASPEF as its design and provisions were not compatible with the requirements of the sector.

Shortcomings in Government Planning

Despite the fact that the Ministry of Agriculture produced elaborate plans for crop financing well in time for discussions with the Ministry of Finance during the *Estimates of Expenditure* exercise, the results of those discussions were disappointing. The Ministry of Agriculture did not receive any obvious priority, and the outturn was always far below 10 percent of the national budget.[12] The resultant allocation was a source of perpetual frustration, as resources made available were grossly inadequate. The Ministry of Agriculture progressively failed to meet its obligations due to inadequate financial resource allocation. This further compromised Zimbabwe's ability to achieve food security at the household and national levels.

Late Resource Allocation to the Ministry of Agriculture from the Ministry of Finance

The few resources that were provisionally allocated to the Ministry of Agriculture by the Ministry of Finance trickled in at an agonizingly slow pace. The reason cited was that the Ministry of Finance needed to match revenue inflows with expenditure forecasts. In the majority of cases, the previously agreed financial flows and forecasts were never followed, resulting in the ministry operating at an enormous deficit.

Rigid Allocation of Resources between Ministries With No Real Growth from Year to Year

Annual allocations to ministries were often static—they did not allow for much expansion or capital expenditure. Most allocations were intended to maintain existing services only, and even in this case, at a reduced level. Despite clear indications from ministry plans that they needed more resources, this call did not materialize. Ministry programs for the Public Sector Investment Program (PSIP) are usually very extensive; however, due to resource limitations, little funding has been provided for new projects over the last ten years. The government could only provide funds to maintain existing services.

Lack of Appreciation of the Significance of Agriculture and Its Role in Household and National Food Security

The significance of food security at the national and household levels was taken for granted. Despite reliable indications from the crop forecasts that grain would be limited, the government did not put together an early importation program. In 2002, for example, the decision to import maize was taken very late, by which time prices had more than doubled. This lack of appreciation of the importance and significance of food security at both the household and national levels led to a further deterioration of the food security status in the country. If there had been this appreciation, Zimbabwe should have tried to implement the Southern African Development Community (SADC) directive to allocate at least 10 percent of national budget to agriculture. For example, despite the hyperinflation, allocations to agriculture should have been significant to at least 10 percent of the national budget.

Poor Levels of Funding and Poor Targeting within the Ministry of Agriculture

The tight budget allocations resulted in poor priority targeting in the Ministry of Agriculture. Budgets had to maintain a large overhead base with little room for operating expenses. As a result, structures within the ministry, such as the extension division, the research division, the agricultural economics division, the livestock production and extension division, and the division of veterinary services, failed to service the agriculture clientele due to budgetary constraints. The long-term result as we now know it was a severe reduction in the food security situation in the country. The fact that Zimbabwe has not been producing enough food on its own indicates that there is a reduction in the food security situation in the country. This reduction becomes severe given the proposal in the STERP document to provide for 80 percent of requirements in order to meet food security needs of the country.

The Champion Farmers Program

With the evident failure of Maguta and the worsening food security situation, the Zimbabwe government introduced the Operation Food Security (Champion Farmers) program starting in the summer of 2008. The food security situation during the 2008 season became even more critical. There were very limited inputs available due to low production in the previous season. There were no inputs in the country other than those imported or purchased by the central bank, and these inputs were not sufficient to meet national demand. Under the Champion Farmers program, the government undertook to provide inputs to targeted farmers capable of producing high yields. The idea was to ensure that the few inputs available would be put to the best use to boost food production and food security. Only farmers with a known production record should have been selected, in order to optimize the few inputs available. It would appear that the program has failed to target potentially productive farmers. The extension service has a very good knowledge of the capable and productive farmers in the country. These farmers should have been selected ahead of everyone else. Some of the shortcomings of the Champion Farmers program include:

- Everyone who filled an application form was considered, regardless of capability or track record.
- Most farmers who registered for the program appeared to have no idea what to expect. There was no awareness program mounted by the government to advertise the program among farmers, hence most of them were not aware of the objectives of the initiative.
- Delays in launching the program affected yields.[13]
- Revision of crop packs and their reduction of fertilizer requirements by 50 percent made projected yields unattainable.
- The staggering of inputs to farmers in an attempt to stretch the availability of inputs compromised yields. Inputs were provided to farmers in small bits to increase distribution, but this did not provide for effective operation at the field level.
- The lack of proper targeting meant that the objectives of achieving food security could not be met in the immediate term. The Champion Farmers program was intended to provide immediate relief within one season.

Multilateral institutions are not against the provision of inputs by the state; however, implementation modalities riddled with corruption and favoritism reduced the significance of the government's good intention to assist farmers.

Subsidized Fuel for Farmers

The idea of providing farmers with subsidized fuel was noble given the cost and availability difficulties. The fuel facility was intended to assist all farmers.

The Role and Effect of the Land Reform Program on Food Security at the Household and National Levels

Critics of the government's land reform program attribute the failure by government to achieve sustainable food security to the manner in which the program was implemented. The government embarked on the land reform program soon after independence to redress the skewed ownership of land in the country. Initially, the program started on a willing buyer, willing seller basis, with the British government compensating the white farmers. A change of government in London resulted in the British government reneging on its promise to pay compensation. Subsequently, the Government of Zimbabwe decided to acquire land through designation, and undertook to compensate farmers for improvements to land only including developments such as dams, irrigation systems, housing facilities, and fencing, and infrastructure, such as tobacco barns, grading shades, and electrical installations. Some of the farmers accepted compensation, while others resorted to the courts to contest both acquisition and compensation.

The land reform program was also characterized by massive land invasions, as people ran out of patience. To date, most of the former commercial land that belonged to white settler farmers has been acquired, although a few white commercial farmers still remain on the land. The new black indigenous farmers have now been allocated land in various models and to various extents. Model A1 is the most extensive, in which farmers have been allocated land ranging from 5 to 30 hectares per family, while Model A2 has been allocated to farmers who can carry out farming on a commercial basis. While it is accepted that the land reform program itself was controversial, it alone cannot be attributed with causing the current failures. The program availed land to more people than ever before. Further, it gave opportunities to people that had never owned land, nor had access to land to engage in production.

Besides, the commercial agriculture sector, prior to the land reform program, did not contribute much to household food security, which was the major responsibility and achievement of the communal sector. In its current form, the land reform program has the capacity to contribute immensely to food security only if the government reviews and pursues more progressive policies. There is a need to refocus the land redistribution program as a productive rather than a sociopolitical program. Numerous audits have been undertaken, whose results have not been implemented. The idea behind the audits was to establish the extent to which occupation had taken pace, as well as the degree of agricultural production and capacity of the new farmers. In all of the audits, there are indications that a lot of land is lying idle despite having been allocated.

If Zimbabwe is to tackle the deteriorating food security situation at both the household and national levels, productive land in resettlement areas that is currently lying idle should be put to good use. This will take more than political will, yet it has to be done in order to achieve food security.

Proposals to Achieve Food Security At the Household and National Levels

Multilateral institutions believe Zimbabwe has tremendous potential to address the food security issue, provided some of the shortcomings in policy and implementation are addressed. The Zimbabwean government has missed opportunities, partly due to its reluctance to engage with multilateral institutions. The following are some of the considered views to achieve food security in the country.

The Need for a Changed Policy Environment

The analysis presented earlier indicates that government policies for achieving household and national food security have been beset by severe limitations and shortcomings. It took the government too long to realize that current policy thrusts were not meeting the objectives. There were other options available to the government that should have been tried. It is imperative that the government support the raw material requirements of the fertilizer industry. There is a need to use policy as a way out of the vicious circle associated with chronic failure. Refocusing on demand growth at both the household and national levels must receive high priority among development policies that enhance food security. The government should, as a matter of priority, enhance the budget reallocation toward rural populations in order to overcome the unaddressed causes of food insecurity. The policy environment needs to be significantly widened. There should be flexibility in the choice of available policy measures in order to tackle the causes of food insecurity that remain unaddressed.

The Need for Proper Planning and Forecasting

The government needs to properly forward-plan its requirements. While there is evidence that proper forecasting was done with respect to the food security situation, there was a problem of self-denial when the government could not admit that there was an impending problem until it surfaced. The government invested heavily in information propaganda to deny that there was a looming problem. This failure to embrace the development partners and some NGOs resulted in the Zimbabwe government not fully appreciating the probable extent of the problem. This unprecedented level of pride has seen a further decline in food security and has contributed to poor policy implementation.

The situation could have been alleviated through, for example, an early importation program or early mobilization of inputs after realizing that the amounts available would not suffice. The government should have embarked on an importation program as early as May. However, the importation program was only put in place in October, by which time chronic food shortages were being experienced in many parts of the country. Some inputs arrived into the country as late as January or February, when they were supposed to have been available at the start of the season in October. Lack of transparency kept would-be helpers at bay. The result has been the embroiling of the Zimbabwean food security situation into a political crisis.

Coping with Implementation Failures

Implementation failures have included rampant corruption among those in charge of the program. In 2005, the Ministry of Agriculture tried to cope with this phenomenon, the root cause of which is that initial access to inputs is free. By making inputs available at some cost, this would serve as a deterrent to would-be pilferers. It will be unattractive to purchase large quantities of inputs only to divert them to the parallel market. In 2006, the government tried to set up a purchase mechanism through the GMB. Those that had previously accessed large quantities for free in 2004 and 2005 complained bitterly, citing inefficiency of the GMB system.

Regrettably, the individual input purchase scheme was discontinued, and those that continued to access large quantities of inputs did so with the full knowledge that they would not be paying for them. Farmers have gone without inputs or have been forced to revert to the expensive black market. Dependence on the government needs to be corrected, and initiative must be placed back on the farmer.

It may be a blessing in disguise that the central bank announced at the end of 2008 that there would be no more quasi-fiscal activities in 2009. One can say that enough damage was done to agriculture by the RBZ. The intentions may have been good, but the implementation modalities proved disastrous. The Ministry of Agriculture and many other ministries under the quasi-fiscal programs of the RBZ became fully dependent on it. The central bank's reluctance and unwillingness to support fertilizer companies is well documented, and so is its meddling in fertilizer imports.[14] Indeed, Zimbabwe has learned its lesson the bitter way, and it is now time to move forward.

Use of Official Development Assistance through Development Partners

Despite the availability of official development assistance (ODA) and the presence of development partners willing to assist the government in achieving food security, Zimbabwe did not embrace these opportunities.[15] The government cited largely political reasons for its reluctance to embrace development assistance partnerships:

- The government accused some development partners of interfering in Zimbabwe's internal affairs through support to opposition parties.
- The government labeled most development partners as averse to the government's land reform program.
- Development partners were viewed with great suspicion, to the extent that the government failed to read any good intentions on their part.
- While there may have been cases of political linkages, their significance did not outweigh the need for food security in the country.
- Despite its apparent failure to adequately provide for food production nationally, the government decided to pursue a *Look East* policy, resulting in mixed fortunes. This policy was the government's response to sanctions that were imposed by the West. The government looked to China and the Far East for assistance.

It is strongly recommended that the government engage development partners to garner resources for production and improvement in the food security situation. The government should make an assessment of genuine development partners, especially now that the land reform program has been largely concluded and cannot be reversed. It is noted that there are development partners who are genuinely concerned about the continued deteriorating food security situation in the country, and the government should constructively engage them. Assistance from development partners should support development efforts to expand and stabilize agricultural production (including irrigation), prevent occurrence of food crisis, and attract foreign investment. This can be done through sustained support to allow the smallholder farmers to produce sufficient food for themselves, while excesses could be sold to the market.

Role of NGOs and Civil Society

From the early years of independence, NGOs and some civil society groups have rendered variable assistance to areas where government activities were severely curtailed. These organizations had managed to provide mechanisms for food security in drought-prone areas. Regrettably, the government viewed their activities as largely political and therefore suspended them. The result has been untold suffering and increased food insecurity among communities that previously benefited from the activities of NGOs and civil society groups. Unfortunately, the government has not been able to close the gap that the NGOs left:

- They were a source of development initiatives for local people.
- They reached areas that the government found otherwise difficult to reach.
- They provided employment to a significant portion of Zimbabwe's professionals in the field of agriculture.
- They also provided transport and other services to people in harsh environments.
- They were a source of hope and sustenance to many communities.

While it cannot be denied that some NGOs and civil society groups carried a political message, the number of such NGOs was quite small. It should also be accepted that the forced withdrawal of NGO services by the government, and its subsequent failure to fill the resultant gap, further alienated the communities who then felt abandoned by government—it is no wonder that some communities found refuge in opposition politics. It is recommended that the government should intensify dialogue with NGOs and civil society to determine what assistance they can provide in order to achieve national and household food security in the country.

Restoring Initiative With the Farmer

Policies pursued by the government have so far created a dependence syndrome that will take time to eradicate. When the government undertook to provide inputs for six years in 2001, they did not realize that they were taking away the initiative from farmers. From then on, farmers increasingly depended on the government to provide them with inputs. The sad thing though is that the government was unable to meet demand for inputs and worsened the situation by crowding out other farmers who may have wanted to source inputs on their own. By commandeering all available inputs to the government program, only one source was available. Furthermore, the use of political patronage to access inputs further alienated those farmers who were apolitical.

Regrettably, some of these inputs found their way back into the black market where they were sold at exorbitant prices in foreign currency. The government would have done better if a percentage of available inputs, 30 percent, for instance, had been allowed into retail outlets. If this had been done, those farmers with resources would have been able to purchase their input requirements. The situation in terms of access to inputs would have been a lot better.

It is strongly recommended that the government restore the farmers' initiative by allowing inputs to flow to commercial retail outlets, where farmers can source their requirements as they see fit. Restoring the farmers' initiative will rekindle the enthusiasm and eliminate the black market that has emerged due to a few privileged farmers accessing inputs free of charge from the government. Farmers would be able to buy their realistic requirements rather than horde free products.

Pricing of Major Food Security Crops

Since independence, the government has controlled the selling price of most major crops, especially food crops such as maize, sorghum, and wheat. The controls were intended to ensure affordable food for the people. The result though has been quite the opposite:

- Many farmers moved away from basic food crop production citing nonviability of the government price. A number of farmers reduced their area under food crop production or moved to crops such as cotton and tobacco.
- Those who remained in production significantly reduced their areas, as they focused on meeting their own requirements only.
- Others who remained in production engaged in side marketing to enhance their incomes.
- The government responded by reviewing prices, but these adjustments always fell below the cost of production.

Special schemes introduced by the government failed because it did not honor its promises. For example, in an attempt to get farmers to increase wheat production, the government, through the central bank, promised to pay in foreign currency, in whole or in part. To date, most farmers who opted for this scheme have still not been paid. In the current season, the government has promised to pay an import parity price. Judging by previous experience, not many farmers (if any) will opt for the scheme.

The government has failed to pay attractive production incentives, preferring instead to pay the foreign farmer through imports. A significant portion of the blame must be apportioned to the central bank because it misled the government through inappropriate policy interventions.

It is recommended that the government seriously consider a policy that provides sustainable incentives to increase the production of food security-related crops. Such incentives should woo farmers back into production with the full confidence that they will get a just reward for their effort. The incentives should also restore the balance in productivity levels of food security-related crops. The government should allow market forces to play their part by abandoning price controls, which have proved to be retrogressive.

The Role of Food Aid

Multilateral institutions were critical of the government's slow response to food aid offers despite clear indicators that the food security situation was deteriorating. The government has only embraced food aid as a last resort, despite indications that the country has been heading toward food insecurity. Agencies such as the WFP and other NGOs have battled for long periods with the government to accept food aid. In a few cases, pledges made for food aid were withdrawn because the government was dragging its feet. It is still too early to determine whether the government will approach donors. The major preoccupation of the government is to raise enough funds to support its balance of payments. The issue of food aid is likely to arise sometime in August 2009 when the country begins to experience food shortages. The amount of money required for food aid can only be determined after a full assessment of the current harvest.

Although food aid is not a permanent solution to food insecurity, it plays an important stop-gap measure, thereby allowing the government to put in place sustainable measures to guarantee food security at both the household and national level. The government should not waste time in the face of an impending crisis in citing unsubstantiated claims of political interference. While the government may be apprehensive about the motives of some of the organizations offering food aid, it is within the capacity of the government to evaluate each case on its own merits. Furthermore, the government can monitor the activities of the agencies offering food aid to ensure that they adhere to the stipulated conditions. The suspicious attitude adopted by the government has severely compromised the food security situation in some rural communities that had received assistance from NGOs and civil society groups over the years. These groups did not only assist with food, but also provided some critical inputs for future production.

It is recommended that the government embrace development partners, NGOs, and civil society groups to chart a food aid course in the short term. The planning could take the form of allocating areas of responsibility to different agencies and relaxing some of the import requirements. It is evident that Zimbabwe is now in an eighteen month cycle of food insecurity, and the food aid program must address food availability and access over that period. With proper planning, a major food insecurity disaster can be avoided.

Creating Capacity for Sustainable Production

The level of food production in Zimbabwe has been falling over the last eight years, and indications are that the fall will continue in the current 2008–2009 season. While a portion of the decline can be explained in terms of natural phenomena such as drought, the greater blame lies in the policies pursued by the government and how these policies have been implemented. The government should take stock of policies pursued since 2000 and implement progressive remedial measures. The most significant negative policy by far has been the government's total control of the source and distribution of inputs, including fuel. There is evidence that exclusive government control has been gravely abused, resulting in the inputs and fuel not reaching their intended targets. Cases of maize seed arriving in the wrong hands, fuel for farmers being diverted, and fertilizer being channeled to the parallel market abound.

The one major reason leading to this rampant abuse is that these inputs are initially obtained free of charge, and in the case of fuel, no checks and balances are in place to ensure that bona fide beneficiaries receive the commodity. The action by the government has taken the initiative away from the farmer, to which initiative must be restored if the capacity for sustainable production is to be restored.

The government must create an enabling environment for all farmers to acquire inputs as they need or can afford. This will ensure the direct acquisition and delivery of various inputs into deserving hands. More importantly, it must be appreciated that Zimbabwe will experience a severe shortage of planting material for the next few seasons. This situation must be carefully planned for. While food aid might address the immediate shortages, a more sustainable program for achieving food security must be put in place. Zimbabwe needs to be enabled to grow and produce its own planting material and fertilizer in the long run. The shortage of planting materials and fertilizer for the next season needs to be addressed.

Role of Irrigation and Agricultural Water Management Interventions

Zimbabwe has a commendable water development infrastructure in the form of large, medium, and small farm dams that can be used for full or supplementary irrigation. Regrettably, some of the dams are grossly underutilized due to a lack of outlet works infrastructure, while others have suffered from years of neglect and lack of maintenance. As drought has become a near-permanent feature of the Zimbabwean agricultural calendar, the use of available water resources and maintenance of water-related infrastructure for irrigation will go a long way in ensuring sustainable crop production in the country.

Current efforts aimed at rehabilitating irrigation systems in newly resettled areas should be strengthened, while development of all identified irrigation potential should also be given priority. It would appear that the government only puts an effort into this area when drought occurs. Not only is it too late to do so, the results are not achieved, and as soon as some semblance of a normal season is attained, irrigation development efforts are abandoned due to poor funding. There are some schemes in Matabeleland that have been perpetually under rehabilitation since independence. This has not helped to ensure food security in this dry area.

Restoring the Food Production Chain

Over the years, the dominant position of maize as the staple food of choice has marginalized other crops that could be grown more successfully in areas where maize does not do well. Furthermore, the distribution of maize grain in areas such as Matabeleland, in western Zimbabwe, has made maize synonymous with drought relief. More significantly, the domineering position of maize has compromised other crops that farmers used to grow, albeit on a small scale. Crops such as cowpeas, edible beans, rapoko, bambara nuts, finger millet, and sorghum in Regions II and III are no longer grown in as large quantities as before. Maize appears to have taken over, yet these crops can make a significant contribution to food security at the household level. The crop production chain that used to exist, particularly in the communal and early resettlement sectors, needs to be restored in order to contribute to the nutritive value of the food available at the household level.

Livestock As a Source of Food Security

Although livestock is a significant agricultural activity in many parts of the country, its contribution to food security has been severely underestimated. Food security programs have concentrated on cropping, while livestock has received a minimal treatment despite its huge potential to complement cropping. In drought years, livestock die in large numbers largely because there are no plans to rescue them. The role and contribution of all forms of livestock to food security has, therefore, been largely by default. Yet with good organizational planning, livestock can play an enhanced role in both food security and nutrition at the household and national levels. The government has attempted to include livestock in the food security basket; however, due to the long gestation periods associated with livestock, particularly cattle, these inclusions have not been very effective. Small stock and poultry have played a more significant role in the livestock-producing areas than cattle. However, large-scale production has been beset by either a shortage of feed or an unaffordable cost of feed. The rearing of free range chicken at the household level has been widespread, but continued reproduction has been hampered by the consumption of eggs before they hatch.

Improved Targeting of Beneficiaries

Policies implemented by the government since 2000 have failed due to poor targeting of beneficiaries. Almost without exception, some of the people who accessed services were undeserving. In the Government Crop Input program, a significant number of people who collected seed and fertilizer ended up selling these commodities late in the season, citing a number of problems unrelated to agriculture. Few cited the problem of lack of tillage facilities. There were others who cited the problem of availability of fuel. In this and subsequent programs where subsidized fuel was made available by the RBZ, a significantly large number of people who obtained the fuel ended up selling it on the black market for quick gains. Despite observations by more serious farmers, no substantive action was taken to mitigate the problem.

Under the Champion Farmers program, some people with no known record of agriculture production were included and allowed to access the scarce seed and fertilizer. There was no attempt to evaluate applicants in terms of their track record. A significant number of bogus farmers who accessed seed and fertilizer are now selling the same goods in hard currency. Failure to target was due to the fact that the Champion Farmers program was hijacked from the original would-be implementers (Agritex) by the Maguta/Inala formation. The inability of the government to implement a credible targeting system will constitute a considerable failure of the Champion Farmers program.

Unofficial statistics recently released by Agritex indicate that only 6 percent of genuine farmers accessed some seed, though not in the right quantities, and approximately 10 percent accessed fertilizer. These statistics spell doom for the agricultural sector in the current season.

Strengthening Institutional Capacity

The effectiveness of the Ministry of Agriculture and its departments must be restored and strengthened in order to achieve success in formulating and managing the purpose of achieving food security at the national and household levels. The marginalization of ministry structures reduced the ministry's response to the needs of various stakeholders, producers, input and output traders, processors, and consumers. There is a need for a well-structured organization with adequate staffing (in numbers and in skills) and resources to operate. There is also the need for policy dialogue between the government and stakeholders in order to adapt to and absorb emerging challenges and changes as they occur in the economy.

The Ministry of Agriculture must be facilitated to adopt improved management practices based on transparency and accountability. The ministry should implement personnel policies that develop individual staff competencies and provide them with adequate performance-related incentives and career development opportunities. It is hoped that such a strategy will mitigate the losses due to "brain drain." Some of these requirements will take long to achieve, but the blueprint should form part of an integrated strategy whose core activity will be to achieve food security at both household and national levels in the short to medium term.

Conclusion

The challenge of achieving food security at the household and national levels in Zimbabwe is real. Simple but effective solutions are required, whereby the government should embrace development partners, NGOs, civil society, and other groups to tackle what has become a chronic problem. Despite its efforts over the last eight years, the government has not been able to achieve food security due to several reasons. In this new endeavor, the government should tackle the corruption scourge, poor planning, and poor beneficiary targeting, and implement incentive-based pricing techniques to facilitate early release and availability of inputs on the market. The government should also deregulate the market to allow market forces to play their part.

Zimbabwe must haul itself out of the grip of the hunger spiral by creating opportunities for the self-generation of agricultural inputs, especially planting material and fertilizers, over the next season, thereby reducing the increased dependence on food aid. The capacity to do so exists—only the will must now be established through the support of development partners.

Notes

Many of the sources used to compile the chapter cannot be disclosed for reasons of confidentiality and because many are unpublished. Simon Pazvakavambwa was not in a position to divulge these sources as he was bound by the terms of his retirement as permanent secretary for the Zimbabwean Ministry of Agriculture. Further, as these sources are largely unpublished, their availability in the public domain is very restricted. However, the observations and ideas put forth in this chapter are those of Mr. Pazvakavambwa alone and should not be interpreted as reflecting the viewpoints of the government of Zimbabwe.

1. Ministry of Lands and Rural Resettlement, 2009.
2. Land audits carried out by the Ministry of Lands, Land Reform, and Resettlement indicate that the percentage of land utilization in the Fast Track Resettlement areas is low. Three land audits have been done, all showing a similar trend of between 20 and 70 percent utilization. These audits have not been published, nor placed in the public domain.
3. Zimbabwe requires two million tones of maize and five hundred thousand tonnes of wheat annually to feed its population.
4. The winter season was almost midway through and no funding for the wheat crop had been made available. Farmers could not procure seed, chemicals, or fertilizer, the latter in short supply and highly priced in U.S. dollars.
5. Not much has been done. A recent retreat of the Ministry of Lands, and Rural Resettlement only managed to outline basic parameters for discussion with stakeholders. There are indications that a land audit will be resisted by a certain section of the community.
6. Seed houses withheld seed from the market while they negotiated prices with the government. Similarly, fertilizer companies did not release fertilizer to the market until some agreement on price had been reached with the government. Invariably, this led to a late start to the season and resultant low yields.
7. For example, the allocation and distribution of agricultural machinery, such as tractors, implements, and animal drawn equipment, was carried out under a political perspective. Cases of undeserving beneficiaries have surfaced, while a proposed audit of the actual distribution has yet to be undertaken.
8. The interest rate was determined by the central bank based on what they perceived as the cost of money for the program. This interest rate had no relationship with the market rates as they existed then.
9. The Agricultural Finance Corporation (AFC) was a parastatal under the Ministry of Agriculture. In 1998 following government review of parastatals, AFC was converted into the Agricultural Development Bank, trading as AGRIBANK. Funding to the development sector (the communal and resettlement farmers) was then handled through a soft window called the Agricultural Development Assistance Fund (ADAF). However, ADAF was soon wound down due to lack of funding as AGRIBANK concentrated on Retail Banking operations. Both commercial and development lending, which was formerly handled by AFC, were now being handled through commercial banks.

10. The sources of information on ASPEF were various RBZ documents and the writer's personal experience.
11. The traditional role of the Ministry of Agriculture is to provide funding to ministries; however, under the quasi-fiscal activities of the central bank, funds were provided directly by the central bank, bypassing the Ministry of Finance. For some reason, the bank wanted to see through the implementation of programs they supported across the government directly.
12. The government estimates of expenditure provide for expected expenditure by the ministries. This is an annual publication.
13. Yield is a function of good land preparation and time of planting. Late planting leads to low yields.
14. The central bank imported fertilizers, although at the same time they were reluctant to support the raw material requirements for the local industry. Some of the fertilizers imported did not meet the required specifications.
15. The fact that development assistance partners, such as the U.K. government, the WFP, the Food and Agricultural Organization (FAO), the U.S. Agency for International Development (USAID), and others were willing to support Zimbabwe is regarded as an opportunity. Included among this group were various NGOs whose work was later to be suspended by the government because of political involvement, such as World Vision and Catholic Relief Services.

References

Boussard, Jean-Marc, Benoit Daviron, Francois Gerard, and Tancrede Voituriez. "Food Security and Agricultural Development in Sub-Saharan Africa: Building a Case for More Support." Background paper to a High-level Workshop by Agricultural Research for Development (CIRAD) for the FAO, Nairobi, Kenya, September 14–16, 2005.

Government of Zimbabwe. Central Statistical Office (CSO). *Quarterly Digest of Statistics.* July 2007.

———. Ministry of Finance. *Short Term Emergency Recovery Programme (STERP).* March 2009.

Jayne, T.S., M. Chisvo, M. Rukuni, and P. Masanganise."Zimbabwe's Food Insecurity Paradox: Hunger Amid Potential." In *Zimbabwe's Agricultural Revolution Revisited.*

Mellor, John W., Christopher L. Delgado, and Malcolm J. Blackie, eds. *Accelerating Food Production in Sub-Saharan Africa.* International Food Policy Research Institute. Baltimore and London: John Hopkins University Press, 1983.

"The Reserve Bank Governor, Dr. G.G. Gono Breaks His Silence On Motor Vehicle Allocations To Parliamentarians and Other Issues Relating to Quasi-Fiscal Operations." *The Herald*, April 18, 2009.

Rukuni, Mandivamba, Godfrey Mudimu, and Thomas S. Jayne, eds. "Food Security Policies in the SADCC Region." Proceedings of the fifth annual Conference on Food Security Research in Southern Africa. University of Zimbabwe/Michigan State Food Security Research in Southern Africa project, Department of Agricultural Economics and Extension, University of Zimbabwe, Harare, October 16–18, 1989.

Rukuni, Mandivamba, Patrick Tawonezvi, and Carl Eicher, eds., with Mabel Munyuki-Hungwe and Prosper Matondi. *Zimbabwe's Agricultural Revolution Revisited.* Harare: University of Zimbabwe Press, 2006.

Tagwireyi, Julia. "The Food and Nutrition Situation in Zimbabwe." In *Zimbabwe's Agricultural Revolution Revisited.*

University of Zimbabwe/Michigan State University. "Food Security Project." Proceedings from the First National Consultative Workshop on Integrating Food, Nutrition and Agricultural Policy, Juliasdale, Zimbabwe, July 15–18, 1990.

World Bank. *Agricultural Growth and Land reform in Zimbabwe: Assessment and Recovery Options.* Environment, Rural, and Social Development Unit. AFTSI Country Department 2 Africa Region. Report No.31699-ZW. 2006.

Zumbika, Naison. *The Challenges of Lending to the Poor.* Harare: Kaycee Printers, 2000.

Chapter 9

Public-Private Partnerships in the Provision of Infrastructure to Redress the Human Resource Shortages in Zimbabwe

Helen Moatshe

Executive Summary

The Government of National Unity (GNU) in Harare suffers from a limited capacity in terms of human resources and skilled personnel, which are key in rebuilding all sectors of the economy. This chapter places emphasis on a holistic approach that gives a historic perspective of the problem, looking backward to 1979 and prior to the country's independence. It also looks at the role regional countries played in exacerbating the human resource challenges in the postcolonial era and assesses what interventions would be needed to create an enabling environment. A closer look is taken at the economic sector nodes, such as agriculture, that could make a difference in stimulating economic growth.

Issues painting a gloomy picture include the Zimbabwean land repossessions, primarily blamed on the unresolved political differences emanating from the Lancaster House Agreement.[1] This agreement did not advocate for land repossessions, but rather highlighted the most difficult challenges that would require a pragmatic approach for economic growth and skills development.

It can also be argued that during periods of extended political strife, the economy declines, social infrastructure decays, and human rights conditions deteriorate, resulting in large volumes of skilled workers leaving the country. Even though in the long run, through the remittance system, the country benefits, this does not match the loss of skilled workers in the public and private sectors, including educators, health workers, engineers, bureaucrats, and financial experts. This chapter provides a perspective on the role the GNU needs to play in creating conditions for investment and growth[2] through the establishment of strategic partnerships, and smart partnership, in the region with other governments (public-public) and/or private (public-private) sectors to redress the infrastructure needs of the country—with the long-term objective of attracting Zimbabwean skills back to Zimbabwe.

Debatably, Zimbabwe's public sector needs to collaborate closely with the private sector to provide the country with the most needed transport, health, education, water, sanitation, and agricultural infrastructure. Although public-private partnership (PPP) and collaboration is not a new phenomenon, the potential for PPPs[3] to build infrastructure and address the human resource skills required for economic growth has not received much attention.

Introduction

Prior to independence, during the period 1978–1979, emigration of small-scale farmers was sped up by a series of events, which include, amongst others, the Viscount (near Kariba) massacre,[4] the Hunyani attack, and the bombing of the Southerton industrial area fuel storage depot in Harare in 1979. During this period of instability, Zimbabwe recorded a net loss of 2771 white farmers. The total loss for the period of 1978–1979 was 13,709, of which most were small-scale producers. The massacre of over 20,000 Ndebele people also contributed to the mass departure of black people. Added to this trend of exodus was the economic crisis, which was a result of the introduction and implementation of the Economic Structural Adjustment Program.[5] This was also coupled with the adoption of violent and repressive policies aimed at curbing political opposition by the Zimbabwean government. Emigration by the black majority has also been instigated by political reasons.[6] Although exact figures are not available, a range of statistical sources suggest that there are up to 1.5 million Zimbabweans in South Africa (as of 2008).[7] This posed a challenge to the government in retaining the skills required for the country's socioeconomic growth.

In 1980, prior to making changes to the social and economic structures that it inherited, the government set up a commission, chaired by Roger Riddell, to deal with the issues of skill retention and the narrowing of wage differentials in postindependence Zimbabwe.[8] The government wanted to reduce and/or freeze wage levels for skilled workers and professionals so that the wages of the unskilled could be raised gradually to reduce the wage gaps. The commission noted that this might result in the emigration of those people with mobile skills and subsequent lack of incentive to train for skilled work.[9]

Between 1980 and 1984, the period after independence, it is estimated that fifty thousand–sixty thousand whites left Zimbabwe due to violent repossessions of farms by the Zimbabwean government. The United Nations Development Programme (UNDP) estimated that one million farm workers and their families lost their homes and livelihoods as a result of the fast-track land reform program, which started in 2000 and led to the near-collapse of the commercial farming sector in Zimbabwe. Approximately five hundred and seventy thousand people were made homeless by the urban demolitions of Operation Murambatsvina (clear the filth) in 2005, while the government also destroyed the homes of thousands of informal mine workers in Operation Chikorokoza Chapera (stop the gold panning) in late 2006 and early 2007.[10]

Unlike farmers, Zimbabwean teachers have formed the Association of Zimbabwean Teachers in Johannesburg. This association hopes to assist its members to obtain accreditation and registration with the South African Qualification Authority (SAQA).[11] This association believes that there are ten thousand Zimbabwean teachers in South Africa.[12] These teachers, like many of the professionals that fled Zimbabwe, left due to severe shortages of basic items and low wages.[13] In the health sector, the Health Professional's Council reported that the numbers of nurses and doctors has remained constant. This contradicts the statement by the director of nursing that estimated that Zimbabwe had, since 1997, lost about thirteen thousand nurses and doctors due to the adjustment program and the subsequent reduction in annual health spending.[14]

In the post-1988 period, price rises were dramatic, with inflation estimated at 24 percent. In 1992, the real inflation rate was estimated at about 52 percent. What became clear is that this economic slump contributed to the migration of skilled and professional workers. Even though there is no reliable information on the effect this inflation has had on specific sectors and groups of skills, there has been an observable outflow of people as a result of acute economic and social deterioration; it is natural in such situations for individuals to emigrate in search for better socio-economic livelihoods. In this instance, migration becomes an important way for households to diversify their livelihood survival strategies.[15]

Zimbabwe not only lost skills, but also suffered a shortfall of investors. According to Besada and Moyo, Zimbabwe's foreign direct investments (FDI) have diminished, and there is a high expectation that southern African investors will step in to fill the void left by Western investors.[16] FDI inflows between 1990 and 2000 dropped from 110 to 107 in 2006, with an outflow dropping from 102 to 101 in 1998.[17] FDI in Zimbabwe totaled US$444 million, and in 2001, it had fallen to US$5.4 million.[18] This had a negative implication on the creditworthiness of Zimbabwe and was also worsened by the suspension of funding by the International Monetary Fund (IMF). The situation became worse in June 2003 when the IMF suspended Zimbabwe's voting rights in the organization for failing to make effective efforts to repay arrears of about US$305 million (Z$251 billion) to the IMF.[19]

To reverse the economic situation in Zimbabwe requires urgent intervention combined with support from southern African countries and their public and private institutions. This calls for the proactive and innovative stabilization of social infra-structure (water, sanitation, health, and education services), as well as the rebuilding of physical infrastructure (electricity, transport, and roads) and retail services. The governments of neighboring countries should take the leading support role in assisting with the development and facilitation of political solutions in order to speed up the rebuilding of social infrastructure. Amongst other efforts to stabilize the movement of Zimbabweans further inland, regional governments could consider providing shared primary health services as well as retail services closer to the border. This would ease the influx and rapid movement of illegal migrants. Furthermore, southern African development funding institutions, such as the Development Bank of Southern Africa (DBSA), the Industrial Development Corporation (IDC), and the Department of Trade and Industry (DTI), should prioritize Zimbabwe's recovery in their regional sector development strategies and plans in order to drive regional social stability and integration. The DTI should also consider other types of cooperative arrangements that may include sectoral cooperative agreements. This does not, however, insinuate departure from their original mandates, but instead these institutions would complement the Southern African Development Community (SADC), which seems to be deficient in implementing its core mandate of regional integration. The SADC has first-mover advantage with respect to the rest of the continent due to its close proximity with Zimbabwe.

In prioritizing the interventions, the Zimbabwean government will have to consider the most crucial and efficient areas of involvement that are required in the short and medium to long term to address skills shortfalls.

Pre-conflict Opportunities for Zimbabweans

Zimbabwe, as with a large number of African states after independence, inherited a society fractured along racial lines and had to struggle to build its education system, as large numbers of its population had been prevented from attending school. The postcolonial era has seen the reversal of discrimination in education, with the government introducing universal primary education through the Education Act of 1979,[20] which made it compulsory for every school-age child to be in school. The positive spin-offs included increased enrollment, and at the end of the sixth year, the secondary, tertiary, and higher education systems were overstretched beyond capacity, demonstrated by space shortages and education budget constraints.[21]

In 1998, there were positive labor developments in South Africa. The South African government passed the Employment Equity Act (EEA) of 1998 that contained provisions for affirmative action.[22] The main objective was to correct the imbalances created by the apartheid government and to generate equal employment opportunities for all previously excluded citizens. The act[23] required that any South African employer who retained more than fifty employees had to meet the standards set for affirmative action (AA) targets, which targeted black workers, women, and the disabled.[24] This posed a challenge to the private companies in South Africa, as there were no immediate sources of qualified workers in the designated groups from which they could pick that would allow them to meet the required standards. The initial candidates were recruited from the neighboring countries, causing Zimbabwe, Malawi, Zambia, Swaziland, and Botswana to benefit. It can therefore be concluded that affirmative action in South Africa has contributed toward Zimbabweans' movements to South Africa in order to market their skills as affirmative action candidates. This might have been the contributing factor to the 2008 xenophobic attacks in South Africa.[25]

However, during this period, employers were not aware of the buildup and brewing of tensions brought about by their affirmative action recruitment spree. Even though there were some elements of internal-country pressures and fear of the eruption of factional fights, the foreign employees' main draws were attractive salaries, better working conditions, higher salaries, a better infrastructure, and social, health, and education facilities.

On the other hand, employers in return paid relocation costs, arranged for working permits, and were satisfied to meet the AA targets. The demand for managerial skills as well as the pressure to meet the AA targets were exacerbated by the outflow of qualified human resources and skills from Zimbabwe. South Africa became the new destination for formal employment for Zimbabweans. This outflow increased in late 2001 with the land seizures,[26] where some 4,000 owners (virtually all white) of Zimbabwe's most productive farms were forced out, along with their 320,000 workers (almost all black) and their families—amounting to between one and two million people. This outflow climaxed in 2007 due to internal conflicts, lack of security, and the deterioration of basic services. The numbers in 1 indicate the total registered migrant population, which includes both skilled and unskilled people. These numbers continued to increase before and after the Zimbabwean elections of 2008. Although exact figures are not available, a range of statistical sources suggest that there are a maximum of 1.5 million Zimbabweans in South Africa.[27] It is unknown how many have left Zimbabwe, as no formal records are available of individuals leaving the country; however, some sources report that out of a population of 13 million, about 3 million have left.[28]

According to Polzer, the South African government currently does not have access to reliable data concerning the number, demographics, or location of Zimbabweans in South Africa, nor about levels of entry, as this information remains undocumented.[29] This undermines the government's ability to plan and provide services and security for both migrants and citizens. The free visa[30] and the special dispensation permit will enable the state to measure the volumes and impacts of migration more effectively. On April 3, 2009, the Department of Home Affairs announced its

Table 9.1 Estimated migrant population, 2001–2007

Year	Population
2001	131,886
2002	175,715
2003	255,604
2004	375,935
2005	522,364
2006	763,425
2007	1,022,965

Source: Daniel Makina, "Risk-sharing, partnerships between banks, development agencies and NGOs can facilitate access to finance for SMMEs," *Africagrowth Agenda*, September–November 2006.

intention to grant Zimbabweans in South Africa a twelve-month "special dispensation permit" on the basis of the 2002 Immigration Act, section 31(2)(b).[31] This permit grants the right to legally live and work in the country. As complementary measures, a moratorium on deportations and a ninety-day free visa for Zimbabweans entering South Africa have been implemented from May 2009.

The relaxation and lifting of the influx laws[32] increased the inflow of illegal immigrants from all the borders. Some immigrants obtained permits to enter South Africa; conversely, the authorities had no control over expatriating the skilled people once the system absorbed them. Census South Africa estimated that over one million Zimbabweans were in South Africa by end of year 2007. The IOM report further estimated that there are about five hundred thousand Zimbabweans living in the United Kingdom and about three hundred thousand in Botswana.[33]

Another labor pull took place after former South African president Thabo Mbeki, in his 2006 state of the nation address, announced that the government would put aside over R370 billion for infrastructure development as part of the Accelerated and Shared Growth Initiative (ASGISA).[34] With South Africa's formal unemployment rate estimated at 19 percent in 2006 and at 24 percent in 2009, the infrastructure program had the added onus of creating and sustaining employment, while at the same time increasing the skills drive. The drive for skills was a critical priority for South Africa, and their lack threatened to derail some of the interventions being undertaken by ASGISA. Mr. Mbeki announced the formation of a task force to push South Africa's growth to 6 percent and said he was considering importing skilled people from abroad to achieve this goal. He further introduced the *Joint Initiative on Priority Skills Acquisition* (JIPSA)[35] in South Africa. According to the South African Government Publications 2008, JIPSA aimed to develop scarce skills in the following areas:

- engineering and planning skills for jobs in transport, communications, and energy;
- engineering projects for cities and towns, as needed by municipalities;
- management and planning skills in education, health, and municipalities; and
- teacher training for mathematics, science, information and communications technology, and language skills.

In response to this call, the DBSA,[36] through the Development Fund,[37] launched a program known as the Siyenza Manje (we are doing it now) Initiative[38] in June 2008. The Initiative focuses on three core areas:

1. Mobilizing and deploying engineering, finance, and town planning experts[39]
2. Providing grant funding for capacity building and institutional development
3. Development facilitation

Over the past year, a cumulative of 189 engineers and technicians, 80 finance experts, 26 planners, 156 young professionals, and 164 artisans were deployed in municipalities in 199 of the participating provinces. Municipalities whose Municipal

Infrastructure Grants (MIG) were not being disbursed were specifically targeted to ensure that allocation translated into delivery. This mobilization of experts to provide professional support for project and program implementation was meant not only to unlock service delivery bottlenecks, but also to sustain the Project Consolidate thrusts. Through the DBSA Development Fund, sixteen young graduates were placed in municipalities and mentored by experts.[40] The aim of the program was to build skills required for municipality service delivery using mentorship by near and retired engineers and accountants. The Fund agreed to cover the cost of placing these graduates for a year, as municipalities had not made provisions for this in their personnel budgets.

Through the Siyenza Manje initiative (table 9.2), 3,825 capital infrastructure projects to the value of R8.9 billion are being implemented in the participating municipalities and 1,237 were completed by 2010. Around 203,125 households have received access to water and 107,195 to sanitation as a result of the hands-on technical support provided by the experts during the project.[41]

What remained a challenge for initiatives such as Siyenza Manje and JIPSA was the unavailability of the targeted skills in South Africa. This did not, however, pose a major threat to these initiatives because efforts were made to recruit engineering, financial, and accounting skills from Zimbabwe and other countries in the SADC (table 9.3) as well as partnering with other oganizations such as Industrial Development Corporation and Department of Public Affairs.

Siyenza Manje, though managed by the DBSA's Development Fund, is a partnership between the DBSA, the South African National Treasury, Cooperative Governance and Traditional Affairs (COGTA), the South African Local Government Association (SALGA), the Department of Water and Environmental Affairs (DWEA), and Higher Education South Africa (HESA). It is one of the DBSA's major PPPs and indeed a groundbreaking response to the shortage of properly qualified professional and technical personnel in many municipalities.[42]

Table 9.2 Siyenza Manje successes

Outputs	2007/08	2008/09	2009/2010
Number of people trained on the job in finance	143	521	1008
Number of people trained on the job in technical areas	338	1,083	1025

Source: DBSA, *Development Fund Annual Report*, Midrand, South Africa, 2008–2009 & 2009/10.

Table 9.3 Total number of deployees from the SADC region by country

Country of origin	Number
Zimbabwean	34
Zambian	3
Swazi	1

Source: DBSA, *Development Fund Annual Report*, Midrand, South Africa, 2008–2009.

Priorities

The Zimbabwean government is faced with competing issues, ranging from the breakdown of public services and the power sector, decaying infrastructure, and the near-collapse of the agricultural sector. It cannot, however, address all of these problems simultaneously due to the demands they pose on its limited funding and human resources. Perhaps its efforts should be focused on creating an enabling environment wherein trade and investment can take place. The *Short Term Emergency Recovery Programme* (STERP)[43] for 2009 focuses on macroeconomic policy and aims to achieve low inflation, address economic decline, and improve socioeconomic conditions. Challenges include how the program will be funded and where the government will get the resources to implement it. The IMF indicates that the authorities expected an economic activity pickup. It also states that the customs duties, excises, and the value-added tax (VAT) are expected to account for 60 percent of budget revenue.[44] The Zimbabwe recovery plan, which needs US$10 billion and US$2 billion of that sum urgently, had managed to secure only US$400 million from African states as of May 2009. Mr. Tsvangirai met with the president of South Africa to request US$5 billion aid for humanitarian crisis in Zimbabwe. The response from South Africa was a US$1 billion loan for retail and US$1 billion toward emergency services in education, health, and municipality services (water and sanitation and other infrastructure). The SADC had undertaken to raise the US$2 billion, with South Africa and Botswana pledging credit lines and budget support of $800 million and $70 million, respectively.

In the quest to raise money for his country, Prime Minister Morgan Tsvangirai approached the European Union (EU), the Netherlands, and other countries in 2009. In Washington, President Barack Obama offered £45 million for good governance and the fight against HIV and AIDS, but the money was to go through aid agencies and not the Zimbabwean government. Germany said it would contribute £17 million to a World Bank (WB) fund promoting democracy, Norway increased its aid by £4 million, and Denmark offered a further £11 million. Sweden declined to provide any extra money, saying more progress was needed.[45] According to Netherlands News Worldwide, the Netherlands and other EU countries will not give any funds to Zimbabwe's transitional government until it meets its own benchmarks, including ending lawlessness and the abuse of human rights. The Dutch minister also called for reforms of the security and justice systems and an opening up of Zimbabwe's media.[46] The general response from most countries was that Zimbabwe has to address its internal political challenges before the FDI could flow in.

In light of the failure on the part of Tsvangirai to secure the funds deemed necessary for Zimbabwe's economic recovery, the SADC, together with state-owned enterprises (SOEs) in the region, could, in an effort to attract direct foreign investors, redirect its support toward Zimbabwe through normalization, identification, and prioritization of basic services projects such as water, electricity, health, and education. According to a report that came out of the Zimbabwe

Roundtable[47] held in Victoria Falls, Zimbabwe, on May 15, 2009, project preparation and prioritization of projects in the pipeline could reduce crowding and the time needed to mobilize funds. The objective is to be able to provide technical grants for the preparation and planning of projects, and simultaneously identify PPPs that could invest funds toward the implementation of these projects.[48] On an emotional level, these efforts could slowly build the confidence of the donor society.

Coupled with these efforts is, for instance, the respect for property rights, which could play a key role in rebuilding investor confidence and increasing investment and savings rates, thereby working to improve dilapidated infrastructure, which is a vital component of rebuilding the productive capacity of the economy. Besides physical capital and infrastructure, rebuilding the human capital needed to drive a sustained economic recovery is equally important. An expanded and well-functioning social sector (health and education) can play an important role in this regard.

According to the UNDP's 2008 discussion document on economic recovery in Zimbabwe, some of the priority areas in Zimbabwe include agriculture, infrastructure, manufacturing, and mining (as shown in figure 9.1).[49] Partnerships exist not only at the national level, but also at the sectoral and project levels. In identifying and prioritizing sector projects, private and public, nongovernmental organizations (NGOs) and other organizations, such as the New Partnership for Africa's Development (NEPAD), will assist to add value in supporting the planning, institutional arrangements, and long-run promotion of investment. The Zimbabwean government should look for assistance in terms of project preparation, packaging, and advice from development funding institutions in the region and embark on marketing the viability of these projects. Parties to the PPPs are the public and the private sectors, with the support of NGOs. The role of government is both to create conditions for growth, focusing particularly on establishing policy, legal, and institutional frameworks that enable the private sector to play the leading role in economic development, and to selectively increase the key public goods that will catalyze broad-based economic growth.[50]

The main players in Zimbabwe's agricultural sector are smallholder producers, and to this effect, it is vital to focus on building the capacity of these producers. Agribusiness is the main private stakeholder, whose primary aim is to make a profit, with lesser importance given to moral and ethical obligations, such as social and corporate responsibility, compliance to environmental principles and political governance, accountability, and equity. NGOs play the crucial role of implementer, collaborator, and lobbyist; however, structural composition, management, funds utilization, and administration should be entrusted to the PPP.[51]

The economic vision of the SADC is to transform the fourteen countries of southern Africa from operating as individual, fragmented markets into a single, integrated, and globally competitive market characterized by the free movement of goods, services, capital, and labor.[52] Road, rail, and airline infrastructure is paramount in developing Zimbabwe as it links it to economic resources in other countries and to coastal ports, perhaps even linking a few nodes along a transportation

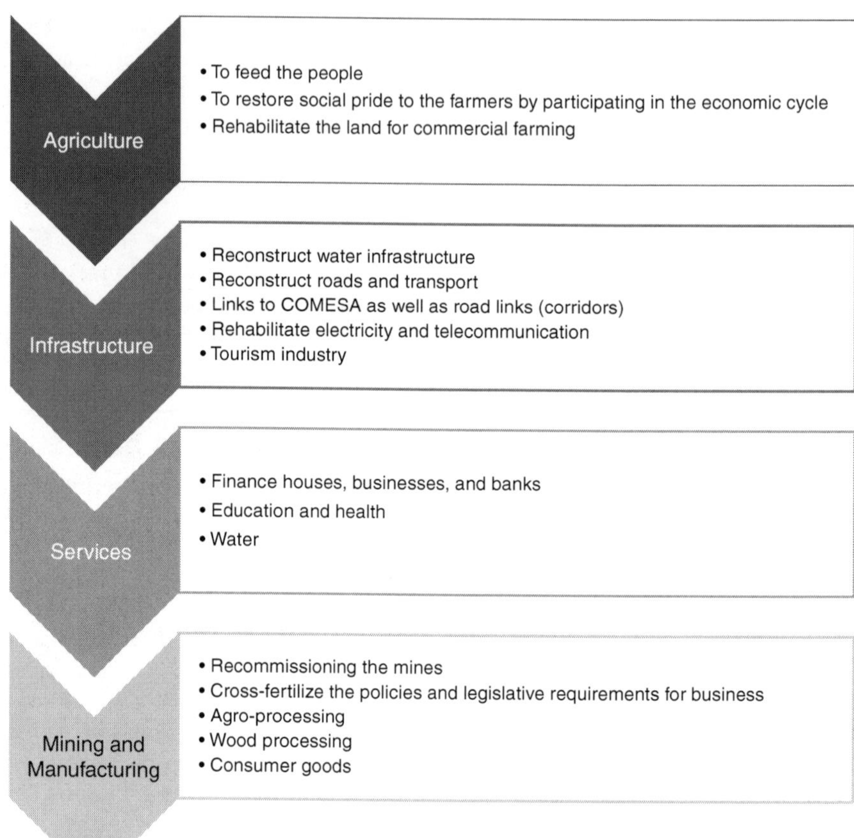

Figure 9.1   Proposed medium to long term priorities per sector for Zimbabwe.

Source: Workshop on Zimbabwe Take-off at Victoria Falls, organized by Development Enterprise Africa Trust (DEAT) and the Centre for International Governance Innovation (CIGI) in cooperation with DBSA, May 2009.

route, which would allow for the exploitation of the variety of other development opportunities that arise along the route. The provision of infrastructure has been dominated by the public sector, with the private sector having been denied the opportunity to be a player in funding infrastructure projects. This has resulted in delays due to a lack of political commitment, with business bearing the high costs of maintenance, loss, and damages of products due to poor roads.

The public sector commonly identifies specific and usually large potential anchor projects along the transport corridor. These anchor projects are usually opportunities for private investment, and they act as catalysts for economic growth in the corridor. In addition, the public sector attempts to remove constraints to private sector investment and business development, and promotes the development of PPPs.[53] Embarking on major projects in mining, water infrastructure, agriculture, electricity, and telecommunications may have a positive spin-off for job creation in the construction industry, which could benefit tourism and medium to long term, gradual economic growth. Some PPP opportunities are jointly conducting feasibility studies and undertaking capacity building and skill building in the sectors identified earlier.

One of the few examples of PPPs is between the Infrastructure Development Bank of Zimbabwe (IDBZ) and the African Development Bank (AfDB), or DBSA, on eligible projects in relation to the development and preparation of projects. Preparation and feasibility studies require funds for pre-investment activities due to long lead times for preparing these projects prior to them reaching their bankable states. The immense infrastructure, growth, and poverty gaps in the region require multi-institutional and multistakeholder responses.[54] The DBSA, together with the IDC and the AfDB, provides strong collective African leadership in development finance in the region.[55]

Key Drivers for Attracting the Skills in Zimbabwe

The GNU is presented with many opportunities to turn around the Zimbabwean economy, even if it has to overcome the inherent challenges of economic slump, declining socioeconomic levels, and the increasing exodus of its resources. Essentially, for the country to drive economic growth, it needs to focus its available efforts on resolving immediate challenges, which are as follow:

- Functional alignment of all land reform[56] initiatives[57] with the capacity development of farmers. Farming as a long-term, high risk, and, volatile industry requires extensive financial support for commercial farming and a considerable amount of technical assistance, planning, and capacity development for small holder producers, strengthening the capacity to organize, access inputs, produce markets, and experiment on different crops.[58] The involvement of NGOs is crucial in promoting rural development, stakeholder and participatory planning, and capacity building. In addition, involving organizations such as agribusiness could broaden and deepen the sentiments of the donor community.
- Stopping all ethnic segregation and discrimination and providing safety and security for all Zimbabweans. This will ensure the direct re-participation and reengagement of all citizens in the country's economic reconstruction efforts,[59] guaranteeing that their skills will be available for all sectors of the economy, either through relocating to their homelands, participating in business initiatives, or taking employment in the formal sector. There is a need for the government to create viable business opportunities for small and medium scale entrepreneurs (SMEs), identify policies and strategies, and support projects and programs that will provide a sustainable basis for empowering local communities.

- Providing a full spectrum of basic needs, such as food, water, sanitation, security, and primary and emergency health care, especially for HIV and AIDS, as well as housing and education.
- Creating jobs by embarking on the reconstruction of infrastructure for transport and roads, information and communication, electricity, water, and sanitation.
- Creating an enabling environment for investors through attractive economic and investment policies and building trade relationships with regional development institutions, such as the ADB, DBSA, and IDC. Through these relationships, Zimbabwe could harness opportunities to mobilize donor and FDI in manufacturing, retailing, and mining, and create opportunities for these institutions to co-fund cross-subsidization and grant funding in the areas of project preparation.[60]
- Investment and risk-sharing cooperation between other direct foreign investors and development funding institutions. This might include cooperation with other international funding institutions, such as the German Development Institution (KFW), *Agence Française de Développement* (AFD), and the AfDB, in order to co-fund and partner on infrastructure projects—as with the DBSA-AFD Project Preparation and Feasibility partnership on the Ghana-Togo-Benin and Zambia-Tanzania-Kenya energy interconnectors, and the Kariba North Bank and Itezhi-Tezhi power generation projects.[61] These cooperations could be used to accelerate the pace of project preparation and planning, financing, and capacity building.
- Resolve the issue of property rights in close cooperation with all the stakeholders.

Conclusion

For Zimbabwe to make substantial inroads in rebuilding its shattered economy, rehabilitating its decaying infrastructure, and addressing deep-seated social problems, it needs to address the bottlenecks that have hindered the flow of foreign investment and the return of its migrated labor. Key to dealing with this is the speeding up of political changes and the bettering of health and education for children.[62] In doing so it cannot apply interventions alone to attempt to address the shortage of skills, but rather must build PPPs with regional SOEs such as the DBSA, IDC, and the Limpopo Development Corporation (LIMDEV),[63] and to some extent other interested organizations from China, India, and southern Africa. These organizations could jointly share the risk, develop or attract the required capacity, develop skills programs in the priority areas, and, where possible, redeploy such skills as an interim measure until such time that Zimbabwe is ready to attract the lost skills.

Paramount to the PPPs are the institutional and operational arrangements. In order to have positive results and to promote accountability, where funding is secured for any projects (e.g., in mining), proper structures should be established to manage the operations of the partnership. Funds should not be disbursed into any government account. Where service providers are identified, they should be paid directly from the source, such as the payment of employees.[64]

It is certain that immigrants at all skills levels have contributed to the much-needed skills in South Africa, and in an effort to build the confidence of these immigrants, the South African government, through its initiatives such as JIPSA and Siyenza Manje, could jointly embark in passive repatriation schemes through the PPPs. What should not be overlooked is the significant emphasis on crowding raised by South African SOEs and private sector, through negotiating guarantees with the Zimbabwean government under the Bilateral Investment Promotion and Protection Agreement (BIPPA).[65]

What remains a challenge is unblocking the aforementioned obstacles in order to build and attract foreign direct investors. The moral obligation that the government of Zimbabwe carries is to serve the citizens of the country and deliver the election promises, including job creation and making Zimbabwe livable. The SADC is also accountable for integration, participation, and support in the region, and should encourage Zimbabwe to speed up the implementation process.

The responsibility remains in the hands of the Zimbabwean government to restore citizens' and investor trust through good governance, keeping its peace obligation, and facilitating changes. If this is in place, it would be appropriate to state that the West owes it to Zimbabweans to lift the sanctions against the country in order for Zimbabwe to rebuild its economy and re-attract the skills it requires to drive the economy.

Notes

1. The Zimbabwean civil war lasted for nearly two decades before negotiations for a settlement were initiated in the late 1970s. The inequalities in Zimbabwe at that time were still very stark. Population densities in the communal areas were three times those in commercial farming areas. There was still a highly visible racial division of land, with six thousand white farmers owning approximately 42 percent of the country. In terms of seeking a resolution to the crisis in Zimbabwe at the time, the land reform experience of Kenya was influential. As with Zimbabwe, Kenya had had a comparable land problem resulting in a guerrilla war. In the case of Kenya, the British sought to defuse the situation by buying out white farmers. The British made available UK£500 million for land acquisition and settlement support in Kenya. It was hoped that a similar solution could be found for Zimbabwe. Thus, during the secret negotiations in the mid-1970s, the notion of an Anglo-American Development Fund for Zimbabwe was promoted. The endowment received broad support (including backing from the then ZANU/ZAPU Patriotic Front). This fund, to which the British agreed to contribute UK£75 million, would be used to buy out farms owned by whites. At the time, the United States hinted it would contribute an extra US$200 million to the fund. However, as we will see in this chapter, the fund failed to materialize. See Tom Lebert, "Backgrounder-Land and Agrarian Reform in Zimbabwe," National Land Committee, Johannesburg, January 21, 2003, http://www.landaction.org/display.php?article=61.
2. The GNU needs to establish policy, legal, and institutional frameworks that enable the private sector to play a leading role in economic development.

3. According to Pflug, the term partnership means "joint initiatives of the public sector in conjunction with the private, for-profit and non-for-profit sectors, also referred to as the government, business, and civic sectors. Within these partnerships, each of the actors contributes resources (financial; human; technical; and intangible, such as information or political support) and participates in the decision-making process." See Tanja Pflug, "Private-Private Partnership in the Framework of Financing for Development," Policy Paper 18, Heinrich Boell Foundation, Beirut, 2002.

4. Zimbabwe People's Revolutionary Army (ZIPRA) guerillas waged their attacks by shooting down a passenger aircraft in protest of segregation policies.

5. JoAnn McGregor, "Professionals Relocating: Zimbabwean Nurses and Teachers, Negotiating Work and Family in Britain," *Geographic Paper* 178, University of Reading, February 2006, 4.

6. International Organization for Migration (IOM), *The Development Potential of Zimbabweans in the Diaspora*, A survey on Zimbabweans Living in the UK and South Africa (IOM: Geneva, 2006), 125.

7. Tara Polzer, "Regularising Zimbabwe Migration to South Africa," Migration Policy Brief, Consortium for Refugees and Migrants in South Africa and University of the Witwatersrand, May 2009, 3.

8. Rudo Gaidzanwa, *Voting with Their feet, Migrant Zimbabwean Nurses and Doctors in the Era of Structural Adjustment,* Research Report no. 111 (Uppsala: Nordiska Afrikaninstituet, 1999), 18.

9. Ibid.

10. Norwegian Refugee Council, "Zimbabwe Internal Displacements," 2008, 1.

11. The South African Qualification Authority Act 58 of 1995 was passed in September 1995, and its purpose is to "provide for the development and implementation of a National Qualification Framework (NQF) and the establishment of the South African Qualification Authority." The function of SAQA is to formulate and publish policies and criteria for the accreditation of bodies responsible for monitoring and auditing achievements in terms of the standards and qualifications. See B.J. Swanepoel, *South African Human Resource Management* (Cape Town: Juta & Company, 1998).

12. "No Welcome, No Let-Up," *The Economist,* Vol. 384, Issue 8541, August 11, 2007, 37.

13. Ibid.

14. Gaidzanwa, *Voting with Their Feet,* 33.

15. Daniel Tevera and Lovemore Zinyama, *Zimbabweans Who Move: Perspectives on International Migration in Zimbabwe,* Migration Policy Series no. 25, South African Migration Project (Cape Town: Idasa, 2002), 12.

16. Hany Besada and Nicky Moyo, "Picking up the Pieces of Zimbabwe's Economy," Technical Paper no. 5, The Centre for International Governance Innovation (CIGI), October 2008.

17. United Nations Conference on Trade and Development (UNCTAD), *World Investment Report: Transnational Corporations, Extractive Industries and Development* (UNCTAD: New York, 2007).

18. Ibid.

19. Encyclopedia of the Nations, 2010.

20. Chengetai J.M. Zvobgo, "African Education in Zimbabwe: The Colonial Inheritance of the New State, 1899–1979," *A Journal of Opinion* 11, no. 3/4, The Re-creation of Zimbabwe: Prospects for Education and Rural Reconstruction (1981): 2–3.

21. "Zimbabwe—Educational System—Overview." StateUniversity.com, http://education.stateuniversity.com/pages/1709/Zimbabwe-EDUCATIONAL-SYSTEM-OVERVIEW.html.

22. Government of South Africa, *Employment Equity Act No. 55 of 1998*. The Employment Equity Act 1998 contains a number of provisions providing for affirmative action and protection against, amongst other things, unfair discrimination and sexual harassment. This act promotes equal employment opportunities to people of all races.

23. Section 5 of the EEA of 1998 provides for the elimination of unfair discrimination by requiring that "every employer must take steps to promote equal opportunity in the workplace by eliminating unfair discrimination in any employment policy or practice." "Employment policy or practice" is widely defined in s. 1 and includes recruitment, job classification, remuneration, employment benefits, terms and conditions, promotion, and dismissal. Section 6 prohibits unfair discrimination: "6(1) No person may unfairly discriminate, directly or indirectly, against an employee, in any employment policy or practice, on one or more grounds, including…gender, sex, pregnancy, marital status, family responsibility."

24. "15(1) Affirmative action measures are measures designed to ensure that suitably qualified people from designated groups have equal employment opportunities and are equitably represented in all occupational categories and levels in the workforce of a designated employer."

25. The May 2008 xenophobic violence in South Africa was primarily directed against black foreigners living in some of the poorest urban areas (black townships) of the country. Most victims were black people from mostly Zimbabwe, Mozambique, Zambia, and Somalia. No incidents were reported against white foreigners living in urban areas. Few incidents were reported from urban areas against foreigners from West Africa. However, this violence has also impacted on those who acquired citizenship by virtue of their specialized skills, including accountants, financial management, academics, scientists, and engineers. And it has also impacted on those with legitimate work and study permits, such as the tens of thousands of Mozambicans working in mines, mathematics teachers from Zimbabwe, and foreign university students. There were more than sixty people killed and about one hundred thousand displaced. See "More than 2,000 Zimbabweans Flee, Fearing Attacks," *humanitarian news and analysis*, November 17, 2009, http://allafrica.com/stories/200911171109.html. Recently in Pietermaritzburg, KwaZulu Natal, South Arica, the premier Zweli Mkhize, in response to the 2008 xenophobia attacks, called on the province to embrace one another irrespective of ethnic background. During Heritage Day celebrations in Pietermaritzburg, Dr. Mkhize told thousands of people that xenophobia and other forms of discrimination had no place in a democracy. "Our people must be taught to accept all people and fight against xenophobia and bring to an end all forms of political intolerance that caused brother to murder brother." See "Mkhize Warns against Xenophobia," *SAPA*, September 25, 2009, http://www.polity.org.za/article/mkhize-warns-against-xenophobia-2009–09–25.

26. Zimbabwean colonization started in the 1890s when the "pioneer column" of John Cecil Rhodes crossed north over the Limpopo. This movement north of European settlers was spurred on by massive gold discoveries on the Rand (now Johannesburg) in South Africa in the 1870s. "Gold hunger" led mining capital to explore for further rich gold fields. These explorations penetrated as far inland as the Zimbabwe highlands, where gold was indeed discovered. The Morris-Carter Commission of 1925 was established to set out a framework for ensuring the emergence of Rhodesia as a self-sustaining white colony. The commission proposed landholding patterns to put the settler economy on a sound footing. This was followed by the Land Appointment Act of 1930, which separated land along racial lines (both in terms of quality and quantity). Race groups were not allowed to acquire land in areas designated for other races. This land structure has largely carried through into the postindependence period. See Lebert, "Backgrounder-Land and Agrarian Reform," 2.

27. Polzer, "Regularising Zimbabwe Migration," 3 and Gaidzanwa, *Voting with Their Feet*.

28. "No Welcome, No Let-Up," 37–8.

29. Polzer, "Regularising Zimbabwe Migration," 2.

30. For a more detailed analysis of the implementation issues relating to the Special Dispensation Permit, see the *Forced Migration Studies Programme (FMSP)* Report, "Immigration Policy Responses to Zimbabweans in South Africa: Implementing Special Temporary Permits," available from tara.polzer@wits.ac.za

31. See http://www.cormsa.org.za/wp-content/uploads/MigrationPolicyBrief/Migration %20Policy%20Brief%201%20-%20Zim%20Special%20Permits.pdf.

32. The *Native (Black) Urban Areas Act No 21 of 1923* imposed a system of segregation that allowed black Africans access to towns only to serve white labor needs. Domestic workers were allowed to live in town, and the rest were restricted to finding housing in townships on the outskirts. Legislation in 1937 restricted black African males a window of fourteen days in which to find employment or return to the reserves. The act was superseded by the Native (Urban Areas) Consolidation Act No 25 of 1945, which was repealed by the Abolition of Influx Control Act No 68 of 1986. The Pass Laws, which ultimately characterized influx control, were abolished by the P.W. Botha government in 1986.

33. IOM, *The Development Potential of Zimbabweans*, 10.

34. ASGISA is a government plan that has identified six priority factors that constrain growth in South Africa. One factor is a shortage of skills. JIPSA is a detailed plan of action to fast tracks skills in support of the ASGISA.

35. JIPSA is a multistakeholder working group, through which government, labor, and business will join forces to fast track the provision of priority skills required to support accelerated and shared economic growth for the country.

36. The DBSA is a development finance institution wholly owned by the government of South Africa that focuses on investments and joint ventures/partnerships in public and private sector financing. Approximately 86 percent of loans are for infrastructural development throughout sub-Saharan Africa. See Development Bank of Southern Africa, *Development Fund Annual Report*, Midrand, South Africa, 2008/2009.

37. The DBSA Development Fund is a Section 21 company that was established by the DBSA in 2001. The Fund's main objective is to address the challenges and development needs of local government, focusing on low capacity municipalities in particular. It operates within the DBSA mandate and has its own board of directors. See ibid.

38. The Siyenza Manje program is a flagship intervention program that is funded jointly by the National Treasury and the DBSA. This initiative aims at improving the capacity of municipalities and to remove performance constraints that hamper sustained service delivery, particularly in low capacity municipalities.

39. The main reason for the focus on engineering, finance, and town planning is the dire shortage of expertise in these three sectors, which consequently negatively impacts municipal performance. These experts support municipalities by providing vital hands-on technical, financial, and planning support. This support includes on-the-job training of municipal officials, as well as young graduates, to build critical skills at the local level of government. See DBSA, *Development Fund Annual Report,* 2008/2009.

40. DBSA, "Siyenza Manje is 'Doing It' for Municipalities Constrained by Lack of Capacity," Media Release, August 30, 2007, http://www.dbsa.org/%28S%284qbu2ey3zsprtm45y cwnpajb%29%29/News/LatestNews/Pages/aManjeis%E2%80%9Cdoingit%E2%80% 9DforMunicipalitiesconstrainedbylackofcapacity.aspx.

41. Ibid.

42. DBSA, *Development Fund Annual Report,* 19.

43. As part of its obligation to address the economic crisis, the Zimbabwean government has come up with the present Short Term Emergency Recovery Programme (STERP), which covers the period February to December 2009. STERP is an emergency, short-term stabilization program whose key goals are to stabilize the macro- and micro-economy; recover levels of savings, investment, and growth; and lay the basis for a more transformative mid- to long-term economic program that will turn Zimbabwe into a progressive developmental state.

44. IMF, "Zimbabwe: 2009 Article IV Consultation," IMF Country Report No. 09/139, May 2009, 11, http://www.imf.org/external/pubs/ft/scr/2009/cr09139.pdf.

45. P. Thornycroft and S. Berger, "Zimbabwe PM Morgan Tsvangirai Struggles to Raise Funds on World Tour," *The Telegraph,* June 21, 2009.

46. Government of Zimbabwe, "Dutch Govt Turns Down Tsvangirai," *The Herald,* June 9, 2009, http://allafrica.com/stories/200906090008.html.

47. The roundtable was organized by the Development Enterprise Africa Trust (DEAT), a Zimbabwe-based nonprofit research and strategy organization, with support from the Zimbabwe Independent Newspaper Group, Africa Sun Limited, Air Zimbabwe, Frontier Advisory, and private sector organizations in Zimbabwe.

48. The eligible partners in this instance would be other regional governments and public utilities in the region.

49. UNDP, *Comprehensive Economic Recovery in Zimbabwe: A Discussion Document,* UNDP Zimbabwe, 2008, http://www.undp.no/assets/Other-publications/UNDP-Comprehensive-Economic-Recovery-in-Zimbabwe-2.pdf.

50. *The Comprehensive Africa Agriculture Development Programme* (Midrand: NEPAD, 2003), http://www.caadp.net/about-caadp.php.

51. Aid/donor funds are managed by NGOs, which in most instances are managed by the resources appointed by the aid source organization. In order to support the creation of job opportunities, the PPPs between agribusiness, small producers, and public sector should ensure that there are established NGOs reporting to the PPPs structure, with skills obtained from the beneficiary's country.

52. I. Thlase, "Concept Note on Regional Integration," unpublished, Development Bank of Southern Africa, 2009, 11.

53. Ibid.

54. DBSA, *Development Fund Annual Report,* 29.

55. Ibid.

56. In terms of the Land Appointment Act, 50.8 percent of the land was reserved for white settlers, with the bulk of it on the arable central highlands. The majority indigenous African population was allocated 30 percent of the land. This 30 percent was located largely on the plateau sloping down into the Zambezi Valley and in the mountainous escarpment regions. This land was designated as African Reserve Areas (now known as communal areas). The remaining 20 percent of the land was either owned by commercial companies or the colonial government (Crown Land), or was reserved as conservation areas. A further very small area (0.05 percent), the Native Purchase Areas, allowed the acquisition of land (through freehold or leasehold) by richer Africans or small groups of African people. It is important to note, however, that not only did white settlers have the pick of land in the best agro-ecological regions of the country, but they were also supported by massive state intervention in the development of the farming economy. Thus, the colonial state provided extensive communication and marketing infrastructure in commercial farming areas and made subsidies and loans available to white farmers.

57. Mellor (2001) cites the example of Malaysia as a success story for agricultural development and poverty reduction. The agricultural growth of Malaysia came from exportable cash crops such as rubber and palm oil, rather than food crops. Malaysia also adopted a policy of support for research and rural infrastructure that led to considerable yield increases and induced large income increases for the many small producers of these products. The intensification of rice production also led to increases in rural incomes that were translated into increased non-farm employment. If improved agricultural productivity leads to higher incomes for the poor who spend it on domestic non-tradable, then agricultural growth will induce non-agricultural rural growth and decreases in poverty via employment multipliers. Thus, the pattern of the distribution of increased incomes from the initial stimulus is the most important determinant of subsequent growth and poverty reduction if the fruits of the initial productivity stimulus are concentrated on those who re-spend it domestically on labor-intensive products with low import dependence.

58. NEPAD Secretariat, *The Comprehensive Africa Agriculture Development Programme,* 46.

59. The ethnic divide between the Ndebele and the Shona has since 1980 resulted in the minority Ndebele leaving Zimbabwe after conflicts that left thousands dead. The divide carried on and was demonstrated by the elections, where most votes for Mugabe were from Matabeleland and for the opposition from Ndebele strongholds.

60. Project preparation entails the collection of data, which will assist in conducting a feasibility study or the appraisal of a document. A consultant is appointed to work with government, civil society, beneficiaries, and a development agency. The government and the funding agent agree on the implementing agent for the project and on reporting lines. The preparation of the feasibility requires extensive funding, and a technical assistance grant could assist. In most cases, this is an expensive exercise as projects might be classified as bankable (feasible) or not feasible, and the cost could be written off as sunk costs. In sharing the risk, government and funding agents agree to jointly pay for the costs and create a pipeline of bankable projects, which makes it easier for investors/business to embark on projects. This is a positive spin-off of PPPs.

61. DBSA, *Development Fund Annual Report,* 29.

62. Alice Bloch, "Emigration from Zimbabwe: Migrant Perspectives," *Social Policy & Administration* 40, no. 1 (2006): 67–87.

63. LIMDEV's mandate is to develop the provincial economy and to promote and manage environmental and tourism activities, as well as to strengthen regional cooperation ties and harness their strategic location as the gateway to Africa. It is in keeping with the objectives of NEPAD and the Provincial Growth and Development Strategy (PGDS) objectives through regional integration initiatives.

64. Irma Weenink, Lessons Learned: Funding NEPAD Projects, AFD/DBSA Project preparation and feasibility study (PPFS) Experiences, Development Bank of Southern Africa, 2008.

65. South Africa and Zimbabwe severed official diplomatic ties in 1980 when Zimbabwe gained its independence. However, during the period between 1980 and 1994, South Africa maintained unofficial relations with Zimbabwe through its trade office in Harare. In 1994, the bilateral relations between South Africa and Zimbabwe were normalized, with the establishment of full diplomatic relations in effect from April 29, 1994. In 2009, South Africa and Zimbabwe signed an agreement that created an enabling and protective environment for investments made by nationals of both countries in each other's territories. See "Emerging Market Business News, South Africa Signs a Bilateral

Investment Agreement," *BuaNews,* Harare, April 9, 2009. The Department of Trade and Industry also made it clear that a driving factor behind South Africa decision to aid Zimbabwe's economic recovery was to alleviate the burden placed on the South African state resources by Zimbabwean immigrants. See J. Brand and M. Krynauw, *Implications and Ramifications on Zimbabwe/SA Agreement on Investment Protection,* BG Attorneys, Articles, February 2010.

Part III

Foreign Direct Investment and Donor Engagement for Socioeconomic Reconstruction

Chapter 10

Multinationals and Foreign Investment in Zimbabwe
A Development and Human Rights Perspective

Dianna Games

Executive Summary

Zimbabwe, up to 2009, was frequently described as the fastest shrinking economy outside a war zone. Its decline has been discussed and debated in detail, and solutions sought for its problems by other countries, mostly western, for nearly a decade. The country's economic decline was driven by a government bent on political survival, buoyed by the support of regional governments; yet the innovative people of Zimbabwe devised ways to survive the state's tortuous economic policies.

Development as a whole in Zimbabwe has suffered under many years of Zimbabwe African National Union—Patriotic Front (ZANU-PF) misrule, with a rapid deterioration in social sectors, infrastructure, services, and macroeconomic fundamentals.

Most foreign investors, notably those from South Africa, which comprise the majority of foreign companies still operating in Zimbabwe, have held the line through the darkest times in Zimbabwe's history, ever hopeful of change. However, there was little new investment as business conditions became ever more difficult and policies increasingly unpredictable and erratic.

Zimbabwean-owned businesses suffered mixed fortunes. Many were unable to survive the economic contraction and closed their doors. Others reduced operations to a fraction of capacity and retrenched workers, while a handful prospered—mostly as a result of government patronage and regional expansion as a hedge against problems at home.

The plight of Zimbabwean workers became dire. With unemployment rising to more than 80 percent of adults, according to anecdotal estimates, thousands of professionals and blue collar workers fled to greener pastures in other parts of the world, mostly the United Kingdom (UK) and South Africa. Many of those who stayed, including skilled and well qualified workers, were forced by the economic climate into the informal sector, and a significant number of Zimbabweans survived on foreign currency remittances, which acted as a buffer against the economic crisis.

Foreign investors were pressured by their home governments and civil society to examine their ethical stance in this compromising situation. Lobby groups and commentators asked whether foreign investors, by staying, were either supporting the pariah government, or helping the people of Zimbabwe—or both. While continued investment in Zimbabwe meant jobs could be saved, multinational companies had to weigh this against the fact that their very presence helped to maintain the political status quo, notwithstanding the fact that their bottom line was being affected by the ruling party's policies and behavior.

The pressure for disinvestment became more intense in 2008 when the violence against the opposition and intimidation of potential voters reached new levels ahead of that year's election. Several multinationals did pull out in 2008, although most continued to operate, citing concerns about workers.

Zimbabweans seemed inclined to believe it was good for multinationals to stay because they provided a lifeline to thousands of people, in terms of jobs and social spending, and their presence helped to keep Zimbabwe on the map. Multinational corporations would also be a resource, it was argued, when a new government finally was able to restore normality in Zimbabwe.

The new multiparty Government of National Unity (GNU), brokered by the Southern African Development Community (SADC) in 2008 and inaugurated in 2009, signaled a new order for Zimbabwe and nullified the disinvestment debate, despite the fact that tensions between the main parties continued to hold back the country's potential.

This chapter examines the recent political and business climate in Zimbabwe, focusing on issues affecting, and of particular concern to, local and foreign multinationals in Zimbabwe. It also looks at the role such businesses can play in the country's economic recovery.

Introduction: The political economy of Zimbabwe's lost decade (1998–2008)

Zimbabwe's economy effectively collapsed during 2008 when normal commercial activity became almost impossible, owing to the collapse of the currency, record-breaking inflation, government price controls, foreign currency and cash shortages, lengthy power cuts, and a breakdown of health and water services.

In the decade since President Robert Mugabe's government began to systematically destroy the country's key agricultural sector and undermine the then emergent opposition, the Movement for Democratic Change (MDC) in 2000, Zimbabwe's economy has contracted by at least 30 percent.[1] The state-owned newspaper, *The Herald*, reckoned in 2008 that it had contracted by almost 50 percent,[2] an unusual admission from a staunch defender of the status quo.

The crisis was the coalescence of problems dating back to the late 1990s. The economy, already under strain from the implementation of the International Monetary Fund (IMF)'s structural adjustment program of the early 1990s and successive droughts, was further undermined by massive spending on the war in the Democratic Republic of Congo in the late 1990s. Former finance minister Simba Makoni estimated the costs of two years of fighting at US$10 billion.[3]

The beginning of the end for the Zimbabwe dollar was November 1997, when Mugabe made huge unbudgeted payments of Z$50,000 each to about 50,000 restive *war veterans* who were to become his private vigilante force.[4] This resulted in the crash of the currency, which overnight lost more than 70 percent of its value against the US dollar as investors pulled out of the stock market.[5]

But the biggest catalyst for economic deterioration has been the state's destruction of the commercial agriculture sector since 2000, the year the ruling party faced the biggest threat to its unchallenged hegemony since it came to power in 1980. This threat was presented by the formation of the trade union-based MDC party and a *no* vote in the referendum on a new constitution drawn up by the government, both occurring in 2000.

The violent seizure of white-owned commercial property and the eviction of farmers and their workers led agricultural production across Zimbabwe to plummet. Many of the newly occupied farms were handed to the political elite, who seldom farmed them, preferring instead to keep the profits from the sale of produce and maintain the farms as weekend retreats. Some were given to small farmers who did not have the inputs and resources to exploit them and were not provided with these by the state.

The strong linkages between the agricultural and manufacturing sectors meant the latter also declined, owing to a lack of locally produced raw materials. The manufacturing sector was further hit by foreign exchange shortages, which curtailed the import of key inputs, and power shortages as the electricity parastatal ZESA succumbed to years of neglect. In 2007, the Confederation of Zimbabwe Industries put manufacturing capacity at just 18.9 percent, down from 33.8 percent in 2006.[6]

The mining sector similarly suffered from power problems, flight of skilled workers (as Zimbabweans sought a normal life elsewhere), foreign currency shortages, and government interference, particularly in gold mining companies—which were traditionally the biggest foreign exchange earners for the state. Another successful sector, tourism, suffered from the country's reputational damage, a situation that was later exacerbated by moral concerns over holidaying in Zimbabwe and by significant shortages of goods and food.

The contraction of key economic sectors was compounded by poor macroeconomic policies that focused on politically expedient short-term rescue plans rather than growth, the collapse of investor and business confidence, and deteriorating relations with external funders. Freedom of speech and association were severely curtailed by legislation, and political arrests and human rights abuses against opposition members became the order of the day.

Exports declined from US$2.19 billion in 2000[7] to US$1.9 billion in 2006,[8] which had a knock-on effect on the currency. The government interfered with export earnings via a series of constantly changing and complex formulas—mandating the portion of foreign earnings that exporters could retain in hard currency and the portion that had to be exchanged for Zimbabwe dollars at official exchange rates, which were a fraction of the black market value.

In addition to a shrinking tax base, the government's obsession with political projects that benefited few citizens drained the treasury and diverted the state's attention from social spending. Such projects included, for example, the reestablishment of the senate, which had been abolished by the president in 1987 because it was deemed unnecessary.

As a result, the biggest deterioration in modern day Zimbabwe, aside from agriculture, has been in key social sectors, notably health, education, water, housing, and municipal services. These sectors, which are primarily the preserve of government in any country, were affected by significantly reduced state spending and by the inability of citizens to pay for services—as a result of unemployment and the erosion of incomes due to inflation. It is estimated that life expectancy in Zimbabwe is 44 for males and 43 for females[9] because of disease and malnutrition, and worsened by increasing unemployment and poverty.

The cholera epidemic of 2008 and 2009, which started in the capital and spread eventually into northern South Africa, was the starkest evidence of the breakdown of basic services. By early February 2009, the death toll had climbed to more than 3,800 people, with more than 80,000 infected,[10] despite Mugabe's bizarre announcement in December 2008 that the epidemic was over.[11] The World Health Organization (WHO) says it is one of the largest cholera epidemics ever reported.[12]

Other development realities in Zimbabwe include the following:

- Unemployment/informal employment at more than 90 percent by 2009
- Rapidly declining disposable incomes to pay for goods and services
- Serious food shortages—by 2009 nearly half of the population needed food aid
- The failure of basic services in cities and the neglect of urban infrastructure
- The collapse of previously supportive economic initiatives, such as rural water, housing and education schemes, agricultural training, and extension services
- A non-existent savings/pension base
- Malfunctioning parastatals, which contributed in large measure to inflation and high domestic debt
- Official constraints on the operations of non-governmental organizations (NGOs), both local and international, to provide food because of the government's reluctance to let outside agencies control these vital vote-buying sectors

In the decade up to 2008, Zimbabwe's economy became a numbers game. According to Zimbabwean economists, higher numbers indicated greater economic decline. The last officially recorded inflation figure, released in July 2008, was 231 million percent, although analysts maintained it had, by then, spiraled up to several trillion percent.[13] Accurate estimates were impossible given the lack of official statistics and the shortage of goods on the shelves with which to measure inflation.

The currency faced a similar fate, with official interbank rates reaching six figures and parallel market rates running into billions of Zimbabwe dollars for one US dollar. The central bank shaved zeroes off the currency to tackle cash shortages—and Zimbabwe's image. The most drastic of these was the removal of 10 zeroes in August 2008 to avoid a conversion rate of one US dollar to 10 trillion Zimbabwe dollars.[14] Talk of trillions and quadrillions was common. The real economy was valued at US$3 billion in 2008, down from about US$12 billion 12 years prior,[15] with money supply (M3) valued at less than US$50 million in 2008, down from US$3.25 billion a decade earlier,[16] reflecting the erosion of the economy. Inflation made saving impossible since the divide between interest rates and inflation grew hourly, and banks could not keep pace. Inflation rendered pensions valueless, and many people lost their life savings through the collapse of insufficiently regulated banks.

The Zimbabwe Stock Exchange (ZSE) became a haven for trapped domestic money trying to maintain value in equities. As a result, the ZSE, on a percentage basis, became one of the best performing stock exchanges in the world. However, just 2 percent of trading on the ZSE was by foreigners in 2008, down from 30 percent in 1998.[17]

Before the *dollarization* of the economy, the government printed money to meet demand for cash on the back of hyperinflation, but rising demand and ongoing cash shortages pushed the government to set strict withdrawal limits for banks. This added to the poor quality of life in Zimbabwe as citizens had to queue at banks for several hours a day to draw sufficient money to pay their daily expenses. In 2008, bartering of goods and services started to replace cash transactions.

Over the years, the Mugabe government, as a response to a crisis of its own making, devised a plethora of economic recovery schemes and programs, all of which were unworkable without political reform, but which imposed an onerous burden on business, which had to adapt to this moving target.

Many government officials were actively engaged in black market practices and corruption, which further diminished the state's desire for structural reform. Ruling party officials became rich through black market currency trading, which provided access to extremely preferential exchange rates and government contracts.[18]

Sanctions

Mugabe blames western sanctions for Zimbabwe's problems; however, there are no broad-based sanctions against Zimbabwe. The European Union (EU), Australian, and American sanctions target the president, senior members of the ruling party and their families and colleagues, as well as a range of companies owned by or linked to party members and those that are actively supporting the regime. They also include an arms embargo on the basis that the government would use the weapons against its own people.

The EU first imposed sanctions on the ruling party in 2002. In January 2009, it added more than sixty companies with links to the Zimbabwe government to its targeted sanctions list, banning them from traveling to or doing business with EU countries. In 2009, there were 203 individuals and forty companies on the list. Among those targeted, for the first time, were shell companies registered in Europe, which EU officials say are being used to channel funds out of Zimbabwe. In February 2010, the EU renewed sanctions, saying the government had not introduced reforms agreed to under the Global Political Agreement (GPA), which underpinned the formation of the unity government in 2009. However, the EU did remove several organizations from the list.[19] In 2003, the U.S. government imposed sanctions against specific Zimbabwean individuals, chiefly immediate family members and targeted entities. It also included anyone providing assistance to a sanctions target.

The sanctions prohibit Americans, wherever they are located, from conducting financial, trade, and other transactions with any entities identified on the list of Specially Designated Nationals. Any of the listed people possessing property in the United States had their assets frozen, and U.S. citizens were prohibited from undertaking any financial transaction with them, including blocking money, checks, bank accounts, and even interests in companies.[20]

In July 2008, the U.S. Treasury added seventeen entities to the list, including several companies in which the Zimbabwe government had an interest, such as the Minerals Marketing Corporation of Zimbabwe, Zimbabwe Iron and Steel Company, the Agricultural Development Bank of Zimbabwe, and ZB Financial Holdings Limited. Omani citizen Thamer Bin Saeed Ahmed Al-Shanfari and his company, Oryx Natural Resources, were also targeted for enabling Mugabe and his senior officials to benefit from mining ventures in the DRC. A statement from the U.S. Treasury said that its targets had been illegally used to "siphon revenue and foreign exchange from the Zimbabwean people." In 2009, President Barack Obama extended the sanctions by a year,[21] but trade between the countries has continued; and in 2008, the U.S.-Zimbabwe trade relationship was in the latter's favor, with US$93 million in goods exported to Zimbabwe and US$112 million in goods imported into the United States.[22]

In 2002, Australia introduced *smart sanctions,* which followed the trend set by Western powers.[23] Moreover, the United Nations (UN) attempted to introduce sanctions in 2007, but was frustrated by the veto power utilized by China and Russia.[24]

Donor countries have continued to deliver humanitarian support to Zimbabwe, mostly through nongovernmental channels. In 2007, for example, the United States delivered more than US$170 million worth of food aid to Zimbabwe,[25] and the United Kingdom has provided £142 million in humanitarian assistance between 2005 and 2010.[26]

Although the sanctions have had an effect on the economy, more significant factors in the lack of foreign inflows have been the withdrawal of aid and the fact that capital has avoided Zimbabwe. Foreign investors, particularly those in traditional investing countries, are concerned about the high risk associated with doing business in the country. This includes investment from countries with no sanctions in place, such as China and other African countries.

The government's knee-jerk economic policy, designed to bolster the political status quo, and constant threats by government officials to seize businesses and interfere with their operations for political gain were strong disincentives to investment. Rapid currency devaluation, foreign exchange shortages, and steep runaway inflation were other problems keeping foreign money out of Zimbabwe.

Multilateral financial institutions stopped delivering aid because of Zimbabwe's failure to pay its dues, setting a trend for other donors to reduce or suspend disbursements on existing loans to the government and parastatal companies. This has had a similar effect to formal sanctions by restricting the amount of new money flowing into the economy, but was linked to the government's own behavior. Even after the installation of the GNU, both the IMF and African Development Bank (AfDB) stated that they would only sign off on new money for Zimbabwe after existing debts had been paid.

A New Era for Zimbabwe?

Political change was the solution business sought with the expectation was that this would return the economy to normality and unlock significant funding and investment. Many analysts predicted that the economy would precipitate change in Zimbabwe and, to a large extent, that is what happened.

The use of foreign currency as a tradable currency gained ground rapidly in 2008 when the Zimbabwe dollar had, in essence, collapsed. It had taken time to reach this point because the state had made the acts of storing and using foreign currency inside the country a criminal offense.

But changing foreign currency on the black market had become an increasingly tortuous affair, with at least four exchange rates operating at any given time, and it became simpler to pay with U.S. dollars or South African rands at an agreed exchange rate. Over time, the usage of foreign currency increased and became more brazen.

In September 2008, the government acknowledged the reality on the streets and said it would license 1000 retailers and 250 wholesalers to sell goods in foreign currencies.[27] This system was unsuccessful as few could afford the licenses, but by January 2009, business had started openly using foreign currency to trade, and even hospitals and public transporters were starting to charge in U.S. dollars. In February 2009, after the unity government was inaugurated, new finance minister Tendai Biti announced that public servants would be paid in U.S. dollar vouchers,[28] a crucial move designed to forestall strikes by employees who were angry about being marginalized from the hard currency economy.

In the same month, the ZSE, which has been forced to suspend trading for three months over allegations of improper activities by brokers, started operating again—this time in foreign currency denominated trades.[29] The stock exchange was one of the avenues through which foreign currency entered the country. Other means included the repatriation back to Zimbabwe of funds that had been externalized funds by business and citizens over several years (despite being illegal), remittances from the diaspora, and earnings from regional business activities.

The currency change was not favored by ZANU-PF officials who had made small fortunes in arbitrage using the highly preferential exchange rates for the Zimbabwe dollar they alone had access to, and they unsuccessfully fought to keep the Zimbabwe dollar alive. They had support in the lower income segments of the population who had little access to U.S. dollars and rands, but the tide had already turned.

The currency change found most favor with the private sector. Scrapping the Zimbabwe dollar brought the country back into the regional economy, and it enabled retailers to import goods into their stores. Slowly, the economy came back to life.

The concurrent political development was the formation of the GNU in September 2009, midwifed by the SADC in the aftermath of the 2008 elections. The elections were won by the MDC, but in effect were hijacked by Mugabe in a presidential runoff vote that Tsvangirai boycotted because of increased violence against his supporters by the ruling party. The GNU was inaugurated in February 2009, led by Mugabe as president, MDC-Tsvangirai (MDC-T) leader Morgan Tsvangirai as prime minister, and splinter MDC movement leader Arthur Mutambara as deputy prime minister.

It was an uncomfortable compromise. From the outset, the two parties struggled to work together, and promised reforms failed to materialize. As a result, Western countries refused to drop sanctions, and many investors adopted a *wait and see* approach. After becoming prime minister in 2009, Tsvangirai estimated that Zimbabwe would need at least US$5 billion to kick-start the economy.[30] His singular lack of success in raising funds on a trip to the United States and Britain in mid-2009 came as no surprise to analysts who predicted that the prime minister would continue to be frustrated by Mugabe.

A year after the government was inaugurated, it was clear that their concerns were not misplaced. Key reforms of the constitution, legal system, electoral system, media, and other areas were not in place, and the security situation, still controlled by the ZANU-PF ministers in the cabinet, remained a problem, with violent takeovers of remaining white-owned commercial farms continuing despite court orders for them to cease. Furthermore, allegations by the MDC of recurrent attacks on its members persisted.

As tensions rose, talk began among politicians about an election in 2011, under reformed electoral laws, to end the transition phase.[31] Despite concerns about violence erupting again if, as is expected, the former ruling party resorted to its old tactics, Zimbabweans increasingly believe the power-sharing façade cannot continue for much longer, as it is affecting the country's chances for real recovery. Much-needed investment, which was poised to stream into a politically free Zimbabwe, has not been forthcoming because of the continuing political uncertainty and high business risk of the transition. However, a ZANU-PF election win that put Mugabe and his coterie of military supporters, war veterans, and old-style politicians back in power would drive investors away, and would likely prompt multinationals to once again examine their options.

Business in Zimbabwe: Challenges and Threats

Despite the direct threat that politics has posed to their bottom line and potentially to their reputations, most companies that were already invested in Zimbabwe in 2000 remained in the country and endured a most challenging operating environment. Group operations were forced to ring fence their Zimbabwean operations in order to keep the hyperinflationary accounting off the books. Listed multinationals struggled to pay dividends from Zimbabwe because of foreign currency restrictions, and profits were generally stored in the ZSE.

Government interference in the private sector through politically inspired policies was an onerous burden for companies already facing high operating risk: agricultural concerns fell victim to land seizures; producers were subjected to state harassment and price controls; the mining sector was threatened with nationalization; and high street banks struggled to maintain their core business. New millionaires were, however, made from inflation-based trading in fuel, currency, and luxury goods, and as the formal economy contracted, so the black market grew in prominence.

Blaming the private sector for problems of the government's own making was commonplace in Zimbabwe, and it gave Mugabe ammunition to intimidate business through the introduction of ad hoc regulations, and policies and threats of seizure. This was most pronounced with the introduction of price controls in the middle of 2007, which almost destroyed what was left of the formal economy.

The controls were a misplaced attempt to rein in inflation, which the government claimed was being driven by private sector greed. Initially, the controls, which forced all suppliers, producers, and retailers to cut prices by 50 percent,[32] were applied only to basic foodstuffs. However, they were later extended to all locally produced goods and services, including hotel rooms, air fares, and mobile phone tariffs. This brought the price of goods well below the cost of production. More than seven thousand people were arrested for flouting the controls, including several hundred executives. But the price bonanza was short-lived as shelves emptied—and it stayed that way. Retailers claimed they could not afford to restock in the depressed and uncertain climate. Manufacturers found it unviable to maintain full production, and most reduced production to between 10 and 30 percent of capacity.[33]

There were several consequences of this ill-considered move by the state. One was that shelves remained empty for eighteen months after the price controls were introduced, and even after most of the controls were reversed. When goods eventually returned to the shelves in late 2008, most were imports, closing the gap for local manufacturers who had become uncompetitive.

Trust between the government and business also broke down and was replaced by fear and resentment. Tripartite and bilateral forums for engagement became dormant, and business chambers were accused of not standing up for the interests of their members, as they preferred to remain on the right side of the unpredictable and toxic state. This legacy of mistrust has flowed into the *new* Zimbabwe under the unity government, particularly in light of ZANU-PF officials' decision to fast-track the indigenization of business, which potentially has major implications for foreign investors.

However, despite their operational difficulties, foreign and local companies failed to speak out about the government's knee-jerk economic policies and its human rights record, its violations of the rule of law, rigged elections and political repression.

South African companies, in particular, were targeted by critics for their silence, especially in light of the South African government's unprincipled stance on the problems of its neighbor. Although no companies have been specifically targeted, there are dozens of South African companies operating in Zimbabwe, including some of the biggest listed stocks on the Johannesburg Stock Exchange (JSE), and their collective voice would have been large enough to make an impact on the situation. Even if public statements did not sway the ZANU-PF, it would have been a useful counter both to the South African government's own inaction, and to the propaganda being disseminated by the government, which proclaimed that all was well in Zimbabwe.

Business aversion to publicly ratcheting up pressure for change was based on three central platforms—fear, self-interest, and survival. In a country run by a government bent on total control, it was easiest to keep below the radar. Business people who challenged Mugabe did not survive. Foreign companies were concerned about forced takeovers of their enterprises by a government that had shown through its violent land seizures that it was neither concerned about the rule of law at home, nor public opinion in the West.

For example, mining magnate Mutumwa Mawere, once an ally of Mugabe's, had his assets expropriated by the government after falling foul of the president and was forced into exile in South Africa.[34] Millionaire U.K. businessman John Bredenkamp, who has companies in Zimbabwe and is reported to be a key financial backer of the government, fled the country in 2006 after Mugabe launched an investigation into his affairs.[35] British property tycoon Nicholas Van Hoogstraten, who lived in Zimbabwe, is another example. Also believed to be a backer of Mugabe, he was arrested in 2008 on charges relating to currency and his businesses.[36]

The issue of whether companies should leave the country, as a protest against the actions of the Zimbabwe government toward its people, gained momentum in 2008 following a wave of state-sponsored violence against the political opposition ahead of both the March elections and the one-man runoff election for president that followed. The British newspapers were particularly vocal on the subject, raising questions about the support being given to the Zimbabwe government by British businesses, albeit indirectly.[37]

Companies had different ideas about their continued presence in Zimbabwe. The main course of action, overall, was for foreign investors to remain in the country on the basis that closing up shop would exacerbate the hardship experienced by ordinary Zimbabweans. But the human rights defense is just part of the story. Companies that believed they had a future in Zimbabwe did not want to squander the opportunity of being part of a reformed country—particularly given the potential cost of reentry in a normalized Zimbabwe, where assets were likely to be more expensive and where first-to-market advantage would be lost to those who had remained in the country through the hard times.

There was also a view that pulling out of Zimbabwe, although a public relations coup for the companies concerned, would not necessarily put too much pressure on the government because the void could be filled by businesses from less scrupulous countries, such as Iran, China, and Russia.

There is little doubt that business has an important role to play in the rebuilding process, in creating wealth, providing employment and linkages to the informal economy, building capacity, and providing revenue for the reconstructing the state. The inauguration of the GNU meant that companies could reevaluate the market, looking at investing or boosting their existing investments.

However, in a short time, two factors threatened to derail this business interest—the global economic crisis, which reduced available funding and credit lines to both business and the government, and the February 2010 gazetting of the regulations that gave effect to the 2008 *Zimbabwe Indigenisation and Economic Empowerment Act.* This mandates foreign and white-owned Zimbabwean companies valued at more than US$500,000 to give a minimum 51 percent stake to black Zimbabweans within five years. The legislation, unilaterally driven by the ZANU-PF, has created new tensions between business and government, and between the parties in the government.

Zimbabwean business people are concerned about the repercussions this onerous legislation will have on the country's economic revival. Already the ZSE has seen significantly lower trades since the regulations were gazetted.[38] Many say indigenization has occurred organically over the past decade, and that there was no need for such draconian legislation, which was passed in 2007.

There are few who believe that the legislation is really about empowerment, but rather most see it as a tool to give the political and business elite stakes in lucrative companies built by others. There are few Zimbabweans outside the political elite who are capitalized enough, after a decade of recession, to afford big stakes in foreign companies.

Predictably, the reaction by business has not been favorable, not because there is opposition to empowerment in principle, but because there are concerns about the size of the stake—foreign companies are unwilling to cede control of their international brands to local companies—and the government's track record in implementing such schemes, as evidenced by the violent land redistribution campaign. Many foreign investors, aware of the growing empowerment drive over the past five years, have already put in place measures toward empowerment credits. In the past, they had also attempted to sell shareholdings to local investors, such as Anglo American, Zimplats, and Metallon. Most attempts failed, partly because of undue political interference, but also because of a lack of local capacity and funding to take advantage of opportunities.

For example, in 2001 Zimplats, a key indigenization target given its foreign ownership and the high international price of platinum, offered a 15 percent stake to indigenous shareholders, but bidding companies failed to find the capital to take up the stake. In 2006, the company, which has plans for a R500 million expansion of its Zimbabwe operations, gave up 36 percent of its Ngezi claim in return for empowerment credits[39] but in 2010, the indigenization minister declared that in trying to use such claims toward its 51 percent target, the company was "crazy."[40] Many companies believe the government will force companies to either cede a portion of the stake for free, or at well below the market price, despite government statements about market-based remuneration.

Although the politically expedient nature of the legislation suggested it would not apply to Mugabe's new friends from the East,[41] the legislation also deterred Chinese investors who had been eyeing investments in Zimbabwe. For example, the purchase of the moribund state-owned steel maker Zisco floundered as the Chinese held back amid concerns about the application of the new law,[42] despite an announcement in 2006 that the Metallurgical Corporation of China was to buy a stake for US$3 billion.[43] In 2009, Indian multinational ArcelorMittal was one of two shortlisted bidders for the parastatal, but in 2010, the company voiced concern about the empowerment legislation, suggesting it might review its interest in the R4 billion deal.[44]

The sale in January 2008 by U.S. company HJ Heinz, one of Zimbabwe's first big foreign investors, of its 51 percent shareholding in Olivine Industries to the privatized Zimbabwean company Cotton Company of Zimbabwe was attributed by government propagandists as being the result of pressure imposed by the state on foreign companies to indigenize. The company, which had written down its Zimbabwe investment in 2006 because of the economic climate, denied this, saying the sale was a strategic decision based on its decision to focus on profitable core businesses.

While no company publicly refused to comply with the legislation, Britain's Standard Chartered Bank and South Africa's Stanbic told a parliamentary committee during a public hearing in 2008 that ceding control of foreign-owned banks to local owners would mean the loss of critical international synergies needed for their growth. Barclays Bank said it would review the situation when necessary, while South Africa's insurance giant Old Mutual, which has operated in Zimbabwe for more than one hundred years, offloaded a 20 percent stake in the company to black employees ahead of the law being passed.[45]

The indigenization issue has been divisive for the unity government, with the ZANU-PF's minister of indigenization Kasukuwere (backed by Mugabe) being uncompromising about the 51 percent ownership despite concerns voiced by the MDC about the effect this would have on investment. In 2010, the unity government seemed to find some common ground on the issue, with sectoral committees appointed to look at a sectoral breakdown in the application of the regulations in consultation with business. The issue for many companies is not the principle of empowerment, but the requirement to cede control to local investors, which has implications for multinationals' brands, reputation, bottom line, harmonization of group operations, and other areas of business.

Corporate Social Responsibility

Large companies in Zimbabwe have used corporate social responsibility (CSR) as a defense for their continued presence in the country. Many argue that their employment of Zimbabweans, as well as company support of health, education, and community development initiatives, signify that business departure would impoverish more locals. But CSR covers a broad spectrum of activities, from in-house health programs to a company's responsibility in terms of human rights and global warming.

Most large companies have funded traditional CSR causes, such as education, support for agricultural training programs, and HIV/AIDS initiatives. The Zimbabwe Business Council on AIDS, launched in 2006, has a number of multinational companies as members, including Standard Chartered Bank, Old Mutual, Unilever East and Central Africa, British American Tobacco, and Zimplats. It aims to reduce the effect of the virus on business through awareness schemes, education, and treatment. Barclays, for example, has a proactive workers committee that is providing counseling and treatment with the help of an NGO,[46] while Zimplats,[47] Standard Chartered,[48] and others say their workers benefit from antiretrovirals and community programs.

Companies, in the past, have had to provide many nontraditional services to workers, such as free lunches, transport to work due to fuel shortages and transport costs, loans, and medical treatment.[49] Employers also faced onerous requirements to keep salaries in line with rapidly increasing inflation, often paying wages weekly, and during the period of cash shortages, paying workers with goods and fuel coupons.[50]

The toxic nature of the government in Zimbabwe prior to 2009 was morally repugnant to the international community, and yet, not only did companies not express their disapproval of the government's policies and human rights behavior, but they actually engaged directly with the government. This was done through loans to the state, giving in to pressure to fund new farmers without collateral, buy Treasury Bills and pay taxes that directly funded ZANU-PF's activities, and had ministers and ruling party officials as clients.

In the broader sense, the mere presence of some of the world's biggest companies in Zimbabwe was useful propaganda material for the state, given the sense of economic normality their presence suggested. The engagement was not necessarily voluntary, but undertaken for fear of repercussions. Having their reputations tarnished by a state quick to play the race card made compliance an easier option than taking on Mugabe.

Curiously, CSR was not used as a stick with which to beat multinationals in Zimbabwe in the way it has been used in other pariah states to push them to disinvest on moral and reputation grounds—as it was, for example, in apartheid South Africa. Initiatives such as the Sullivan Principles[51] of corporate governance coerced companies to either disinvest from South Africa, or risk themselves becoming pariahs by association with the apartheid regime. Activists pushed U.S. cities and states to refuse to buy goods from companies with South African operations and to sell their shares in the country. The movement forced out multinational giants such as General Motors.

But the South African case was clear-cut in the international community in regard to notions of right and wrong. In the case of Zimbabwe, it was a black government, led by someone regarded as a liberation hero, that was repressing and impoverishing its citizens. The ZANU-PF's land strategy, which generated an emotional response from other Africans, helped to obscure the government's *power at any cost* rule.

So, while many Western countries believed that, on moral and ethical grounds, companies should not be operating in such a repressive and dysfunctional state, few African countries—including some members of the SADC—supported such action. South Africa, a direct beneficiary of the Sullivan Principles movement, failed to take a stand against events in Zimbabwe, to put pressure on its companies to disinvest, or to even speak out against rights abuses in the country.

South Africa is the biggest investor in Zimbabwe,[52] and many companies have investments in Zimbabwe dating back half a century and more. Most investment was in the mining sector, reaching hundreds of millions of dollars up until 2008, but also in the retail sector, tourism, financial services, insurance, manufacturing, commercial agriculture, and others. South African companies active in Zimbabwe include: Anglo American; Impala Platinum; Metallon Gold; Standard Bank, whose Zimbabwean subsidiary is Stanbic; clothing retailers Edcon and Truworths; sugar producer Tongaat Hulett; Old Mutual, which is involved in real estate and insurance; PPC cement company; construction company Murray and Roberts; general retailer Massmart, which owns the Makro store in Zimbabwe; and SAB Miller, which has a stake in Zimbabwe's Delta Beverages.

Business ties remain strong, which made it even more curious that South African officials appeared to support the government that was, in effect, destroying value for those companies, among other costs to South Africa, namely, a serious refugee problem. Its reputation as a regional power also suffered as a result of its inaction on the problems of its neighbor.

It took more than five years for Zimbabwe to agree to sign an investment protection agreement with South Africa due to conflict over a clause providing for adequate compensation in the event of the appropriation of assets. Eventually the compromise that sealed the deal was the removal of a clause that backdated compensation for the nationalization of agricultural assets. South Africa is competing with countries such as China, India, Russia, and Iran, which are gaining influence in Zimbabwe because of their stated unwillingness to put pressure on Mugabe's regime to respect human rights and political freedom.

In 2007, China was said to be the second largest investor in Zimbabwe after South Africa, taking the position long held by the United Kingdom. This was according to China's ambassador to Zimbabwe Nasheng Yuan told Zimbabwean journalists that bilateral trade between the countries had increased by 72.6 percent from 2003 (US$197 million) to 2007 (US$340 million).[53] He states the aggregate investment by Chinese companies in engineering and contracted projects totaled US$1.6 billion.[54]

The extent of Chinese investment has been exaggerated by Zimbabwe, and many deals have consisted of exchanges of commodities, such as minerals and tobacco for buses, aircraft, arms, building materials, machinery, and cheap goods that have only served to undermine local manufacturers. China has expressed a keen interest in gold and platinum mines, but to date has completed only one major mining deal, Sinosteel Corporation's purchase of 92 percent of Zimasco, Zimbabwe's biggest ferrochrome producer, in September 2007.[55] High-profile energy projects that were announced several years ago, as well as the rehabilitation of the national railway, have not yet begun. Chinese companies have, as mentioned earlier, been concerned about nationalization threats, the government's ability to pay, and the poor state of utilities, such as steel parastatal Zisco.

Disinvestment Debate

Foreign investment in Zimbabwe is quite significant. A survey undertaken by the Zimbabwe Institute for Development Studies in 1989 found that of 667 firms surveyed, 56 percent were at least half-owned by foreigners and 21 percent were foreign-owned.[56] By 2008, many of the same companies still had a presence in Zimbabwe, although shareholding percentages may have changed over the years. A subsequent study by London-based Ethical Investment Research Services claimed that Britain was the largest foreign investor in Zimbabwe in 2008, with holdings in more than a quarter of the 82 companies that had their parents listed on overseas stock exchanges. It is not clear if South African companies were included in the study as it is generally accepted that the country is the largest investor in Zimbabwe but reliable figures are difficult to get.

From 2000 to 2008, almost no new investment came into Zimbabwe (table 10.1). Most companies waited out the bad times, hoping for a change that always seemed to be just out of reach. From about 2005, many citizens and foreign businesspeople believed the economy could not get much worse and would eventually implode, toppling the Mugabe government and ushering in a new era of normality. This belief kept companies from withdrawing their investments from Zimbabwe.

The disinvestment debate was fairly muted until 2008, when the much publicized violence that characterized both the March elections and the subsequent one-man runoff resulted in increasing pressure on European multinationals to pull out of Zimbabwe.

Table 10.1 Investment in Zimbabwe

Year	Total investment (US dollars, in millions)
1998	$436
2001	$5.4
2005	$103
2006	$40
2007	$69

Sources: US Department of State (http://www.us.state.gov); Reserve Bank of Zimbabwe (www.rbz.co.zw); and UNCTAD (www.unctad.org/sections/dite_dir/docs/wir08_fs_zw_en.pdf).

Anglo American became an early target with its announcement in June 2008 that it planned to go ahead with a US$400 million investment in the Unki platinum mine in Zimbabwe.[57] Anglo, with a primary listing in London, is subject to U.K. pension fund ethical guidelines on investment, which discourage investment in Zimbabwe. In response to calls to disinvest, Anglo issued a statement saying: "Anglo American has been an investor in Zimbabwe for 60 years [and] is deeply concerned about the current political situation, and condemns the violence and human rights abuses that are taking place."[58] The company, which employs nearly 200 people at Unki and 450 contractors, stated that the mining project had been in development since 2003,[59] and that it was not likely to generate income for several years,[60] suggesting that the situation in Zimbabwe might be different by then and the ethical problem solved.

However, behind these statements was an altogether more sinister story. News reports suggested that state officials were threatening to take away their jobs if Anglo American officials did not start the project on time. In early 2008, the company had already been strong-armed into giving up two of its platinum concessions in return for empowerment credits under the new indigenization law.[61] However, the government sold on the stakes, not to Zimbabweans, but to British mining company Central African Mining and Exploration Company (CAMEC) for US$120 million in 2008,[62] a company that suffered little of the disinvestment pressure piled onto Anglo.

In the CAMEC deal, a further payment of US$100 million was extracted from the company for the firm brokering the deal, Virgin Islands-registered Lefever Finance,[63] to comply with its "contractual obligations to the Government of the Republic of Zimbabwe." In other words, this was an unsecured loan at best, and a donation at worst.[64] Given the timing of the deal—April 2008—it was generally assumed the money would be used to finance Mugabe's election campaign, which involved serious human rights violations.

Other British companies with involvement in Zimbabwe, for example, Barclays Bank, which has a 67 percent stake in Barclays Bank Zimbabwe, were asked to comment on their involvement in the country. Barclays, lambasted by British newspapers for funding the Zimbabwean government, said it would continue its operations in Zimbabwe but not expand its business. Although questions were raised in Britain about whether Barclays had violated sanctions by lending money to the government, it defended its actions by saying the loans had been granted by Barclays Bank Zimbabwe, which was incorporated in the country.[65]

Standard Chartered Bank, which said it was committed to the Zimbabwe market and did not want to jeopardize the livelihoods of more than eight hundred employees and their families by leaving Zimbabwe, was also accused of violating sanctions. It was also the subject of an inquiry by Britain's Foreign Office into whether it had done so by providing large loans to government officials. It denied these accusations and insisted that it complied with all sanctions.[66] Other companies that pledged to stay in Zimbabwe despite pressure to disinvest included Unilever, mining giant Rio Tinto, and British American Tobacco.[67] British Petroleum and Shell have been trying to sell their assets to South African company Engen since 2009 but the sale ran into problems of outstanding debts and issues relating to the indigenization legislation and it had yet to be completed by late 2010.[68]

Swiss firm Nestle was one of the most recent casualties of association with the Mugabe government. In 2009, news leaked that Nestle Zimbabwe sourced 15 percent of its milk from a farm owned by the president's wife, Grace Mugabe, who is now the owner of at least six seized farms.[69] The company did so not out of moral concern and not because of sanctions, since Switzerland is not an EU member and thus not bound by sanctions. Rather it did so because of the negative publicity and boycott threats that followed the disclosure of this relationship. It defended its actions by claiming that half of its regular suppliers had closed down, and that if it did not source from her, her farm may have had to close, therefore causing job losses and hardship for its workers.[70]

The activism over disinvestment was not entirely without result. A few companies that had overt dealings with the government have given in to disinvestment pressure. For example, international advertising agency Young & Rubicam, a subsidiary of WPP, sold its 25 percent stake in a Zimbabwean subsidiary in 2008 after discovering that a senior member of the Zimbabwean company had been advising Mugabe in a personal capacity.[71]

German company Gieseke & Devrient, which had supplied banknote paper to the Reserve Bank of Zimbabwe (RBZ) for forty-five years, was pressured by the German government and stopped selling to Zimbabwe in July 2008.[72] The company said it had made the decision after a "political and moral assessment" of the conditions in Zimbabwe.[73] An Austro-Hungarian software company that has supplied the licences and software used to design and print the Zimbabwe dollar, Jura JSP, then came under pressure to cancel the Zimbabwe license. The company said it would comply if required to do so in terms of international sanctions, but there were not sanctions in place to force it to act.[74]

Supermarket group Tesco, which came under fire over the years for importing foodstuffs from illegally seized Zimbabwe farms, announced in June 2008 that it would no longer be doing business with Zimbabwe, while voicing concern about the plight of the workers it had dealt with. The company sourced approximately US$2 million worth of goods annually from the country.[75] Two other UK retailers Sainsbury's and Waitrose both buy fish from Zimbabwe. Waitrose said that while it supported international efforts to resolve the problems in Zimbabwe, it believed its "limited relationships" with two Zimbabwean suppliers enhanced, rather than undermined, these efforts, and withdrawing would have a negative impact on the workers and their families.[76]

Wilf Mbanga, editor of the U.K.-based newspaper *The Zimbabwean*, said he was shocked to find food produced in Zimbabwe being sold in the United Kingdom when Zimbabweans themselves were starving. Mbanga told the *Daily Mail* in Britain that the foreign currency raised by the government—as a result of a policy requiring exporters to lodge a significant percentage of their profits with the central bank in exchange for Zimbabwe dollars—essentially meant that exporters were automatically funding the regime. "Once the government has the foreign currency, it can do what it likes with it, whether that involves buying luxury cars for the military or guns from China," Mbanga is quoted as saying.[77] Mbanga raised the moral issues that many who believed that multinationals should disinvest held.

Michael Holman, a Zimbabwean and former Africa editor of *Financial Times*, concurs:

> After 25 years in office, has Robert Mugabe's regime become so corrupt, and sleaze so endemic, that nearly every company in the country has to be complicit, if only to survive? And if that indictment is correct, are overseas partners not tainted by association? Has the regime become so persistent in flouting the norms of democracy that to do business with it demeans the participant?[78]

When serving as the official opposition, the MDC frequently criticized companies in Zimbabwe for propping up the government, whether they were dealing directly with the government or not, on the basis that any investment provided a lifeline to the regime. The MDC further promised that once in power, it would scrutinize deals completed by companies with the ZANU-PF during its tenure as the ruling party.[79] However, on assuming power, the MDC has not referred again to this, preferring to court business and donors in order to help it rebuild the country.

But there were equally strong views that disinvestment would cause hardship for Zimbabwean workers, which had to be weighed against the perceived benefits to the state that impoverished these workers by companies remaining. The London-based Ethical Corporation,[80] an independent media company launched in 2001 to create debate on responsible business, suggested that companies needed to stay invested to provide stability and assist in rebuilding the country.[81]

> Businesses in Zimbabwe must act as islands of sanity; they must keep their heads when all about are losing theirs. Business as usual, as far as is possible, should be every firm's priority. This demonstrates commitment to local staff, their families and communities, and to local business partners. It shows that companies can be trusted; that they will not cut and run at the first flicker of trouble.[82]

Alyson Warhurst, an academic and corporate consultant to multinationals, takes a similar view.

> Multinational corporations operating in such countries as Myanmar, Zimbabwe, and China are easy targets for critics who accuse them of supporting totalitarian regimes. Of course, business should be accountable. But it is a mistake to undermine a responsible company's reputation through ill-informed "trial by media." In fact, forcing companies to divest their holdings in these countries could ultimately harm the very people who most need help. Private enterprise is one of the best ways to lift people out of poverty.[83]

Addressing Anglo's situation, she says:

> Should it go? That would be a pity. Anglo American has been in Zimbabwe for 60 years and has extensive business and social networks. And it has a good reputation. Year after year, verified reports show it is a responsible employer and corporate citizen. If it withdraws, its employees would suffer and its networks would crumble, reducing opportunities for business engagement with future governments. And if Anglo American leaves, the Mugabe government would seek investment from

others—notably, from Russian and Chinese mining companies, which may have lower human-rights standards and lack transparency. If prices are fair, wages are just, working conditions are decent, transactions are transparent, and community initiatives are sustainable, should we not trust responsible global businesses to stay, so long as they operate by the principles we have asked them to adopt?[84]

Business and the Redevelopment of Zimbabwe

Business has a crucial role to play in the rebuilding of Zimbabwe, and companies will need to rise to the challenge of exploiting the multiplier effect of their activities. Rebuilding a shattered and distorted economy will require solutions that break the mould of traditional applications and models, in the same way that surviving in the broken economy has done.

Since 1980, 80 percent of all poverty reduction globally has been attributable to economic growth.[85] This suggests that investment and entrepreneurship are the most effective ways out of poverty, and these typically are driven by the private sector. Thus, business, in creating wealth for itself, has a major role to play in generating downstream wealth in the societies in which it operates; therefore, there is a good business case for reducing poverty.

Already half of the health care in sub-Saharan Africa is being delivered directly by the private sector, and private education is following the same trend to offer alternatives to poor quality services at state facilities, due to lack of funding, mismanagement, and skill shortages.[86]

In Zimbabwe, private education has managed to survive relatively well, narrowly escaping the interfering hand of politics by dint of the fact that many ZANU-PF politicians educate their children in private schools. Private health facilities, on the other hand, have not fared as well.

The answer to the rehabilitation of these sectors and other key social sectors is not just an injection of money, which is likely to come from donors and increased CSR activities, but also an increase of staff and capacity building. The case for public-private partnerships is compelling, although its success is dependent on the political will of the public sector to work for the greater good. Large companies can motivate growth by creating linkages with, and investments in, small and medium enterprises, thereby developing the capacity of businesses to participate more profitably in the supply chain. Retailers and manufacturers can also unlock value at the bottom of the pyramid by using multiple suppliers, in addition to direct and indirect employment.

Companies in the agriculture sector have a particularly important role to play in the rebuilding of Zimbabwe due to the multiplier effects of farming. The outgrower schemes already in place are both a good building block for future expansion, and a model for new entrants. Zimbabwe also has strong companies in this sector and retains skills and knowledge of export markets. However, its development is dependent on the emergence of a land system that has security of tenure at its heart, as well as the restoration of law and order, which still seems to be a long way off, even under the new political dispensation.

Tourism is another important sector in terms of its linkages to the rest of the economy, employment, and potential to raise foreign exchange revenues. Although it has taken a serious knock in the past decade, companies are gearing up for expansion and growth in anticipation of change. Operators at Victoria Falls, formerly a top international destination, have already ring fenced the area in marketing terms and have experienced some success, despite Zimbabwe's negative image. It will not take much to build on this.

There are a number of global initiatives that Zimbabwe can become a part of, such as HIV/AIDS programs and the Business Alliance Against Chronic Hunger (BAACH), launched in 2006 to mobilize business solutions to hunger and poverty, which also builds on a version of the farmer outgrower model.[87]

Conclusion

This chapter shows that business in Zimbabwe has been a casualty of the ZANU-PF government's political madness. Companies, even those close to Mugabe at times, have been threatened, intimidated, arrested, undermined, and bullied by state officials. They have been used as scapegoats for the state's failed policies and problems of its own making. Many have not survived this onslaught, and those that have survived have often had to compromise their preferred way of doing business in the process. Consequently, the concept of corporate governance became something of a luxury for most companies over the past decade—although disinvestment has been an option, even if few took that route.

But for the reasons listed in this chapter, most companies, including multinationals with historical links to Zimbabwe, are still there, and they have an important role to play in the redevelopment of the country. The inherent strength of the private sector, recent memory of success, remaining trade and market linkages internationally, and a commitment to the market are factors that give Zimbabwe an advantage over most other African states emerging from crisis of trading its way out of trouble.

The unity government is also focused on getting the private sector back on its feet. On March 18, 2009, the GNU announced measures for economic recovery as part of its *Short-Term Economic Recovery Programme* (STERP), which includes the introduction of a stimulus package for troubled industries through a US$1 billion external credit facility. This would provide finance to restock raw materials, acquire equipment, and perform other measures to stimulate the supply side of the economy. It aims to increase capacity utilization from the current 10 percent, to about 60 percent within six months.[88]

The danger is that the donor community and international NGOs, in their rush to a new trouble spot, will overwhelm the efforts of business to pull the country out of its current mess. While the importance of donor money in the rebuilding effort cannot be underestimated, particularly in social sectors and in the normalization of macroeconomic fundamentals, donor activities can have the unintended consequence of undermining private enterprise. There is also a role for development institutions, such as the Development Bank of Southern Africa and the AfDB, to lend money to Zimbabwe, particularly for rebuilding infrastructure and parastatals, like the power utility ZESA, although these institutions will not lend without previous payments to the outstanding debt.[89]

Zimbabwe still has a long way to go. The political terrain is still far from conducive, despite some gains made by the GNU. An election in 2011 is likely to stall much new investment because of the country's poor record in this regard, and the political instability and human rights abuses this might precipitate in the short term. The violent land seizures, uncertainty about property rights, and lack of progress in rebuilding agriculture are also factors holding Zimbabwe back, as is the fact that the rule of law has yet to be restored.

A lack of policy clarity on the indigenization process is likely to deter investors, particularly if it involves relinquishing a majority stake.

For business to play a meaningful role, not just in the recovery of companies but of the whole economy, broad multigroup and multisector coordination and cooperation will be required. The injection of official development assistance into budgetary processes will allow the government to begin the process of infrastructure rehabilitation, stimulate government departments into working, provide support for exports, and reduce pressure on the banks, which will provide opportunities for business to renew its economic activity.

The most serious infrastructure needs are in sewage and sanitation and power, and there may be opportunities for business to develop projects in partnership with the government in these and other sectors. As much of the infrastructure has held up reasonably well, it can be rehabilitated rather than rebuilt. The GNU is to reinstitute privatization, stalled by the ZANU-PF since 2000, opening up opportunities for investment[90]; but the success of this initiative will depend on the several factors listed earlier.

Given the extreme politicization of the public service, institutions such as the central bank, government departments, parastatals, marketing organizations, training colleges, the media, and many other facets of Zimbabwe will have to be unraveled. The business interests of politicians will need to be scrutinized and contracts reexamined. Otherwise, rebuilding cannot start in earnest.

The continued hold on power by Mugabe and some of his more hard-line ministers, even in a GNU, will continue to be a major constraint to recovery. Many businesses, NGOs, and donors will find it difficult to work with key players whom they cannot trust.

Notes

1. Most research on Zimbabwe estimates the Gross Domestic Product (GDP) contraction since 1999 to be just over one-third of the economy. See World Bank (WB), "Zimbabwe—Country Brief," March 2008, http://go.worldbank.org/RFP74M2PK1. The accelerated economic decline in 2008–2009 has not been measured. Hyperinflation and the plunging rate of the Zimbabwe dollar made statistics a guessing game over the past decade. As a result, many of the estimates used by economists are based only loosely on facts.

2. Sebastien Berger, "Zimbabwe Inflation Hits 231 Million Per Cent," *Telegraph.co.uk*, October 9, 2008, http://www.telegraph.co.uk/news/worldnews/africaandindianocean/zimbabwe/3167379/Zimbabwe-inflation-hits-231-million-per-cent.html.

3. Simba Makoni, in answer to a parliamentary question in August 2000, said that in the first four months of 1998, Zimbabwe spent US$260 million, but this had sharply risen to US$4 billion in 2001, rising again in 2002. "DRC War Costs $10bn," *Daily News*, August 31, 2000.

4. C. Mangongera, "Will Mugabe Survive This Time Around," *Zimbabwe Independent*, August 10, 2007.

5. Dianna Games, "Making Up for Wasted Time after Zimbabwe's Lost Decade," interview with the CEO of the Zimbabwe Stock Exchange, Emmanuel Munyukwi, *Business Day* (South Africa), March 18, 2010.

6. Dumisani Ndlela, "Zim Manufacturing Sector Declines Further," *Bizcommunity.com*, July 23, 2008, http://www.bizcommunity.com/Article/410/19/26645.html.

7. International Monetary Fund (IMF), "IMF Concludes 2003 Article IV Consultation with Zimbabwe," Public Information Notice No. 03/89, July 28, 2003, http://www.imf.org/external/np/sec/pn/2003/pn0389.htm.

8. United Nations Statistical Division, "Exports, Merchandise, f.o.b., US$ (IMF)," UN Data, http://data.un.org/Data.aspx?q=zimbabwe&d=CDB&f=srID%3A6190%3BcrID%3A716

9. World Health Statistics 2008, "Zimbabwe," World Health Organization (WHO), http://www.who.int/countries/zwe/en/.

10. "Zimbabwe's Cholera Crisis Worsens As Number of Dead, Infected Rises—UN," *UN News Centre*, February 20, 2009, http://www.un.org/apps/news/story.asp?NewsID=29972&Cr=zimbabwe&Cr1=cholera.

11. Celia W. Dugger, "Cholera Epidemic Sweeping Across Crumbling Zimbabwe," *The New York Times* (Africa), December 11, 2008, http://www.nytimes.com/2008/12/12/world/africa/12cholera.html.

12. WHO, "Global, National Efforts Must Be Urgently Intensified to Control Zimbabwe Cholera Outbreak," News Release, January 30, 2009, http://www.who.int/mediacentre/news/releases/2009/cholera_zim_20090130/en/index.html.

13. Jono Waters, CEO of Zimbabwean financial newswire service Zfn at the Zimbabwe: The New Investment Frontier conference, Johannesburg, South Africa, October 21, 2008.

14. Synodia Bhasera, "RTGs—Wise Technology Put to Wrong Use," *Financial Gazette* (Harare), October 18, 2008, http://allafrica.com/stories/200810240230.html.

15. S. Gammon, managing director of Imara Capital Zimbabwe, speech made at the Zimbabwe: The New Investment Frontier conference, Johannesburg, South Africa, October 21, 2008.

16. D. Munatsi, CEO of African Banking Corporation, speech made at the Zimbabwe: The New Investment Frontier conference, Johannesburg, South Africa, October 21, 2008.

17. Games, "Making Up For Wasted Time," interview with the CEO of the ZSE.

18. In 2001, a lucrative contract for the building of a new airport in Harare was awarded to a company that involved Leo Mugabe, the president's nephew. Several government officials were implicated in allegations of bribe-taking related to the awarding of the contract to the winning bidder, Air Harbour Technologies, a director of which was former UN secretary general Kofi Annan's son Kojo. Media reports reported that the Zimbabwe ministers included Emmerson Mnangagwa, Herbert Murerwa, and Simon Moyo. See "The Harare Airport Scam and the Annan Connection," *Sokwanele*, June 21,

2004, http://www.sokwanele.com/articles/sokwanele/harareairportscamandtheannanc onnection_21june2004.html.

19. "EU Extends Zimbabwe Sanctions For Another Year," *Reuters*, February 16, 2010.

20. U.S. Department of the Treasury Office of Foreign Assets Control, *Zimbabwe: What You Need To Know About U.S. Sanctions,* November 23, 2005. http://www.treas.gov/ offices/enforcement/ofac/programs/zimbabwe/zimb.pdf.

21. "Obama Renews Zimbabwe Sanctions," *BBC News,* March 5, 2009, http://news.bbc. co.uk/2/hi/7925240.stm.

22. Foreign Trade Statistics, "Trade in Goods (Imports, Exports and Trade Balance) with Zimbabwe," U.S. Census Bureau, http://www.census.gov/foreign-trade/balance/c7960. html.

23. Australian Government Department of Foreign Affairs and Trade, "Zimbabwe: Targeted Sanctions Regime," 2002, http://www.dfat.gov.au/un/unsc_sanctions/zimbabwe.html.

24. "Russia, China Veto UN Sanctions on Zimbabwe," *CNN.com/world,* July 12, 2008, http://www.cnn.com/2008/WORLD/africa/07/11/zimbabwe.sanctions/.

25. U.S. Department of State, "President Bush Nominee's Statement at his Senate Confirmation Hearing," Embassy of the United States—Harare, Zimbabwe, http:// harare.usembassy.gov/senate_mcgee.html.

26. British High Commission Pretoria, "UK in South Africa—UK Policy on Zimbabwe," http://ukinsouthafrica.fco.gov.uk/en/about-us/working-with-south-africa/ uk-policy-zimbabwe/.

27. Jeslyn Dendere, "Price Distortions Likely—NECF," *Zimbabwe Independent,* September 18, 2008, http://allafrica.com/stories/200809190996.html.

28. Jan Raath, "Zimbabwe State Employees To Be Paid in US Dollars," *The Times,* February 19, 2009, http://www.timesonline.co.uk/tol/news/world/africa/article5762439.ccc.

29. Banya Nelson, "ZSE Restarts, Trades in US Dollars," *Mail & Guardian Online,* February 19, 2009, http://www.mg.co.za/article/2009–02–19-zse-restarts-trades-in-us-dollars.

30. "Tsvangirai Puts Recovery Costs at $5bn," *Financial Times,* February 22, 2009, http://www.ft.com/cms/s/0/b9783934-ff81–11dd-b3f8–000077b07658,s01=1. html?ftcamp=rss&nclick_check=1.

31. Ntungamili Nkomo and Patience Rusere, "Zimbabwe Leaders Talk 2011 Elections— But Others Say Country Not Ready," Voice of America, *voanews.com,* March 8, 2010, http://www1.voanews.com/zimbabwe/news/Zimbabwe-Leaders-Talk-Election-In-2011- But-Critics-Say-Country-Not-Ready-For-Another-Poll-86932532.html.

32. "Zimbabwe: Price Controls Backfire Again," *IRIN Africa,* July 3, 2007, http://www. irinnews.org/Report.aspx?ReportId=73064.

33. Ibid.

34. "Zimbabwean-Borne Businessman Sues Blair," *Zimonline,* June 1, 2007, http://www. zimonline.co.za/Article.aspx?ArticleId=1472>http://www.zimonline.co.za/Article. aspx?ArticleId=1472.

35. Andrew Meldrum, "Tycoon Flees Zimbabwe after Falling Foul of Mugabe," *The Guardian,* June 9, 2006, http://www.guardian.co.uk/world/2006/jun/09/zimbabwe. topstories3.

36. "Nicholas van Hoogstraten—Zimbabwe Arrest," *Telegraph.co.uk,* January 26, 2008, http://www.telegraph.co.uk/news/uknews/1576679/Nicholas-van-Hoogstraten—- Zimbabwe-arrest.html.

37. For example, *The Independent* in Britain carried a story, "Blood Money: The MPs Cashing In On Zimbabwe's Misery." It said Tory frontbenchers, including six Conservatives and one Liberal Democrat, were found to have investments collectively worth more than £1 million in firms trading in Zimbabwe despite the call by party leader David Cameron

for all companies with dealings in Zimbabwe to ensure they were not propping up the government in some way. The companies include Anglo American, Rio Tinto, Standard Chartered, Barclays, Shell, and BP.

38. Games, "Making Up For Wasted Time," interview with the CEO of the ZSE.

39. Stuart Doran, *Zimbabwe's Economy: A Report Card Mid-2009,* Discussion Paper 8/2009 (Johannesburg: The Brenthurst Foundation, 2009), http://www.thebrenthurstfoundation.org/Files/Brenthurst_Commisioned_Reports/BD0908-Zimbabwe.pdf.

40. Sure Kamhunga, "Zimplats Expansion Faces Further Delays," *Business Day* (South Africa), April 13, 2010, http://allafrica.com/stories/201004130314.html.

41. The Iran Tractor Manufacturing Company was the first new investment after the legislation was passed, yet the statutory 51 percent indigenous shareholding requirement was waived, with the Iranian company keeping a 54 percent share in the company.

42. Oscar Ncala, "Bill Giving Potential Suitors For Zim Steel Mill Cold Feet," *Engineering News,* October 5, 2007, http://www.engineeringnews.co.za/article/bill-giving-potential-suitors-for-zim-steel-mill-cold-feet-2007–10–05.

43. The Economist Intelligence Unit, "Zimbabwe: Manufacturing," *ViewsWire,* June 20, 2007, http://www.eiu.com/index.asp?layout=VWArticleVW3&article_id=742296259®ion_id=&country_id=1250000325&channel_id=180004018&category_id=410004041&refm=vwCat&page_title=Article&rf=0.

44. "Zisco Suitor Flags Empowerment Laws," *New Zimbabwe,* March 7, 2010, http://www.newzimbabwe.com/business-1967-Zisco+suitor+flags+empowerment+laws/business.aspx.

45. *The Zimbabwean,* August 30, 2007, http://www.thezimbabwean.co.uk/index.php?option=com_content&task=view&id=5977&Itemid=104.

46. "Zimbabwe: Workplace AIDS Programmes Feel the Pinch." PlusNews: Global HIV/AIDS news and analysis, *IRIN*, November 22, 2007, http://www.plusnews.org/Report.aspx?ReportId=75459.

47. See http://www.implats.co.za/cr/reports/2007/hiv.htm.

48. See http://www.standardchartered.com/zw/about-us/en/.

49. Interviews conducted in Harare during 2006 with companies.

50. Ibid.

51. The Sullivan Principles were created in the mid-1970s to put pressure on American companies doing business in apartheid South Africa. Their founder was the Rev. Leon Sullivan, a U.S. church minister and a member of the General Motors board.

52. Solidarity Peace Trust, *A Difficult Dialogue: Zimbabwe-South Africa Economic Relations Since 2000,* a preliminary report, October 23, 2007, http://www.solidaritypeacetrust.org/reports/difficult_dialogue.pdf.

53. "China-Zimbabwe Trade Relations Improve," *The Zimbabwe Guardian,* May 19, 2008.

54. Ibid.

55. "China's Sinosteel Takes 92 pct Stake in Zimbabwe Chrome Cirm Zimasco," Forbes.com, *AFX News Limited,* December 25, 2007, http://www.forbes.com/feeds/afx/2007/12/25/afx4473564.html.

56. Patrick Bond, *Uneven Zimbabwe: A Study of Finance, Development and Underdevelopment* (New Jersey and Eritrea: Africa World Press Inc, 1998).

57. "Zimbabwe: Mining between a Rock and a Hard Place," humanitarian news and analysis, IRIN, June 30, 2008, http://www.irinnews.org/Report.aspx?ReportId=79019.

58. "Unki Platinum Mine Dilemma," *Miningreview.com,* June 27, 2008, http://beta.miningreview.com/node/13369.

59. Ibid.

60. "Zimbabwe: Mining between a Rock and a Hard Place," *IRIN.*

61. "Doing Business in Zimbabwe—Time to Stand and Deliver," Ethical Corporation, *Ethics Watch,* September 1, 2008, http://www.ethicalcorp.com/content.asp?ContentID =6049&ContTypeID=49.

62. Brendan Ryan, "Anglo 'Shaken Down' in Zimbabwe," *Fin24.com,* June 26, 2008, http:// www.fin24.com/articles/default/display_article.aspx?ArticleId=2347629.

63. Lefever Finance was the 60 percent owner of the Zimbabwe company that had the mineral rights to the concessions; the remaining 40 percent was owned by state-owned company Zimbabwe Mineral Marketing Corporation, which was placed on the expanded U.S. sanctions list in 2008.

64. Brendan Ryan, "Camec's Zimbabwe Platinum Project Threatened," *Miningmx,* July 18, 2008, http://www.miningmx.com/platinum/674062.htm.

65. David Connett, "Standard Chartered At Centre of Zimbabwe Sanctions Inquiry," *The Independent,* June 15, 2008, http://www.independent.co.uk/news/business/news/standard-chartered-at-centre-of-zimbabwe-sanctions-inquiry-847312.html.

66. Ibid.

67. Paul Lewis and David Pallister, "Shell Ready to Quit Zimbabwe as Mugabe Cronies Hoard Fuel," *The Observer,* July 6, 2008, http://www.guardian.co.uk/world/2008/ jul/06/zimbabwe.southafrica1.

68. David Robertson, "Outrage Over £200m UK Investment in Zimbabwe," *The Times,* June 25, 2008, http://www.timesonline.co.uk/tol/news/world/africa/article4207971. ece.

69. Katherine Glover, "Nestle Zimbabwe Conveniently Dumps Grace Mugabe Farm as Supplier," *BNET,* October 5, 2009, http://industry.bnet.com/food/10001037/nestle-zimbabwe-conveniently-dumps-grace-mugabe-farm-as-supplier/.

70. Ibid.

71. Dumisani Ndlela, "Global Ad Agency Dumping Firm Over Mugabe Campaign?" *Biz*-Community (Cape Town), June 23, 2008, http://allafrica.com/stories/200806240582. html.

72. "No Paper for Zimbabwe Banknotes," *BBC News,* July 2, 2008, http://news.bbc.co.uk/2/ hi/business/7484838.stm.

73. Ibid.

74. Basildon Peta and Daniel Howden, "Zim Regime May Lose 'Licence' to Print Money," *Independent Online,* July 24, 2008, http://www.iol.co.za/index. php?sf=126&set_id=1&click_id=68&art_id=vn20080724112235174C689499.

75. "Tesco to End Aid with Zimbabwe." *BBC News Online,* June 30, 2008, http://news.bbc. co.uk/1/hi/business/7482383.stm.

76. Ibid.

77. Sean Poulter and Ian Drury, "We're Eating Zimbabwe's Food…As Its People Starve." *Daily Mail,* June 25, 2008, http://www.dailymail.co.uk/news/worldnews/article-1029223/Tesco-Morrisons-Waitrose-condemned-selling-Zimbabwes-produce-people-starve.html.

78. Michael Holman, "Should UK Banks Do Business in Zimbabwe?" *Times Online,* November 1, 2005, http://www.timesonline.co.uk/tol/comment/article585360.ece.

79. Martin Zhuwakinyu, "Business Deals Struck with Mugabe's Gvt Will Be Reviewed, MDC Warns," *Mining Weekly,* June 24, 2008, http://www.miningweekly.com/article. php?a_id=136380.

80. See http://www.ethicalcorp.com.

81. "Zimbabwe—Doing Business in a Failing State," *Ethical Corporation,* editorial, September 1, 2008, http://www.ethicalcorp.com/content.asp?ContentID=6046.

82. Ibid.

83. Alyson Warhurst, "Engagement vs Divestment: Forcing Multinational Corporations to Pull Out of Totalitarian Countries Can Yield Disastrous Results," *Bloomberg Businessweek,* August 11, 2008, http://www.businessweek.com/globalbiz/content/aug2008/gb20080811_573922.htm.

84. Ibid.

85. Background paper, World Economic Forum on Africa, June 2008.

86. Ibid.

87. World Economic Forum, "Business Alliance Against Chronic Hunger: A Public-Private Partnership Managed by the World Economic Forum," www.weforum.org/pdf/BAACH/Hunger_2008_final.pdf.

88. Bernard Mpofu, "US$1bn Stimulus Package for Industry," *Zimbabwe Independent,* March 19, 2009, http://www.thezimbabweindependent.com/index.php/business/22229-us1-billion-stimulus-package-for-industry.

89. Nelson Banya, "Gono: Zim Must Repay Debt, Reform Economy," *Mail & Guardian Online,* March 15, 2009, http://www.mg.co.za/article/2009–03–15-gono-zim-must-repay-debt-reform-economy.

90. Dumisani Muleya, "Zimbabwe: Mugabe Makes Surprise Plea to 'Friends' for Foreign Funds," Business Day, March 20, 2009, http://allafrica.com/stories/200903200096.html.

Chapter 11

South African Corporate Expansion into Zimbabwe

Weathering the Storm and Reaping the Benefits

Sanusha Naidu

In future, the recovery of Zimbabwe will bring significant benefits to the South African economy through increased employment, export earnings as well as remittances from profits earned by subsidiaries situated in Zimbabwe. Therefore, the assistance advanced to Zimbabwe by the South Africans will result in a win win situation for both countries.

—Elton Mangoma, Zimbabwean minister of economic planning and investment promotion, March 30, 2009

Some South African companies are even using the crisis, or are planning to use the crisis, to take over large swathes of the Zimbabwean economy. They are not alone in attempting to do so. British, French and Chinese companies are attempting to do exactly the same thing. Time will tell which countries' capital will benefit the most out of this macabre race. One thing that is certain, however, is that the corporate vultures are descending; and this is happening at the cost of Zimbabwe's remaining, and limited, sovereignty.

—Shawn Hattingh, October 4, 2007

Introduction

As the terms of Zimbabwe's negotiated political settlement were being concluded between the ruling Zimbabwe African National Union-Patriotic Front (ZANU-PF) and the Movement for Democratic Change (MDC) in the latter half of 2008, much of the concern focused around the dynamics of the power-sharing formula. With battle lines drawn over who should control significant portfolios such as the security forces and home affairs, it seemed that the protracted negotiations resolving the crisis over Zimbabwe's acute political and economic decline had reached another stalemate. While the political pundits were trying to tease out an acceptable power-sharing framework, the dynamics of Zimbabwe's post-conflict economic reconstruction had also become the subject of much debate.

Undoubtedly, Zimbabwe's economic reconstruction remains a pivotal point in reversing Harare's misfortunes and restoring political and economic stability. At the center of the debate is the nature of the stimulus package required to kick-start the Zimbabwean economic confidence. The political deal brokered by the Southern African Development Community (SADC) in late 2008[1] only signified one aspect of Zimbabwe's arduous road to recovery. And that was the easy part. Now the real test for Zimbabwe's economic revival from its financial morass is whether to follow an aid-based, trade-led, or mixed structural economic program. And herein lies the dilemma. With Zimbabwe's transitional government facing daunting challenges in restoring the once booming economy to a semblance of respectability, policymakers, mainstream commentators, and experts remain divided over how this should be achieved.

Tony Hawkins, an expert and economics professor at Harare University, argues that while there seem to be some guarantees from the international community toward assisting the economic reconstruction of the country,[2] it remains to be seen whether "Zimbabwe will get the much needed funds that are central for an economic turnaround."[3] Such cautiousness is perhaps because donors are still not confident that the new coalition government is undertaking far-reaching political and economic reforms, particularly since the Government of National Unity (GNU) seems barely functional, civil society abuses are still continuing, and property rights are no closer to being restored, while the government is moving toward enforcing an indigenization policy that serves to reinforce old patterns of economic control.

It is unfortunate that Zimbabwe's economic reconstruction comes at the most inconvenient time in the global economy—the most severe economic crisis since the Great Depression of 1929—with a price tag of approximately US$5 billion in foreign aid and US$1.6 billion in financial aid.[4] On the other hand, economic analysts are confident that if the Zimbabwean economy is to achieve the projected Gross Domestic Product (GDP) rate of 7 percent in 2010, then a sustained growth-led strategy with the right market fundamentals, and notwithstanding increased foreign direct investment (FDI) flows to the value of over US$1 billion, can provide the right path to follow.[5]

Yet the certainty in investment flows is unhinged by current uncertainties in the global financial markets. According to the United Nations Conference on Trade and Development (UNCTAD), FDI flows to Africa declined by 36.2 percent in 2009.[6] This makes the spread of foreign investment leaner, while attempts at an export-led growth strategy are arrested by not only the depressed global demand and supply chains, but also weaker international commodity prices: "Between July 2008 and February 2009, the U.S. dollar price of energy plummeted by two-thirds, and that of metals dropped by more than 50 percent, from earlier highs. Dollar prices of agricultural goods retreated by more than 30 percent, with the prices of fats and oils dropping 42 percent."[7]

While there seems to be a slight recovery in current global commodity prices, predicated, amongst other things, on China's billion-dollar domestic stimulus package that is re-catalyzing demand for raw material and other commodities for new infrastructure projects in China, this appears to be a gradual increase. For instance, in the first two months of 2010, commodity prices were volatile, responding to speculative demand from China for base metals and the severe winter in the North, which increased the global price of oil and other energy-related products.

So if there is to be an economic recovery in Zimbabwe, where would this stimulus come from? The answer, it seems, points most notably toward South Africa, and in particular, the corporate sector.

South Africa's corporate profile in Zimbabwe is well documented[8] and even during the height of the political and economic crisis, South African corporations remained committed to their investments and projects. This confidence, or "weathering of the storm," seems to have well-positioned South African corporations to become industry shapers in Zimbabwe's post-conflict economic reconstruction. And while this may seem an ideal position, they are also seen as capitalizing on the Mbeki administration's "quiet diplomacy," which appears to be interpreted as opening spaces for South African capital to take advantage of opportunities created by the negotiated settlement.[9]

Therefore this chapter will explore the South African capital investment trajectory in Zimbabwe's economic recovery. It will highlight the salient issues that underscore its presence in Zimbabwe's economy and assess how it can actually be a stimulus for Harare's economic revival. Moreover, it will examine postapartheid South Africa's foreign policy in the continent and the competing image of whether Pretoria promotes a genuine development/African renaissance project or, as some analysts contend, a sub-imperialist agenda, especially now under the Zuma presidency. Finally, the chapter will assess whether South African corporations will face competition from other actors, particularly as the transitional government hedges its bets in attracting foreign investors into its economy. In short, this chapter will analyze if by weathering the storm, corporate South Africa will reap the benefits.

Postapartheid Corporate Expansion

Following South Africa's negotiated settlement, debates around the postapartheid Africa policy were caught between the advocates of the policy rhetoric of South Africa forging development partnerships with the continent and opponents who opined and accused Pretoria of perpetuating the apartheid regime's style of realpolitik and mercantilist interests. In fact, some commentators such as Patrick Bond, executive director of the Centre for Civil Society based at the University of KwaZulu-Natal in South Africa, were bold enough to assert that democratic South Africa's agenda in Southern Africa mirrored a sub-imperialist framework, while others such as Shawn Hattingh, a researcher based with the International Labour Research and

Information Group (ILRIG) in South Africa, argued that the political transition had, in fact, only truly liberated South African capital.[10] And so the discourse and scholarship around the nature of post-apartheid South Africa's engagement north of Limpopo focused around whether the "leopard had changed it spots."[11]

The response to the preceding question has not, in fact, led to any conclusive deductions and still remains a contentious issue amongst analysts and policymakers. While this debate continues, there is hardly any doubt that South African capital will use the democratic space to push ahead across the continent. After all, Africa became a fertile ground for market-seeking strategies, given the Structural Adjustment Programmes (SAPs) of the 1980s, which had liberalized African economies, depressed African states from pursuing sustainable industrial policy programs, and created the impetus for private sector investors to become significant drivers of growth and development within these economies. This was an opportunity that South African corporations took advantage of in the 1990s as international capital was primarily shifting their investments toward the former Soviet empire of eastern Europe following the end of the Cold War.

In the immediate regional neighborhood of southern Africa, the vestiges of Pretoria's apartheid dominance and destabilization policy,[12] notwithstanding the historical economic linkages[13] forged under British colonialism, had strengthened the commercial spaces for South African capital to consolidate its presence in regional economies after 1994. Therefore, as Daniel et al. observe, "in structural terms, the South African economy in the early 1990s reflected a paradox of comparative regional strength and growing international weakness."[14]

Yet, the implications of South African corporations' investment trajectory into the southern African subcontinent and beyond were considered to be exploitative. That apartheid South Africa had deliberately destroyed the region's infrastructure as part of its aggressive and interventionist total strategy counterinsurgency policy[15] against the antiapartheid struggle, which was aimed at stubbing out base camps of the "enemy," was condemned. But that South African corporations under a post-apartheid regime were poised to rehabilitate the region through reconstruction and development infrastructure projects was seen to be chauvinistic.

Despite such challenges and criticisms, the penetration of regional economies by South African capital moved with rapid pace, underpinned by large inflows. For instance, during the 1994–2004 period South African capital had invested US$8.7 billion in southern Africa.[16] Part of this could be attributed to the Southern African Customs Union (SACU),[17] but it was the need to capture new markets that was perhaps the overriding incentive.

The Gamble

This reawakening of corporate South Africa's interests was not lost on Zimbabwe, even though, in essence, the main conglomerates of South African capital, such as Anglo-American, had an entrenched presence in the Zimbabwean economy through historical business linkages.[18]

Undoubtedly, this provided South African businesses with a strategic platform to remain in the Zimbabwean economy amidst the call for withdrawal by other foreign investors as the political crisis began to set in and threaten their investments. Some of the companies that stayed on included Tongaat-Hulett in the agricultural sugar sector; Impala Platinum (Implats) through its Zimbabwean division Zimplats, where it recorded a gross profit of R854.6 million in 2007, up from R317.6 million in 2006; Tourvest, a hotel and tour operator, which offered international clientele direct flights to Victoria Falls from Johannesburg; and the black economic empowerment mining company Metallon, which also continued to invest in the mining sector.[19] SAB-Miller invested US$16 billion into Delta Beverages to expand its canning factory production and increase beer demand, and African Rainbow Minerals (ARM) invested about US$300 million exploring for new coal and platinum projects. Yet some, such as Pick 'n Pay in the retail sector, through its 25 percent stake in the TM chain, were challenged by price controls and runaway inflation.

In addition, it would seem that while other investors, especially in the mining sector, were caught in the web of Mugabe's assertion of state monopoly, nationalization of industries, and industrial indigenization policy,[20] South African businesses appeared to navigate through these displays of state coercion. Richard Saunders, associate professor at York University in Toronto, Canada, acknowledges that the "steadfast presence of dozens of South African companies [during] the deepening crisis [was a result of] a certain residual protection [for subsidiaries by appealing] to headquarters in Johannesburg for political help."[21] While Zimbabwean industry insiders asserted that this was an attempt by South African businesses to ring fence their operations by separating their financial sheets from parent companies, to protect against foreign currency losses and shifting taxation rules, these remain unsubstantiated claims given that they are difficult to measure and assess.

At the same time, whereas international sanctions against Zimbabwe prompted foreign companies to disinvest from the country, South African companies remained in the economy, as illustrated earlier. This is reflected in the trade statistics shown in table 11.1.

Even though the trade balance declined in the same period, it still remained in South Africa's favor, thereby indicating that even at the height of the economic crisis, two-way trade between Harare and Pretoria was strong. However, it must be noted that in terms of South Africa's top ten trading partners across the continent,

Table 11.1   South Africa-Zimbabwe trade, 2002–2007 (in million rands)

	2002	2003	2004	2005	2006	2007
Exports						
Annual total	7,309,455	6,551,409	6,182,317	7,486,859	7,410,602	8,501,124
Imports						
Annual total	2,159,775	2,656,012	2,795,783	3,131,518	4,633,368	6,036,490

Source: Department of Internationals Relations and Cooperation (South Africa), 2009: http://www.dfa.gov.za/docs/2009/zimb0316.html.

Table 11.2   South Africa-Zimbabwe trade balance, 2002–2007 (in million rands)

Trade Balance	2002	2003	2004	2005	2006	2007
Annual total	5,149,681	3,895,396	3,386,534	4,355,341	2,777,234	2,464,634

Source: Department of Internationals Relations and Cooperation (South Africa): http://www.dfa.gov.za/docs/2009/zimb0316.html.

Zimbabwe, which occupied the top spot in 2005, dropped to second place in 2006 and slipped another position in 2007 (table 11.2).[22]

Nevertheless, Pretoria's trade dynamic with Zimbabwe was significant: South Africa's retail sector became a lifeline to an ailing commodities sector; South African companies such as Zimplats, Implats, and Metallon profited from the resource/mining sector due to the boom in global commodity prices before the onset of the financial crisis in late 2008; and others, such as Tongaat-Hulett in the sugar sector, took advantage of the de-Zimbabwenization of the local economy. Of course in all of this, the attraction of bargain assets enabled South African corporations to buy them at basement prices, putting them on hold while waiting for a tenable situation to return to the Zimbabwean economy to reap the benefits.

Has the Tide Turned?

Now that the tide has turned with a transitional government in place, South African corporations seem well positioned to play an integral part in the revitalization of Zimbabwe's socioeconomic development.

In May 2009, the United Kingdom's *Financial Times* reported that as an interim measure Zimbabwe's neighbors South Africa and Botswana were stepping in with financing to revive the country's ailing private sector in order to assist the government's targeted credit line of US$1 billion from African countries.[23] In the same report it was noted that from the South African side a US$30 million trade finance package was being finalized, with Botswana offering a loan of US$70 million to "fund opportunities in Zimbabwe."[24] As much as there is talk of this South African finance package deal with Zimbabwe, there is very little detail around what the terms of this package entail. Some speculation is that the deal would be aimed at revitalizing the Zimbabwean economy and providing for reduced tariff barriers and market access to the South African economy. But this is not to detract from the reality that this would be also about South Africa's private sector playing a significant role in this economic reconstruction.

In addition, in December 2009, the governments of South Africa and Zimbabwe signed an agreement on the Promotion and Reciprocal Protection of Investments, which is aimed at offering investors from both countries increased security and certainty under international law when undertaking investments or setting up businesses in each other's countries.

With a strong presence in the mining, retail, and financial sectors, there are between twenty and thirty South African companies who stand to gain from this economic development assistance package and economic cooperation, including companies such as Standard Bank, FNB, Nedbank, Zimplats, Old Mutual Insurance, African Rainbow Minerals, Jet Stores, Pep Stores, Famous Brands, Massmart, and Shoprite Group, as well those from the telecommunication sector such as MTN and Vodacom. Not only would these companies have access to the contracts under this package, but they could also serve as a catalyst to finance projects that were dormant under the ring fencing phase and initiate operations in those assets that were bought at bargain prices. Some of the projects may include agro-processing, infrastructure, energy, transport, and mining.

At the same time, Zimbabwe's economic revival offers a boost to other sectors of the South African economy. For instance, within the information, communication, and technology (ICT) sector, stakeholders are anticipating that rebuilding Zimbabwe's infrastructure would reap benefits that could lead to a resurgence in cross-border trade in personal computers, Internet connectivity in schools, government sectors, and households, and fixed line telephony, notwithstanding the attraction of a large mobile consumer base.

Another sector with potential opportunities is the infrastructure and construction sector. The experience of South African corporations in this sector is well demonstrated by their expansion in the late 1980s and early 1990s into the continent, especially in rehabilitating deficient infrastructure in war-torn economies such as Mozambique—where they have played a vital role in renewing the economic impetus of the country. In similar fashion, these companies can assist Zimbabwe's economic revival not only in the reconstruction and development of new infrastructure, but also in upgrading old or defunct construction projects that reconnect the Zimbabwean market to the regional SADC free trade zone.

In this regard South Africa's financial development agencies, such as the Industrial Development Cooperation (IDC) and the Development Bank of Southern Africa (DBSA), may play a significant role in assisting the unity government with economic reconstruction. In January 2010, the Zimbabwean government approached the African Development Bank (AfDB) and the DBSA for a loan to increase the country's moribund electricity supply. The DBSA promised a loan of US$81 million while the AfDB is considering a loan of US$51 million that will assist the Zimbabwean Electricity State Authority (ZESA) with upgrading electricity generators at the Hwange thermal power station. Other projects that the IDC and DBSA are considering include Indian company Jindal Steel and Power's potential bid to acquire ZISCO, the Zimbabwean state-owned steel company.

It is clear then that South African corporate activity in Zimbabwe involves a coordinated sectoral investment strategy in which each industry relies on the other to advance its operations and mechanisms in the market. Seen as drivers of a market-led development engagement, South African businesses are observed as primary actors in leading this process, particularly in taking advantage of Pretoria's economic largesse and development assistance.

But, as much as South African companies are ideally poised to play a significant role in Zimbabwe's economic reconstruction, they face increasing competition from

China's deepening involvement in Africa,[25] and more specifically from Beijing's close relations with Zimbabwe's president Robert Mugabe and his ZANU-PF party.

The China Factor

China, regarded as an emerging actor or a revisionist partner in Africa, has remained a steadfast ally of Mugabe and the ZANU-PF even at the height of Zimbabwe's political and economic crisis. This is attributed to Beijing's policy of noninterference and respect for the internal sovereign right of another state. But perhaps it also has to do with the fact that China objects to the what it sees as bully tactics, such as sanctions, which have been the punitive actions that Western countries such as Britain, the European Union (EU), and the United States have pursued against Harare as part of their responsive strategy in trying to restore a credible civilian government in Zimbabwe. For Beijing, sanctions would complicate the situation rather than resolve the crisis; instead, trying to find a negotiated settlement with the relevant parties seems to be the more attractive option.

As much as Pretoria, and Mbeki in particular, is credited with being the appointed SADC power broker that undid the stalemate and enabled the transitional government, China's own quiet diplomacy toward resolving the Zimbabwean meltdown cannot be ignored. The fact that Beijing also showed solidarity by vetoing sanctions against the Mugabe regime in the United Nations (UN) Security Council in 2008, and pushed for a negotiated settlement at all times in reply to the deadlock, reflects a consistency with Mugabe's *Look East* policy, which was introduced around 2002, just after the presidential elections.[26] This demonstrates China's behind-the-scenes play, and perhaps even strategic influence over the Mugabe regime, in accepting a transitional power-sharing deal with the MDC. Of course this raises a significant question for Pretoria and its corporations in terms of what impact this will have for its economic interests in post-conflict Zimbabwe.

Already the Chinese have astutely used the West's inertia and its wait-and-see attitude toward assisting Harare's much-needed reform program to its own advantage. This was evident during Prime Minister Morgan Tsvangirai's visit to Washington and the EU in June 2009 where, despite accepting the fragile political reform settlement, these Western governments were unwilling to commit toward economic reforms—instead handing the prime minister US$500 million for humanitarian assistance only. This, indeed, opened a door for Beijing.

China's commitment of a US$950 million[27] line of credit facility to Zimbabwe for its economic reconstruction program highlights what has become an underlying philosophy of Beijing's engagement in Africa, namely that development can been driven through market reforms. A media report in March 2010 by Reuters cast doubt about whether the much-needed aid that Zimbabwe requires will be disbursed by Western donors.[28] The fact that President Mugabe remains at the helm of the power-sharing deal continues to be an obstacle for Western donors who prefer that Mugabe be removed from political office. Nevertheless in 2009, of the Western donors, only Norway had resumed aid disbursements to Harare by committing US$9.17 million to nongovernmental organizations, the World Bank (WB), and the International Monetary Fund (IMF).[29] The money was aimed toward revitalizing the health care sector and supporting the GNU.

Also in 2009, the WB announced a grant of US$22 million, while Britain promised humanitarian assistance to the value of US$23.90 million. The United States has also channeled humanitarian assistance through food donations disbursed via the U.S. Agency for International Development (USAID). But, as Zimbabwe's financial minister Tendai Biti remarks in the Reuters report of March 2010: "It is very unlikely that donors will fulfill the US$810 million, we're on our own."[30] Therefore Beijing's aid package signals and reaffirms the perceptions of the Look East policy that, in spite of the global financial crisis, China has the economic resources and the financial muscle to provide bailout packages and become an alternate source of credit.

While Western commentators see this as a race for influence in Zimbabwe with the West,[31] closer home it represents a more strategic competition with South Africa, which is actually considered a significant African actor across the continent.[32] This is because South Africa is perceived, mainly in Western political circles, and now by emerging powers such as China, Brazil, and India, to be the continent's most stable democracy (especially in terms of its institutional strength), while also being Africa's economic powerhouse. Tables 11.3 and 11.4 reflect how much of South Africa's global trade footprint is still dominated by its engagement with Europe, and more recently with Asia. Nevertheless, what these figures mask is the presence of South African corporations in African economies and the nation's highly developed structural economic conditions, which make it a significant economy vis-à-vis other African markets.

The emergence of China as a competing development partner to many African countries tends to raise the China factor in South Africa's continental foreign policy, even though both governments may claim that there is no intrinsic competition between them in African markets.

Table 11.3 South African exports by continent, 2006–2009 (in million rands)

Region	2006	2007	2008	2009	Global exports 2006 (%)	Global exports 2009 (%)
Europe	134,969,480	158,066,133	208,563,006	148,019,467	39	33
Asia	102,414,192	134,693,195	190,889,348	162,036,473	29	36
Africa	50,129,773	64,494,505	99,016,216	86,328,583	14	19
Americas	50,289,112	65,648,804	79,899,610	51,635,826	14	11.3
Pacific	9,721,003	10,895,867	13,714,522	7,193,064	3	1.6
Total	347,523,560	433,798,504	592,082,702	455,213,414		

Source: South African Department of Trade of Industry's economic database: http://www.thedti.gov.za/econdb/raportt/rapcont.html.

Table 11.4   South African imports by continent, 2006–2009 (in million rands)

Region	2006	2007	2008	2009	Global imports 2006 (%)	Global imports 2009 (%)
Europe	168,382,196	200,578,583	244,835,362	186,442,979	36	35
Asia	193,633,684	228,906,770	314,219,866	231,540,844	42	43
Africa	29,423,734	40,886,843	73,549,591	40,378,117	6	8
Americas	58,985,660	74,803,676	99,946,388	69,786,507	13	13
Pacific	10,836,309	12,522,721	15,536,311	10,592,011	2	2
Total	461,261,582	557,698,593	748,087,518	538,740,458		

Source: South African Department of Trade of Industry's economic database: http://www.thedti.gov.za/econdb/raportt/rapcont.html.

Nevertheless, the fact that Beijing can issue a credit line facility that is more than thirty times the value of Pretoria's illustrates China's economic largesse for distressed African states in need of economic and social reform. While this comparative advantage may be at odds with issues of transparency, human rights norms, good governance, and even linked to supporting illegitimate regimes, it is undeniable that Beijing's financial capacity is something to be reckoned with in Africa and the global economy.

Second, the meltdown in the global economy has provided the impetus for this growing financial influence. This is evidenced by the fact that Chinese companies are in the next stage of their "going global," or "going out" strategy, backed by the Chinese government[33] and the US$2.4 trillion foreign reserve,[34] well as other financial instruments such as the sovereign wealth fund[35] (China Investment Corporation) and the US$5 billion China-Africa Development Fund (CADF).[36] The underlying factor is that Chinese corporations are on the hunt for more long-term accumulation of resource commodities and mineral assets, made cheaper by the slump in global prices. Not only does this enable China to buy offshore assets but to also have direct access and control of these commodity assets to be able to influence and negotiate prices. This was demonstrated by the rumored US$5 billion platinum-backed deal with the China EXIM Bank.[37] Even though it is unclear whether the deal has been signed, Zimbabwe provides a litmus test for the finance for resource strategy, given the fact that Harare might be desperate to mortgage assets to finance its economic recovery program. See figures 11.1 and 11.2 illustrating China's trade dynamic with Zimbabwe.

Finally, with tensions still marking the relations between ZANU-PF and the MDC-Tsvangirai (MDC-T) faction, it would be interesting to see how China and South Africa maneuver around this, especially since Beijing is seen to lean more toward the ZANU-PF side, while the Zuma administration has a more engaging relationship with Tsvangirai's MDC. On the Chinese side there has definitely been a strategic calculation to woo Tsvangirai, which probably fits with Beijing's

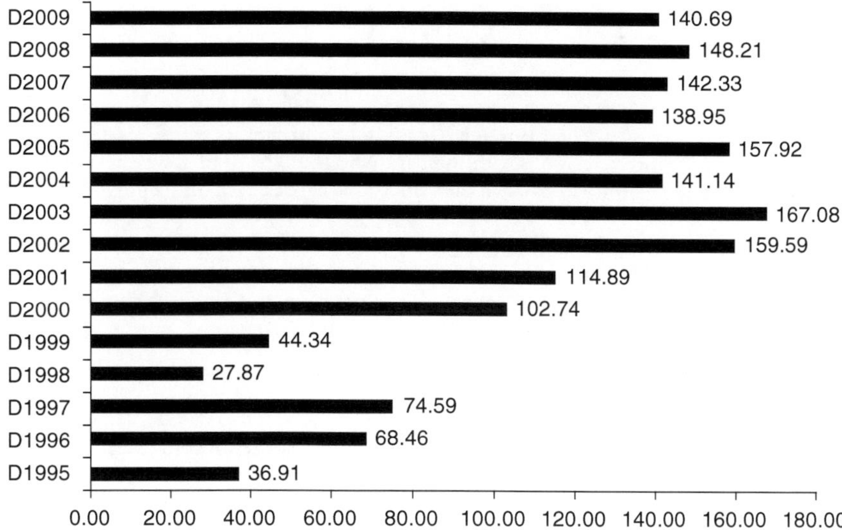

Figure 11.1   China's total imports from Zimbabwe, 1995–2009 (US$ million).

Source: World Trade Atlas on Tralac: http://moodle.kimmagedsc.ie/file.php/1/moddata/forum/6/81/ South_Centre_Newsletter_Oct_08.pdf.

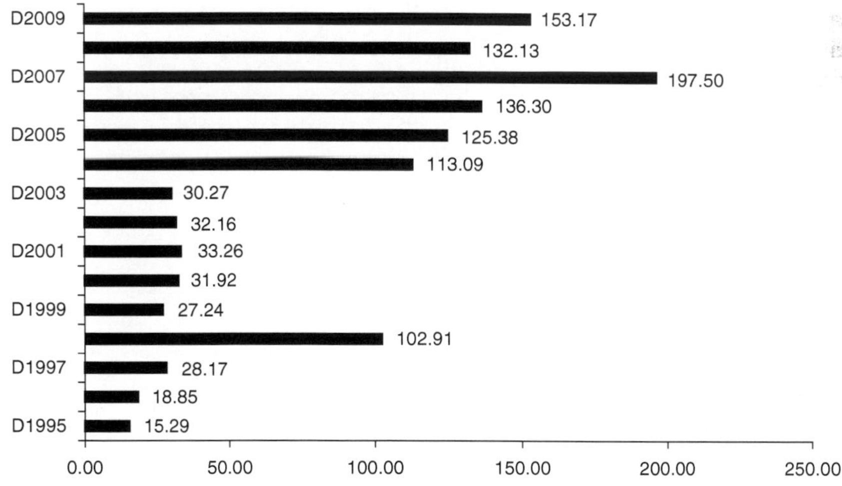

Figure 11.2   China's total exports from Zimbabwe, 1995–2009 (US$ million).

Source: World Trade Atlas on Tralac: http://moodle.kimmagedsc.ie/file.php/1/moddata/forum/6/81/ South_Centre_Newsletter_Oct_08.pdf.

long-term thinking that sees Tsvangirai as the future president elect. This has been observed by some Western commentators who have argued that:

> China's decision to activate the financial package right now, during the tenure of the inclusive government, and through Tsvangirai, illustrates its will to strategically position itself for future relations with someone who could be Zimbabwe's next president. It also allows China to balance the criticism it has received for its proximity to Mugabe.
>
> China is effectively having its cake and eating it too: its relationship with both parties is flourishing. Plans are afoot to invite the MDC to Beijing for political and investment talks. By choosing to engage the government as a whole, China will be able to exert leverage on both ZANU-PF and the MDC, something western donors might not achieve.[38]

The question is whether Pretoria can develop the same strategic calculus with ZANU-PF even if Mugabe is no longer at the helm. Somehow this seems a much more difficult task given Pretoria's postapartheid relationship with regional neighbors and its engagement in the region with what Peter Kagwana, president of the African Policy Institute (API) based in Kenya and South Africa (Pretoria), highlights as interregional trilateral rivalry between Pretoria on the one hand and Harare and Luanda on the other hand for dominance in the SADC.[39] While the political and economic crisis in Zimbabwe has eclipsed this rivalry to some extent, its residual effects still linger over whether Pretoria's true intentions of an African renaissance under the Mbeki administration were intended to benefit the continent, or provide an opening for South African corporations to dominate regional and African economies.

Perhaps the Zuma presidency will heal such political divisions and mistrust, considering that while President Zuma's Africa policy[40] represents continuity with the Mbeki administration, it also signifies a return to President Mandela's foreign principles of justice, democracy, and human rights. Whether President Zuma succeeds depends on how he manages to build sustainable partnerships with African countries and how he refocuses South Africa's image as an African partner and not a hegemon.

Conclusion

Returning to the question raised at the beginning of this chapter about whether South African corporations are reaping the benefits after weathering the storm, the answer certainly seems positive. Part of this is linked to their geographical proximity and their proclivity at underwriting risk even during times of deep economic crises. Their experience in Zimbabwe during the political and economic decline, indeed, reflects this and undoubtedly assists them, even though perceptions of South African corporations may not always be well perceived. This suspicion derives from some views within the general populace that companies are exploiting economic opportunities, while those government officials who may have their own business interests with other economic actors might perceive South African businesses as competitors.

South African capital showed tenacity in withstanding the economic decline, which distinguished it from the rest. And so it is unmistakable that for those new market-seeking investors, and even existing ones, wanting to capture a share of Zimbabwe's post-economic recovery, the attractiveness of South African corporations as viable business partners may be hard to ignore. South African corporations have a reputation for being trendsetters in terms of commercial learning, cross-border cultural experiences, and brand building, as well as for advocating corporate social responsibility programs as part of their commitment to socioeconomic development.

Clearly, the reputation of South African corporations being considered as African MNC Champions has caught the attention of Asian National Champions. This is already evident with Chinese and South African banking institutions joining forces—examples include the recent ICBC-Standard Bank deal and the Memorandum of Understanding (MOU) signed by First Rand and China Construction Bank to jointly finance resources and other manufacturing projects while sharing the equity exposure. Moreover, South Africa, and in particular Johannesburg, serves as a strategic commercial hub for launching this investment trajectory across the Limpopo River into Zimbabwe, into other regional economies, and ultimately across the continent.

Yet South African businesses are also cautious. While they may be anticipating the windfall from investing in Zimbabwe's economic recovery, they are also astutely aware that for them to affect any firm commitment on their part, the Zimbabwean transitional government must equally provide guarantees against political and expropriation risks, especially in respect of the Zimbabwe Indigenisation Act. Such protection is imminent given past experiences. In terms of the latter, the Bilateral Agreement for the Promotion and Reciprocal Protection of Investments (BIPPA), signed in November 2009 between the South African and Zimbabwean governments, provides a security framework for South African investors. According to South African minister of trade and industry Rob Davies:

> the aim of the BIPPA was to provide security for any South African investor in any sector, including agriculture.[41] This security would create certainty for investors in Zimbabwe to boost economic recovery and stabilization, thereby contributing to political stability. However, the BIPPA's aim was not to "reopen old wounds" which is why, said Davies, it was impossible for South Africa to negotiate a retrospective property rights clause.[42]

Yet South African corporations remain watchful of BIPPA because some believe that the South African government did not follow the proper consultative processes, which does guarantee the legal dimensions and legitimacy of BIPP. Moreover, by the end of 2009, the constitutional elements of the agreement had not been made public and, therefore, remain unenforceable.

Finally, Zimbabwe represents another opportunity for South African corporations. South Africa's domestic environment has become somewhat of a battleground around intense socioeconomic disputes. While socioeconomic strikes continue to characterize the Zuma presidency, with more acute tensions mounting between the labor force and government concerning wage increases, inflation-targeting, and employment protection, and more generally service delivery protests because of the slow pace of distribution, South African businesses seem caught in the middle of these actions; more importantly, they are losing significant productivity output. These shifts in South Africa's political landscape may in fact prompt South African firms to consider relocating production sites to Zimbabwe to avoid further disruptions to production and operations, as well as sidestep the rigidity of South Africa's industrial relations. While this may raise intense debate amongst South Africa's labor antagonists, the fact of the matter is that Zimbabwe has a skilled workforce keen on finding employment opportunities.

However, such a consideration signals a negative impact for South Africa's fragile employment sector (creating less job opportunities), which the alliance partners, COSATU and SACP, may react aggressively toward since these partners now have a stake/voice in government and parliament to enforce policies that protect the interests of their constituencies.

Moreover, while such a strategic maneuver by South African corporations might actually offer the skilled Zimbabwean in South Africa an opportunity to return home,[43] it could nevertheless make the South African government uncomfortable since the Zuma administration is facing serious challenges against government performance in the arena of social services delivery, public sector employment, and shortages of sustainable private sector job opportunities.

Therefore as much as this move is further exemplified by fact that the rand is being considered as a possible trading currency for the Zimbabwean economy, it could very well be that Zimbabwe could become an enclave economy for South African business interests. Yet such intentions will definitely become a sensitive political issue in terms of South Africa's corporatization of the Zimbabwean economy. The South African government may want to advise corporate South Africa that revitalizing the socioeconomic reconstruction of Zimbabwe is better poised since it could trigger greater social justice struggles in South Africa that could affect the ANC-led government's electoral support in the 2014 national elections.

In conclusion, South African corporations seem to have a strategic advantage in Zimbabwe, like they do elsewhere in other African economies. Whether the South African state will drive this process remains to be seen, since what is becoming increasingly clear is that the geography of multinationals compared to the geography of the state leans heavily in favor of corporations. Therefore, from this perspective, South African corporations may actually be pushing the agenda. They might be pressing to become more firmly entrenched in the Zimbabwean economy, but not necessarily without looking toward Pretoria to negotiate political guarantees and others forms of stability that are vital to the sustainability of their investments.

Notes

1. Subsequent to the initial power-sharing deal negotiations, an agreement that provided for a government of national unity was signed in February 2009; this included the MDC

as well. While this represented a structural change to Zimbabwe's power structure, ZANU-PF still remained in control of significant cabinet portfolios that continued to strengthen the ruling party's power at the center. Therefore, as much as the coalition government was an attempt to bring in the MDC, the old guard of ZANU-PF still remained dominant, which did not resolve tensions between MDC and ZANU-PF with violence on the ground between supporters still being rife and rampant. As it stands now the coalition government remains fragile and characterized by intense suspicion and ongoing battles around power and effective governance.

2. In January 2010, the IMF restored Zimbabwe's voting rights. This has enabled Zimbabwe to qualify for US$510 million loan package as part of the IMF's global assistance package to help countries to cope with the 2009 financial crisis. According to Minister of Finance Tendai Biti, US$210 million of this IMF would be used for infrastructure development. Biti also announced that donors had pledged US$800 million toward Zimbabwe's 2010 budget. See MacDonald Dzirutwe, "Zimbabwe Economy on Mend, 7 Pct Growth Seen in 2010," *Reuters News,* December 2, 2009, http://www.alertnet.org/thenews/newsdesk/GEE5B11GP.htm.

3. "Zimbabwe: Unity Government Going Nowhere Slowly," *IRIN,* March 24, 2009, http://www.irinnews.org/Report.aspx?ReportId=83616.

4. See United Nations Development Programme (UNDP), *Comprehensive Economic Recovery in Zimbabwe: A Discussion Document,* Working Paper Series (UNDP Zimbabwe, 2008). http://www.undp.org.zw/images/stories/Docs/Publications/CompEconoRec2008.pdf.

5. See Brent Cloete and Greg Mills, "Scan of Zimbabwe Economic Recovery Literature," Brenthurst Discussion Paper 4/2009, Johannesburg, April 2009.

6. See "Foreign Direct Investment Faces Modest Recovery," *Forbes,* January 26, 2010, http://www.forbes.com/2010/01/25/africa-asia-latin-america-business-fdi-oxford.html

7. See World Bank (WB), "Global Economic Prospects 2010: Commodity Markets," http://web.worldbank.org/WBSITE/EXTERNAL/EXTDEC/EXTDECPROSPECTS/EXTGBLPROSPECTS/0,,contentMDK:20666027~menuPK:612516~pagePK:2904583~piPK:2904598~theSitePK:612501,00.html.

8. See Dianna Games, "A Nation in Turmoil—The Experience of South African firms doing Business in Zimbabwe," Business in Africa Report no. 8, South African Institute of International Affairs, Braamfontein, SA.

9. Solidarity Peace Trust, "A Difficult Dialogue: Zimbabwe-South African Economic Relations Since 2000," A Preliminary Report, October 23, 2007, http://www.solidaritypeacetrust.org/reports/difficult_dialogue.pdf

10. See Patrick Bond, "Zimbabwe Under a Sub-imperial, Neo-liberal Thumb," *Pambazuka News,* March 26, 2009, http://www.pambazuka.org/en/category/comment/55156; Shawn Hattingh, "South Africa in Zimbabwe: The Vultures Have Descended," Centre for Civil Society, Durban 2007: http://www.ukzn.ac.za/ccs/default.asp?3,28,11,3162; William G. Martin, "South Africa's Subimperial Futures: Washington Consensus, Bandung Consensus or Peoples Consensus?" *Africa Files,* http://www.africafiles.org/article.asp?ID=19153; and "South African Companies Unlock Sub-Saharan Africa," *Business Week,* December 4, 2008, http://www.businessweek.com/magazine/content/08_50/b4112052173000.htm?campaign_id=rss_topStories.

11. See John Daniel, Varusha Naidoo, and Sanusha Naidu, "The South Africans Have Arrived: Post Apartheid Corporate Expansion," in *State of the Nation: South Africa 2003–2004,* eds. John Daniel, Adam Habib, and Roger Southall (Cape Town: HSRC Press, 2004).

12. During the apartheid regime's fight against majority rule, the minority Afrikaner Nationalist government embarked upon a regional military strategy that extended

beyond its borders toward protecting the regime against external threats. The strategy was aimed at rooting out the training camps of the African National Congress (ANC) through military incursions and other forms of attacks in order to weaken attacks from the ANC and more specifically the liberation struggle. As a result because southern African countries offered the ANC base camps in their countries, these countries suffered the onslaught of the South African Defense Force, which destroyed infrastructure and contributed other structural damages. This became known as the destabilization policy of the apartheid regime.

13. The emergence of South African capital in southern Africa is rooted in the development of the mining and industrial sectors of the South African economy. With the discovery of gold in the 1820s, the development of corporate South Africa was through the formation of companies such as Anglo-American by Cecile John Rhodes, under the yoke of British colonialism. The region was significant as a reservoir of cheap labor to the mines in South Africa.

14. Ibid., 327.

15. The support that Zimbabwe and other neighboring countries lent to the antiapartheid struggle was to provide an exit route for combatants to leave South Africa and allow the ANC to set up training camps in their countries. The governments in the region supported the antiapartheid struggle because of the dominance of the white minority regimes in the regional political and economic spaces by getting directly involved in intra-state conflicts such as in Namibia, Angola, and Mozambique. As a result in the early 1980s the countries in the region formed the Southern African Development Coordination Conference (SADCC) as a political and security organization response to coordinate their political and military efforts against the apartheid government. They argued that the total strategy and total onslaught policy of Pretoria toward undermining the liberation movement implied that the countries were at the frontline of the attack. Hence they formed the Frontline States against apartheid South Africa. In this regard Zimbabwe became a significant voice with Mugabe at the helm representing the voice of these states against the white minority regime.

16. "South in Africa: Articles to the African Diamond Workers Network," International Labour Research and Information Group, Vol. 3, Cape Town, 2007.

17. The Southern African Customs Union (SACU) is the oldest customs union in the world. Initiated as part of the trade agreement between the British Colony of Cape Town and the Orange Free State Boer Republic in 1889, a new agreement was signed in 1910 between the Union of South Africa and the British High Commission of Territories (HCTs) of Lesotho, Botswana, and Swaziland. Because South West Africa (now Namibia) was administered by South Africa it became a de facto member of SACU. The aim of SACU was to coordinate regional trade and economic development. For more information see www.sacu.int.

18. The presence of South African capital in the region dates back to the 1920s through the activities of Anglo-American where, for instance, the company acquired its first mines in what then known as Northern Rhodesia (now Zambia) in 1928.

19. John Daniel and Nompumelelo Bhengu, "South Africa in Africa: Still a Formidable Player," in *A New Scramble for Africa? Imperialism, Investment and Development,* eds. Roger Southall and Henning Melber (Scottsville, SA: University of KwaZulu Natal Press, 2009).

20. The indigenization policy was introduced by the Mugabe regime toward the end of 2005–2006. The legislation is a type of Black Economic empowerment policy that relates to foreign-owned mining groups investing in Zimbabwe. The legislation advocates that foreign companies have to cede 51 percent control of their holdings to state

and local stakeholders without compensation. The policy entrenches large sums of tax revenues to an essentially bankrupt state but also gives political elites access to engage in corruption and nepotism.

21. Richard Saunders, "Crisis, Capital, Compromise: Mining and Empower in Zimbabwe," *African Sociological Review: Special Issue: South Africa in Africa: African Perceptions, African Realities* 12, no.1 (2008): 67. See also Dianna Games, "A Nation in Turmoil," 2006; and "The Experience of South African Firms Doing Business in Africa: A Preliminary Survey," SAIIA Business in Africa Research Project Report No. 1, Braamfontein, 2004.

22. Daniel and Bhengu, "South Africa in Africa,"

23. Tom Burgis and William Wallis, "Harare to Receive African Credit," *Financial Times*, May 4, 2009.

24. Ibid.

25. By the end of 2008 China's trade with Africa reached US$106,7 billion up from US$73 billion in 2007 and just US$10 billion in 2000, making it the continent's second trade partner after the United States, while between 2006 and 2008 Chinese companies had invested approximately US$5 billion across Africa.

26. Essentially the "Look East" policy was aimed at recalibrating Zimbabwe's foreign policy toward Asia at a time when trade and investment partners from the West were less forthcoming because of the deepening political and economic crisis. The Mugabe regimes used this policy as a rationale to say that Zimbabwe would find trade and investment partners from the East and develop synergies with Asian countries to forge strategic partnerships.

27. Haru Mutasa, "China Buys The World: Zimbabwe's Special Relationship," *Aljazeera. net*, August 10, 2009.

28. See "Zimbabwe Struggles to Attract Foreign Aid—Finmin Biti," *Reuters*, March 11, 2010, http://www.alertnet.org/thenews/newsdesk/LDE62A204.htm.

29. See "Norway Resumes Aid to Zimbabwe, Despite Mugabe," *Reuters*, May 25, 2010, http://www.reuters.com/article/idUSLP449530.

30. Ibid.

31. See François Grignon, "The Race for Influence in Zimbabwe," *The Guardian*, July 25, 2009, http://www.guardian.co.uk/commentisfree/2009/jul/25/zimbabwe-aid-china-west.

32. For instance, during Hilary Clinton's seven nation African visit in August 2009, one of the key issues on the agenda during her meeting with President Zuma was to discuss Pretoria's continued pressure on Harare for more effective political reform since Washington does not recognize the transitional government representing any fundamental change with Mugabe and his cronies still at the helm.

33. This has been explicitly stated by Premier Wen Jiabao: "We should hasten the implementation of our 'going out' strategy and combine the utilization of foreign exchange reserves with the 'going out' of our enterprises." See Stephen Marks, "Rio Case Could Signal a Shift," *Pambazuka News,* Issue 443, July 23, 2009, http://www.pambazuka.org/en/category/africa_china/57937.

34. See "China's Forex Reserves Account for 30% of World Trade," *China Daily,* February 20, 2010, http://www.chinadaily.com.cn/bizchina/2010–02/20/content_9477391.htm

35. Sovereign Wealth Funds are state owned investment funds that are made up of financial assets including bonds, stocks, property, precious metals (such as gold). China Investment Corporation (CIC) is a sovereign wealth fund.

36. The China-Africa Development Fund (CADF) was announced as one of the eight measures unveiled at the 2006 Forum on China-Africa Cooperation in Beijing. The fund

was established to financially support Chinese companies to invest in African markets and enter into cooperation with African companies. The fund is administered by the China Development Bank and has opened offices in Johannesburg and recently in Ethiopia. More information can be accessed at: http://www.cadfund.com/en/.

37. See "Biti Signs US$5 Billion Deal with China," *The Zimbabwean Independent,* July 2, 2009, http://www.thezimbabweindependent.com/index.php/local/22974-biti-signs-us5b-deal-with-china.

38. Grignon, "The Race for Influence in Zimbabwe."

39. See Peter Kagwanja, "An Encumbered Regional Power? The Capacity Gap in South Africa's Peace Diplomacy in Africa," Democracy and Governance Research Programme Occasional Paper no. 6, Cape Town, 2009.

40. Postapartheid South Africa Africa's policy is based on reintegrating democratic South Africa into the continent. Based on principles of mutual interest and development, democratic South Africa sought to project an African policy that articulates an image resonating with the African renaissance and pushing for African peace, stability, and development. Yet this approach is seen in certain quarters as ambivalent since Pretoria is trying to reconcile South Africa's political power with its economic footprint that tends to reflect deep suspicion by African governments around whether democratic South Africa is behaving like its apartheid predecessor and importantly about whether it really represent the voice of the continent. See Chris Alden and Garth Le Pere, "South Africa in Africa: Bound to Lead?" *Politikon: Special Edition on Africa's Relations with Emerging Powers: Charting a New Direction in International Engagements* 36, no. 1 (2009) (guest editors Sanusha Naidu, Lucy Corkin, and Hayley Herman).

41. John Brand and Mieke Krynauw, "Implications and Ramifications of Zimbabwe/SA Agreement on Investment Protection," February 15, 2010, http://www.bowman.co.za/LawArticles/Law-Article-Content-Implications%20ramifications%20Zimbabwe.asp.

42. Ibid.

43. South Africa is home to approximately three million Zimbabweans, many of whom are illegal migrants.

Chapter 12

Donors and the Crisis in Zimbabwe
Experiences and Lessons Learned

Holger Bernt Hansen

Many Catholics in high office have fallen woefully short in their performance in office. The synod calls on such people to repent, or quit the public arena and stop causing havoc to the people and giving the Catholic Church a bad name.

—From the statement issued by the Synod of Bishops for Africa, October 23, 2009

No one was in doubt as to who the primary addressee was when the African Bishops issued their strong words from the Synod in the Vatican in October 2009. Over the last couple of years the Catholic Church in Zimbabwe has suffered from various kinds of restrictions and threats from the Mugabe regime, all with the purpose of weakening its critical voice against those in power. This is seen as a symptom of the suffering that the majority of Zimbabwean people experience. In their statement, the Synod of Bishops moved beyond the usual request for repentance and went straight to say: quit the arena. They could just as well have used the term "regime change," for that is what they really meant, and that was what the Zimbabwean bishops said outright in a statement a year earlier. "Regardless of whether he is a former 'liberator' or an 'Elder African Statesman,' he must be forced to step down… No solution to the crisis in Zimbabwe is possible as long as he is there."[1]

The term regime change echoes what most international donors, such as the United States and the European Union (EU), have asked for, both tacitly and vocally, for almost ten years. Correspondingly, regime change is also at the center of President Robert Mugabe's repeated counterattacks when he criticizes the donors for aiming at exactly that, even in the most imperialistic way. What is interesting is that a leading civil society organization (CSO), such as the Catholic Church, speaks in these terms. Without identifying themselves with the donors, the churches in Zimbabwe find themselves caught in the dilemma between their Christian obligation to defend people's rights and prevent abuses, and the limitations on their advocacy role caused by increasing violence and restrictions on humanitarian workers. The churches have reached the point where the only solution to the dilemma is a regime change.

It is exactly the same solution that most Western donors consider to be the only way out of their increasingly painful dilemma between the humanitarian imperative and the political realities in Zimbabwe. This chapter presents a key to the understanding of donor governments' policies toward the long drawn-out crisis in Zimbabwe. It is within this dichotomous framework that this chapter will analyze the donors' policy toward Zimbabwe, and eventual engagement in Zimbabwe's reconstruction.

The International Context

A first step in this analysis will be the establishment of the context within which international donors act. A relevant point of departure is the declaration on the Millennium Development Goals (MDGs) passed by the United Nations (UN) General Assembly in 2000. The ultimate goal is the reduction of poverty, as spelled out in eight MDGs, mainly within the social sectors, health and education, and with a special emphasis on women's and children's rights to a decent living. The declaration is based on two preconditions: developing countries integrate this agenda into their budgets and long term plans; and donor countries should gear their aid programs to achieving the MDGs by 2015. In the case of Zimbabwe, the first of the two preconditions has spiraled downward over the last ten years because of budget cuts, which has raised one of many dilemmas for donor governments in their dealings with Zimbabwe: How to give priority to development goals when a government's policy is destructive? Or, should the driver of change be the private sector through foreign investments, and not assistance channeled through the state?

Assistance channeled through the state is related to the discussion of the importance of economic growth as the necessary condition for achieving the MDGs, a subject on which the Millennium Declaration is strangely silent. This leads to the question of the role of the state vis-à-vis the private sector, which reflects the well-known dilemma between official aid and private investments. In general, the whole issue of aid modalities and aid effectiveness in situations like the Zimbabwean one is the subject of an increasingly critical debate over the role of aid,[2] made even more poignant during a time of economic crisis when aid volume is under pressure and a degree of aid fatigue is observable in donor circles.[3] A recurring theme in the discussion is the curtailment of Africa's own development efforts and entrepreneurial spirit caused by the many conditionalities attached to foreign aid. Even after many years of aid, a static situation emerged, characterized by aid dependency in the sense that foreign aid in some countries constitutes 40 percent or more of the national budget.

The whole debate around aid and donor roles influences the approach to situations like the Zimbabwean one, and raises the question of the extent to which Zimbabwe's progress can be measured by this same standard since it exhibits all the signs of a malfunctioning state. There is a feeling of uncertainty about how to navigate and move along on a scale where, at the one end, there is great need to reduce poverty and meet developmental needs, while at the other there is an acute challenge for the donors to play a normative role by emphasizing human rights, democratic values, and good governance practices. There is a real dilemma in bringing the two ends to meet and adjust to each other.

One move to repair and improve the prevailing aid regime came in 2005 with the well-known Paris Declaration on Aid Effectiveness,[4] which was seen as an answer to much of the criticism from the international debate on aid. It addressed the obvious lack of ownership in the developing world, not least because the many conditionalities attached to development assistance were seen as limiting the space for partner countries to exercise effective leadership. But the main part of the Paris Declaration is directed toward the donors because of the overcrowding of donor agencies in many countries. The complexity of the international aid system has grown over time, seriously affecting the success of aid and accounting for the lack of results. As the most important remedy, the Paris Declaration called for an extensive harmonization of donor activities, in order to avoid overcrowding, and better coordination, with a clear focus on the desired results.

In spite of extensive harmonization and alignment efforts, at the end of the day donors are still setting the agenda, strongly influenced by their normative role. In order to achieve unity among the many actors, it is often the lowest common denominator that prevails; but even if donors act together, the conditions for obtaining the desired results depend on a conducive environment at the receiving end. If this is not the case, as in Zimbabwe, robust donor collaboration will often be counterproductive in the sense that donors will easily be accused of pursuing an agenda biased in favor of their own self-interests. This is exactly the case in present-day Zimbabwe, where such criticism is expressed through a strong anti-Western vocabulary.

The initiative to reform the well-known aid regime was contrasted by new actors on the African stage. China became an increasingly important partner for a number of African countries, later followed by Brazil, India, and a number of other countries. Their approach was quite different as they did not come with an aid agenda full of conditionalities, norms, and values, such as democracy, good governance, and human rights. These new donors have instead focused on business, trade, and investments. To a limited extent, they have offered aid, but outside the prescriptions of the Paris Declaration and without normative guidance. This has meant that countries like Zimbabwe, for the first time, have been presented with alternative choices, offering them more space to maneuver in pursuit of the government's own preferences.

Consequently, traditional donors will now have to operate under different circumstances and under new kinds of pressure. In the case of Zimbabwe the situation is further complicated by the fact that its southern neighbor, South Africa, with its great economic and political muscle, is an actor with its own interests in Zimbabwe, and has strengthened its claim of a southern African sphere of interest, which Zimbabwe would belong to. With new actors emerging outside the process of harmonization, it is not easy to pursue the usual aid agenda; traditional donors have, so to speak, lost their monopoly.

The context outlined earlier, within which international donors operate, is not static. An aid agenda under strain from external developments and internal dilemmas can be observed over the period so far examined. The dilemma between the need for political change and economic growth, on the one hand, and the difficulties in bringing the actions on the ground to reflect the basic values and norms ingrained in the prevailing idea of development, on the other, can be seen in terms of the implementation of a salient development assistance policy. Zimbabwe exposes these dilemmas to an extent hardly seen elsewhere.

The Beginning of the Crisis between Zimbabwe and Donors

It is difficult to point to a specific year as the beginning of the crisis, but increasingly strained relations between donors and the Zimbabwean government became visible during the 1990s. The Danish experiences illustrate the course of events and the fact that many of the dilemmas identified here started at an early stage.

After its liberation and independence in 1980, Zimbabwe became one of the twenty major recipient countries (later referred to as program countries) enrolled in the full-fledged Danish development assistance program, centered on the social sector and agriculture. The program amounted to about US$25 million annually.[5] During the 1990s, the cooperation became more difficult, mainly due to the government's handling of the land reform issue, but first and foremost because of restrictions on democratic procedures and the decreasing respect for human rights. This meant that development activities in rural areas and within the health sector, which, from a donor's perspective, still worked fairly well, were rearranged and increasingly channeled through local authorities and nongovernmental organizations (NGOs), with the explicit goal of benefiting poor people in the countryside. This model for granting assistance by bypassing the central government was already working in Kenya, a country that in many ways was, and still is, comparable to Zimbabwe.

The liberal-conservative government that came to power in Denmark in late 2001 cut down on the aid budget (from about 1 percent to 0.8 percent of Gross National Product or GNP), necessitating a reduction in the number of program countries and, apart from some clear cut cases, there came a choice between Zimbabwe and Kenya. The latter was retained while the former was left out. Two main reasons are worth mentioning as characteristics of donor thinking. First, while Kenya did not let politics totally overshadow economic development, Zimbabwe downscaled the latter and gave almost absolute priority to the political field, an approach motivated by the liberation ideology that it expressed strongly in anticolonial terms. Hence, aid could only have a limited impact in Zimbabwe and required a constant compromise with the normative elements ingrained in Denmark's aid program, while it made sense to continue working with Kenya.[6] Second, Kenya's position was strengthened when the prospect of regime change was included in policymaking. Regime change was much more likely in Kenya, vindicated by the National Rainbow Coalition's replacement of the Daniel arap Moi regime that was in power for twenty-four years, accompanied by reforms to strengthen institutions such as the electoral commission, the judiciary, and the human rights commission, all of which are central to a proper democracy. Events in Zimbabwe, with the referendum on the draft constitution in February 2000, followed by parliamentary elections in June of the same year and presidential elections in March 2002, turned things in the opposite direction and made regime change highly unlikely.

For these two reasons the Danish government closed the official aid program and went a step further in the middle of 2002 by closing its embassy in Harare. However, these steps did not neutralize the painful dilemma between political realities and the humanitarian imperative. The Danish government responded to the latter challenge by channeling relief through UN organizations and NGOs over the following years, while it responded to the political restrictions and rights violations by supporting CSOs in their advocacy work, amidst increasingly tense relations with the Zimbabwean authorities.

The Danish policy was indicative of the line followed by most donors. The initial response may not have been as strict and consequent as the Danish one, but other Western donors acted within the same dilemma and on the same premises. In 2001 most donors, including the World Bank (WB) and the International Monetary Fund (IMF), made cuts in aid and loans and strongly criticized the deterioration of law and order and the violations of human rights in Zimbabwe. In February 2002 some Western donors, with the EU in the lead, introduced travel and foreign asset sanctions against the core members of the ruling elite. The donors started to advocate for the need for a regime change as the best way to bring relations back to normal.

The deterioration of living conditions at all levels meant that the humanitarian imperative was felt even stronger. At the same time, the mismanagement of the economy (to a large extent caused by the breakdown of the farming sector), the violation of democratic procedures, and the misbehavior of the security forces meant that donors would not, in spite of declining social conditions and food shortages, resume aid programs and cooperate with the government. Instead, with the EU and the United States in front, they renewed sanctions against members of the ruling hierarchy, and in 2005, U.S. secretary of state Condoleezza Rice labeled Zimbabwe as one of the world's six "outposts of tyranny."[7]

The more conditions deteriorated in both the economic and political fields, the more donors believed in and advocated for regime change as being the formula that could brake the vicious cycle and relieve the fundamental dilemma in which they were caught.[8]

The Escalation of the Crisis and the Donors' Dilemmas

As the downward spiral continued and affected all corners of state and society, donors felt the humanitarian imperative to be even stronger, while at the same time actions in the field became more and more difficult. Political conditions hardened, especially around and after the elections in 2005, when violence and rigging became the order of the day. Security forces (including a number of militias) and the judicial system were indiscriminately misused to persecute supporters of the opposition party, the Movement for Democratic Change (MDC), especially its leader Morgan Tsvangirai. With inflation reaching world record levels and the currency and monetary system run down to wretched dimensions, Zimbabwe's economy turned into a sad laughing stock. But the real tragedy was the suffering of ordinary people, both in rural and urban areas. Water and sanitation systems, health services, and the educational system were hardly functioning, with rising food prices and food shortages adding to the tragedy. An estimated three million voted with their feet and went into exile in neighboring countries, primarily South Africa.[9] The situation was aptly summed up by a neighboring head of state when he described Zimbabwe to be in the process of meltdown.

With the resumption of any kind of aid program being out of the question, Zimbabwe's *meltdown* strongly urged donors to act in accordance with the humanitarian imperative. But relief programs had their own problems. First, the regime politicized emergency aid to an extent rarely seen by diverting supplies to their own supporters in selected regions, while depriving opposition strongholds of any assistance.[10] Second, as is commonplace with humanitarian assistance, middlemen demanded their own share of the money. All funds had to be channeled through the Reserve Bank of Zimbabwe (RBZ), where the governor acted against all corporate social responsibility standards by tapping accounts indiscriminately and channeling relief money into the pockets of both the civilian and military elite.[11] Protests against these illegal "transaction costs" had no effect, and donors (including UN organizations and humanitarian NGOs) had to accept such special "conditionalities," as it was out of the question not to assist the desperate people of Zimbabwe who were forced to return to a subsistence economy.

For most donors it was natural to point to regime change as the only realistic solution to get out of such a contradictory environment. At this point there were several weaknesses in Western donor strategies and their handling of the situation. One such weakness was that Western donors employed the concept of regime change in a manner much too personalized by identifying it with the exit of one person: Robert Mugabe. Such an approach was likely to divert attention away from the essential elements in regime change: the change of structures and central institutions (such as the judiciary and security forces), respect for the role of parliament, and the division of powers as fundamental for the working of a proper system of democracy.

By personalizing their request for change, Western donors were employing a strategy that often proved counterproductive in the African context. Growing skepticism toward Western dominance provided fertile ground for Robert Mugabe to appeal to fellow Africans, especially to the southern African region, that Africa was once again experiencing a case of the West's imperialistic behavior—through their lack of recognition of African independence and lack of respect for Africans' ability to run their own countries.[12] His anti-imperialistic rhetoric became even more vociferous each time representatives from the United Kingdom voiced their criticism and referred to their special obligations toward the people of Zimbabwe. Mugabe's stance as a liberation hero has a special appeal to *comrades* from other liberation movements in southern Africa, and when under attack from the West, their primary solidarity and loyalty will be with Mugabe, which has been evident at several Southern African Development Community (SADC) summits.

Most Western donors have difficulty understanding this kind of solidarity. They argue that people overlook and downplay Mugabe's miserable record in bringing the country to a catastrophic meltdown. Most donors are still surprised when their appeals for action to member countries of the SADC get little or no response, with Botswana as the only notable exception. Western donors tend to overlook the emerging polarization of world order whereby Africa no longer looks solely to the West, but also to the East, to China as a powerful partner to cooperate with. Zimbabwe has used this alternative outlet over a number of years. Not in the least, mining deals, investments in the energy sector, and delivery of military hardware have contributed substantially to the endurance of the Mugabe regime. Indirectly, China, together with Russia, supported the regime in June 2008 when they vetoed a Western-backed UN Security Council resolution to impose sanctions.[13] (For a detailed account see chapter eleven, 236–240).

Global Political Agreement of September 2008

Electoral drama (not to say a tragedy) unfolded from March to June 2008, when the opposition won both the parliamentary and presidential elections, although the Electoral Commission fabricated the results of the latter, preventing the opposition's candidate, Morgan Tsvangirai, from being credited with the necessary 50 percent of the vote. The period until the runoff in late June was plagued by so much violence and persecution of the opposition that Tsvangirai pulled out shortly before the poll. In spite of protests from donors and others, the runoff took place with only one candidate, and Robert Mugabe was reinstated as president.

The period of electoral turmoil had implications for the entire donor setup and made it necessary to revise the strategy. In the highly politicized (almost poisonous) climate, it was important for the donor community to voice their criticism and recommendations with great care. The United States continued to be in the lead, but the EU was assuming a more prominent role as a leading actor in terms of donor policy.[14] The United Kingdom still thought that it had a role of its own to play, but its utterances have often turned out to be less helpful, causing ferocious outburst from Robert Mugabe and his cronies.[15]

This acute situation forced Western donor governments to put their policy on regime change on standby. They had to accept the "nine lives of Mugabe" and, for the time being, opted for a softer version like system change, with focus on the acceptance of basic democratic values and principles, reform of central institutions, such as the judiciary and the security apparatus, a guarantee for the enforcement of law and order, and respect for human rights. This should be done by a power-sharing agreement guaranteed by an external authority.[16] In this respect, representatives from the United States and the EU drew a parallel to Kenya, where six months earlier a similar arrangement was the main instrument in solving the severe postelectoral crisis, just before ethnic tensions threatened to pull the whole country apart. The chief mediator and negotiator was former

UN secretary general Kofi Annan, who acted under the auspices of the African Union (AU).[17]

While a kind of power-sharing agreement was generally accepted, the procedures turned out quite differently in the Zimbabwean case, much to the dismay of the donor community. President Mugabe and his party outright refused to allow international mediators to be involved, possibly because of warning signals from the Kenyan experience that external mediation would mean a loss of initiative and a reduction of room for maneuvering. In view of its many ties with Zimbabwe, it came as no surprise that South Africa stepped in and introduced a different formula. President Thabo Mbeki became the chief mediator and head of negotiations and the SADC (of which Zimbabwe had been an influential member from the start), not the AU, became the responsible authoritative body. In the eyes of most donors, this was a weak and watered-down version of the Kenyan model.

Thabo Mbeki's mediation work went through many stormy sessions and several high-level SADC meetings until the Global Political Agreement (GPA) was signed in September 2008. In general, the donor community took a pessimistic view of the GPA. There were many holes and loose ends, like control of the security sector, the relationship between the presidency and the government, and the reorganization of the financial sector. These issues posed even more problems as the MDC had lost trust in Mbeki's nonpartisanship and had severe doubt that he was prepared to take issue with his old associate in the liberation struggle, "Comrade Mugabe." In addition, Western donors found the SADC—with a few exceptions—entangled in the liberation ideology and weakly responsive to actively pursuing democratic values. This arrangement left them with limited leverage. The main reason for Western donors' acceptance of the GPA was that they were anxious about the alternative: the risk of a military takeover, followed by unrest and more suffering for the people.[18]

Furthermore, the GPA was seen as a chance to soften the dilemma between the humanitarian imperative and the political realities. It gave space to think in terms of the reconstruction of society and of the economy, and to introduce some longer term developmental perspectives.[19] In 2007, a group of Harare-based donor representatives, most of them signatories to the Paris Declaration, had started to draw up plans for a tentative program that could start a process whereby assistance could gradually move beyond the humanitarian concern toward reconstruction and development-oriented activities.[20]

Ahead of such a planning process it is important to address two issues. First, which category of state were the donors dealing with? It is noteworthy that the answer to this question of categorization had already been discussed some three years earlier during consultations in the international donor community. In 2005, under the auspices of the Organisation for Economic Co-operation and Development/Development Assistance Committee (OECD/DAC), leading donor agencies drew up the "Principles for Good International Engagement in Fragile States."[21] Listed among the fragile states was Zimbabwe, alongside Sudan, the Democratic Republic of the Congo (DRC), Guinea-Bissau, and Somalia. A pilot exercise was initiated in each country, with the European Community (EC) delegation as the facilitator in Zimbabwe, the primary aim being to secure aid effectiveness and cooperation between donors. However, the process did not go very far before the *Interim Country*

Report clearly stated that "the exercise has been strongly hampered by the mentioning of Zimbabwe as a 'fragile state'…They are worried on the eventual impact this notification might have on their good, technical relations with Government." The conclusion was that it did not make sense to carry out the exercise based on a classification of Zimbabwe as a fragile state, and it was premature to fine-tune present aid to the country "under present restricted aid conditions" and in view of "the entrenched political situation."[22]

Hence, in view of the endorsement of the GPA, the planning of a reconstruction program could not start from the assumption that Zimbabwe was a fragile state similar to post-conflict states. This leads to the second issue: How run down was Zimbabwe? The symptoms described earlier point to a poor state of affairs in most corners of society. But since Zimbabwe is not considered a fragile state, it is more useful to rephrase the question: Have the people of Zimbabwe the ability and the will to rise again and utilize support from outside to regenerate society and its institutions? The answer differs from one sector to another. It may be easier to rebuild the infrastructure within sectors such as health, education, water supply, and transport, where technical aspects supplement human resources. An important factor to consider is to what extent the large number of people who have gone into exile will return and take part in the rehabilitation process.

But the most important question will be if people, after years of uncertainty, harassment, and demoralization, can mobilize community spirit, optimism, and hope for a better livelihood. It is a difficult question to answer, and experiences from other parts of Africa point in both positive and negative directions. Yet experiences from Kenya provide some cause for optimism that, in spite of all kinds of disaster, there is still the ability and will to catch up. Donors may provide some incentives, but the real driving force will have to come from within, through the mobilization of communities and the development of their entrepreneurial spirit.[23]

It is within this whole range of uncertainties that donor representatives came forward toward the end of 2008 with a provisional assistance program.[24] The humanitarian concern was the overriding principle, but the program also looked carefully ahead to the time when political conditions would allow donors to introduce real development-oriented activities without restricted aid conditions. These wider plans carefully reflect the principles of the Paris Declaration. The activities were divided into phases, with both ownership and accountability written into each phase, but also with an emphasis on results and aid effectiveness. The cooperation with Zimbabwean counterparts was emphasized, but just as much was the harmonization and division of work among donors. Rooted in the Paris Declaration, the suggested program reflected (not surprisingly) a common donor thinking through the emphasis of a controlled pro-poor growth. To a large extent the program still reflected a donors' agenda, and as its authors had to be careful not to engage too much with the government, the activities were at a risk of being mainly donor driven, potentially resulting in an aid-dependent economy.

Two responses to the reconstruction of Zimbabwe are of special interest. First, South Africa was not convinced that it would be suitable to let the traditional donors take the lead. In view of its rational self-interest in Zimbabwe, South Africa, as a close neighbor, felt that it was better suited to take charge of the coordination. It planned to call a meeting, and in addition to the usual donors, South Africa also invited new actors, such as China and Brazil. An attempt to break the dominance of the traditional donors can be observed here, as well as an effort to open up space for new ideas by including new actors who are not limited by traditional donor thinking, but rather are open to exploring new avenues.[25]

Similarly, the second response questioned the usual practice for development aid, which is based on the "government-to-government" principle. Rather, it was suggested that the private sector should be recognized as the driver of economic growth and development due to its ability to attract foreign investments. The business sector should be crucial both for economic recovery and for meeting one of the biggest future challenges, the creation of jobs for young generations. Again, South African businesses have their own interests, although they maintain a low profile at present. Nonetheless, South Africa has traditionally been Zimbabwe's most important investor and largest trading partner. As already touched upon, this brings the discussion to a very topical issue in the current debate on development. The question is not about finding an alternative between aid and private investment, but rather about recognizing the importance of the business sector and promoting a better balance between the state and the private sector. This again means that donors should act accordingly by reorienting aid to create an enabling environment for the private sector's leading role. This would also mitigate the danger of Zimbabwe becoming an aid-dependent economy.

Clearly reflecting the current international debate on aid, the GPA has opened up space for discussions on the role of donors and aid in the reconstruction of Zimbabwe; however, this has scarcely had an effect on the ground. International donors are still stuck trying to balance the humanitarian imperative against restricted aid conditions because of the unchanged political realities. Substantial reforms of the political and financial systems were the necessary condition for a return to the flow of aid money in support of the implementation of GPA.

The Government of National Unity

The GPA laid the foundation for power-sharing and the formation of a Government of National Unity (GNU), but it took five months before a unity government could be sworn in, and during these five months all kinds of delay tactics and dirty tricks were played. This chain of depressive incidences has been described elsewhere. Western donors felt uncertain about the outcome, but, like earlier, they hoped for the best as they feared the worst. They supported Morgan Tsvangirai morally and in other ways, not least in his appeals for help from South Africa and the SADC, but these efforts proved unsuccessful as Zimbabwe's neighbors maintained their earlier supportive attitude toward the president and tended to assess the situation in alternative terms: Mugabe or chaos.

The formation of the unity government in February 2009 moved the political platform to another level and made the political processes more visible, but rather than change the power structures, the division of key ministries cemented them.

This situation can be described as a "Potemkin democracy," behind which there is a determined lack of will to share power and to implement the provisions written into the GPA. Seen from the point of view of Western donors, the democratic deficit was increasing as the lawlessness and human rights abuses were continuing unabatedly, with the freedom of the media hardly existing.

Hence the conditions for resuming support for development activities and giving desperately needed financial support to the unity government have not been met, and Western donors are left with the option of continuing to give their assistance on the basis of the humanitarian imperative. They have recognized the urgency of the situation and the special obligation they should rightfully honor after the formation of the GNU, a commitment they have shown by their quick response and by the substantial increase in the volume of humanitarian assistance.[26]

The formation of the unity government has facilitated the humanitarian exercise with regard to distribution, accountability, and results. Assistance is still channeled through multilateral agencies and NGOs, but it can now be done with the guidance and authority of the new MDC ministers, whose portfolios mainly cover the "soft" political areas, like health, education, water and sanitation, food, and so forth; in other words, the areas having caused people the most suffering and in greatest need of improvement in order to help people regain their livelihoods and resume normal functions. The otherwise disadvantageous distribution of ministries has been turned into a great advantage.

This change has created two important differences in the provision of development aid. First, the distribution of assistance has now been depoliticized. It is no longer possible to favor districts that are staunch supporters of the old ruling clique and punish supporters of the opposition. Neither is it possible for wandering groups, like militias, to serve themselves unconstrained. Second, the pipeline from the RBZ to the civilian and military elites is no longer fully operational as the Ministry of Finance has been assigned the overall responsibility for managing incoming funds, and an agreement has been reached on the establishment of a special donors' fund, administered by the WB, in consultation with Zimbabwe's Ministry of Finance. These changes have already been felt by the ruling clique, which is campaigning for a return to the old practice, with RBZ Governor Gideon Gono in charge.

The effects of the mainly humanitarian efforts are visible. Health and education services and water supplies have started to work as the salaries of nurses, doctors, and teachers are paid from the relief money.[27] In addition, the economy has been stabilized, with galloping inflation under control, thanks to currency reform[28] and credit lines from some of the neighboring countries. In addition, under special crisis schemes, limited loans from the WB and the IMF have made it possible for the GNU to halt economic collapse.[29] But all actors agree that Western aid money of much larger proportions—an amount of US$10 billion over five years has been mentioned—is indispensable for any real reconstruction. Yet Western donors are still asking for substantial political and macroeconomic reforms. Until the unity government tackles this challenge, the donors will not show much willingness to move beyond the humanitarian imperative.

This position has been maintained in spite of many appeals to donor representatives and donor governments for a policy revision from both Minister of Finance Tendai

Biti and Prime Minister Morgan Tsvangirai himself—the most significant attempt being the latter's visit to the United States and to a number of EU countries in June 2009. He was received at the highest level in all countries, and he argued in persuasive terms for the necessity to get substantial aid and investments in order to start the economic recovery and the political reform process. He was warmly welcomed and given a lot of moral support, but he did not manage to reverse the order of things. The United States and the EU maintained that under present conditions they could not proceed beyond humanitarian assistance.[30] Direct financial support on a massive scale would cement the present appalling state of affairs and act as a blockage against the necessary overhaul of the economic and political structures, with their many corrupt practices.

At home Morgan Tsvangirai was scorned for his failure to attract the much-needed money from Western donors, and immediately after his return, a ZANU-PF minister boasted that he had made a much better deal by securing US$950 million in credit lines from China[31] (although nothing has been heard about substantial Chinese assistance since then). Morgan Tsvangirai has also been blamed for not advocating the lifting of the targeted sanctions, a claim that the Mugabe clique increasingly, and without any formal justification, has put forward as a condition for implementing the remaining parts of the GPA—most likely running parallel with the drying-up of other dubious forms of income, such as diamond mining and farm grabbing.

The responses that Tsvangirai met on his tour are characteristic of the sentiments of most donor governments just six months after the formation of the unity government. Donor countries maintain a distinction between humanitarian and development assistance, and they are still caught in the dilemma between the humanitarian imperative and political realities. It should be recalled that the policy of granting humanitarian assistance to Zimbabwe under present circumstances is based upon the so-called *Hague Principles* drawn up in 2005 in connection with the guidelines for dealing with fragile states.[32] Any divergence from the Hague Principles would mean a major shift in policy, which could not be justified by the situation on the ground, characterized by the Mugabe regime's frequent return to the violation of human rights, misuses of the judiciary, farm grabbing, and outright disengagement from the GPA. The necessary regime change is far out in the horizon, while regime endurance seems to be the order of the day.

Hence it comes as no surprise that Minister of Finance Tendai Biti, in a speech to parliament in November 2009, summarized the actual situation by the following statement: "As I speak to you, we have failed to attract a single cent for budget support. The first thing that the donors ask is 'are you going to put our money through the central bank' and I have no answer to that."[33]

Humanitarian Plus—A Softening of the Donors' Dilemma

Soon after the formation of the unity government in February 2009, voices emerged, especially from the agencies, questioning whether the donor policy is the most suitable and responsible in view of the bleak and politically static situation in Zimbabwe. They argued that the time has come to move on and commit to taking risks against all omens from recent experiences. First, they argued, it is necessary to assist in a way that enables the GNU to deliver to the people and move the country forward out of the crisis. It is particularly necessary to support Prime Minster Tsvangirai and his MDC colleagues in order to give them sufficient means to realize their political goals. They have taken a risk in signing the GPA and entering the government, and they should be given a chance to justify their move and show that they are able to deliver and move things in a new direction that is different from the old Mugabe regime. In order to get this very difficult operation started right away—which cannot wait for the reform of various institutions such as the police and the judiciary—donors have to run the risk and involve themselves ahead of the reform process. The donors should engage in some kind of dialogue with the government and help to kick-start the democratic reform process. It is important that donor governments are proactive and make use of the breathing space that the unity government has created.[34]

The approach used to extend the humanitarian domain and narrow the gap between humanitarian and developmental assistance has been named *Humanitarian Plus*. In relation to Zimbabwe, the concept was first introduced by the International Crisis Group (ICG) in its April 2009 report, where they refer to the Humanitarian Plus program that the EU initiated in Sudan in 2002. The reason for naming the program Humanitarian Plus was its emphasis not only on immediate needs, but on medium-term operations that could bridge the gap between humanitarian and development funding.[35] In transferring the concept to Zimbabwe, the ICG has particularly emphasized that donors should move beyond humanitarian relief to reconstruction assistance and "help make the reform process irreversible" by engaging with the government.[36]

The same Humanitarian Plus aid strategy was soon after advocated with even greater authority by a group of eminent global leaders referred to as "The Elders."[37] With Archbishop Desmond Tutu as chairman and Kofi Annan, Jimmy Carter, and Graca Machel as members, the Elders wrote to eighteen donor countries and the EC, pleading with them to respond more swiftly, generously, and creatively to Zimbabwe's needs by providing Humanitarian Plus-type assistance. Now is not the time for donors to take a wait-and-see approach, but rather they should start bridging the gap between relief and longer-term development assistance. In Kofi Annan's words, "A rapid infusion of 'Humanitarian-Plus' resources is needed to help stabilize the country at this vulnerable stage of its recovery. Supporting the inclusive government to deliver better services will foster much needed change."[38] Similar strong support for the concept of Humanitarian Plus activities came soon thereafter in a revised appeal from humanitarian agencies, including UN organizations, in 2009.[39]

Parallel with the growing support for the Humanitarian Plus concept there was a growing awareness on the donor side of the need for a softening of policies based on the humanitarian imperative. Representatives from a number of EU countries had listened carefully to Morgan Tsvangirai's arguments and appeals, and in order to enable his government to keep up the momentum and to deliver to the people, they were open for more active engagement with the government by supporting other kinds of activities besides the humanitarian ones. The lead was taken by Danish minister for development Ulla Toernaes when she (to the surprise of other EU countries) paid a visit to Zimbabwe in March 2009. During meetings with both sides of the government, she discussed various areas of cooperation, while at the same time emphasized the urgent need to fully implement the GPA and get a wide-ranging reform process started.[40] The visit was followed by the release of US$18 million in grants for the education and health sectors and for food security.[41] In addition, the 2010 Danish aid budget allocated another US$20 million, with the specific aim of "supporting the democratic forces and [giving] Tsvangirai a chance to succeed."[42]

Support for the Danish initiative also came from other international donors when they attended an informal meeting on Zimbabwe called by Denmark and Norway. There was a general agreement that new approaches were needed by working through the government—"the risk by not engaging in the development of the country is greater than by supporting it." The suggested program is very similar to the Elders' Humanitarian Plus program, with the emphasis on medium term operations intended to bridge the gap between humanitarian and development funding, and on the need for an active engagement with the unity government.[43]

This means that not only are NGOs and UN agencies supporting the Humanitarian Plus initiative, but donor governments are also arguing in favor of expanding the program in accordance with the Humanitarian Plus concept, and thereby softening the principles otherwise guiding their dealings with the unity government. The fact that some governments are on the move may have been spurred by their respective diplomats in Harare, who have been calling on headquarters to consider a "strategic re-engagement" and not limit themselves to pure humanitarian aid.[44] It is not clear whether they would be willing to go as far as former South African finance minister Trevor Manuel recommended when he urged donors to go beyond humanitarian aid and inject cash directly into the treasury rather than through foreign agencies.[45] However, at least one government followed the many calls as only a few months later the Australian minister for foreign affairs claimed that "Australia was one of the first countries to deliver assistance in a manner that has become known as 'Humanitarian Plus.'"[46]

Toward a New Agenda?

As already pointed out, the responses that Prime Minister Tsvangirai received during his June 2009 visit to a number of Western governments did not indicate much willingness to listen to the calls for a change of policy by adopting the Humanitarian Plus concept. Over the following months, high-ranking officials from leading Western donors maintained the position outlined in the *Statement by Participants in Zimbabwe Like-Minded Meeting* in Washington in March 2009, in which they promised an increase in the current levels of humanitarian assistance. Further moves would be dependent on the implementation of the specific goals set out in the GPA, but in the meantime the international financial institutions should start developing an appropriate framework for reengagement.[47]

On the U.S. side, this policy of caution was confirmed by the outgoing ambassador to Zimbabwe in a wind-up interview and by newly appointed assistant secretary of state for Africa Johnnie Carson. The former referred specifically to the *Five Principles* from 2007[48] and refused to start a development assistance program or remove sanctions against Zimbabwe unless there was a verifiable movement on these principles.[49] Similarly, in his address to the Senate Committee on Foreign Relations, Johnnie Carson emphasized that in view of "the anti-democratic and abusive practices of Robert Mugabe and his followers"[50] the United States could not go much beyond the humanitarian aid directed through NGOs. The United States supported those working for the implementation of the GPA "without aiding those forces who cling to power through repression and corruption."[51] The difficult position in which the United States found itself was reiterated by the State Department a month later.[52]

On the EU side, high-level policy and decision makers expressed themselves in parallel terms. In May 2009, the incoming chair of the rotating EU presidency, Sweden, used the opportunity to translate the Five Principles into a number of requirements to be adhered to before any real reengagement could start; in the meantime, the like-minded donors were willing only to increase their humanitarian and technical support.[53] The EU position was repeated in an even stronger way during a visit to Zimbabwe by the European commissioner for development and the Swedish EU presidency in September 2009, the first official visit by a high-level EU delegation since the first sanctions were imposed in 2002. Sanctions were at the center of discussions and the EU representatives restated firmly that those sanctions not directed against the people of Zimbabwe would not be lifted before real progress was made toward the full implementation of the GPA.[54] A month later the European commissioner for development made it absolutely clear that lifting of the EU-targeted measures and reengagement in developmental aid would be clearly linked to progress "on the ground."[55]

In view of the positions clearly stated by the United States and the EU, it came as a surprise that only some weeks later, after a meeting in Berlin in late October 2009, a group of like-minded donors issued a statement that seemed to revise the six-month-old Washington statement. This opened up the question of whether there has been move toward a new agenda resulting from the repeated calls for policy change among agencies and donor governments.

Notably, local representatives from some of the donor governments seem to have exerted mounting pressure for the softening of the conditions required for a reengagement with the Zimbabwean government. Eleven bilateral donors in Harare, in addition to the EC, had for some time conducted a consultation process to review the operating environment and design a collective approach for providing assistance. While they all agreed on the Five Principles and were cautious of not feeding into the ZANU-PF patronage system, for example, by retaining the targeted sanctions, they nonetheless believed that "there is also a risk of doing too little." Hence, "consistent with the strongly unified position on the concept of 'Humanitarian Plus' of the donor community," they were conducting "some programming now under the rubric of humanitarian plus." But none of this was to be delivered either in the form of budget support, or directly through the government—a full development assistance program was considered premature.[56] It is interesting to observe that this transition to move beyond the humanitarian imperative very much reflected contemporary appeals from Prime Minister Tsvangirai, as he also called for a "move away from humanitarian support to development needs" and for the need to "expedite the EU's rapid dialogue."[57]

As a result of the mounting pressure, two features are of special interest in connection with the Berlin meeting of October 26, 2009. In the first place, seventeen states were present, as well as representatives from the EU and from the international financial institutions, including the African Development Bank (AfDB). These seventeen states, of which ten are EU member countries, all represent Western donors, while new donors, such as China, India, Brazil, and the regional power, South Africa, have not been invited. Second, this long-established donor group took the significant step of renaming themselves "the Friends of Zimbabwe," which in itself signals a change of direction.

In the *Declaration by Friends of Zimbabwe Group* there is an opening for reengagement and for working closer with the inclusive government in its task to implement the GPA and to build long-term stabilization and recovery. The new direction is outlined by the signatories: "we as a group have increased our support for the people of Zimbabwe, gradually shifting from measures aimed at purely humanitarian relief to substantial longer term assistance in a number of sectors."[58] While the targeted sanctions are not mentioned at all, the donors are not going as far as entering into a full reengagement—"at this point in time support is not distributed via the Government budget."[59]

Although the Berlin Declaration was held in diplomatic terms and was not widely publicized, it was seen as a significant change of donor policy. As the Declaration did not include a specific endorsement of the Humanitarian Plus concept, there was a need for an operational clarification, and as the sanctions were not mentioned, there was also a need for a clarification of which "political conditionalities" were still maintained by the donors. Regarding the first issue, as spokesman for the donor group, the German ambassador made it absolutely clear that Western countries had changed their engagement with the country's inclusive government during the past few months in response to greater political stability, and that the Friends of Zimbabwe Group, in the October meeting, had agreed to a new formula for shifting international funding toward developmental projects. As the sanctions did not allow government-to-government aid, donor support could not be lent through classical instruments, such as financial or budgetary aid. Instead, the money was to be held in a multi-donor trust fund administered by the WB, and assistance was to be provided for various infrastructure projects and the agriculture and education sectors. The donors also promised to reestablish lending rights from the IMF and the WB, and the German ambassador pointed to the implementation of the GPA and the completion of the constitutional and electoral processes as the road map for full engagement of the international community.[60]

Parallel with the growing engagement with the unity government on developmental issues, there was also a need to clarify whether regime change was still an item on the donors' agenda. Since sanctions were introduced in 2002, regime change had been seen as the essential element in changing the political realities in Zimbabwe, and calls for Robert Mugabe to vacate the presidency had been numerous over the years. As late as December 2008 the EU Council of Ministers called on Mugabe to step down,[61] and one of President Obama's first initiatives in relation to Africa was to call for a fresh approach to topple the regime.[62] But dissenting voices could also be heard. In June 2009, the outgoing U.S. ambassador to Zimbabwe stated, somewhat surprisingly, that regime change was not part of U.S. policy,[63] and in October, the ICG recommended that donor governments leave out regime change as an option.[64]

As the Berlin Declaration did not address the issue of regime change, the EU ambassador to Zimbabwe took the earliest opportunity to clarify this and other political issues at stake in the reengagement and normalization process. In plain language he stated, "There is no such thing as a regime change agenda." The EU was ready to reengage with the inclusive government of President Robert Mugabe and Prime Minister Morgan Tsvangirai. According to the agreed-upon methodology, Zimbabwe was to demonstrate GPA implementation through a road map, and the EU was to respond with its own road map of progressive normalization. The ambassador also distanced himself from the often-voiced accusation that "all the wrongs of this country are the result of illegal sanctions imposed by the West." They would be gradually lifted following progress of the normalization process.[65]

The statement about regime change signifies the extent to which donor governments adopted a new agenda and moved from earlier positions. Looking closer at the whole context, it becomes clear that donors have been influenced by a growing awareness that reengagement and support for the implementation of the GPA is the only solution to gradually bring Zimbabwe back to normal and avoid a chaotic alternative. The move away from the strategy of regime change has been influenced by Morgan Tsvangirai's strong appeals. His statement during his visit to the EU in Brussels that "although President Mugabe was part of Zimbabwe's problems, he was also key to solving the country's ten-year crisis" has been important in convincing donors to change the agenda by leaving out some items and include new ones.[66]

Lessons Learned

If we look at the development over the ten-year period examined in this chapter, it is a matter for discussion how big the donors' change of policy and strategy really is. The most significant change is connected with the softening of the dilemma between the humanitarian imperative and political realities. The forces at work have created a movement beyond traditional humanitarian work and an effort to bridge the gap between humanitarian and developmental assistance. There has been a parallel reassessment of political realities and a change of attitude toward political processes and actors in Zimbabwe, manifested both in the shelving of the demand for regime change, and by increasing engagement with the government. This leaves donors with two lessons regarding their chances of influence: First, external actors have to recognize that they cannot be the driving force, politically or economically, for a sustainable recovery process. There has to be a climate for genuine change and a committed leadership to ally with. Second, the carrot and stick strategy has its limitations. In the case of Zimbabwe, the employment of targeted sanctions has not produced any noticeable results. They have not served their purpose of driving the diehards to grant major concessions, nor did they produce any spirit of reconciliation. In fact, they have had the opposite effect by becoming a hot political issue, and the sanctions have shown themselves to be easy to introduce, but difficult to administer and even more difficult to lift.

The dilemma faced by donors over the years has not left much room for the start of a development program. A group of like-minded donors began to prepare a fully fledged aid program based on the rather detailed principles guiding international donor cooperation, with special emphasis on poverty reduction and sustainable growth, situated within a government-to-government framework. But the crisis situation and the need for matching conditionalities with political and economic realities have set narrow limits for any engagement with the government. In spite of the softening of the donors' dilemma, only little room is left for a traditional aid program based on a government-to-government model and for the employment of traditional instruments, such as budget support and sector-wide support.

This situation raises three issues for further consideration. The first is whether it is the best solution to think in terms of traditional aid programs in a crisis situation occurring in a weak and dysfunctional (if not fragile) state such as Zimbabwe. Will it not be more suitable to select other instruments directly geared toward rehabilitation and reconstruction of the existing, but weakened structures and institutions of the society?

This leads to the second issue. Which instrument is the best driver in such a situation: foreign investments or aid money? How should the linkage between the two be defined? Do they work together and supplement each other, or should one of them be given priority in creating an enabling environment for the other?

Finally, the last and wider issue: Who are the foreign actors? In discussing the issue of aid money, whatever the purpose may be, this chapter has examined the often like-minded donors, most significantly those who gathered at the Berlin meeting in October 2009. They represent a long-established aid regime, knitted together by the Paris Declaration, but are they the only relevant actors in connection with the reconstruction of Zimbabwe, and do they represent the world order of today and tomorrow? Missing in all the discussions have been South Africa, the regional power with special interests and strong capacities to assist Zimbabwe, and new donors such as China, which may bring new and nontraditional ideas to bear on the rebuilding of a conflict-ridden and weakened nation such as Zimbabwe.

Notes

1. Statement from Southern African Catholic Bishops' Conference, December 18, 2008.
2. The titles of two recent books illustrate the growing scepticism. The most critical position has been taken by the Zambian economist Dambisa Moyo in her book *Dead Aid: Why Aid is Not Working and How There is Another Way for Africa* (London: Allen Lane, 2009), whereas a collection of essays with the title *Africa Beyond Aid* reflects on the exit of donors and Africa's own potentials after the end of the present aid regime: Holger Bernt Hansen, Greg Mills, and Gerhard Wahlers, eds., *Africa Beyond Aid* (Johannesburg: Brenthurst Foundation, 2008).
3. The EU countries are fairly representative in this respect.
4. For a short summary of the Paris Declaration and for further references, see Guido Ashoff, "Implementing the Paris Declaration on Aid Effectiveness: Where Does Germany Stand?" Briefing Paper 5, German Development Institute, Bonn, 2008.
5. Cf. Annual Reports from the Danish Foreign Ministry.
6. For an outline of the Danish policy toward Zimbabwe in 2002, see Holger Bernt Hansen, "Partnership Visions and Realities: Donors, Democracy and Good Governance in the New Aid Regime," in *The New Partnership for Africa's Development (NEPAD). Internal and External Visions*, eds. Rachel Hayman, Kenneth King, and Simon McGrath (Edinburgh: Centre of African Studies, University of Edinburgh, 2003).
7. Lauren Ploch, "Zimbabwe" (RL 32723) *CRS Report for Congress,* Congressional Research Service, Washington, March 11, 2005.
8. In 2004 the new American ambassador to South Africa, Jendayi Frazer, called for the building of a "coalition of the willing" to push for regime change. See Peta Basildon, "US Seeks 'Coalition' to Force Zimbabwe Change," *The Independent,* August 25, 2004.
9. There are numerous reports about people going into exile, not least from the crossing point at Beitbridge. The most significant account of the number of people involved can be seen from the reports on the xenophobic attacks in South Africa in May 2008, for instance UN information agency *IRIN,* May 23, 2008.
10. Oral information from agencies. See also Ploch, "Zimbabwe" (RL 32723) *CRS Report for Congress,* 7.
11. Personal information from sources in Zimbabwe.
12. See "Zimbabwe's Mugabe Vows to Combat 'Regime Change,'" *Monsters and Critics,* February 24, 2007, http://monstersandcritics.com; and "Mugabe Blasts West for Seeking 'Regime Change,'" *Mail & Guardian,* June 3, 2008.
13. In Hany Besada, email to author, January 6, 2010, Mr. Besada, CIGI (Canada), gives a detailed outline of Zimbabwe's current political and economic engagement with China. See also Ian Taylor, *China's New Role in Africa* (Boulder, CO: Lynne Rienner, 2009); and Pádraig Carmody, *Globalization in Africa. Recolonization or Renaissance?* (Boulder, CO: Lynne Rienner, 2010), chapter 2.
14. Ingrid Melander, "EU Extends Zimbabwe Travel Ban, Demands Mugabe Quit," *Reuters,* December 9, 2008; and "EU Extends List of Banned Mugabe Allies and Companies," *Reuters,* January 23, 2009.
15. Examples are numerous in the government-owned newspaper *The Herald* from the period.
16. The position of Western governments in the postelection period has been summarized in Lauren Ploch, "Zimbabwe: The Power Sharing Agreement and Implications for U.S. Policy," RL 34509, *CRS Report for Congress,* Congressional Research Service, Washington, October 27, 2009.

17. Regarding the parallel between Kenya and Zimbabwe, see Holger Bernt Hansen, "Elections in Kenya and Zimbabwe: Similarities and Paradoxes" (in Danish), *udenrigs* (the Danish foreign policy magazine) no. 2 (2008).

18. The donor position has been summarized in Ploch, "Zimbabwe: The Power Sharing Agreement."

19. For an overview of documents and plans dealing with an economic recovery in Zimbabwe, see Brent Cloete and Greg Mills, "Scan of Zimbabwe Economic Recovery Literature," Brenthurst Discussion paper 4, Johannesburg, April 2009.

20. The group is named the Fishmongers after the restaurant where they regularly meet. The eleven members are from ten countries and the European Commission. See press release from the Swedish development agency SIDA, May 2009.

21. Drafted in January 2005 by a Senior Level Forum on Development Effectiveness in Fragile States under the auspices of OECD/DAC and field tested in nine countries before the endorsement in 2007. OECD, *Principles for Good Engagement in Fragile States and Situations*, Paris, 2007.

22. OECD, "Principles for Effective International Engagement in Zimbabwe," Interim Country Report, Paris, 2006. The pilot was carried out by a core donor group including the main donors active in Zimbabwe. For the overall pilot project, see Oxford Policy Management, "Support to Piloting the Principles for Good International Engagement in Fragile States," Synthesis Report, Oxford, September 2006.

23. For a useful account of the donors' response to the protracted crisis, see Kate Bird and Stefanie Busse, "Re-thinking Aid Policy in Response to Zimbabwe's Protracted Crisis," Overseas Development Institute Discussion Paper, London, 2007.

24. Three representatives from the Fishmongers (Australia, The Netherlands, and the United Kingdom) presented the provisional program at the Zimbabwe Reconstruction Workshop in Johannesburg, October 2–3, 2008, organized by Hany Besada, the Centre for International Governance Innovation (CIGI) and Nicky Moyo, Development Enterprise Africa Trust (CEAT).

25. The plans for such a meeting were advertised at the conference in October, but to my knowledge it has not taken place probably influenced by the continued stalemate in the situation in Zimbabwe.

26. It is difficult to establish the exact figures for the humanitarian assistance. The United States raised its assistance by 40 percent from 2008 to 2009 and by 30 percent in the budget request for 2010. See Lauren Ploch, "Zimbabwe: The Power Sharing Agreement and Implications for U.S. Policy," RL 34509, *CRS Report for Congress*. The EU has as the biggest donor raised its contributions accordingly.

27. Denmark has been a lead donor in this respect, but most other donors have followed suit not least after appeals from the minster of education David Coltart.

28. An excellent overview has been provided by the Zimbabwean economist John Robertson in his paper "The Zimbabwe Economy. Rebuilding Productive Activity" (presented at the AEGIS International Africa Conference in Leipzig, Germany, June 4–7, 2009). See also Stuart Doran, "Zimbabwe's Economy: A 2009 Report Card," Brenthurst Discussion Paper 8, Johannesburg, October 2009.

29. As of April 2009 only US$400 million have been pledged in credit lines by African governments according to "Mid-Year Review/Revision. Consolidated Appeal for Zimbabwe from Humanitarian Partners," Office for the Coordination of Humanitarian Affairs, Geneva, May 2009, 3.

30. A *Reuters* article dated June 22, 2009, summarizes the results of Tsvangirai's tour to United States and Europe. He did get some extra money in "transitional support," but to be distributed via the charities and UN agencies. See also *Reuters,* June 30, 2009.

31. *Reuters,* June 30, 2009.

32. See OECD, "Principles for Effective International Engagement in Zimbabwe," 2006.

33. *Reuters,* November 10, 2009.

34. A good example of the call on donor governments to involve themselves more directly in the reform process by engaging with the unity government is the report from the Zimbabwean office of MS Action Aid Denmark *Breathing Space. Zimbabwe's Golden Opportunity for Reform?* (Copenhagen, October 2009). Other humanitarian agencies too support the need to go beyond pure humanitarian efforts, cf. policy briefing from International Crisis Group, "Zimbabwe: Engaging the Inclusive Government," April 20, 2009, 11.

35. The European Commission's Delegation to the Sudan, *Humanitarian Plus Program (HPP)* (note dated, presumably 2007). "Aide-Mémoire—Donor Models to Funding Transition," prepared for the Second International Meeting on Good Humanitarian Donorship, October 21–22, 2004.

36. See International Crisis Group, "Zimbabwe: Engaging the Inclusive Government," April 20, 2009, 10.

37. The Elders are a group of global leaders brought together by Nelson Mandela in July 2007 who offer their experience and independent voices to support the resolution of conflict and the alleviation of human suffering.

38. Alice Chimora, "Zimbabwe: The Elders Intervene in Humanitarian Crisis," May 8, 2009, http://en.afrik.com/article15664.

39. Dated May 29, 2009, see "Mid-Year Review/Revision," Office for the Coordination of Humanitarian Affairs, May 2009, 3.

40. Press release from the Danish Foreign Ministry March 13, 2009. The Danish minister's surprise visit was covered even by the correspondent from the Chinese press agency Xinhua, March 18, 2009.

41. Press release from the Danish Foreign Ministry, June 12, 2009; see also *Reuters,* June 17, 2009, on Tsvangirai's visit to Denmark.

42. *Priorities in the Danish Government's Development Policy 2010–2014,* Copenhagen. Danish Foreign Ministry, August 2009.

43. Press release from the Danish Foreign Ministry, April 26, 2009.

44. See International Crisis Group, "Zimbabwe: Engaging the Inclusive Government."

45. *Mail and Guardian,* March 22, 2009, cf. Crisis Group, *Zimbabwe...,* 11.

46. Australian minister for foreign affairs, speech at the annual Australian Council for International Development dinner, Canberra, October 28, 2009.

47. U.S. Department of State, Bureau of Public Affairs, March 27, 2009. The meeting was held on March 20 and attended by twenty-four donors including the international financial institutions and the United Nations. Regarding the IFIs activities in Zimbabwe the vice president for the Africa Region in the World Bank emphasized at a press conference on May 22, 2009, that the right conditions had not yet been created for a reengagement with the government, and that humanitarian assistance was currently been provided through NGOs and aid agencies.

48. See OECD, *Principles for Good Engagement in Fragile States and Situations,* Paris, 2007; OECD, "Principles for Effective International Engagement in Zimbabwe," 2006; Oxford Policy Management, "Support to Piloting the Principles," September 2006; and World Bank (Harare Office), *Operational Guidelines. Zimbabwe Multi-Donor Trust Fund,* July 1, 2008. The Hague Principles are in Zimbabwe called the Five Principles.

49. James McGee (Ambassador), interviewed by Violet Gonda, Nehanda Radio, SW Radio Africa transcript June 23, 2009.

50. Johnnie Carson, opening remarks from hearing in Senate Committee on Foreign Relations, Washington, September 30, 2009.

51. Ibid.

52. Ian Kelly, State Department spokesman, Daily Press Briefing, October 7, 2009.

53. Press release from the Swedish International Development Agency (SIDA), May 2009.

54. Press releases from the European Commission, September 10 and 13, 2009, and from the Embassy of Sweden in Harare September 12, 2009.

55. Press release from the European Commission, October 16, 2009.

56. For a full account of the consultations among donor representatives in Harare and their activities in accordance with the concept of *Humanitarian Plus*, see the Testimony to Senate Committee on Foreign Relations by USAID Acting Assistant Administrator, September 30, 2009.

57. Morgan Tsvangirai, interview with *African Free Press,* October 9, 2009, during a visit to Spain to receive an award.

58. The Declaration was published by the German Ministry of Foreign Affairs, October 26, 2009 (http://aktion-europa.diplo.de) and by the U.S. State Department, October 30, 2009. See also *Times Live* (Johannesburg), November 2, 2009.

59. Ibid.

60. Media briefing from December 4, 2009, printed in *The New African Times* and *VOA News*; and printed in *The Standard,* December 5, 2009, and in *Daily News,* December 8, 2009.

61. *Xinhua News Agency,* December 8, 2009.

62. *The Times* (London), January 28, 2009.

63. Interview, June 23, 2009. See OECD, *Principles for Good Engagement in Fragile States and Situations*, Paris, 2007; OECD, "Principles for Effective International Engagement in Zimbabwe," 2006; Oxford Policy Management, "Support to Piloting the Principles," September 2006; and World Bank (Harare Office), *Operational Guidelines. Zimbabwe Multi-Donor Trust Fund*, July 1, 2008. The Hague Principles are called the Five Principles in Zimbabwe.

64. International Crisis Group, *CrisisWatch,* October 1 and November 1, 2009.

65. Opening remarks from Ambassador Xavier Marchal at a seminar on Economic Partnership Agreements, December 10, 2009. The remarks on regime change caught the headline in the Chinese *People's Daily Online,* December 10, 2009.

66. German ambassador in media briefing, December 4, 2009. See the Testimony to Senate Committee on Foreign Relations by USAID Acting Assistant Administrator, September 30, 2009.

Chapter 13

South Africa's Role in Providing Development Assistance to Zimbabwe

Policy Options and Strategies

Steven Gruzd, George Katito, and Elizabeth Sidiropoulos

Introduction

South Africa has played many roles in the complex and multifaceted relationship with its neighbor across the Limpopo River—apartheid-era antagonist, liberation-struggle comrade, financial investor, electricity supplier, chief trading partner in Africa, endorser-in-chief of questionable elections, protector in international forums, and conflict mediator—and is now poised to take on a new role of development partner in reconstructing Zimbabwe.

The long history between South Africa and Zimbabwe arguably entered a new era when the political power-sharing deal known as the Global Political Agreement (GPA) was signed in September 2008. Under the agreement, the Zimbabwe African National Union-Patriotic Front (ZANU-PF), Zimbabwe's ruling party since 1980, committed to a division of key government functions between itself and the two factions of the Movement for Democratic Change (MDC), following controversial and inconclusive elections in March and June 2008. South Africa brokered the GPA, under the mediation of former South African president Thabo Mbeki, on behalf of the Southern African Development Community (SADC). The GPA provides for a broad range of political, social, and economic changes—foremost among them commitments to constitutional reform, redress of Zimbabwe's controversial land reform policy, and the removal of economic sanctions.

Indeed, within the first one hundred working days of the Government of National Unity (GNU),[1] Pretoria mooted the possibility of enacting a broad range of interventions to lend budgetary support to buttress Zimbabwe's economy as it recovered from a decade of economic decline. South Africa indicated an interest in making finances available to revitalize Zimbabwe's crumbling physical infrastructure, on condition that Zimbabwe's economy exhibit compelling evidence of improved governance and robust recovery.[2]

Unsurprisingly, however, the implementation of the GPA has been marked with contention and deep rifts. It took three months, from the controversial presidential run-off poll in June to September 2008, for the parties to sign the GPA, and then a further five months for MDC leader Morgan Tsvangirai to be inaugurated as prime minister in February 2009. Disagreement erupted over the formation of a National Security Council, partly owing to the unwillingness of conservative sections of Zimbabwe's security forces to acknowledge the joint leadership of Tsvangirai. Similar clashes developed over the appointment of provincial governors and other key posts. Article 6 of the GPA,[3] calling for constitutional reform, has been equally divisive as the coalition partners clash over the politics and process of reforming Zimbabwe's constitution.

Nonetheless, South Africa's hopes are pinned on the successful implementation of the GPA, not only because it played a key role in negotiating this deal, but also because reconstructing Zimbabwe's economy must be a priority for South Africa's own stability and prosperity. Despite efforts such as the Great Limpopo Transfrontier Park, operated jointly between South Africa, Mozambique, and Zimbabwe to promote tourism and animal migration, meltdown in Zimbabwe has hampered most attempts at regional integration[4] and has had profound consequences in South Africa in terms of migration, health (through repeated foot-and-mouth disease and cholera outbreaks), commerce, and diplomacy. Arguably the most poignant illustration of the impact that Zimbabwe's economic decline has had on its southern neighbor was the eruption of xenophobic violence across South Africa in May 2008. The events left at least sixty-two people dead, hundreds injured, and thousands displaced.[5] For several observers, the outburst of violence targeted at other African nationals was fueled by the increasing influx of economic immigrants—an estimated three million of whom are believed to be Zimbabwean.[6] Large immigration flows, this line of thinking would argue, exacerbate conflict among various working class communities competing for access to severely strained economic resources and social services.

However, should the coalition in Zimbabwe hold, it may vindicate the years of criticism that former president Thabo Mbeki endured for his policy of "quiet diplomacy"[7] toward President Robert Mugabe and create conducive conditions for Zimbabweans in South Africa to return home.

This chapter will trace the history of South Africa as an emerging donor in Africa, its plans to assist in the recovery of a post-settlement Zimbabwe, and some of the challenges it is likely to face.

The Development of Development Assistance in South Africa

The notion of South Africa as a development partner may seem counterintuitive. After all, like almost every other African country, South Africa has been a recipient of development assistance since the early 1990s. Between 1999 and 2005, it received US$4 billion in donor aid.[8] Its liberation movements in exile—the African National Congress (ANC) and Pan-Africanist Congress (PAC)[9]—depended on contributions from eastern European states in the Soviet era, and (mainly) progressive European states and institutions. The strength and diversity of the South African economy and its prudent economic management, however, mean that Pretoria is much less dependent on external aid than many other states on the continent, with development assistance making up only about 1 percent of Gross Domestic Product (GDP),[10] compared to approximately 10 percent in Mozambique, Ethiopia, and Uganda in 2008.[11]

Like other emerging powers around the world, such as China, India, and Brazil, South Africa has been growing its investment and assistance within its immediate neighborhood and beyond. The country's efforts to mediate the protracted conflict in the Democratic Republic of Congo that began in 1997 vividly demonstrate its strategically driven foreign policy. The peace deal brokered by South Africa in December 2002 not only created conducive conditions for investment by its telecommunications giant Mobile Telephone Networks (MTN) and other key commercial South African interests, but also for the firms of other countries, especially in mining.

Apartheid-Era Support: Trying to Win Friends and Influence Countries

Pumping money into the continent is not just a postapartheid phenomenon.[12] From the early 1960s when British prime minister Harold Macmillan identified the winds of change blowing independence to former colonies in Africa, the apartheid state recognized that financial support might win it friends and buy it influence in the United Nations (UN) General Assembly, and/or prevent the liberation movements from using newly independent states as military bases. Prime Minister B.J. Vorster's outward bound policy of the late 1960s was predicated precisely on this notion of buying friendship from the few countries, such as Kamuzu Banda's Malawi, that were in the market.

Malawi's sprawling new capital, Lilongwe, was largely built with South African money, evident in the austere apartheid-era architecture of the government compound on Capital Hill and its airport. Other countries that received economic support in this largely failed policy included the Comoros, Côte d'Ivoire, Equatorial Guinea, Gabon, and Lesotho. This development assistance fell under the *Economic Co-operation Promotion Loan Fund Act* of 1968, and was also used to fund development projects, construction of government buildings, and employment creation schemes in the homelands, the quasi-independent ethnic statelets created under grand apartheid. A chief directorate in South Africa's former Department of Foreign Affairs [DFA; renamed the Department of International Relations and Cooperation (DIRCO) in May 2009], the Development Assistance Programme (DAP) managed this project-related support, generated by direct requests from recipient countries or the homelands for technical and other forms of development assistance. Subsequently, the act formed the basis of an amended 1998 document of the same name that stipulated the allocation of unused loan amounts into South Africa's National Revenue Fund.

Augmenting an African Renaissance

The DAP continued after the political transition in 1994; but it was replaced in 2000 by the African Renaissance and International Co-operation Fund (ARF), which was shaped to reflect the new priorities and direction of South Africa's foreign policy, the latter having a strong African focus. President Thabo Mbeki, who succeeded Nelson Mandela in 1999, promoted the idea of an African Renaissance, which sought "to build [a new African world which] is one of democracy, peace and stability, sustainable development and a better life for the people, non-racism and non-sexism, equality among the nations and a just and democratic system of international governance."[13]

The ARF's key sectors reflect central aims of the country's foreign policy:

- Cooperation between South Africa and other countries;
- promotion of democracy and good governance;
- conflict prevention and resolution;
- socioeconomic development and integration;
- humanitarian assistance; and
- human resource development.[14]

However, the ARF comprises only a fraction of South Africa's overall development assistance—just an estimated 3.8 percent in 2002, 3.3 percent in 2004, and 3 percent in 2009.[15] Research undertaken by the South African Institute of International Affairs (SAIIA) in 2006 and 2007 indicated that in fact at least half of South African national government departments—apart from DFA/DIRCO—were active in various African endeavors, using funds from their own budgets and considerably exceeding the funds provided by the ARF. According to Braude, Thandrayan, and Sidiropoulos, "ARF spending was R50 million in 2003–2004 and 2004–2005, R100 million in 2005–2006, R150 million in 2006–2007 and R215 million in 2007–2008. The estimated allocation by the [then] Department of Foreign Affairs [alone] in 2008–2009 [was] R275.9 million."[16] They also note, "South Africa paid 15 percent of the total AU budget from January 2006, an increase from 8.2 percent. These contributions totaled R155 million in 2006, and R161 million in 2007, and [were] expected to increase to R172.5 million in 2008."[17]

As Sidiropoulos notes,

Although not regarded as a "donor" and objecting to the moniker, under President Mbeki South Africa built up a sizeable outreach to African countries in the form of development co-operation. However, apart from the Fund, the government is only now beginning to put in place an overarching framework for this development co-operation, which has been proliferating across many government departments.[18]

Indeed, South Africa's preferred term is *development partner*, to connote equity and play down fears that it will try to dominate other states economically or politically—given its far more advanced economy, the potential for neoimperialist accusations, and its apartheid-era history of militarily attacking neighboring states that supported liberation movements. On a symbolic level, the change of its foreign affairs department's name to the Department of International Relations and Cooperation is largely attributed to South Africa's eagerness to emphasize its preference to act in partnership with African and other states in its foreign policy. More substantively, the government has indicated its commitment to establishing a South African Developmental Partnership Agency (SADPA), which will focus on building development partnerships as the basis of South Africa's development policy framework.

There is currently no single agency driving South Africa's overall development assistance efforts, which are instead split between three main groupings:

1. The ARF, which operates out of DIRCO.
2. Other government departments (spearheaded by the Departments of Defence, Education, Safety and Security, Minerals and Energy, Trade and Industry, but also including Agriculture, Justice, and Constitutional Development, Arts and Culture, Public Service and Administration, Public Enterprises, Public Works, and Science and Technology).
3. A collection of statutory bodies, agencies, and parastatal companies [including the Development Bank of Southern Africa (DBSA), Independent Electoral Commission (IEC), Industrial Development Corporation, Human Sciences Research Council (HSRC), National Research Fund (NRF), and the South African Management Development Institute (SAMDI)].

In 2006, the National Treasury undertook a mapping exercise to identify the volume and locus of assistance provided outside South Africa by various government ministries. In the absence of an overarching policy framework for development assistance, the research undertaken found that the monitoring of development assistance disbursements lacked rigor: there was no central database tracking disbursements, no overarching aid strategy, no separate reporting on development assistance in departmental budget lines, and no operational guidelines outside the ARF. This diffuse system and lack of institutional memory makes precise research on figures and, indeed, the effects and impact of aid difficult to ascertain.[19] However, the National Treasury is exemplary in its system for tracking incoming development assistance,[20] and the division responsible, the International Development Co-operation Chief Directorate, plans to develop a similar system to track outgoing funds. Nevertheless, to do this effectively will require the adoption of a coherent and uniform system across all government departments, with clearly articulated objectives.[21]

A trend of trilateral assistance—where South Africa and Western donors work together in a third African country—is also gaining importance since the model pioneered the delivery of flood relief to Mozambique in 2000. This proposed trilateral approach to development assistance could be particularly crucial in providing assistance to Zimbabwe, given that the rocky start to Zimbabwe's GNU has not eliminated traditional donors' mistrust. In a June 2009 trip to raise funds by Zimbabwe's prime minister Morgan Tsvangirai, various potential development partners [among them the United States of America and members of the European Union (EU) such as Germany and Sweden] expressed reluctance to engage bilaterally with Zimbabwe as democratic conditions remained unsatisfactory.[22]

China's increased interest in Africa's resources has made it an important player on the continent. Its policy of noninterference in other countries' internal affairs, including governance issues, means that China has put fewer political conditions on its investments and assistance to African governments than traditional donors, providing a lifeline to beleaguered regimes such as the ZANU-PF. In July 2009, China extended US$950 million in credit lines to Zimbabwe, the largest loan secured by Harare's GNU up until that point.[23] South Africa's engagement with Zimbabwe will, therefore, increasingly occur in a competitive context—where Chinese aid and business interests could prove more agile and proactive in contributing to Zimbabwe's reconstruction.

Toward a South African Development Partnership Agency

A move toward a more entrenched development assistance system in South Africa—to address some of the weaknesses identified here—was discussed at the ANC's fifty-second National Conference in Polokwane, Limpopo Province, in December 2007 (building on a policy conference held in June 2007).[24] The *Polokwane Resolutions* on international relations encourage African self-sufficiency in financial assistance, focusing on strengthening the Pan-African Infrastructure Development Fund (PAIDF), launched to generate capital of US$1 billion from the private sector and African governments. The PAIDF is a large-scale, long-term fund managed by the South African firm Harith, aimed not only at driving infrastructural development through governments across the continent, but also at seeking to promote private-public partnerships toward the same goal.[25] Many viewed the fund as an important instrument for reaching the Millennium Development Goals (MDGs) on the continent and the start of weaning Africa off (non-African) aid. The policy document states:

> The idea of a Developmental Partnership is one of the key strategies that could assist the ANC and government in pursuit of our vision for a better Africa. The Development Partnership will enhance our agenda on international relations which rests on three pillars namely; (i) consolidation of the African agenda, (ii) South-South and (iii) North-South cooperation. The national budgetary processes should commit the necessary resources to such a developmental partnership. The fund should be

located in the Department of Foreign Affairs as is the current situation, functioning as the African Renaissance Fund.[26]

Braude, Thandrayan, and Sidiropoulos[27] estimate that in 2006 total development assistance from South Africa may have amounted to between R3 billion and R5 billion (US$360 million and 600 million), including transfers of approximately R2 billion to the Southern African Customs Union (SACU) in the higher figure.[28] This would put assistance at between 0.18 and 0.29 percent of GDP in that year. In the discussion document for the Polokwane Resolutions, the ANC proposed pegging assistance at between 0.2 and 0.5 percent of GDP, which would make South Africa proportionately one of the most generous countries in the world, and suggests a doubling or tripling of current levels.[29]

The new administration in South Africa has expressed its commitment to implementing the Polokwane Resolutions. In June 2009, DIRCO announced the establishment of the South African Development Partnership Agency (SADPA), which will possess a similar mandate to the ARF and various government departments in supporting both South Africa's engagement with Africa, and the work of traditional donors seeking to engage with the continent on a trilateral basis.[30] SADPA will presumably build on a draft white paper on development assistance, itself partly based on the review conducted by the National Treasury in 2006 of development assistance provided by different ministries to other African states.

However, with the global recession, significant political changes in South Africa, and most importantly, renewed commitment to increase domestic spending on social services as a developmental state,[31] South Africa could face formidable challenges to the delivery of funds needed to be a serious development partner, despite its low national debt levels.

Some officials feel that there should be a more direct advantage for South Africa from the country's peacemaking, capacity building, and financial assistance in Africa. Deputy Minister of International Relations and Cooperation Sue van der Merwe, in a June 2009 speech, discounted the premise that South Africa's foreign policy should be primarily altruistic, and instead underscored that the key drivers of foreign policy should be South Africa's national interest and the economic and social needs of its citizens. Indeed, Pretoria's actual engagement with Zimbabwe strongly suggests that Zimbabwe-South African relations are driven by self-interest. In 1998, Pretoria signed a bilateral trade agreement with Harare, ostensibly to facilitate free trade between the two countries, but, in effect, also to protect and entrench South African capital and secure South Africa's corporate interests in Zimbabwe's extractive industries. Sidiropoulos writes, "This [regional engagement] usually implies greater economic and political influence for South Africa in other African countries, and some South Africans see development cooperation as one means to create greater leverage."[32]

Interestingly, on Zimbabwe, the Polokwane Conference simply stated, "The people of Zimbabwe in the main would find a solution to their current problems. The conference expressed support for South Africa's mediation effort as mandated by the SADC region."[33] In comparison, ten paragraphs were devoted to Western Sahara and nine to Palestine.

Rebuilding Zimbabwe: South Africa's Choices

There is clearly an economic and political imperative for South Africa—the government, the private sector, and civil society—to participate actively in rebuilding Zimbabwe. If the GPA negotiated by Thabo Mbeki is successfully implemented, it will be the first step in beginning the reconstruction process, provided it allows for the return of the rule of law and the normalization of the political environment.

South Africa has been developing engagement plans for Zimbabwe for some time, although they are not yet freely available in the public domain. The Polokwane Resolutions' mention of Zimbabwe echoes similar, albeit scanty, sentiments in the Department of Foreign Affairs' Strategic Plan for 2008–2011. In her introduction, former foreign minister Nkosazana Dlamini-Zuma wrote:

> We certainly and furthermore will pursue the mandate given to us by SADC to assist the sister peoples of Zimbabwe to find a speedy resolution to their political and economic challenges moving from the understanding that only the people of Zimbabwe acting with the support of the region can find a resolution to their challenges.[34]

The only other significant mention of Zimbabwe in this plan is:

> South Africa will play a role in the socio-economic development of Zimbabwe within the framework of the SADC Plan and through the structured bilateral mechanisms that exist between the two countries…South Africa will strengthen its co-operation with Namibia, Botswana and Zimbabwe in Joint Commissions on Defence and Security in pursuit of regional peace, security and stability.[35]

Now that it seems that the settlement is entrenched, any direct financial assistance that South Africa might provide is likely to be dwarfed by that of traditional multilateral and bilateral donors if they can overcome a decade of hostility by President Mugabe. In 2008, the European Commission (EC) pledged to commit €64 million, in line with the Organisation for Economic Co-operation and Development (OECD) Principles for Effective International Engagement with Zimbabwe—focused on a broad range of sectors (including agriculture and food security, for which €25 million was earmarked—for democratic governance and community development.[36]

The International Monetary Fund (IMF), World Bank (WB), African Development Bank (AfDB), and the UN Development Fund established a Multi-Donor Trust Fund, which has carried out analytical work and that might be a channel for managing aid to Zimbabwe, although apparently only US$5 million has been contributed thus far.[37] Various commitments from European countries and the United States in June 2009 totaled US$500 million, with the prospect of further aid pledges conditional upon the unity government's success.[38] Notably, pledges of assistance are largely on condition that aid is channeled through aid agencies as opposed to Zimbabwe's central bank. Proponents of this stance applaud this approach as a means of ensuring that aid reaches its intended recipients. Skeptical observers view the approach as a strategy that grants nongovernmental organizations (NGOs) and foreign governments a disproportionately large influence over Zimbabwe's internal politics.[39] Aid channeled to Zimbabwe through NGOs might indeed come under increasing scrutiny and attack from within the GNU. Furthermore, any assistance not already fully budgeted and passed through parliaments might be less substantial than envisaged in the context of the global economic slump. Finally, the engrained antipathy between the ZANU-PF and these Western powers will not evaporate overnight.

While South Africa could never match these amounts, its role as a development partner can be significant in other respects. Among other functions, South Africa could increasingly play a vital role in driving Zimbabwe's monetary policy—given Zimbabwe's adoption of a multiple currency regime in which the South African rand is a key medium of exchange. Zimbabwe's industry and commerce minister Welshman Ncube has mooted the prospect of Zimbabwe joining the Common Monetary Area.[40]

Furthermore, a medium term option that could see South Africa's role in Zimbabwe expand further is the latter's possible integration into the SACU.[41] Unfortunately, the South African Treasury would face an uphill battle convincing fellow SACU member states Namibia, Lesotho, and Swaziland of the merits of this approach; and joining the SACU and/or the Common Monetary Area would mean Zimbabwe effectively ceding autonomy over its monetary policy.

The most crucial and feasible role that South Africa could assume would be to act as a catalyst to encourage the South African private sector to invest heavily in the reconstruction of Zimbabwe. As the research by Dianna Games shows, the two economies are already heavily intertwined. In 2005, twenty-seven companies listed on the Johannesburg Securities Exchange (JSE) had Zimbabwean operations, 60 percent of the listed companies on the Zimbabwe Stock Exchange (ZSE) were from South Africa, and South African corporations owned or part owned over 90 percent of Zimbabwean platinum mines.[42] South Africa has traditionally been the top export destination for Zimbabwean goods and with the economic meltdown in Zimbabwe, there has been enormous demand for South African imports.[43] Furthermore, two of the largest investors in Zimbabwe are the South African-based Implats Group, via a controlling stake in Zimplats, and the South African-listed mining house Anglo Platinum, which has a 51 percent controlling stake in the Unki Mine in southern Zimbabwe.[44] In 2006, Implats ceded 36 percent of its shares to the Zimbabwean government in return for a license to undertake a long-delayed expansion of output from its current ninety thousand ounces per year. In 2007, the operating profits of Implats' Zimbabwean-controlled operations were close to US$150 million, and in its 2007 annual report to shareholders, Implats indicated that its Zimbabwean operations represented the ultimate "blue sky" growth opportunity for the company over the long term.[45]

While South African companies might have ring fenced their Zimbabwean operations in the hyper-inflationary environment and written off or mothballed operations, they have not disinvested, believing that a political settlement will eventually be solidified, and that the Zimbabwean economy will bounce back to become profitable. They are thus well-poised to reengage given the right political and economic conditions. Of South Africa's forty major companies, twenty-seven still hold a presence in the country according to director of Development Enterprise Africa Trust, Nicky Moyo. Arguably, this attests to a conservative South African approach to doing business that could augur well for stimulating investment in Zimbabwe's economy. In other contexts, such as Mozambique, South African businesses, and most notably energy giant SASOL have been willing to reengage in investment at the first signs of improved country credit ratings. At this point, it is unclear whether the South African government has any formal policies to stimulate investment.

South Africa's formidable parastatal companies in the energy sector—Eskom, for example—could also play a potentially catalytic role in a post-settlement Zimbabwe, where there are untapped gas, coal, and uranium supplies. Zimbabwe's proven gas reserves in the south, for example, could supply the SADC's energy needs if the reserves are commercially viable to exploit. At the least, the parastatals could play a critical role in injecting capital into the resuscitation of its energy sector; however, in interviews in late 2008, senior Eskom officials pointed out that South Africa did not currently have any specific strategy in place to boost Zimbabwe's energy generation capacity. They also claimed that South Africa's formidable domestic energy security constraints would remain the main area of focus for the utility.

Since early 2004, following a cabinet decision to allow Eskom to increase domestic generation capacity (which reversed a previous moratorium on new, local capital investments), Eskom has substantially reduced its business footprint in Africa. At the time, Eskom enterprises had a presence in about thirty-five African countries (such as Mali and Uganda), in areas such as consulting, engineering, managing power utilities, and various power-related joint ventures. Today, it has refocused primarily on southern Africa. Eskom has a long-standing agreement with the Zimbabwe Electricity Supply Authority (ZESA)—known as a non-firm purchase and sale agreement—which gives South Africa a large degree of discretion as to whether it trades electricity with Zimbabwe. Given the domestic electricity shortfalls in South Africa and Zimbabwe's profound economic problems, including dramatic foreign currency shortages and hyperinflation, Eskom has neither sold electricity to Zimbabwe, nor bought power from it for three years.

The prospects of Eskom investing in Zimbabwe will depend on an improved country credit rating, decreased investment risk, and likely the leveraging of capital from development finance institutions.[46] These prospects are linked to an economic turnaround in the country and increased foreign investment, expected fruits of a genuine political settlement, and international reengagement. The business case—as opposed to the political case—will have to be sound. Zimbabwe's strategic geographic position as a conduit for electricity supply to the region could also nudge South Africa's Eskom to play a pronounced role in the reconstruction of a post-settlement Zimbabwe.[47]

In the medium to long term, South Africa is likely to drive and pursue multilateral engagement through the SADC or other multi-donor arrangements with the Development Bank of Southern Africa (DBSA) or the AfDB. For example, at a special SADC Summit on March 30, 2009, Zimbabwe reportedly requested US$10 billion.

One month later, South Africa and Botswana had reportedly pledged "credit lines and budget support of US$800 million and US$70 million respectively," with US$200 million pledged by both SADC and the Common Market for Eastern and Southern Africa (COMESA), but other states involved said they "need[ed] more time to consult."[48]

Focus on Food Security

In the short term, the South African government has identified food security and agriculture as the foci of its planned interventions. The immediate resuscitation of this sector is recognized as extremely important as the country can then begin to address the challenge of food security, as well as the rebuilding of Zimbabwe's export base. Reviving agriculture, although fraught with its own difficulties, not the least of which will be the adoption of a well-thought-out land policy dealing with the shortcomings of the past and present land use configurations, will also play a significant catalyzing role for the whole economy.

In Zimbabwe, agriculture accounted for 18 percent of GDP and 41 percent of total exports in 1998.[49] In the following seven years, due to a combination of drought, productivity declines, and the controversial fast-track land reform program, this sector contracted by half, and between 65 and 80 percent of Zimbabweans are now dependent on food aid.[50] South Africa believes critical interventions are needed to revitalize the agricultural sector and foster food security, to mitigate the effects of successive droughts, poor investment in production, and inadequate equipment, and to provide inputs that cannot be purchased with Zimbabwe's worthless currency.

The October 2008 *Medium-Term Budget Policy Statement* (MTBPS) delivered by then South African finance minister Trevor Manuel explicitly mentioned R300 million to assist Zimbabwe. He said: "Madam Speaker, the adjustments budget also makes provision for R300 million to assist in meeting Zimbabwe's short term food requirements, subject to acceptance of an appropriate role for international food relief agencies by a recognised multi-party government."[51] Though short on detail, it suggests that the South African government felt that the time was right to make a considerable sum available for food security in Zimbabwe, as (at the time) the MTBPS followed on the heels of the deal signed by the ZANU-PF and both MDC factions in September 2008. This agreement would later form the basis of Zimbabwe's incumbent unity government. Subsequently, however, South Africa reversed the precondition for aid, citing the urgency of humanitarian need in Zimbabwe.[52] In December 2008, South Africa announced its decision to disburse agricultural and humanitarian assistance worth an estimated R300 million through a Zimbabwean nonpartisan coalition of civil society and public and private sector representatives.[53] Apparently the SADC was to play an oversight role with regard to the mechanism, and it had embarked on disbursing agricultural inputs to Zimbabwe in early January 2009.[54] However, other reports suggest this organizational structure was never properly implemented.

Support... With Strings Attached

South Africa's intention to extend substantial financial assistance to Zimbabwe is not without precedent. In August 2005, news broke that South Africa's cabinet had agreed in principle to extend a US$412 million loan targeted to help Zimbabwe repay US$295 million in debt owed at the time to the IMF and to revitalize its agricultural sector, along with US$58 million in food aid.[55] The proposed financial assistance was directly tied to a set of political conditions.

According to a report in *Business Day*, these "conditions" included the "restoration of the rule of law, economic reforms, the repeal of repressive laws and, crucially, the resumption of talks with the MDC."[56] According to the *South African Press Association*, "There has been widespread speculation that President Robert Mugabe's government is not happy with the conditions South Africa may want to attach to the loan. [Justice Minister Patrick Chinamasa] told parliament... that Harare would not accept any loan 'that has political conditions attached to it.'"[57] The article says South African sources denied reports that one of the conditions of the loan was for talks between the ZANU-PF and the MDC. South Africa stipulated that the Zimbabwean government institute constitutional reforms to repeal repressive laws, restore media freedoms, reinvigorate dialogue on aspects of the constitution, and embark on restructuring the economic system. Conditions were also proposed for the ruling ZANU-PF to resume negotiations over constitutional reforms with a broad set of actors, including the MDC.

This proposed loan ultimately failed to materialize amidst heavy criticism from within South Africa, Zimbabwe's ruling ZANU-PF, and Zimbabwean civil society. ZANU-PF officials rejected the offer, contending that the conditional loan amounted to Western-style interventionism and would place undue pressure upon the ZANU-PF to come to an unwelcome negotiated political settlement with the MDC. There is also speculation that the then Zimbabwe finance minister Dr. Herbert Murewa had no credible economic plan acceptable to South Africa, and that this led to his being fired by President Mugabe. South Africa's opposition parties also expressed overt and sustained opposition to the loan as a whole, arguing that such a bailout would divert funds from domestic service-delivery needs and come at an unnecessary cost to taxpayers.[58] Furthermore, civil society organizations in Zimbabwe viewed the proposed loan as at the very least a stop-gap measure, and at the most a morally unjustifiable proposal—given the extent of humanitarian need in the aftermath of the Zimbabwean government's *Operation Murambatsvina* in May 2005 that left seven hundred thousand homeless and in need of emergency aid.[59]

The South African government, fearing that reengagement beyond emergency food aid by the international community would take too long, established an Agriculture Task Team in late 2008 that, according to officials and some donors, had secured agreement from all principals in the negotiations to engage officials (principal secretaries and directors' general) and technical experts in the relevant Zimbabwean ministries on an agriculture roll-out plan. South Africa would drive this program as the aforementioned SADC initiative. The R300 million for agriculture announced by the finance minister in October 2008 was intended to kick-start the initiative (notionally with inputs from other regional players to follow). The distribution of this aid would be overseen by an SADC-based monitoring mechanism, possibly in cooperation with an international agency such as the UN's Food and Agriculture Organization (FAO). South Africa apparently intended to use the promise of this aid as a carrot to break the deadlock at the time.

How well-thought-out was this South African rescue process? And was it too late? According to Bill Kinsey, an agricultural economist from Zimbabwe, November is a very late stage for donors to salvage the growing season. Kinsey argued that delivering seed and fertilizer would be overdue given that commercial farmers previously secured these inputs in June, while small-scale farmers bought theirs in October and early November (although changing rainfall and climate patterns mean that some planting of maize happens as late as December). More importantly, delayed delivery of maize would compromise the quality and volume of yield.[60] Furthermore, there is the very real threat that seed delivered for planting would be used as food, given the dire food shortage at present.

Incidents of rural communities soaking off antifungal chemical coatings from scarce stocks of maize seed and grinding the stocks for consumption have been reported, although the precise scale of such practice is yet to be determined. "So, if maize seed is distributed, it has to be delivered along with maize meal so people have something to eat as they prepare land and plant," according to Kinsey.[61] Given time and transportation infrastructure constraints, provisions would need to be made to airlift supplies, contract transporters and efficient clearing agents, and develop networks with local NGOs to ensure that supplies reach their intended recipients.[62] Some argue that these logistical challenges could be overcome, and that South Africa's agricultural assistance should not be seen as a short-term palliative. Furthermore, even if the assistance missed the 2008–2009 season, it should be supplied in the 2009–2010 season as the Zimbabwe seed and fertilizer industries still face structural supply chain bottlenecks and fuel shortages that will take time to resolve.

DIRCO offers modest detail of how its planned intervention in Zimbabwe will overcome these various challenges. A package to meet fertilizer, seed, and farm implement needs, in liaison with SADC finance ministers, was under consideration at the time of writing.[63] However, the mechanics of how such a rescue plan would work in practice was not clear.

One of the first priorities of the GNU should be the issue of a new land policy, which must tackle the structural and political problems that have plagued land reform since independence. This will be extremely difficult given the balance of forces in the new cabinet. Critics have indicated that appointment of a transitional administration is likely to constrain decision-making, fostering consensus-style compromises that both delay and undermine reforms. Internal strife and turf battles will likely partially paralyze parliament, a number of ministries, the justice system, and the security services. Cabinet is already bloated to accommodate various interests; because the politicians will be aware of the shortened electoral cycle, they will be less willing to implement radical reforms for fear that the benefits will not materialize within the timeframe set by the GPA for constitutional reform.

However, if development assistance from South Africa, and indeed any other country, is to have a longer term impact, other structural reform is critical. Land reform in particular is vital given its centrality to both Zimbabwe's political and economic fortunes. However, there are several complicating factors.[64] As the 2008 UN Development Programme (UNDP) discussion document *Comprehensive Economic Recovery in Zimbabwe* noted, there are currently five different ministries dealing with aspects of land and agriculture in Zimbabwe: Land policy is tasked to the Ministry of Lands, Land Reform, and Resettlement and the Minister of State for Special Affairs responsible for the Land Reform, and Rural Resettlement Programmes. The Ministry of Agriculture, the Ministry of Agricultural Engineering, Mechanization and Irrigation, and the Ministry of Water Affairs and Infrastructure are together tasked with dealing with agricultural matters.[65]

In order to obtain a better understanding of state thinking, the SAIIA conducted interviews with senior South African government officials and those working in parastatals in October and November 2008. A senior National Treasury representative stated that multipronged, long-term South African development assistance to Zimbabwe will be vital, but that it is also likely to be extremely costly and protracted, given that it is the first engagement of its kind for South Africa.[66] This official mentioned three key strands of South Africa's involvement: first, agriculture and food security are likely to define immediate South Africa-Zimbabwe engagement. Second, South Africa would implement an *Economic Strategy Programme* for post-conflict reconstruction (which would include elements such as exchange rate correction; incrementally working toward market liberalization; tackling price controls; and revising inflation and fiscal policies). Third, and most intriguingly, South Africa, as current chair of the SADC, might be in a position to coordinate donor efforts to reengage with Zimbabwe and to continuously assess levels of need and levels of commitment. To date, South Africa has overseen the establishment of an economic assistance plan through the SADC. Whether it would infringe upon Zimbabwe's sovereignty, what right would South Africa have to call any such meeting, and would Mugabe assent are questions that merit consideration.

Cholera Crisis Spurs Some Action

The international and regional responses to the outbreak of cholera in Zimbabwe in August 2008 stand as a rare example of a relatively swift reaction by the international community to a crisis in Zimbabwe. The outbreak stemmed in large part from deteriorating health and water and sanitation infrastructure. According to figures from the UN's Office for the Coordination of Humanitarian Affairs (OCHA), from August 2008 to July 15, 2009, 98,592 cases of cholera were reported in Zimbabwe, with 4,288 deaths,[67] but the rate of infections and fatalities has declined dramatically of late. Perhaps realizing the urgent humanitarian need to contain the epidemic and the spillover of cholera cases into South Africa and other neighbors, the response has been markedly prompt compared to similar crises, such as the displacement of 700,000 Zimbabweans in 2005 under a government sponsored "clean-up" operation.[68]

Among other donors, the EC pledged US$12 million toward medical supplies and water treatment chemicals.[69] Similarly, the World Health Organization (WHO) and others lent prompt and substantial assistance through the provision of emergency relief supplies and drugs. Domestically, Zimbabwe's shrinking private sector—and notably platinum mining company Zimplats—pledged financial assistance toward health supplies. South Africa, which had previously resolved to withhold the earlier-mentioned aid to Zimbabwe until the installation of the GNU reversed the decision, pledged to channel medical emergency supplies to tackle the epidemic and provide the R300 million in agricultural aid that it had previously withheld due to the impasse over cabinet posts. Among other states in the region, Tanzania, Zambia, and Namibia also responded to the SADC's call to the fifteen-member organization to provide aid toward mitigating Zimbabwe's cholera outbreak.

Conclusion

The depths to which Zimbabwe has sunk in terms of the state of its socioeconomic infrastructure, as well as the erosion of constitutionalism and the integrity of state institutions, implies a long period of reconstruction to attain late 1990s levels of economic and social indicators. Herbst, Mills, and McNamee write that "if Zimbabwe's rate of economic decline has averaged over 8 percent per annum since 2000, it will take the same rate of growth for the same period to get back to the moment of decline."[70] The UNDP estimates that recovery could take twelve years if growth averages 5 percent annually.[71] Other estimates believe that the cost of recovery over the next five–ten years could exceed R100 billion, which is approximately US$12 billion.[72]

South Africa has clear political and economic interests in the economic and social resuscitation of Zimbabwe. Indeed, in the past Zimbabwe proved to be a dynamic, profitable market for South African retail, banking, and energy sector companies, evidenced by the large scale investment of (among others) South Africa's Pick 'n Pay, Shoprite, and Massmart groups in the 1990s.[73] The two economies are intertwined—a great deal of political capital has been expended by the South African government toward Zimbabwe's cause, and any efforts at regional integration and stability are hamstrung if a major player in the area is subject to the level of crisis that has steadily built up in Zimbabwe over the last decade.

Other than financial resources, South Africa's strong political and economic institutions potentially have a lot to offer to Zimbabwe. Technical assistance could be availed to its Zimbabwean counterparts to rebuild their institutions, such as public financial management systems, local government, the central bank, the revenue authority, and so forth. In addition, South African assistance could support areas of science, technology, and infrastructure, the development of a new constitution, justice sector reform, and the sustainable indigenization of business.

South Africa has also experienced social pressures because of the crisis occurring in Zimbabwe, including large-scale migration, strains on socioeconomic delivery, and the spread of health risks such as cholera. It is therefore in South Africa's interests to adopt a constructive and decisive approach to address Zimbabwe's post-conflict reconstruction. Nonetheless, aid on its own will not be enough for Zimbabwe, although it might act as a spur for the return of fixed investment to the country.

The portion of the South African corporate sector that has retained a significant presence in Zimbabwe is an engine of growth, and its role is expected to expand once the macroeconomic and political situation has stabilized. For both aid and private investment to work a "reconstructed and reformed environment"[74] will be vital.

However, the reluctant hegemony of South Africa, manifestly the most powerful state in the region, but one careful not be seen to openly bully or scare its neighbors, has also been at play in its relations with Zimbabwe and is likely to continue when South Africa provides development assistance. Before 1994, President Mugabe was seen as the leader of southern Africa. Since the start of the current crisis in 1999, Mugabe has appeared to have consistently broken agreements made with presidents Mandela and Mbeki. The current power-sharing agreement legally provides for a division of executive and other power between the ZANU-PF and the MDC, perhaps most notably through a Joint Monitoring and Implementation Committee. Yet creating a functional coalition has proved problematic. Within the first few months of the coalition, the SADC and the African Union (AU) had already been summoned to exercise their role as guarantors to the agreement. This because the two parties failed to break deadlocks over the unilateral appointment of an attorney general by the ZANU-PF and the reinstatement of Reserve Bank governor Gideon Gono, despite strong reservations expressed by the MDC. The tenuous relationship between the GNU's component parts will subject the leverage Pretoria has in driving recovery in Zimbabwe to constraints and probably more tortuous diplomatic acrobatics than had the MDC taken power fully in Harare.

The global economic downturn might also negatively affect the dollar value of funds that South Africa can direct toward Zimbabwe. While its impact on South Africa-Zimbabwe investment is yet to be determined,[75] some steadfastly maintain that funds of about US$10 billion earmarked for assisting Zimbabwe remain on the books.

The South African domestic political context has become increasingly inward-looking. Political debate has focused on the internal challenges facing South Africa, not the least of which is service delivery. Indeed, South Africa's domestic challenges may continue to divert high-level political attention from Zimbabwe, and South Africa was particularly focused on hosting a successful football World Cup in mid-2010. Nevertheless, South Africa's fortunes are tied to Zimbabwe's, and, therefore, Zimbabwe will not fall off the agenda entirely. This may be especially so if the Congress of South African Trade Unions (COSATU), long a vocal opponent of Robert Mugabe's actions and a member of the tripartite alliance along with the ANC and the South African Communist Party, has a stronger say in South Africa's Zimbabwe policy under the new Zuma administration.

It will be in South Africa's interests to allocate both financial and human resources to help rebuild Zimbabwe. As South Africa also begins to further refine its development assistance framework, aid to help post-conflict reconstruction in Zimbabwe might also become a useful first case study of a coordinated South

African development approach. Yet domestic pressures on a new South African administration dealing with high unemployment, high crime rate, social dissatisfaction, and recession might necessitate a more conservative stance toward the resources made available to its northern neighbor. The imperative, then, of providing assistance within a strong and reliable policy framework will be more important than ever.

Notes

1. The GNU came into effect only on February 9, 2009, although the GPA had been signed in September 2008.
2. Remarks by senior Development Bank of Southern Africa Board Member, July 8, 2009.
3. Government of the Republic of Zimbabwe, *Global Political Agreement,* Harare, September 15, 2008, http://www.thezimbabwetimes.com/documents/agreement091508.pdf.
4. While regional integration would serve South Africa well, there is growing concern among regional economists that Zimbabwean industry and economic growth would suffer in the absence of targeted policy measures by Zimbabwean authorities to protect local industries and aggressively push for a slower, manageable pace of integration into the region. The SADC Free Trade Agreement signed in August 2008 would arguably stand to damage Zimbabwe's fragile economy even further.
5. African Free Press, "Toll from Xenophobic Attacks Rises," *Mail & Guardian Online,* May 31, 2008, http://www.mg.co.za/article/2008–05–31-toll-from-xenophobic-attacks-rises.
6. Tichaona Sibanda, "South Africa Want Mugabe and Tsvangirai to Speed Up Talks on GPA," *SW Radio Africa (London),* September 3, 2009, http://allafrica.com/stories/200909030852.html.
7. Quiet diplomacy is the policy that South Africa pursued in relation to conflict in Zimbabwe, particularly during Thabo Mbeki's presidency from May 1999 to September 2008. It refers to the refusal to condemn the Mugabe regime in public, preferring to pressure for change in private, behind closed doors, At rhetorical level, the Mbeki administration attributed its policy stance to a respect for Zimbabwe's sovereignty. Vocal critics in South Africa, Zimbabwe, and internationally have called it laissez-faire, if not pandering to Mugabe.
8. Available statistics show that between 1999 and the year 2005, South African government departments received in excess of $20 billion in technical assistance, grants, and other forms of development assistance. More notably, South Africa receives significant amounts of development assistance channeled through nongovernmental organizations and other private institutions that is largely unrecorded. The absence of a clear definition of "Official Development Assistance" also often implies that total ODA inflows into South Africa are often grossly underreported.
9. The African National Congress (ANC) was formed in 1912 as the South African Native National Congress to increase the rights of South Africa's black population. It emerged as the major force opposing apartheid after 1948. The PAC was formed in 1959 from a split within the ANC. Both movements were banned in 1960 and their leaders were arrested, went underground, or were exiled. Both were unbanned in 1990, and the ANC has been the country's ruling party since April 1994, while the PAC has almost disappeared from the political landscape, holding just a single seat in the National Assembly after the April 2009 elections.

10. Development Co-operation Information System, "ODA in the Context of South Africa's Reconstruction and Development Priorities," in *Policy Framework and Guidelines for the Management of ODA,* 2003, http://www.dcis.gov.za/Modules/PolicyFrameworkGuidelines/ODAINSAContextPrinted.htm.

11. Sanjeev Gupta, Robert Powell, and Yongzheng Yang, *The Macroeconomics of Scaling Up Aid to Africa: A Checklist for Practitioners,* International Monetary Fund (Washington, 2006): 3.

12. Wolfe Braude, Pearl Thandrayan, and Elizabeth Sidiropoulos, *Emerging Donors in International Development Assistance: The South Africa Case,* International Development Research Centre (Canada, 2008): 4, http://www.idrc.ca/uploads/user-S/12066375471SouthAfrica_Final_Summary.pdf.

13. Thabo Mbeki, speech given at the African Renaissance conference, Republic of South Africa, Johannesburg, September 28, 1998, http://www.dfa.gov.za/docs/speeches/1998/mbek0928.htm.

14. The *African Renaissance and International Co-operation Fund Act* (51 of 2000), Republic of South Africa.

15. Braude, Thandrayan, and Sidiropoulos, *Emerging Donors,* 4, and own calculations.

16. Ibid., 12.

17. Ibid., 16–17.

18. Elizabeth Sidiropoulos, "South African Foreign Policy in the Post-Mbeki Period," *South African Journal of International Affairs* 15, no. 2 (2008): 110.

19. National Treasury, "South Africa as a Partner in Africa: A Review of South Africa's Development Assistance to Africa" (workshop presentation at the South African Institute for International Affairs, November, 2006).

20. Indeed, the Development Cooperation Information System (DCIS), available at http://www.dcis.gov/za, tracks and monitors incoming ODA funds to South Africa. The OECD hailed this database as an example of good practice for ODA management for recipient countries. It thus provides a good foundation for a tracking system for outgoing ODA once the system is in place in that regard.

21. Although South Africa has enhanced its cooperation with the Organization for Economic Cooperation and Development (OECD), at this point—along with other emerging donors—it is extremely unlikely to join the OECD's Development Assistance Committee (OECD-DAC).

22. In a subsequent discussion with the authors in July 2009, a senior diplomat from a European Union country noted that the prime minister's trip had been perceived by the Europeans as the first step in re-engaging with Zimbabwe, rather than as one of a "beggar with a begging bowl." It had signaled the end of Zimbabwe's isolation (see Jonah Fisher, "Scant Return from Tsvangirai Tour," *BBC News,* Johannesburg, June 28, 2009, http://news.bbc.co.uk/2/hi/8123096.stm.

23. Godfrey Marawanyika, "Zimbabwe Receives $950 Million Loan from China," *Associated Freedom Press,* June 30, 2009.

24. African National Congress, "Resolutions," fifty-second National Conference of the African National Congress, Polokwane, South Africa, December 16–20, 2007, 39.

25. See "Welcome to the Pan-African Infrastructure Development Fund." http://www.harith.co.za/.

26. Ibid., paragraphs 21–22.

27. Braude, Thandrayan, and Sidiropoulos, *Emerging Donors,* 14.

28. The National Treasury notes that SACU and Common Monetary Area (CMA) financial transfers accounted for 87 percent of overall transfers to Africa in 2004. Inclusion of such transfers is apparently normal practice among international donors in reporting overall international aid—although it would probably be counted under the OECD's

Development Assistance Committee definitions as other official flows (OOF) and not official development assistance (ODA). These OOF transfers are not meant for development, but they are still directed to developing countries.

29. Ibid.

30. Minister of International Relations and Co-operation Maite Nkoana-Mashabane, address to the National Assembly on the occasion of the Department of International Relations and Co-operation Budget Vote, Republic of South Africa, June 18, 2009.

31. President of the Republic of South Africa Jacob Zuma, "State of the Nation Address," Joint Sitting of Parliament, Cape Town, June 3, 2009.

32. Sidiropoulos, "South African Foreign Policy," 114.

33. ANC, "Resolutions," 41.

34. Minister of Foreign Affairs Nkosazana Dlamini-Zuma, "Message from the Minister of Foreign Affairs," in Strategic Plan, 2008–2011, Republic of South Africa, 2008. http://www.dfa.gov.za/department/stratplan2008–2011/strategic_plan08.pdf.

35. Department of Foreign Affairs, Strategic Plan, 2008–2011, Republic of South Africa, 18.

36. European Commission, "Draft Zimbabwe-EC Country Strategy Paper and Short-Term Response Strategy," 2008.

37. According to Nicky Moyo, director, Development Enterprise Africa Trust, Zimbabwe, in comments on an earlier version of this chapter, July 2009.

38. "Donors Pledge US$500m for Zimbabwe," *Panafrican News Agency,* July 1, 2009.

39. Remarks by Elinor Sisulu, Crisis Coalition of Zimbabwe Activist.

40. Reuters Africa, "Zimbabwe to Discuss Adopting Rand, Says Minister," *Mail & Guardian Online,* July 7, 2009, http://hades.mg.co.za/article/2009–07–07-zim-to-discuss-adopting-rand-says-minister.

41. Peter Draper and Andreas Freytag, "What Future for Monetary Policy in Zimbabwe?" South African Institute for International Affairs, March 4, 2009, http://www.saiia.org.za/development-through-trade-opinion/what-future-for-monetary-policy-in-zimbabwe.html.

42. Solidarity Peace Trust, *A Dialogue: Zimbabwe-South Africa Economic Relations Since 2000,* a preliminary report, October 23, 2007, http://www.solidaritypeacetrust.org/reports/difficult_dialogue.pdf.

43. Dianna Games, *Zimbabwe: A Pre-election Overview and Recovery Scenarios,* South African Institute of International Affairs (2005).

44. Anglo-Platinum Corporation, *Annual Report 2004: Sustainable Development Report,* volume 2, http://www.angloplatinum.com/investor_media/im_annual_rep/ar_04/pdf/sustainable_dev.pdf.

45. According to Nicky Moyo, director of Development Enterprise Africa Trust (DEAT), in comments on an earlier version of this chapter, July 2009.

46. Leveraging of patient capital from development finance institutions such as International Finance Corporation (IFC), African Development Bank, and the World Bank will be crucial particularly if the debt arrears situation is resolved and business environment is reformed in Zimbabwe.

47. Andrew Etzinger and Mark Sims, interview with Eskom Trade Account Manager, November 12, 2008.

48. Dumisani Muleya, "Zimbabwe: Country Still Far Short of US$10 Billion in Aid," *Business Day,* April 30, 2009.

49. United Nations Development Programme (UNDP), *Comprehensive Economic Recovery in Zimbabwe: A Discussion Document,* Working Paper Series (UNDP Zimbabwe, 2008).

50. World Food Programme, "Zimbabwe Needs Most Food Aid," *The Times,* May 26, 2009.

51. Minister of Finance Trevor A. Manuel, speech on the *Medium-Term Budget Policy Statement,* Republic of South Africa, October 21, 2008.

52. African Free Press, "South Africa Ends Block on Aid to Zimbabwe Official," *The Mthwakazian,* December 29, 2008. http://www.mthwakazian.com/economy/297-safrica-ends-block-on-aid-to-zimbabwe-official.html.

53. Ayanda Ntsaluba, Department of Foreign Affairs Media Briefing, Republic of South Africa, January 14, 2009.

54. Presidential Spokesperson Thabo Masebe, media statement, Republic of South Africa, January 14, 2009.

55. National Treasury, "South Africa as a Partner."

56. Karima, Brown, Vukani Mde, and Dumisani Muleya, "Harare 'No' to Key Loan Condition," *The Star.* August 5, 2005.

57. "SA offered Zimbabwe a Loan—Harare Minister," *SAPA (Independent Online),* August 26, 2005, http://www.zimbabwesituation.com/aug27_2005.html#link5.

58. "DA Wants Parliamentary Debate on Zim Loan," *Mail & Guardian Online,* August 11, 2005.

59. Basildon Peta, "SA Loan for Mugabe Would Be a Mistake," *Mail and Guardian Online,* August 5, 2005.

60. Subsequently, however, the availability of maize seed contributed to a slight increase in Zimbabwe's maize yield, which is expected to total 1.2 million tones—double that of the previous year according to Zimbabwe's Ministry of Agriculture. While South Africa's intervention and indeed those of other stakeholders was ultimately critical—Zimbabwe's expected yield is expected to meet only a fraction of its national requirements. See USAID, "Zimbabwe Food Security Update," http://www.reliefweb.int/rw/RWFiles2009.nsf/FilesByRWDocUnidFilename/VDUX-7U2SYF-full_report.pdf/$File/full_report.pdf.

61. Private correspondence.

62. Private correspondence.

63. Makhaya Xolisa, interview with the director of the Department of Foreign Affairs of the Republic of South Africa, September 22, 2008.

64. Some proposals on the table regarding post-conflict reconstruction phase include the creation of an international commission tasked with various priority areas, and this utilizes African experts to coordinate policy formulation. Zimbabwean civil servants and members of parliament (or people proposed by parliament) would also form part of these policy coordinating bodies. See Denis Worrall, *The Reconstruction of Zimbabwe: A Proposed Strategy for Africa,* January 2009, http://omegainvest.co.za/downloads/The%20Reconstruction%20of%20Zimbabwe%20-%20January%202009.pdf.

65. UNDP, *Comprehensive Economic Recovery,* 165.

66. Neil Cole, telephone interview with the chief director of the National Treasury of the Republic of South Africa, October 1, 2008.

67. United Nations Office for the Coordination of Humanitarian Affairs (UNOCHA), "Zimbabwe Bi-monthly Cholera Situation Report," July 15, 2009, http://ochaonline.un.org/OchaLinkClick.aspx?link=ocha&docId=1112226.

68. Anna Kajumulo Tibaijuka, UN special envoy on human settlements issues in Zimbabwe, *United Nations, Report of the Fact-Finding Mission to Zimbabwe to Assess the Scope and Impact of Operation Murambatsvina,* UN Habitat, http://www.unhabitat.org/downloads/docs/297_96735_ZimbabweReport.pdf.

69. Abgus Shaw, "Zimbabwe Declares National Health Emergency," *Mail and Guardian Online,* December 4, 2008, http://www.mg.co.za/article/2008–12–04-zimbabwe-declares-national-health-emergency.

70. Jeffrey Herbst, Greg Mills, and Terence McNamee, "Zimbabwe: After The Election: A Path to Economic Stabilisation, Recovery and Growth," The Brenthurst Foundation Discussion Paper 1, April 2008.

71. This is not unheard of in economies emerging from recent conflict, but is likely to be made more difficult because of the global economic crisis.

72. Raymond Parsons, "After Mugabe Goes: The Economic and Political Reconstruction of Zimbabwe," presidential address at the Economic Society of South Africa Biennial Conference, Johannesburg, September 12, 2007, 17.

73. Besada, H and Moyo, N, "Picking Up the Pieces of Zimbabwe's Economy," CIGI Technical Paper #6, 2008.

74. Worrall, *The Reconstruction of Zimbabwe*, 11.

75. African Free Press, "World Bank Gears Up Aid Amid Global Financial Crisis," *The Economic Times*, November 11, 2008, http://economictimes.indiatimes.com/News/International-Business/World-Bank-gears-up-amid-global-financial-crisis/articleshow/3701186.cms.

Index